THE
INSTITUTIONAL
INVESTOR
SERIES IN FINANCE

Current Topics in
Investment Management

The Institutional Investor Series in Finance

Implementing Capital Budgeting Techniques, Revised Edition
Harold Bierman, Jr.

Solving the Global Debt Crisis: Strategies and Controversies by Key Stakeholders
Christine A. Bogdanowicz-Bindert, editor

Thrifts Under Siege: Restoring Order to American Banking
R. Dan Brumbaugh, Jr.

The Institutional Investor Focus on Investment Management
Frank J. Fabozzi, editor

Managing Institutional Assets
Frank J. Fabozzi, editor

Current Topics in Investment Management
Frank J. Fabozzi and T. Dessa Fabozzi, editors

The Financial Manager's Guide to Evaluating Bond Refunding Opportunities
John D. Finnerty, Andrew J. Kalotay, and Francis X. Farrell, Jr.

The Debt/Equity Choice
Ronald W. Masulis

International Corporate Finance, Second Edition
Alan Shapiro

Managing Financial Risk
Clifford W. Smith, Jr., Charles W. Smithson, and D. Sykes Wilford

Corporate Restructuring and Executive Compensation
Joel M. Stern, G. Bennett Stewart III, and Donald H. Chew, Jr., editors

Marketing Financial Services
David B. Zenoff, editor

Customer-Focused Marketing of Financial Services
David B. Zenoff, editor

Current Topics in Investment Management

EDITED BY

Frank J. Fabozzi

Visiting Professor of Finance
Sloan School of Management
Massachusetts Institute of Technology

and

Editor
The Journal of Portfolio Management

T. Dessa Fabozzi

Vice President and Manager
Client Analytics
Financial Strategies Group
Merrill Lynch Capital Markets

1817

Harper & Row, Publishers, New York

BALLINGER DIVISION

Grand Rapids, Philadelphia, St. Louis, San Francisco
London, Singapore, Sydney, Tokyo, Toronto

International Standard Book Number: 0-88730-406-0

Library of Congress Catalog Card Number: 89-37652

Printed in the United States of America

Library of Congress Cataloging-in-Publication Data

Current topics in investment management / edited by Frank J. Fabozzi
and T. Dessa Fabozzi.
   p.   cm. — (The Institutional investor series in finance)
Includes bibliographical references.
ISBN 0-88730-406-0
1. Investments. 2. Portfolio management. I. Fabozzi, Frank J.
II. Fabozzi, T. Dessa, 1960-   .
HG4521.S35784   1990
332.6 – dc20
                                                              89-37652
                                                                 CIP

90 91 92 93 HC 9 8 7 6 5 4 3 2 1

List of Contributors

Robert D. Arnott First Quadrant
Jeffery V. Bailey Richards & Tierney, Inc.
Zvi Bodie Boston University
Andrew S. Carron The First Boston Corporation
T. Daniel Coggin Virginia Supplemental Retirement System
Bruce M. Collins The First Boston Corporation
Ravi E. Dattatreya Sumitomo Bank Capital Markets, Inc.
Frank J. Fabozzi Massachusetts Institute of Technology
T. Dessa Fabozzi Merrill Lynch Capital Markets
William J. Gartland Drexel Burnham Lambert
Gary L. Gastineau Salomon Brothers Inc
Floyd J. Gould Investment Research Company and
    University of Chicago
Lakhbir S. Hayre Prudential-Bache Capital Funding
Eric I. Hemel The First Boston Corporation
Joanne M. Hill PaineWebber
Andrew D. Langerman Drexel Burnham Lambert
Kenneth Lauterbach Prudential-Bache Capital Funding
Donald L. Luskin Wells Fargo Investment Advisors
Richard W. McEnally University of North Carolina–Chapel Hill
Llewellyn Miller Drexel Burnham Lambert
Cyrus Mohebbi Prudential-Bache Capital Funding
Edgar E. Peters The Boston Company, Inc.
Uday Rajan Drexel Burnham Lambert
Marc R. Reinganum University of Iowa
Thomas M. Richards Richards & Tierney, Inc.
Prakash A. Shimpi Drexel Burnham Lambert
David E. Tierney Richards & Tierney, Inc.

Contents

/ **ix**

Preface

Current Topics in Investment Management is designed for use as a supplementary book for an undergraduate or graduate course in investment management. This book differs from other readings books in that it is not merely a collection of articles reprinted from academic journals. Thirteen of the 20 articles are adapted from original articles that appeared in *Institutional Investor Focus on Investment Management* and *Managing Institutional Assets,* edited by Frank Fabozzi as part of The Institutional Investor Series in Finance. The other articles are adapted from the writings of Frank Fabozzi that have appeared in several of his books. None of the articles has appeared in an academic or professional journal.

The topics covered in this book were based on decisions we made after reviewing a majority of the textbooks on investment management. The topics that we felt did not receive adequate coverage in some textbooks and are covered here include: asset allocation and policy setting; determination of benchmark portfolios for setting investment objectives and evaluating investment performance; stock index futures and their use in portfolio management; measuring stock price volatility and bond price volatility (duration and convexity); the evaluation of bonds with embedded options, mortgage-backed securities (pass-throughs, collateralized mortgage obligations and stripped mortgage-backed securities); and interest-rate risk control tools (interest rate options and futures, interest rate swaps, and interest rate agreements).

The articles in this book are written by practitioners. In fact, of the twenty-seven contributors to this book, only four are full-time academicians. Even the four academicians have had extensive experience in either managing money, consulting for major financial institutions, or serving on the board of directors of investment companies. It is our hope that the insights provided by the contributors will merit the additional cost of a supplementary book.

Frank J. Fabozzi
T. Dessa Fabozzi

Current Topics in
Investment Management

Overview of the Investment Management Process

Frank J. Fabozzi, Ph.D., CFA
Visiting Professor of Finance, Sloan School of Management
Massachusetts Institute of Technology
and
Editor, *The Journal of Portfolio Management*

T. Dessa Fabozzi, Ph.D.
Vice President, Financial Strategies Group
Merrill Lynch Capital Markets

Regardless of the type of financial institution, the investment management process involves the following five steps:

1. Setting investment objectives
2. Establishing investment policy
3. Selecting the portfolio strategy
4. Selecting the assets
5. Measuring and evaluating performance

The purpose of this chapter is to describe each of the steps. At the end of this article we provide an overview of the book.

I. Setting Investment Objectives

The first main step in the investment management process is setting investment objectives. The investment objective will vary by type of financial institution.

For institutions such as pension funds, the investment objective will be to generate sufficient cash flow from the investment portfolio so as to satisfy its pension obligations. Life insurance companies sell a variety of products. Basically, most of the products guarantee a dollar payment at some time in the future or a stream of dollar payments. The premium that a life insurance company will charge a policyholder for one of its products will depend on the interest rate that it can earn on its investments. To realize a profit, the life insurance company must earn a higher return on the premium it invests than the implicit (or explicit) interest rate it has guaranteed policyholders. The investment objective of the life insurance company is therefore to satisfy the obligations stipulated in the policy and generate a profit.

For institutions such as banks and thrifts, funds are from the issuance of certificates of deposits. These funds are then invested in loans and marketable securities. The objective is to earn a return on invested funds that is higher than the cost of those funds.

For the three institutions we discussed above, the investment objectives are essentially dictated by the nature of their liabilities. For investment companies (mutual funds), the investment objectives will be set forth in the prospectus. While there are no liabilities that must be satisfied by the fund, a target dividend payout typically will be established.

II. Establishing Investment Policy

The second step in the investment management process is establishing policy guidelines to satisfy the investment objectives. Setting policy begins with the asset-allocation decision; that is, the decision as to how the institution's funds should be distributed among the major asset classes (cash equivalents, equities, fixed-income securities, real estate, and foreign securities).

Client and regulatory constraints must be considered in establishing an investment policy. Examples of constraints that might be imposed by the sponsor of a pension fund are: No funds may be invested in a bond of an issuer whose credit rating is below some specified level; no more than a predetermined percentage of the fund's assets may be invested in a particular industry; or options and futures may be used only to protect asset values, not for speculative purposes. For state-regulated institutions such as insurance companies (both life and property and casualty companies), regulators may restrict the amount of funds allocated to certain major asset classes. Even the amount allocated within a major asset class may be restricted based on the characteristics of the particular asset. For investment companies, restrictions on asset allocation are set forth in the prospectus when the fund is launched and may only be changed with approval of the fund's board.

Tax and financial reporting implications must also be considered when adopting investment policies. For example, life insurance companies have certain tax advantages that make investing in tax-exempt municipal securities generally unappealing. Since pension funds are exempt from taxes, they too are not particularly interested in tax-exempt municipal securities.

Financial reporting requirements, in particular Statements of Financial Accounting Standards Board Nos. 87 and 88 and the Omnibus Budget Reconciliation Act of 1987, affect the ways in which pension funds establish investment policies. Unfortunately, financial reporting considerations sometimes cause institutions to establish investment policies that may not be in the best interest of the institution in the long run.

III. Selecting a Portfolio Strategy

Selecting a portfolio strategy that is consistent with the objectives and policy guidelines of the client or institution is the third step in the investment management process. Portfolio strategies can be classified as either active strategies or passive strategies. Essential to all active strategies are expectations about the factors that influence the performance of an asset class. For example, with active equity strategies this may include forecasts of futures earnings, dividends, or price/earnings ratios. With active, fixed-income portfolios this may involve forecasts of future interest rates, future interest rate volatility, or future yield spreads. Active portfolio strategies involving foreign securities will require forecasts of future exchange rates.

Passive strategies involve minimal expectational input. A popular type of passive strategy is indexing. The objective of an indexing strategy is to replicate the performance of a predetermined benchmark. While indexing has been employed extensively in the management of equity portfolios, the use of indexing for managing fixed-income portfolios is a relatively new practice.

Between these extremes of active and passive strategies have sprung strategies that have elements of both. For example, the core of a portfolio may be indexed with the balance managed actively. Or, a portfolio may be primarily indexed but employ low risk strategies to enhance the indexed portfolio's return. This strategy is commonly referred to as "enhanced indexing" or "indexing plus."

In the fixed-income area, several strategies classified as *structured portfolio strategies* have been commonly used. A structured portfolio strategy is one in which a portfolio is designed to achieve the performance of some predetermined benchmark. These strategies are frequently used when funding liabilities. When the predetermined benchmark is to have sufficient funds to satisfy a single liability, regardless of the course of future interest rates, a strategy known as immunization is often used. When the predetermined benchmark is multiple future liabilities that must be funded regardless of how interest rates change, strategies such as immunization, cash flow matching (or dedication), or horizon matching can be employed.

Even within the immunization and cash flow matching strategies, low-risk, active management strategies can be employed. For example, a contingent immunization strategy allows the portfolio manager to actively manage a portfolio until certain parameters are realized. If and when those parameters are realized, the portfolio is then immunized.

Indexing can be considered a structured portfolio strategy where the benchmark is to achieve the performance of some predetermined index. Portfolio insurance strategies — where the objective is to insure that the value of the portfolio does not fall below a predetermined level — are also viewed as structured portfolio strategies.

Which is the Best Strategy?

Given the choice among active, structured, or passive management, which should be selected? The answer depends on (1) the client or money manager's view of the pricing efficiency of the market and (2) the nature of the liabilities to be funded. First let's consider the pricing efficiency of a market.

Efficient pricing refers to a market in which prices at all times fully reflect all available information that is relevant to the valuation of securities. When a market is price efficient, active strategies will not *consistently* produce superior returns after adjusting for (1) risk, (2) transaction costs, and (3) management advisory fees.

What strategy should be pursued by an investor who believes that the market is sufficiently efficient so that superior risk-adjusted returns can not be consistently realized after accounting for transaction costs and management advisory fees? In this case, a passive approach should be followed. But which is the best passive approach to pursue?

Capital market theory tells us that in an efficient market the "market" portfolio offers the highest level of return per unit of risk because it captures the efficiency of the market. The theoretical market portfolio should be a capitalization-weighted portfolio of all risky assets. As a proxy for the theoretical market portfolio, an index that is representative of the market should be used. But this is nothing more than indexing. Thus, there is strong theoretical support for an indexing strategy in an efficient market.

What is the evidence on the pricing efficiency for the stock and bond markets? For the stock market, empirical evidence up to the early 1980s suggested that the market is efficient. These studies, coupled with the poor performance of money managers relative to the Standard & Poor's 500 index, led to the rise of indexing as an investment strategy. However, recent evidence suggests that there are pockets of inefficiencies (referred to as "market anomalies") that may permit abnormal risk-adjusted returns after adjusting for transaction costs.

Turning to the fixed-income market, studies of the U.S. government bond market suggest that it is efficient, yet there are instances where trading opportunities can enhance returns. As for the corporate, municipal, and mortgage-backed securities market, there is insufficient evidence to draw any conclusion about market efficiency. Yet, the poor performance of many money managers relative to commonly accepted benchmarks has pushed more institutional funds in the direction of indexing some or all of their fixed-income portfolios. Because there are sectors of the bond market that tend to be less efficient, indexing-plus strategies have been employed.

But pricing efficiency is not the sole determinant of the type of investment strategy that should be employed. The nature of the liabilities is also extremely important. While indexing may be a reasonable strategy for an institution that does not have a future liability stream that must be satisfied, consider the situation faced by pension funds. If a pension fund indexes its portfolio, then the fund's return will be roughly the same as the index. However, the index may not provide a return that is sufficient to satisfy the fund's obligations. Consequently, for some institutions such as pension funds and life insurance companies, structured portfolio strategies such as immunization or dedication may be more appropriate to achieve their investment objectives. Within these strategies, an active or enhanced return strategy may be employed.

IV. Selecting Assets

Once a portfolio strategy is selected, the next step is to select the specific assets to be included in the portfolio. This requires an evaluation of individual securities. In an active strategy, this means identifying mispriced securities. In the case of fixed-income securities, the characteristics of a bond (that is, coupon, maturity, credit quality, and options granted to either the issuer or bondholder) must be carefully examined to determine how these characteristics will influence the performance of the bond over some investment horizon.

It is in this phase that the investment manager attempts to construct an *optimal* or *efficient* portfolio. An optimal or efficient portfolio is one that provides the greatest *expected* return for a given level of risk, or equivalently, the lowest risk for a given *expected* return.

V. Measuring and Evaluating Performance

The measurement and evaluation of investment performance is the last step in the investment management process. (Actually, it is improper to say that it is the last step, since investment management is an ongoing process.) This step involves measuring the performance of the portfolio, then evaluating that performance relative to some benchmark. The measurement standard selected for evaluating performance is called a *benchmark* or *normal portfolio*.

The benchmark portfolio may be a popular index such as the S&P 500 for equity portfolios or one of the bond indexes published by the major investment banking firms. Recently, pension sponsors have worked with money managers and pension consultants to establish customized benchmark portfolios.

Evaluating the performance of a money manager is not simple. A client will typically rely on the services of a firm that specializes in evaluating money managers.

While the performance of a portfolio manager when compared to a benchmark portfolio may demonstrate superior performance, this does not necessarily mean that the portfolio satisfied its investment objective. For example, suppose that a life insurance company established as its objective the maximization of portfolio return and allocated 75% of the fund to stocks and the balance to bonds. Suppose further that the portfolio manager responsible for the equity portfolio of this pension fund earned a return over a 1-year horizon that is 4% higher than the established benchmark portfolio. Assuming that the risk of the portfolio was similar to that of the benchmark portfolio, it would appear that the portfolio manager outperformed the benchmark portfolio. However, suppose that in spite of this performance the life insurance company cannot meet its liabilities. Then the failure was in establishing the investment objectives and setting policy, not the portfolio manager's performance.

VI. Overview of the Book

The two articles that follow this article focus on the first two steps of the investment management process. The article by Robert Arnott and Frank Fabozzi discusses the asset-allocation decision and the article by Zvi Bodie looks at the investment policy decision for pension funds.

There are nine articles that appear in the section on equity portfolio management. The first article by Marc Reinganum summarizes the evidence on market anomalies. The role market efficiency plays in the selection of money managers by pension funds and its potential for adverse financial consequences are explained in the article by Floyd Gould. Daniel Coggin's article describes the role of the analyst in the investment management process. Benchmark portfolios and the relationship between money managers and plan sponsors are the subjects of the article by Jeffrey Bailey, Thomas Richards, and David Tierney.

The article by Frank Fabozzi, Bruce Collins, and Ed Peters describes how stock index futures are priced and how they can be used to hedge a stock portfolio. An index fund can be constructed by buying individual stocks or by using stock index futures. The article by Bruce Collins and Frank Fabozzi describes how to construct an indexed portfolio using stock index futures. Gary Gastineau's article discusses program trading, index-related strategies (index arbitrage and portfolio insurance), and other uses of stock index futures, taking a close look at the impact of these futures on the equity markets.

"Composite assets" refer to diversified aggregates of assets such as portfolios of stocks and bonds. The article by Donald Luskin describes the revolution in composite asset trading. The volatility of the stock market is important in evaluating the potential performance of the stock market and the relative riskiness of the stock market compared to other major asset classes. In addition, volatility is the key input in an option pricing model. The article by Joanne Hill describes how volatility can be measured and interpreted.

The last eight articles in the book focus on fixed-income portfolio management. The article by Richard McEnally looks at the setting of investment objectives and policies for fixed-income portfolios. Background material on the volatility of bonds (duration and convexity) is presented in the article by Frank Fabozzi and Ravi Dattatreya. A framework for analyzing debt instruments is presented in the article by Lakhbir Hayre and Kenneth Lauterbach. The pricing and portfolio considerations involved when investing in callable corporate bonds are explained in the article by Andrew Langerman and William Gartland. In the article by Llewellyn Miller, Uday Rajan, and Prakash Shimpi, an optimization framework for achieving a targeted total return is explained and illustrated.

The fastest growing sector of the fixed-income market is the mortgage-backed securities market. Two articles in this book are devoted to this market sector. The first, by Lakhbir Hayre, Kenneth Lauterbach, and Cyrus Mohebbi, covers mortgage pass-through securities and explains how they should be evaluated. The article by Andrew Carron and Eric Hemel explains mortgage derivative products (collateralized mortgage obligations and stripped mortgage-backed securities) and their role in the portfolio of certain institutions.

The last article by Frank Fabozzi provides an overview of interest-rate risk control tools—futures, options, interest rate swaps, and interest rate agreements (caps, floors, and collars). The relationship between futures and interest rate swaps and between options and interest rate agreements are explained. How these contracts can be used to control interest rate risk is illustrated.

The Many Dimensions of the Asset Allocation Decision*

Robert D. Arnott
President & Chief Investment Officer
First Quadrant

Frank J. Fabozzi, Ph.D., CFA
Visiting Professor of Finance, Sloan School of Management
Massachusetts Institute of Technology
and
Editor, *The Journal of Portfolio Management*

Asset allocation. Everyone's talking about it, but what is it and what are people doing? One of the puzzles in asset allocation is that the asset-allocation decision is *not* one decision. Much of the confusion and mystique that surrounds asset allocation stems directly from this fact. The term *asset allocation* means different things to different people in different contexts. Asset allocation can loosely be divided into three categories: *policy* asset allocation, *tactical* asset allocation, and *dynamic* strategies for asset allocation, designed to reshape the distribution of returns. There are many variants on each of the three themes, which we review in this article.

I. Policy Asset Allocation

The policy–asset mix decision can loosely be characterized as a long-term asset-allocation decision, in which the investor seeks to identify an appropri·ate long-term normal asset mix that represents an ideal blend of controlled risk and enhanced return. The strategies that offer the greatest prospects for strong long-term rewards tend to be inherently risky strategies. The strategies

---

*Adapted from Robert D. Arnott and Frank J. Fabozzi, "The Many Dimensions of the Asset Allocation Decision," in *Asset Allocation: A Handbook of Portfolio Policies, Strategies & Tactics,* ed. Arnott and Fabozzi (Chicago, IL: Probus Publishing, 1988), chap. 1.

that offer the greatest safety tend to offer opportunities for only modest returns. The balancing of these conflicting goals is what we call "policy" asset allocation.

Even within this definition of policy asset allocation, there are many considerations the investor must address. Policy asset allocation is the balancing of risk and reward in assessing a long-term normal asset mix. But *what* risks and *what* rewards are to be contemplated in this evaluation? For the investor with a short investment horizon and a need to preserve capital, the relevant definition of risk is very different than for a long-horizon investor such as a pension fund or an endowment fund. Ironically, the lowest risk strategy for a short-horizon investor may be a high-risk strategy for a long-horizon investor.

For many investors, there is more than one definition of risk that may have a bearing on the policy asset allocation decision. For example, the pension sponsor needs to be concerned with volatility of assets, volatility of liabilities, volatility of the surplus (or difference between assets and liabilities), volatility of the expense ratio or contribution rate for funding the pension plan, as well as a handful of other factors. But risk is not just volatility. Under the new pension-accounting guidelines for United States–based corporations, risk also can be defined in terms of shortfall. After all, upside risk is a risk that no one fears. But downside risk is to be avoided. Notably in pension management, there is the need to avoid any risk of a net, unfunded liability. No pension officer wants to be tagged as the individual responsible for a new liability appearing on the balance sheet!

There is a host of different tools at the investor's disposal for assessing the policy asset allocation decision. Should the investor use optimization techniques?[1] Should optimization techniques with a shortfall constraint be the basis for the policy–asset mix decision?[2] How does the suitable policy mix shift with different investor circumstances? All of these are questions that can and must be addressed in assessing the policy-asset-allocation decision.

II. Dynamic Strategies

Some of the more intriguing and controversial strategies to emerge in recent years are the *dynamic strategies,* in which the asset mix is mechanistically shifted in response to changing market conditions. The most well-publicized

1. H. Fong and Frank J. Fabozzi, "Asset Allocation Optimization Models," in *Asset Allocation,* ed. Arnott and Fabozzi, chap. 8, and Martin L. Leibowitz, Roy D. Henriksson, and William S. Krasker, "Portfolio Optimization within a Surplus Framework," in *Asset Allocation,* ed. Arnott and Fabozzi, chap. 9.
2. Martin L. Leibowitz and Roy D. Henrikkson, "Portfolio Optimization Under Shortfall Constraints," in *Asset Allocation,* ed. Arnott and Fabozzi, chap. 13.

variant of these dynamic strategies is certainly portfolio insurance.[3] However, dynamic strategies can be used for a whole host of purposes that go well beyond simple portfolio insurance, for all of its potential merits or demerits. In essence, these dynamic strategies enable the investor to reshape the entire distribution of returns. By dynamically shifting the asset mix, investors can control both downside risk and surplus volatility; can directly build *shortfall constraint* into their strategy; and in essence can reshape the return distribution as they see fit. Dynamic strategies are notable for their mechanistic nature and for their potential impact on policy asset allocation. They are mechanistic in the sense that any action in the capital markets triggers a prescribed reaction in the portfolio of assets.

Dynamic strategies have an interesting implication for the policy-asset-allocation decision. If a dynamic strategy is employed, it can represent a long-term policy-asset-allocation *response* to changing market conditions. Many advocates of portfolio insurance have also been advocates of a more aggressive asset-allocation stance, leaning more heavily toward equities in response to the protection offered by portfolio insurance. Other investment practitioners have argued for the opposite strategy: selling portfolio insurance. Such a process involves boosting equity exposure after a decline and lowering it after a rally, thereby ostensibly providing a built-in policy response to changing market conditions. Such strategies clearly provide greatly increased flexibility in investment management and greatly improved control over the nature of the portfolio, *if the dynamic strategy can be implemented at a reasonable cost*. This last issue has been the focal point of much of the controversy regarding dynamic strategies in the wake of the October 1987 market crash.[4]

III. Tactical Asset Allocation[5]

Once the policy asset allocation has been established, and once the use of dynamic strategies, if any, has been decided upon, the investor can turn attention to the issue of tactical asset allocation. Here again things are not as simple as they appear on the surface. Tactical asset allocation is not a single,

3. Hayne Leland, "Portfolio Insurance," in *The Handbook of Stock Index Futures and Options,* ed. Frank J. Fabozzi and Gregory M. Kipnis (Homewood, IL: Dow Jones–Irwin, 1989), chap. 12; and Richard M. Bookstaber, "Dynamic Hedging and Asset Allocation Strategies," in *Asset Allocation,* ed. Arnott and Fabozzi, chap. 10.
4. For a criticism of portfolio insurance, see Mark Kritzman, "What's Wrong with Portfolio Insurance," *Journal of Portfolio Management* (Winter 1986), and Gary L. Gastineau, "Surplus Protection and Portfolio Insurance," in *Asset Allocation,* ed. Arnott and Fabozzi, chap. 11.
5. For a review of tactical-asset-allocation techniques, see Charles H. DuBois, "Tactical Asset Allocation: A Review of the Current Techniques," in *Asset Allocation,* ed. Arnott and Fabozzi, chap. 14.

clearly defined strategy. There are many variations and nuances involved in building a tactical-allocation process.

Attention must first be paid to the whole puzzle of semantics. One of the problems in reviewing the concepts of asset allocation is that the same terms are often used for different concepts. The term *dynamic asset allocation* has been used to refer to some of the dynamic strategies noted above, as well as to tactical asset allocation. The term *strategic asset allocation* has been used to refer to both the long-term policy decision and intermediate-term efforts to strategically position the portfolio to benefit from major market moves, as well as to aggressive tactical strategies. Even the words *normal asset allocation* convey a stability that is not consistent with the real world. As an investor's risk expectation and tolerance for risk change, the normal or policy asset allocation stance may change. It is critical in exploring asset allocation issues to know what *element* of the asset-allocation decision is the subject of discussion, and to know *in what context* the words "asset allocation" are being used.

Tactical asset allocation broadly refers to active strategies that seek to enhance performance by opportunistically shifting the asset mix of a portfolio in response to the changing patterns of reward available in the capital markets. Notably, tactical asset allocation refers to disciplined processes for evaluating prospective rates of return on various classes of assets and establishing an asset-allocation response intended to capture higher rewards. However, there are different investment horizons and different mechanisms for evaluating the asset-allocation decision. These also merit a brief review.

Tactical asset allocation can refer to either an intermediate-term or a short-term process. There are tactical processes that seek to measure the relative attractiveness of the major classes of assets and to participate in major movements in the stock or bond markets. Other approaches are more short-term in nature, designed to capture short-term movements in the markets. The shared attributes of these tactical-asset-allocation processes are several:

- They are typically objective processes, based on analytic tools, such as regression analysis or optimization, rather than relying on subjective judgment.
- They are primarily driven by objective measures of prospective values within a class of assets. We *know* the yield on cash, we *know* the yield to maturity of long bonds, and the earning yield of the stock market represents a reasonable and objective proxy for long-term rewards available in stocks. These objective measures of reward lead to an inherently value-oriented process.
- Tactical-asset-allocation processes normally promote buying after a market decline and selling after a market rise. Hence, they are

inherently contrarian. By objectively measuring which classes of assets are offering the greatest prospective rewards, tactical-asset-allocation disciplines measure which classes of assets are most out of favor. In so doing, they steer investments into unloved classes of assets. These assets are priced to reflect the fact that they are out of favor and the corresponding fact that investors demand a premium reward for an out-of-favor investment. *Therein lies the effectiveness of tactical-asset-allocation disciplines.*

The structure of tactical-asset-allocation disciplines covers a wide spectrum. Some are simple, objective comparisons of available rates of return. Others seek to enhance the timeliness of these value-driven decisions by incorporating macro-economic measures, sentiment measures, measures of volatility, and even technical measures. In essence, the users of these more elaborate approaches would argue that, just as an undervalued stock can become more undervalued, so too an undervalued class of assets can grow more undervalued. The investor who buys an asset as soon as it becomes undervalued does less well than the investor who buys that same class of assets shortly before it rebounds.

In conclusion, we reiterate that there is not one asset-allocation decision, but many.

Pension Fund Investment Policy*

Zvi Bodie, Ph.D.
Professor of Finance
Boston University

I. Introduction

The purpose of this article is to explore the investment policy of pension funds. In the United States today, assets of pension plans amount to almost $1.8 trillion, which makes them the largest single pool of investable funds. An understanding of the principles and practices of pension fund investment management is critical for plan sponsors, for their professional money managers, and for the government officials charged with regulating and/or insuring pension funds.

This article addresses several questions:

- What are the unique features of pension plans that might cause their managers to adopt investment policies different from those of other investors?
- What does academic research tell us about the theory and practice of pension fund investment policy?
- What are the likely future trends in pension plan asset allocation?

II. Defined Contribution versus Defined Benefit Plans

Although employer pension programs vary in design, they usually are classified into two broad types: defined contribution (DC) and defined benefit

---

*This article was prepared under Department of Labor Contract Number J-9-P-8-0097.

(DB). These two categories are distinguished in the law under the Employee Retirement Income Security Act (ERISA).

The DC arrangement is conceptually the simpler of the two. Under a DC plan, each employee has an account into which both the employer and the employee (in a contributory plan) make regular contributions. Benefit levels depend on the total contributions and investment earnings of the accumulation in the account. Defined-contribution plans are in effect tax-deferred savings accounts held in trust for the employees.

Contributions usually are specified as a predetermined fraction of salary, although that fraction need not be constant over the course of a career. Contributions from both parties are tax deductible, and investment income accrues tax free. At retirement, the employee typically receives an annuity whose size depends on the accumulated value of the funds in the retirement account.

The employee often has some choice as to how the account is to be invested. In principle, contributions may be invested in any security, although in practice most plans limit investment options to various bond, stock, and money market funds. The employee bears all the investment risk; the retirement account is by definition fully funded, and the firm has no obligation beyond making its periodic contribution.

For defined-contribution plans investment policy is not much different from an individual deciding how to invest money in an Individual Retirement Account (IRA). The guiding principle is efficient diversification, that is, achieving the maximum expected return for any given level of risk exposure. The special feature is that investment earnings are not taxed as long as the money is held in the pension fund. This consideration should cause the investor to tilt the asset mix of the pension fund toward the least tax-advantaged securities such as corporate bonds.

In a DB plan, the employee's pension benefit entitlement is determined by a formula that takes into account years of service for the employer and, in most cases, wages or salary. Many defined-benefit formulas also take into account the Social Security benefit to which an employee is entitled. These are called "integrated" plans.

In a typical DB plan, the employee might receive retirement income equal to 1% of final salary times the number of years of service. Thus, an employee retiring after 40 years of service with a final salary of $15,000 per year would receive a retirement benefit of 40% of $15,000, or $6,000 per year.

The annuity promised to the employee is the employer's liability. The present value of this liability determines the amount of money that the employer must set aside in order to fund the deferred annuity that commences upon the employee's retirement.

Alternative Perspectives on DB Plans

Defined-benefit pension funds are pools of assets that serve as collateral for the firm's pension liabilities. Traditionally, these funds have been viewed as separate from the corporation. Funding and asset-allocation decisions are supposed to be made in the best interests of the beneficiaries, regardless of the financial condition of the sponsoring corporation.

Beneficiaries presumably want corporate pension plans to be as well funded as possible. Their preferences with regard to asset-allocation policy, however, are less clear. If beneficiaries are not entitled to any windfall gains — if the defined-benefit liabilities were really fixed in nominal terms — rationally they would prefer that the funds be invested in the least risky assets. If beneficiaries have a claim on surplus assets, though, the optimal asset allocation in principle could include virtually any mix of stocks and bonds.

Another way to view the pension fund investment decision is as an integral part of overall corporate financial policy. Seen from this perspective, defined-benefit liabilities are part and parcel of the firm's other fixed financial liabilities, and pension assets are part of the firm's assets. From this point of view, any plan surplus or deficit belongs to the firm's shareholders. The firm thus manages an extended balance sheet, which includes both its normal assets and liabilities and its pension assets and liabilities, in the best interests of *shareholders*.

Investment Strategy in DB Pension Plans

The practitioner literature seems to view a firm's pension liabilities as divided into two parts, retired and active. Benefits owed to retired participants are nominal, and benefits accruing to active participants are real. The nominal benefits can be immunized by investing in fixed-income securities with the same duration or even exactly the same pattern of cash flows as the pension annuities.

Accruing benefits, on the other hand, call for a very different investment policy, whose essence can be summarized as follows: In estimating the liabilities to active participants, the firm's actuaries make an "actuarial interest rate" assumption that becomes the target rate for the pension asset portfolio. Managers of the pension fund should view the possibility of receiving a rate of return below the actuarial assumption as having a greater negative weight than the positive weight associated with a return above the actuarial assumption. This factor will affect the asset-allocation decision.

Portfolio insurance is an investment strategy that developed in response to this view. It calls for maintaining an asset portfolio with a truncated and positively skewed probability distribution of returns. The probability of getting returns below the actuarial rate is zero, while the probabilities of returns above the actuarial rate are positive.

Portfolio insurance can be accomplished in a number of ways. The most direct method is to invest in common stocks and buy protective puts on them, which eliminates downside risk while maintaining upside potential. Another method is to invest in T-bills and buy call options.

The third way of providing portfolio insurance is to pursue a dynamic strategy with stocks and T-bills. The strategy uses continuous portfolio revision to replicate the payoff structure of the two previous strategies. It involves selling stocks when their price falls and buying them when their price rises.[1]

While it reduces downside risk, the adoption of portfolio insurance principles should lead to a lower average rate of return than on uninsured portfolios. Indeed, if pension funds have been insuring to any significant extent by pursuing even limited dynamic hedging strategies, one should expect to find that their average performance falls short of the average performance of conventionally managed portfolios.

This may help to explain the results reported in a study by Berkowitz and Logue.[2] They found that the average risk-adjusted performance of ERISA plans from 1968 to 1983 was lower than returns experienced by other diversified portfolios in U.S. financial markets. Reallocation among stocks, bonds, and cash equivalents had a significant deleterious effect on the portfolio performance of ERISA plans. It should be noted that the risk-adjusted performance measure used by Berkowitz and Logue is not really appropriate for measuring the performance of insured portfolios because it ignores the positive skewness of the distribution of returns that is the main objective of portfolio insurance strategies.

Recent changes in accounting rules may have a profound effect on the investment policies of pension funds, reinforcing the trend toward the use of immunization and portfolio insurance strategies. According to Rule 87 of the Financial Accounting Standards Board (FASB 87), corporations must report their unfunded pension liability on the corporate balance sheet. They previously reported this liability only in the footnotes to their financial statements. Furthermore, the interest rate they use in computing the present value of accrued benefits must be the current rate on long-term bonds.[3] The result is that fluctuations in long-term interest rates will produce large swings in

---

1. For a more complete discussion of dynamic hedging, see Chapter 20 of Zvi Bodie, Alex Kane, and Alan J. Marcus, *Investments* (Homewood, IL: Richard D. Irwin, 1989).
2. Berkowitz, Logue and Associates, Inc., "Study of the Investment Performance of ERISA Plans" (paper prepared for the Office of Pension and Welfare Benefits, Department of Labor, July 21, 1986).
3. Corporations retain the right to use an interest-rate assumption in their actuarial calculations for funding decisions different from what they use for financial reporting purposes.

reported pension liabilities that could, in the absence of offsetting actions by the corporation, play havoc with the firm's debt ratios.

Generally, security analysts and other observers of corporate financial behavior expect that, in order to offset this effect of FASB 87, corporations are likely to hedge the impact of interest rate fluctuations on reported pension liabilities by a strategy of duration matching, which will minimize the net effect on unfunded pension liabilities.[4] The impact on pension fund asset allocation could be profound; there may be a significant shift away from equities toward fixed-income securities.

The Black–Dewhurst Proposal

In 1981 Fischer Black and Moray Dewhurst created a stir among pension plan finance specialists with a proposal that carries to a logical extreme the notion that a pension plan is a way to shelter investment income from corporate income taxes.[5] That is, in order to maximize the value of a firm to its shareholders, a firm should fully fund its pension plan and invest the entire amount in bonds.

Black and Dewhurst propose that the firm reduce its tax liability by substituting bonds for stocks in the pension fund. The simple form of the proposal consists of four operations carried out at the same time:

1. Sell all equities, $X, in the pension fund;
2. Purchase on pension account $X of bonds of the same risk as the firm's own bonds;
3. Issue new debt in an amount equal to $X; and
4. Invest $X in equities on corporate account.

The net effect of these operations is that the firm has more debt outstanding owed on corporate account and more bonds owned on pension account. The market value of the firm's own shares should thereby increase by as much as the corporate tax rate times the amount of new debt taken on in the maneuver.

The plan adds value because the firm earns close to the pretax rate of return on the bonds in the fund but pays the after-tax rate on the debt issued to support the procedure. Given that only 20% of the dividends from the common stock are taxable, and that the tax on the capital gains can be deferred indefinitely by not selling appreciated stock, the effective tax rate on the equities held on corporate account will be very low. Thus, the after-tax

---

4. For a discussion of the investment implications of focusing on the pension surplus, see Martin L. Leibowitz and Roy D. Henriksson, "Portfolio Optimization within a Surplus Framework," *Financial Analysts Journal* (March-April 1988).
5. See Fischer Black and M.P. Dewhurst, "A New Investment Strategy for Pension Funds," *Journal of Portfolio Management* (Summer 1981).

TABLE 1. *Hi-Tek Corporation Balance Sheets Before Black–Dewhurst Manuever.*

a. Corporate Balance Sheet ($ million)

Assets		Liabilities and Owners' Equity	
Current Assets	$ 2	Debt	$10
Property, Plant & Equipment	48	O.E.	40
Total	$50		

b. Pension Fund Balance Sheet ($ million)

Assets		Liabilities and Fund Balance	
Equity	$10	PV of Accrued Benefits	$10
		Fund Balance	0

return on the equities will not be reduced significantly if they are switched from pension account to corporate account. If all value accrues to the firm's shareholders, if the effective corporate tax rate on equities is zero, and if the stocks held on corporate account are equivalent to the stocks previously held by the pension fund, the gain to shareholders has a present value of TX where T is the firm's marginal corporate income tax rate.

An example will clarify this proposal. The Hi-Tek Corporation is a relatively new company with a young work force and a fully funded defined-benefit pension plan. Hi-Tek's total corporate assets are worth $50 million, and its capital structure is 20% debt and 80% equity. Its pension assets consist entirely of a well-diversified portfolio of common stocks indexed to the S&P 500 and worth $10 million. The present value of its pension liabilities is $10 million. Table 1a shows the corporate balance sheet, and Table 1b shows the pension fund's balance sheet.

Hi-Tek's treasurer, who is in charge of the pension fund, reads the Black-Dewhurst article and decides to implement the proposal. The pension fund sells its entire $10 million stock portfolio to the corporation and invests the proceeds in corporate bonds issued by other high-tech companies. The corporation pays for the stock by issuing $10 million of new bonds. The resulting balance sheets appear in Table 2.

According to Black and Dewhurst, the result of these transactions should be an increase in the market value of owners' equity of as much as $10 million times the corporate tax rate, currently 34%. In other words, the market value of the outstanding shares of Hi-Tek's common stock should increase by $3.4 million.[6]

To see why, let r be the interest rate on the debt. As a result of the four operations above, the company now earns $r \times \$10$ million per year in interest

---

6. If the corporate tax rate on equities is greater than zero, the gain in shareholders' equity will be smaller.

TABLE 2. *Hi-Tek Corporation Balance Sheets After Black–Dewhurst Manuever.*

a. Corporate Balance Sheet ($ million)

Assets		Liabilities and Owners' Equity	
Current Assets	$ 2	Debt	$20
Property, Plant & Equipment	48	O.E.	40
Stocks	10		
Total	$60		

b. Pension Fund Balance Sheet ($ million)

Assets		Liabilities and Fund Balance	
Bonds	$10	PV of Accrued Benefits	$10
		Fund Balance	0

on the bonds it bought on pension account, while paying from its after-tax cash flow $(1-T)r \times \$10$ million per year on the debt it issued on corporate account. The net cash flow to the firm will be $0.34r \times \$10$ million per year, the tax saving on the interest. The present value of this saving in perpetuity is $3.4 million:

$$\frac{(0.34r \times \$10 \text{ million})}{r} = \$3.4 \text{ million} \tag{1}$$

Note that even though Hi-Tek's debt ratio has increased from 0.2 to 0.3, the overall risk of the firm has not changed. If we accept the theory that the pension fund assets and liabilities belong to the shareholders, the risk of the assets does not change when the $10 million of stock in the pension fund is, in effect, transferred to corporate account.

This plan implies that the company should increase its contributions to the pension plan up to the limits allowed by the IRS. This is because for every dollar of assets added to the pension fund, invested in bonds, and supported by issuing new bonds, the tax saving increases by rT per year, and the present value of shareholders' equity increases by $T. Thus if T is 0.34, shareholders' equity rises by $0.34 for every dollar added to pension assets or for every dollar switched out of stocks into bonds.

III. Research on Corporate Pension Policy

The financial aspects of corporate pension plans have increasingly attracted the attention of academics. Much of this attention has focused on theoretical analysis of the tax and incentive aspects of corporate pensions. Models of optimal capital structure have yielded testable implications for plan funding and investment strategy,[7] while advances in option-pricing theory have high-lighted the perverse incentives created by Pension Benefit Guarantee Corporation (PBGC) insurance.[8]

As yet, however, empirical work has failed to decisively confirm or reject these effects. Below we provide a brief overview of the relevant theory and of previous empirical work designed to test that theory.

Theory of Corporate Pension Plan Funding and Asset-Allocation Policy

The academic literature more and more views pension decisions as an integral part of overall corporate financial policy. From this perspective, employee benefits accrued under a defined-benefit pension plan are a long-term liability of the firm. Pension assets, while collateral for these liabilities, are assets of the firm in that the surplus/deficit belongs to the firm's shareholders. This integrated perspective requires managing the firm's extended balance sheet, including both its conventional assets and liabilities and its pension assets and liabilities, in the best interests of the shareholders.

Such a corporate financial perspective explicitly ignores the interests of the beneficiaries, in part because their defined benefits are insured by the PBGC. According to this view, if the beneficiaries are protected by the government, corporate pension decisions become what amounts to a game between the corporation and various government agencies and interests, a game that can be and should be thought of as an integral part of corporate financial policy.

The first pension decision of interest is the level-of-funding decision: Are there incentives for the firm to over- or underfund its pension liability? The tax effects are the first, and for most companies, the most important, part of this game. In closely related papers, Black[9] and Tepper[10] argue that the unique feature of pension funds from this integrated perspective is their role as a tax shelter. Because firms can effectively earn a pretax rate of return on any assets held in the pension fund and pass these returns through to shareholders, much as if the pension fund were an IRA or Keogh plan, the comparative advantage of a pension fund lies in its ability to be invested in the most heavily taxed assets. As Black and Dewhurst have demonstrated,

---

7. See Fischer Black, "The Tax Consequences of Long Run Pension Policy," *Financial Analysts Journal* (September-October 1980), pp. 17-23, and Irwin Tepper, "Taxation and Corporate Pension Policy," *Journal of Finance* (March 1981), pp. 1-13.
8. See William F. Sharpe, "Corporate Pension Funding Policy," *Journal of Financial Economics* (June 1976), pp. 183-193, and Jack Treynor, "The Principles of Corporate Pension Finance," *Journal of Finance* (May 1977), pp. 627-638.
9. Black, "The Tax Consequences of Long Run Pension Policy."
10. Tepper, "Taxation and Corporate Pension Policy."

the potential increase in the value of shareholders' equity resulting from a tax-sheltering strategy is substantial.

This means that pension funds should be invested entirely in taxable bonds, instead of common stock, real estate, or other assets that in effect are taxed at lower marginal tax rates for most shareholders, and that the corporation should fund its pension plan to the maximum extent allowed by the IRS so as to maximize the value of this tax shelter to shareholders. The tax effects of pensions should therefore induce corporations to follow extreme policies. Fully funded or overfunded pension plans should place their assets entirely in taxable bonds.

A second effect that may influence the level of funding, the "pension put" effect, is associated with the work of Sharpe,[11] Treynor,[12] and Harrison and Sharpe.[13] Briefly, the PBGC's insurance of pension benefits in effect gives the firm a put option. As with any option, the value of this put increases with the risk of the underlying asset. Thus, as long as the PBGC neither regulates pension fund risk nor accelerates its own claim at the first sign of financial distress, the firm has an incentive to undermine the PBGC's claim. It can do so and maximize the value of its put option by funding its pension plan only to the minimum permissible extent and investing the pension assets in the riskiest possible securities. This of course is the exact opposite policy from the decision suggested by the tax effects described above.

These two theories point to specific firm characteristics as the key determinants of corporate pension policies: profitability, risk (including leverage), and tax-paying status. Two major studies have explored the empirical relationship between the financial characteristics of corporations and their asset-allocation policies. They are described in detail below.

Empirical Studies

Friedman was the first to test empirically for the impact of firm financial characteristics on pension policy. Integrating data from the Standard & Poor's Compustat file and from Form 5500 data for 1977, he examined the relationship between asset allocation and measures of business risk and leverage.[14] He estimated a number of relationships of the following form: The dependent variable was some aspect of the pension decision such as unfunded

---

11. Sharpe, "Corporate Pension Funding Policy."

12. Treynor, "The Principles of Corporate Pension Finance."

13. M.J. Harrison and W. F. Sharpe, "Optimal Funding and Asset Allocation Rules for Defined Benefit Pension Plans," in *Financial Aspects of U.S. Pension Systems,* edited by Bodie and Shoven (Chicago: University of Chicago Press, 1983).

14. Benjamin M. Friedman, "Pension Funding, Pension Asset Allocation and Corporate Finance: Evidence from Individual Company Data," in *Financial Aspects of the U.S. Pension Systems.*

liabilities or the proportion of pension assets invested in bonds; independent variables included measures of conventional financing, such as ordinary balance sheet liabilities, plus one other control variable such as firm profitability, risk, and tax-paying status.

Friedman concluded that pension decisions are indeed related to other aspects of the corporate financing decision. He found that unfunded liabilities and the proportion of pension assets invested in bonds are both positively related to ordinary balance sheet liabilities. He also found that a reverse relationship holds, with balance sheet leverage depending positively on unfunded pension liabilities, regardless of the control variable used—a "risk-offsetting effect."

Results with tests of individual variables such as tax-paying status, however, do not favor any strong conclusion (and often change sign with specification), thus raising rather than resolving questions. This may be the result of bias induced by firm-to-firm variability in the actuarial assumptions used in calculating reported liabilities. That is, reported liabilities may have differed across firms in the sample solely as a result of discount-rate assumptions.

Bodie et al. demonstrated that reported liabilities were systematically biased because of the way firms chose the discount rates that they used in calculating the present value of accrued benefits.[15] They examined the asset allocation choices for 215 firms using data collected in 1980 and estimated reduced-form relationships between pension decisions and the firm's tax-paying status, profitability, and risk. Their data came from FASB 35 filings for 1980, which included interest-rate assumptions, so they were able to adjust reported liabilities roughly to a common rate. In this initial adjustment, they found that the reporting of pension fund liabilities was systematically linked to company profitability through the choice of a discount rate. More profitable firms tended to choose lower discount rates and thus report greater pension liabilities.

The first pension decision examined in Bodie et al. was the extent of funding, measured by pension assets as a fraction of vested pension liabilities. There was strong evidence that firm profitability is positively related to funding, but there was no statistically significant relationship between funding and risk or tax-paying characteristics. Some evidence of the pension put effect was found when the sample was split by riskiness of the firm.

The study also examined asset allocation. The proportion of assets held in fixed-income securities was related to the same firm characteristics listed above. A significant fraction of firms invested their pension assets entirely

15. Zvi Bodie; Jay O. Light; Randall Morck; and Robert H. Taggart, Jr., "Corporate Pension Policy: An Empirical Investigation," in *Issues in Pension Economics,* ed. by Bodie, Shoven, and Wise (Chicago: University of Chicago Press, 1987).

in fixed-income securities, and the proportion of assets allocated to fixed-income securities was positively related to the level of funding.

IV. Hedging Against Inflation

As we pointed out earlier, DB pension funds often view their accruing pension liabilities to active employees as fixed in real as opposed to nominal terms. In that case, a portfolio is efficient if it offers the minimum variance of real rate of return for any given mean real rate of return.

Most textbook expositions of portfolio selection theory, however, and indeed most real-world applications of that theory, are cast in nominal terms. Typically, Treasury bills are taken as the risk-free asset, and the optimal combination of risky assets is constructed on the basis of the covariance matrix of nominal returns. All efficient portfolios are combinations of cash and the optimal nominally risky portfolio.

Since January 1988, however, U.S. investors have had available to them the possibility of investing in virtually risk-free securities linked to the U.S. consumer price level. The new securities were issued by the Franklin Savings Association of Ottawa, Kansas in two different forms. The first is certificates of deposit, called Inflation-Plus CDs, insured by the Federal Savings and Loan Insurance Corporation (FSLIC), and paying an interest rate tied to the Bureau of Labor Statistics Consumer Price Index (CPI). Interest is paid monthly and is equal to a stated real rate plus the proportional increase in the CPI during the previous month. As of this writing (September 1988), the real rate ranges from 3% per year for a one-year maturity CD to 3.3% per year for a ten-year maturity.

The second form is twenty-year, noncallable collateralized bonds, called Real Yield Securities, or REALs. These offer a floating coupon rate of 3% per year plus the previous year's proportional change in the CPI, adjusted and payable quarterly. A recent issue of similar bonds includes a put option.

Two other financial institutions have recently followed the lead of Franklin Savings.[16] It seems as if we have reached a milestone in the history of the financial markets in the United States. For many years prominent economists from all ends of the ideological spectrum have been arguing in favor of the U.S. Treasury's issuing such securities, and scholars have speculated about why private markets for them have not hitherto developed.[17]

---

16. In August 1988 Anchor Savings Bank became the second U.S. institution to issue REALs, and in September 1988 JHM Acceptance Corporation issued modified index-linked bonds subject to a nominal interest-rate cap of 14% per annum.
17. See, for example, the analysis in Stanley Fischer, "On the Nonexistence of Privately Issued Index Bonds, in the U.S. Capital Market," in *Indexing, Inflation, and Economic Policy* (Cambridge: MIT Press, 1986).

The existence of CPI-linked bonds makes possible inflation-protected retirement annuities. Retired people have long been considered the most vulnerable to inflation risk, but proposals for private-market solutions to their problem have been stymied by the lack of a real risk-free asset.[18]

Bodie, for example, proposed the idea of a variable annuity offering at least limited protection against inflation risk, but his proposal lacked appeal primarily because of the low mean real rate of return available on money market instruments (between 0 and 1% per year), the best available inflation hedge at that time.[19] With the availability of virtually risk-free securities offering real rates in excess of 3% per year, the situation is markedly different. Pension funds and other providers of retirement benefits, which currently offer only nominal annuities, could also offer attractive real annuity options to retirees.

To illustrate how such a real annuity option might work, assume that you are an individual who at retirement is entitled to a benefit with a present value of $100,000. Your retirement plan currently offers you a conventional nominal annuity computed on the assumption of a nominal interest rate of 8% per year and a life expectancy of 15 years. Assuming the first payment is to be received immediately, the annual benefit is $10,818. The plan hedges its liability to you by investing in risk-free nominal bonds paying a nominal rate of 8% per year.

From your perspective the real value of this stream of benefits is uncertain. Consider the purchasing power of the final benefit payment to be received 14 years from now. If the rate of inflation turns out to be 5% per year, the real value of the final benefit will be $5,464, about half the value of the first payment. If the rate of inflation turns out to be 10% per year, the real value of the final payment drops to $2,849.

Contrast this with a hypothetical real annuity. Since your plan can now invest your $100,000 to earn a real risk-free rate of 3% per year it could offer you a real annuity computed on the assumption of 3% per year. Your annual benefit would be $8,133 guaranteed in real terms. While the initial payment is lower than under the nominal option, the real value of the benefit is insured against inflation.

---

18. Feldstein and Summers have both argued that the elderly may in fact already be over-indexed because of their claims to Social Security benefits and their ownership of real estate. See Martin Feldstein, "Private Pensions as Corporate Debt," in *Changing Roles of Debt and Equity in Financing U.S. Capital Formation,* edited by Benjamin Friedman (Chicago: University of Chicago Press, 1982), and Lawrence Summer, "Observations on the Indexation of Old Age Pensions," in *Financial Aspects of the U.S. Pension System.*

19. Zvi Bodie, "An Innovation for Stable Real Retirement Income," *Journal of Portfolio Management* (Fall 1980), pp. 5–13. Bodie suggested improving the inflation protection afforded by money market instruments by hedging them against unanticipated inflation with a very small position in a well-diversified portfolio of commodity futures contracts.

It is important to realize that the real annuity need not start at a lower value than the conventional nominal annuity. Bodie and Pesando have shown how real annuities can be designed with the same starting value as conventional nominal annuities.[20] Such a real annuity would have to have a downward tilt to the benefit stream, just like the expected real value of the benefit stream from the nominal annuity. The essential difference would then be that the real annuity would be insured against inflation while the nominal annuity would not.

The idea of indexing retirement annuities after retirement is only one aspect of inflationproofing private pension plans. Another is indexing benefit accruals under private defined-benefit (DB) plans. The accrual patterns and real benefit streams under virtually all private DB plans in the United States are extremely sensitive to inflation. Inflation reduces the real value of DB entitlements because pension benefits are fixed in nominal terms once an employee stops working for the plan sponsor or once the sponsor terminates the plan. This reduces the value of accrued benefits to all participating employees, but it especially affects those who switch employers during their working careers.

For example, suppose you are 45 years old and have worked for the same employer for 20 years. Assume that your DB plan promises 1% of final salary per year of service; that your most recent salary was $50,000; that normal retirement age is 65, and that your life expectancy is age 80. Your claim on the pension fund is a deferred annuity of $10,000 per year starting at age 65 and lasting for 15 years.

If you leave your current employer, what do you have? Since the benefit is not indexed to any wage or price level as Social Security benefits are, the benefit will be losing real value as the price level goes up. Assuming inflation of 5% per year, the value of $1 will have fallen to $0.38 by the time you retire, so that your first year's benefit of $10,000 will have a real value of only $3,800, and that value will continue to fall each year as inflation continues. If, however, you stay with your employer, and your salary increases at the rate of inflation, and if your employer indexes your benefit to the cost of living after retirement, then you will have an annuity worth $10,000 of today's purchasing power per year for life.

Looking at the situation in terms of present values and assuming a nominal discount rate of 8% per year and a real discount rate of 3% per year, your accrued benefit if you switch jobs or if the plan is terminated has a present value of $18,364. If the job and plan continue, with complete indexation both before and after retirement, the accrued benefit has a present value of $66,097.

---

20. Zvi Bodie and J. Pesando, "Retirement Annuity Design in an Inflationary Climate," in *Financial Aspects of the U.S. Pension System.*

One simple alternative to the current system of DB pensions is to offer pension benefits whose value is defined in real terms. This is most readily accomplished by indexing the starting level of benefits either to an index of wages (the way Social Security benefits are indexed) or to an index of prices like the CPI, even for employees who leave the firm. Similarly, a cost-of-living provision could be included in the benefit formula after retirement.

To the extent that pension plans actually were to offer indexed benefits to their employees, pension fund asset allocation could be profoundly affected. A switch to indexed pensions would probably result in hedging strategies involving investment in long-term securities linked to the price level.

V. Summary and Conclusions

The main points and conclusions of this article are:

(1) Pension fund investment policy depends critically on the type of plan: defined contribution versus defined benefit. Both types of plan normally are exempt from taxation, but defined-benefit plans have unique features that can lead their sponsors to pursue investment policies that differ radically from those of defined-contribution plans.

(2) For defined-contribution plans investment policy is not much different from an individual deciding how to invest the money in an IRA. The guiding principle is efficient diversification, that is, achieving the maximum expected return for any given level of risk exposure. The special feature is that investment earnings are not taxed as long as the money is held in the pension fund. This consideration should cause the investor to tilt the asset mix of the pension fund towards the least tax-advantaged securities, such as corporate bonds.

(3) For defined-benefit plans the practitioner literature seems to advocate immunization strategies to hedge benefits owed to retired employees and portfolio insurance strategies to hedge benefits accruing to active employees.

(4) Academic research into the theory of optimal funding and asset-allocation rules for corporate DB plans concludes that, if their objective is shareholder wealth maximization, these plans should pursue extreme policies. For healthy plans, the optimum is full funding and investment exclusively in taxable fixed-income securities. For very underfunded plans, the optimum is minimum funding and investment in the riskiest assets.

(5) Empirical research has so far failed to decisively confirm or reject the predictions of this theory of corporate pension policy.

(6) Recent rule changes adopted by the Financial Accounting Standards Board regarding corporate reporting of defined-benefit plan assets and liabilities may lead to a significant shift to fixed-income securities.

(7) The recent introduction of price-level indexed securities in U.S. financial markets may lead to significant changes in pension fund asset allocation. By giving plan sponsors a simple way to hedge inflation risk, these securities make it possible to offer plan participants inflation protection both before and after retirement.

PART I

Equity Portfolio Management

The Collapse of the Efficient-Market Hypothesis
A Look at the Empirical Anomalies of the 1980s*

Marc R. Reinganum, Ph.D.
Phillips Professor of Finance
College of Business
University of Iowa

I. Introduction

The last decade witnessed an explosion in research that demolished widely held beliefs about the price behaviors of stock-market securities. As a group this research comprises the "market anomaly" literature. Of course, an anomaly can only exist relative to a given benchmark, and by the mid-1970s such a benchmark clearly existed: the efficient-market hypothesis. By the mid-1970s a preponderance of academic research suggested that capital markets were informationally efficient, so that stock prices fully reflected all available information. Operationally, this meant that changes in stock prices were unpredictable from one day to the next and that returns earned by stocks over time were commensurate with their levels of risk. Thus stock returns were characterized as being independently and identically distributed over time, and differences in expected or mean returns among stocks were attributed to their risks as measured by beta, a covariance measure of risk with the market. This view seemed reasonable and much empirical work supported it.[1]

By the mid-1980s this efficient-markets view of stock-price movements came under serious seige on two fronts. First, a body of research emerged

---

*The title for this paper was selected prior to the stock market crash of October 19, 1987.
1. For example, see Eugene F. Fama, *Foundations of Finance: Portfolio Decisions and Securities Prices* (New York: Basic Books, Inc., 1976).

that documented that differences in average rates of returns among securities are not completely explained by their betas. A striking finding in this literature is that a firm's stock market capitalization seems to be a better predictor of future returns than a firm's estimated beta. On the second front, another group of papers revealed that stock returns are *not* identically distributed over time. In particular, this research uncovered systematic patterns in stock returns that vary with certain calendar periods. The purpose of this article is to survey the major research findings in these two areas.

II. The Failure of Beta

In the 1960s two articles by Nicholson suggested that firms with low price/earnings (P/E) ratios outperform firms with high P/E ratios.[2] Among his findings, Nicholson reported in 1960 that the three-year appreciation of the five stocks with the lowest P/E ratios averaged 56%, whereas the equivalent appreciation for the five stocks with the highest P/E ratios equaled only 21%. At that time Nicholson's results were surprising, because most financial analysts assumed high P/E stocks were bought for growth.

Modern portfolio theory, and the capital-asset-pricing model (CAPM) in particular, would offer an alternative interpretation of Nicholson's findings. According to the CAPM, the reason that low P/E stocks could experience average rates of return greater than those of high P/E stocks is that low P/E stocks may be riskier than their high P/E counterparts. Because the risk of a security within the CAPM is measured by its beta, the CAPM could explain Nicholson's findings as long as the betas of low P/E companies were sufficiently greater than the betas of high P/E companies.

Nearly 10 years after Nicholson's second article, Basu resurrected the P/E effect in a way that seriously challenged the efficient-market hypothesis.[3] Unlike Nicholson, Basu had at his disposal the paradigm of the CAPM, and the CAPM dictated how to measure risk using beta. In addition, Basu had the advantage of computerized data files from COMPUSTAT and CRSP, so that he could analyze 1,400 industrial firms that traded on the New York Stock Exchange between September 1956 and August 1971. Thus Basu's effort represented a large-scale study of the potential P/E effect that carefully controlled for risk as measured by beta. Figure 1 plots the average annual abnormal returns for Basu's five P/E portfolios. Basu reported that, on a risk-adjusted basis, the difference in average annual returns between low and

2. S. Francis Nicholson, "Price-Earnings Ratios," *Financial Analysts' Journal* 16 (July–August 1960): 43–45; and S. Francis Nicholson, "Price Ratios in Relation to Investment Results," *Financial Analysts' Journal* 24 (January–February 1968): 105–109.
3. S. Basu, "Investment Performance of Common Stocks in Relation to Their Price-Earnings Ratios: A Test of the Efficient Market Hypothesis," *Journal of Finance* 32 (June 1977): 663–82.

FIGURE 1. *Basu's Computation of Annual Average Abnormal Portfolio Returns Based on Jensen's Differential.*

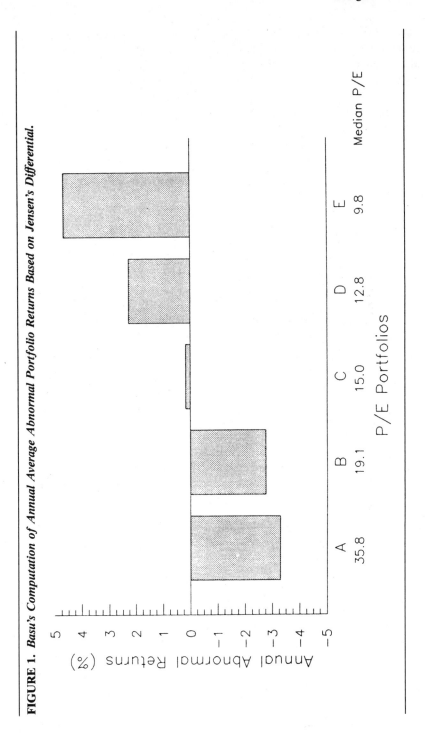

high P/E securities exceeded 7%. Furthermore, this return differential seemed to be stable between the two seven-year periods of Basu's study. Basu looked at potential factors other than beta risk differentials (for example, differential taxes and transaction costs) that might explain the differential return between low and high P/E stocks but still concluded that both tax-exempt and tax-paying investors could profit by acquiring low P/E stocks. Beta failed in the sense that, on an annual basis, low P/E portfolios earned superior rates of return after controlling for risk.

The real deluge of evidence reporting major deficiencies in the CAPM did not begin until 1981. Papers by Banz and Reinganum, appearing in the *Journal of Financial Economics* in March of that year, suggested that economically and statistically significant abnormal returns could be earned by grouping securities on the basis of their stock-market capitalizations (price per share multiplied by number of shares outstanding).[4] In particular, both authors reported that the average returns of small capitalization stocks significantly exceeded the average returns of large capitalization stocks, even after adjusting returns for beta risk.[5]

Banz analyzed the monthly returns of New York Stock Exchange (NYSE) stocks over the period 1931–1975. During this period Banz found that the 50 smallest NYSE stocks outperformed the 50 largest companies by 1.01% per month on average. Banz also presented evidence that suggest the so-called size effect was not linear; that is, the large, positive abnormal returns were clustered among the very smallest NYSE companies.

Reinganum studied the size effect over a shorter interval of time, 1963–1977, but included all the firms that traded on the American as well as New York stock exchanges. He reported a median capitalization for his small-firm portfolio of only $8.3 million. As might be expected, the magnitude of the effect increased as one dipped further down the capitalization scale. Reinganum's evidence indicated that the smallest-firm portfolio earned a mean

---

4. Rolf W. Banz, "The Relationship between Return and Market Value of Common Stocks," *Journal of Financial Economics* 9 (March 1981): 3–18; and Marc R. Reinganum, "Misspecification of Capital Asset Pricing: Empirical Anomalies Based on Earnings' Yields and Market Values," *Journal of Financial Economics* 9 (March 1981): 19–46.
5. An offshoot of the research on the size effect concerned the question of whether the size effect and the P/E effect were two independent phenomena or manifestations of just one effect. Reinganum's 1981 article presented evidence that suggested the size effect subsumed the P/E effect. Basu ["The Relation between Earnings' Yield, Market Value and Return," *Journal of Financial Economics* 12 (June 1983): 129–56] later disputed Reinganum's claim. Thomas Cook and Michael Rozeff ["Size and Earnings/Price Ratio Anomalies: One Effect or Two?" *Journal of Financial and Quantitative Analysis* 19 (December 1984): 449–66] replicated Reinganum's findings using his methods but were unable to corroborate Basu's assertion that the P/E effect subsumed the size effect. Cook and Rozeff argued for both a P/E and a size effect. Regardless of the outcome of this debate, the evidence clearly points out the inability of beta to explain cross-sectional differences in average returns.

excess return of 0.05% per trading day whereas the largest-firm group experienced a mean excess return of −0.034% per trading day. Furthermore, Reinganum's evidence displayed a virtually monotonic relationship between the market capitalization and mean excess returns (see Figure 2). Based on annual data, Reinganum calculated the difference in unadjusted returns between small and large firms to be 23.3% on average.[6] Of course, both Banz and Reinganum recognized that the size effect varied from subperiod to subperiod and in fact, in some subperiods, was negative. The variability of the size effect was emphasized in a subsequent paper by Brown, Kleidon, and Marsh.[7]

The importance of the research by Banz and Reinganum is that it clearly establishes differences in average returns cannot be explained by differences in estimated betas. The discrepancies between what small stocks actually earn and what small stocks are predicted to earn, based on their level of beta risk, are significant both statistically and economically. Naturally, other researchers attempted to explain these anomalous findings using a variety of arguments. Some researchers questioned whether beta risk was appropriately estimated.[8] Others investigated whether transaction costs might eliminate profitable exploitation of the size effect.[9] More recent research has attempted to reconcile the size effect with measures of risk alluded to in the arbitrage-price theory, but this evidence is mixed. In any event the empirical evidence from the 1980s has clearly shown that estimated betas fail to explain important differences in average returns between small and large companies. The failure of beta to account for cross-sectional differences in average returns opened the door to those who have devised simple trading strategies that systematically beat well-accepted investment benchmarks. This research constitutes one branch of the empirical anomalies.[10]

6. Marc R. Reinganum, "Portfolio Strategies Based on Market Capitalization," *The Journal of Portfolio Management* 9 (Winter 1983): 29–36.
7. Philip Brown, Allan W. Kleidon, and Terry A. Marsh, "New Evidence on the Nature of Size-related Anomalies in Stock Prices," *Journal of Financial Economics* 12 (June 1983): 33–56.
8. For example, see Richard Roll, "A Possible Explanation of the Small Firm Effect," *Journal of Finance* 36 (September 1981): 879–88. Also see Marc R. Reinganum, "A Direct Test of Roll's Conjecture on the Firm Size Effect," *Journal of Finance* 37 (March 1982): 27–35.
9. For example, see Hans R. Stoll and Richard E. Whaley, "Transaction Costs and the Small Firm Effect," *Journal of Financial Economics* 12 (June 1983): 57–80. Also see Paul Schultz, "Transaction Costs and the Small Firm Effect: A Comment," *Journal of Financial Economics* 12 (June 1983): 81–88.
10. Other research also explores potential deficiencies in beta, such as studies of the Value Line ranking system [for example, Fischer Black, "Yes, Virginia There Is Hope: Tests of the Value Line Ranking System," *Financial Analysts Journal* 29 (September–October 1973): 10–14] and studies of a dividend-yield effect [for example, Robert H. Litzenberger and Krishna Ramaswamy, "The Effects of Personal Taxes and Dividends on Capital Asset Prices: Theory and Market Equilibrium," *Journal of Financial Economics* 7 (June 1979): 163–95]. However, the magnitude of the size effect seems much larger than either of these two effects.

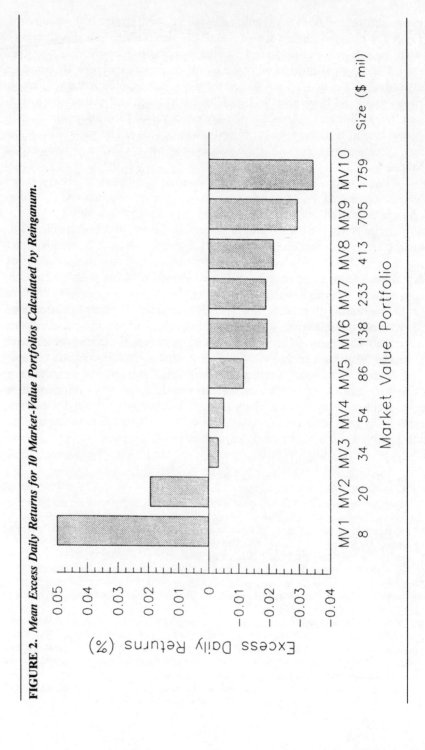

FIGURE 2. *Mean Excess Daily Returns for 10 Market-Value Portfolios Calculated by Reinganum.*

III. Systematic Patterns in Stock Returns

The second set of research papers that drove a stake into the heart of the classical interpretation of the efficient-market hypothesis analyzed predictable changes in expected returns. Through the mid-1970s, most academic researchers probably accepted the proposition that stock returns are independently and identically distributed, at least as a very good first approximation. This view of stock returns grew out of research that suggested stock prices follow a random walk. By the mid-1980s this view of stock price movements imploded. As researchers scrutinized the data more and more closely, four fascinating patterns in stock emerged:

1. A month-of-the-year effect
2. A week-of-the-month effect
3. A day-of-the-week effect
4. An hour-of-the-day effect

Perhaps with the next several years "minute-of-the-hour" and "second-of-the-minute" papers will be written! The month-of-the-year effect is commonly referred to as the January effect. As early as 1976, Rozeff and Kinney documented that the mean returns in January exceed the mean returns of the other months for a market index of NYSE stocks over the period 1904–1974.[11] However, it was not until seven years later that research returned to this topic with a vengeance. In 1983 Keim, investigating the size effect earlier documented by Banz and Reinganum, discovered that this effect is not uniform throughout the calendar year.[12] That is, although small firms outperform large ones on average, the differential return varies by calendar month. Keim reported that, over the 1963–1979 period, nearly 50% of the average magnitude of the size effect occurs in January. Furthermore, Keim found that small firms *always* outperformed large ones in January, even in years in which large firms experienced higher average returns than small ones. Figure 3 displays the differences in average daily excess returns between the smallest and largest portfolios by calendar month. The pattern of January returns is unmistakably different from those of the other months. In January the returns of small firms surge

11. Michael S. Rozeff and William R. Kinney, Jr., "Capital Market Seasonality: The Case of Stock Returns," *Journal of Financial Economics* 3 (October 1976): 379–402. Following up on the research of Rozeff and Kinney, Seha Tinic and Richard West ["Risk and Return: January vs. the Rest of the Year," *Journal of Financial Economics* 13 (December 1984): 561–74] discover that January is the *only* month in which a consistently positive, statistically significant relationship between risk and return exists. At least within the framework of the CAPM, they find investors are compensated for bearing risk only in January.
12. Donald B. Keim, "Size-Related Anomalies and Stock Return Seasonality: Further Empirical Evidence," *Journal of Financial Economics* 12 (June 1983): 13–32.

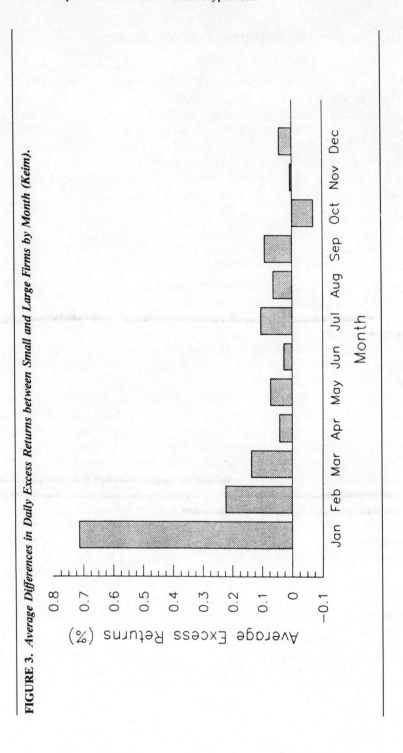

FIGURE 3. *Average Differences in Daily Excess Returns between Small and Large Firms by Month (Keim).*

ahead of those of their larger brethren. Thus the January effect is primarily a phenomenon found among smaller-capitalization stocks. The dramatic shifts in mean returns are not observed among the very largest stocks.

Keim's research begged an explanation, and the tax-loss–selling hypothesis emerged as the leading contender. The folklore behind the tax-loss–selling hypothesis is that individuals sell their losers, which reduces their tax liability. This selling pressure, according to this reasoning, lowers the price of the stock at the end of December. In January the motive for tax selling is eliminated, the selling pressure is relieved, and stock prices rebound resulting in a high January return. Though this explanation does not seem to argue for equilibrium, some earlier empirical work supported it. For example, Branch reported that abnormal profits could be earned if one bought the stock of companies whose prices reach yearly lows in the last week of December, and sold these stocks in January.[13]

In 1983 Reinganum investigated the tax-loss–selling hypothesis as it applied to small and large firms.[14] Based on a measure of potential tax-loss selling, he classified firms into four groups ranging from the previous year's losers to the previous year's winners. Reinganum concluded that the abnormally high returns witnessed during the first few days in January appeared to be consistent with the tax-loss–selling hypothesis. However, tax-loss selling could not explain the entire January effect, because the small firms least likely to be sold for tax reasons also experienced large average January returns relative to other months.[15] After eliminating a list of possible spurious causes of the turn-of-the-year effect, Roll reported a negative relationship between the turn-of-the-year return and the return during the preceding year. Though such evidence is consistent with a tax-loss–selling story, Roll concluded that transaction costs and low liquidity probably prevent the elimination of the seasonality of returns. Schultz enhanced the credibility of the tax-loss–selling hypothesis. He detected no evidence of a January effect in small stock returns prior to the War Revenue Act of 1917.[16]

The search for an explanation of the January effect led to investigations of the returns of stocks traded on international markets. Gultekin and Gultekin surveyed stock-return indexes from most major industrial countries and found evidence of seasonality that is manifested at the turn of the tax year,

13. Ben Branch, "A Tax Loss Trading Rule," *Journal of Business* 50 (April 1977): 198–207.
14. Marc R. Reinganum, "The Anomalous Stock Market Behavior of Small Firms in January: Empirical Tests for Tax-Loss Selling Effects," *Journal of Financial Economics* 12 (June 1983): 89–104.
15. Richard Roll, "Vas ist das?" *The Journal of Portfolio Management* 9 (Winter 1983): 18–28.
16. Paul Schultz, "Personal Income Taxes and the January Effect: Small Firm Stock Returns before the War Revenue Act of 1917: A Note," *Journal of Finance* 40 (March 1985): 333–43.

usually January.[17] They also reported that the stock-return seasonality did not seem to be related to size. Brown, Keim, Kleidon, and Marsh studied the returns of securities listed on the Australian stock exchange.[18] They discovered a January seasonal in returns among Australian stocks. Their smallest portfolio earned 8.86% on average during January. Unlike that of the United States, however, the Australian tax year ends on June 30. Thus Brown and others challenged the assertion that the January effect is tax-driven, although they did recognize the possibility that some of the effect may be caused by the integration of capital markets worldwide (that is, with the United States). Interestingly, Brown and others also found large average returns in July for the Australian stock. In fact, among the smaller portfolios, the July average returns tended to be slightly larger than the January returns.

Berges, McConnell, and Schlarbaum analyzed returns of Canadian stocks over the period 1951–1980.[19] The Canadian data also exhibited a strong seasonal in January. However, the Canadian returns displayed a strong January effect even during the period in which there were no taxes on capital gains. Berges and others concluded that this evidence does not support the tax-loss–selling hypothesis as the sole explanation of the January effect. Kato and Schallheim studied returns of securities that trade on the Tokyo Stock Exchange.[20] They detected the presence of both the January and size effects. Their data also revealed somewhat larger returns in June. Reinganum and Shapiro examined seasonality in the London Stock Exchange.[21] Prior to the introduction of a capital-gains tax in England, the authors could not reject the hypothesis that the mean monthly returns for all months are identical. After the introduction of a tax, the authors reported two months stand apart from the rest, January and April. Reinganum and Shapiro concluded that the April evidence is consistent with the tax-loss–selling hypothesis (because the tax-year end is April 5), but the January returns are not.

The January or month-of-the-year effect has been extensively examined using stock return data from the United States as well as a host of other industrialized countries. The evidence overwhelmingly indicates that the mean

17. Mustafa N. Gultekin and N. Bulent Gultekin, "Stock Market Seasonality: International Evidence," *Journal of Financial Economics* 12 (December 1983): 469–82.

18. Philip Brown, Donald B. Keim, Allan W. Kleidon, and Terry A. Marsh, "Stock Return Seasonalities and the Tax-Loss Selling Hypothesis: Analysis of the Arguments and Australian Evidence," *Journal of Financial Economics* 12 (June 1983): 105–28.

19. Angel Berges, John J. McConnell, and Gary G. Schlarbaum, "The Turn-of-the-Year in Canada," *Journal of Finance* 39 (March 1984): 185–92.

20. Kato Kiyoshi and James S. Schallheim, "Seasonal and Size Anomalies in the Japanese Stock Market," *Journal of Financial and Quantitative Analysis* 20 (June 1985): 243–60.

21. Marc R. Reinganum and Alan C. Shapiro, "Taxes and Stock Return Seasonality: Evidence for the London Stock Exchange," *Journal of Business* 60 (April 1987): 281–95.

monthly return in January is substantially different from the mean returns of most other months. In particular, the January returns are the largest. The reasons for the exceptional performance of stocks in January, especially small ones, is still debated. Some evidence suggests that the pattern of stock returns in January may be tax-induced, but the evidence is mixed. In any case the January effect marks a real departure from the view that stock returns are independently and identically distributed. The mean returns in January are significantly different from those of other months, both in a statistical and an economic sense.

The next anomalous pattern might be termed the week-of-the-month effect. This anomaly actually refers to the pattern of returns earned by firms within a trading month. Over the period from 1963 through 1981, Ariel divided trading months into two equal periods.[22] A trading month starts on the last trading day (inclusive) of a calendar month and extends to the last trading day (exclusive) of the following calendar month. Ariel reported that, using an equal-weighted market index, the 19-year cumulative returns attributable to the first half of a trading month were 2,552.40%. In contrast, the 19-year cumulative returns earned during the last half of the trading month were a paltry −0.25%. The results are truly astounding. Perhaps Ariel's own summation is the most dramatic: "During the nineteen years studied, all of the market's cumulative advance occurred during the first half of the trading months, with the last half of the trading months contributing nothing" (p. 173). Furthermore, Ariel rules out the possibility that this effect is just another manifestation of the January effect. Even when Januaries are removed from the sample, Ariel calculated a statistically significant difference between the mean returns from the first and second halves of a month. Ariel's finding of a week-of-the-month effect in stock returns is still unexplained.

A much larger body of evidence investigates the day-of-the-week effect. This effect refers to the unusual behavior of stock prices from the close of trading on Friday to the close on Monday. Under the calendar-time hypothesis, one might expect the return from Friday close to Monday close to be three times as large as the returns for any other one trading day. But, based on the daily returns of the S&P 500 composite portfolio over the period from 1953 through 1977, French found that Monday's returns are actually negative on average.[23] In fact the mean returns on Monday were negative in 20 of the 25 years. Ignoring transaction costs, French calculated that a trading rule that sold on Friday afternoon, held cash over the weekend, and

22. Robert A. Ariel, "A Monthly Effect in Stock Returns," *Journal of Financial Economics* 18 (March 1987): 161–74.
23. Kenneth R. French, "Stock Returns for the Weekend Effect," *Journal of Financial Economics* 8 (March 1980): 55–69.

repurchased on Monday afternoon would net an investor an average annual return of 13.4%. Gibbons and Hess independently reached similar conclusions.[24] Gibbons and Hess studied not only various market indices, but the 30 individual securities that comprise the Dow Jones 30. From the period July 1962–December 1978, they reported a negative Monday return for their various indexes as well as for each of the 30 individual securities. Gibbons and Hess also found below-average returns for T-bills on Mondays. Keim and Stambaugh documented average negative Monday returns back through 1928.[25] Jaffe and Westerfield extended the study of this phenomenon to the United Kingdom, Japan, Canada, and Australia.[26] They detected a weekend effect in each country, although the lowest mean returns in Japan and Australia occurred on Tuesday.

The initial studies of the day-of-the-week effect confined themselves to an analysis of the returns from the close of trading on Friday to the close on Monday. These studies prompted inquiry into another question: Exactly when do these negative returns develop? From the Friday close to the Monday open? From the Monday open to the Monday close? Rogalski split daily close-to-close returns into trading day (open-to-close) and nontrading day (close-to-open) returns.[27] For the Dow Jones Industrial Average and the Standard and Poor's 500 Composite Index, Rogalski found that the negative component of the Friday-close-to-Monday-close return actually occurs between the Friday close and the Monday open. He attributed the entire phenomenon to the nontrading period. Rogalski also reported that the Monday returns are positive on average in January, particularly for small firms.

Smirlock and Starks disputed Rogalski's conclusion using data on the DJIA for the 21-year period 1963–1983.[28] In the period that overlaps with Rogalski's study (1974–1983), the results reported by Smirlock and Starks concur with those of Rogalski: the weekend effect occurs entirely during the nontrading period. But in the prior sample periods, the results are reversed; the entire effect is observed during the active trading time on Monday. For the overall period Smirlock and Starks found that part of the negative Monday return occurs during trading hours and part during nontrading hours. Figure 4 displays the mean daily returns that Smirlock and Starks calculated.

24. Michael Gibbons and Patrick Hess, "Day of the Week Effects and Asset Returns," *Journal of Business* 54 (October 1981): 579–96.
25. Donald B. Keim and Robert F. Stambaugh, "A Further Investigation of the Weekend Effect in Stock Returns," *Journal of Finance* 39 (July 1984): 819–35.
26. Jeffrey Jaffe and Randolph Westerfield, "The Week-End Effect in Common Stock Returns: The International Evidence," *Journal of Finance* 40 (June 1985): 433–54.
27. Richard J. Rogalski, "New Findings Regarding Day-of-the-Week Returns over Trading and Non-Trading Periods: A Note," *Journal of Finance* 39 (December 1984): 1603–14.
28. Michael Smirlock and Laura Starks, "Day-of-the-Week and Intraday Effects in Stock Returns," *Journal of Financial Economics* 17 (September 1986): 197–210.

FIGURE 4. *Close-to-Close, Close-to-Open, and Open-to-Close Daily Returns for DJIA, 1963–1983 (Smirlock and Starks).*

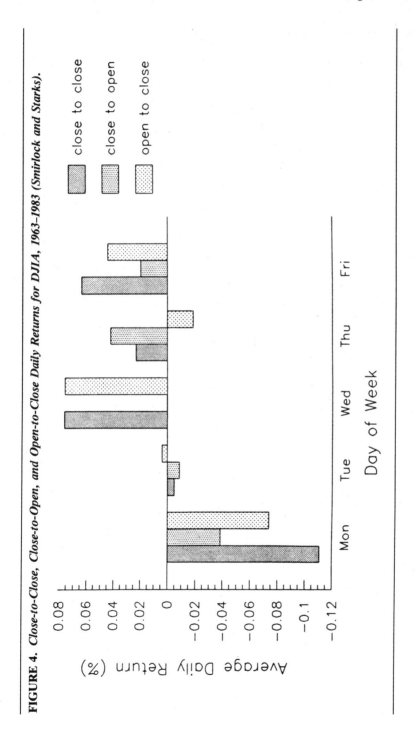

Despite the debate about precisely when the negative returns occur, one fact remains undisputed: the average daily return from Friday close to Monday close is negative whereas for all other trading days it is positive.

Research did not stop after daily returns were broken into close-to-open and open-to-close components. Rather, the level of time disaggregation continued and investigation into a potential hour-of-the-day effect developed. Smirlock and Starks collected hourly observations on the Dow Jones Industrial Average over the 1963–1983 period. They reported that during the first hour of trading the Monday returns are negative on average, but for the other days of the week the average returns in that first hour are positive. Harris, using transactions data for NYSE companies for the 14-month period between December 1981 and January 1983, calculated returns for 15-minute intervals during the trading day.[29] He found that during the first 45 minutes of trading on Mondays prices tend to drop. In contrast, on the other weekday mornings, they tend to rise. Yet, perhaps the most intriguing result described by Harris is one that all days share in common: during the last 15 minutes of trading, prices tend to jump up dramatically. Harris reported that this end-of-day phenomenon is not unduly influenced by just a couple of observations. Rather, it occurs in more than 90 percent of the cases. The evidence from Smirlock and Starks and from Harris clearly reveals intraday patterns in stock returns.

IV. Conclusion

During the 1960s and 1970s, the efficient-markets hypothesis marshalled much evidence in its favor. Stock prices seemed to fluctuate randomly and differences in mean returns between stocks were attributed to their riskiness as measured by beta. But the research of the past decade challenged both of these fundamental tenets. One branch of research documented that stock prices did not change in a manner that could be described as statistically independent and identical. Predictable patterns in stock prices emerged. The mean returns in January stood apart from those of other months. Small firms in particular experienced unusually large January returns especially at the beginning of that month. Other research unearthed the fact that the positive advances made by the market over long periods of time occur almost exclusively in the first part of the month and almost never in the second part of the month. Stated differently, the average returns in the first half of a month are positive and in the second half are zero.

Patterns of price changes by trading day also surfaced. On Mondays, returns tend to be negative. In contrast, the other weekdays possess positive

---

29. Lawrence Harris, "A Transaction Data Study of Weekly and Intraday Patterns in Stock Returns," *Journal of Financial Economics* 16 (May 1986): 99–117.

returns as one might expect. The dissection of intraday returns also began. Indeed the tendency for stock prices to rise during the last 15 minutes of trading is one of the most fascinating discoveries from this nascent research.

The failure of beta to explain differences in average returns over long periods also manifested itself in research during the past decade. Several different investment strategies seem to earn unusually high rates of return even after adjustments for beta risk are taken into account. The two strategies that have garnered most of the attention are those based on price/earnings ratios and those based on stock-market capitalizations. On average, low P/E stocks significantly outperform high P/E securities. Similarly, small-capitalization stocks experience much higher average returns than large-capitalization stocks. Some research suggests that the P/E and size effects may not be independent of each other. In any case the empirical evidence reveals that beta-based benchmarks can be beaten.

Why has the classical view of efficient classical markets begun to collapse at this time? The answer does not lie in the quality or caliber of earlier research. Indeed, much of the earlier work on random walks and the capital-asset-pricing model unveiled important insights into the behavior of stock market prices. Rather, the answer lies, at least in part, in technological change; the tools available to researchers in the late 1980s are much more powerful than those available just 20 years earlier. For example, the mainframe computing capabilities of the 1960s now fit on desktops. Similar advances have been made with respect to databases. In the 1960s collecting data for 30 securities by hand was a major undertaking. By the 1980s researchers culled computer tapes filled with transactions data for all listed securities. As technology advances so will the discoveries in capital markets.

The collapse of the classical efficient-market hypothesis does not mean that information is ignored in the pricing of assets. Indeed a myriad of event studies shows just the opposite. But the collapse, caused by the mountain of empirical anomalies, does mean that the modeling efforts must become more sophisticated. No longer can stock prices be viewed as following a random walk, even approximately. The predictable patterns in stock returns cry out for a coherent, unified explanation. Perhaps that is what the next decade will reveal.

Efficient Markets, Investment-Management Selection, and the Loser's Game

Floyd J. Gould, Ph.D.
Principal, Investment Research Company
and

Hobart W. Williams Professor of Applied
   Mathematics and Management Science
Graduate School of Business
University of Chicago

I. Introduction

All of what follows is expository. Some of it is distilled from a lecture I have had the opportunity to give to MBA students for 15 years, and some of it is distilled from recent research from many sources.[1] The lecture material is from a quantitative models course — one of those courses that the faculty at Chicago decided was good gristle for the students. It is also a course that most of the students decide is neither palatable nor in their interest, and so they tolerate it only with monumental impatience. They don't like math, the course is too hard, they don't see its relevance, they will hire others to do it for them, etc., etc.

1. K. French and R. Roll, "Stock Return Variances: The Arrival of Information and the Reaction of Traders," *Journal of Financial Economics* (September 1986): 5–26; F.J. Gould, "The Re-Emergence of Relative Strength Tactics in Active Asset Allocation — New Evidence" (invited address, Portfolio Risk Management Course — Alternative Strategies for Capital Preservation, Executive Enterprises, New York, 5 October 1987); C.P. Jones and B. Bublitz, "The CAPM and Equity Return Regularities: An Extension," *Financial Analysts' Journal* (May–June 1987): 77–80; D.B. Keim, "The CAPM and Equity Return Regularities," *Financial Analysts' Journal* (May–June 1986): 19–34; A.W. Lo and A.C. MacKinlay, "Stock Market Prices Do Not Follow Random Walks: Evidence from a Simple Specification Test," *Review of Financial Studies* (Spring 1988): 3–40; and B. Rosenberg, K. Reed, and R. Lanstein, "Persuasive Evidence of Market Inefficiency," *The Journal of Portfolio Management* (Spring 1985): 9–16.

This lecture material is rephrased here for those involved with various aspects of financial markets. The discourse points out the importance to the community of having an educated understanding of the role played by quantitative models, and in particular the efficient-market model, along with what we call inefficiencies, also referred to as distortions or anomalies.

Following some general reflections, I show some relevance of these conceptual topics to the concrete and difficult job of the pension-plan sponsor in his or her role as a selector of investment managers. This will involve a comparison of real-world track records (of a manager's trading strategy) versus the importance of simulations and backtesting. I will demonstrate that many if not most plan sponsors — in the process of selecting managers — pursue what basically is, for the organization they work for, a self-destruct strategy. I then conclude with several conjectures as to why a sponsor would adopt such a strategy.

II. Models and Distortions

In order to describe observed phenomena in the physical and biological world, scholars devise models. Scholars also devise models to describe economic phenomena. In this spirit we have the efficient-market theory of equity prices, which implies that past price behavior can provide no information about future prices or future rates of return. An efficient market is one in which the prices behave in accordance with this model.

An *anomaly* is defined to be a departure from a model. The history of all models is such that, initially, a wide body of research produces evidence that tends to support (and indeed leads to the formulation of) the model. A model is a haven for those seeking refuge from chaos. It provides an orderly focus for thought, for discussion, for further research, and what is most interesting to the scholar, a model is a context for the discovery of counterexamples, meaning exceptions to the model. As the state of knowledge matures, these exceptions, or anomalies, are discovered. Those discoveries are then challenged, debated, and finally some of those discoveries will be accepted as facts. Eventually, continued maturation producing more and more in the way of counterexamples leads to the articulation of new models that incorporate and formally extend the previous models and theories.[2]

Of course, some models (such as the flat-earth hypothesis) are eventually totally rejected. But more typically we find that models are generalized or extended (e.g. Newtonian physics, extended to general relativity, extended to unified field theory, extended most recently to superstring theory).

---

2. For a detailed discussion, see T. Kuhn, *The Structure of Scientific Revolutions* (Chicago: University of Chicago Press, 1970), pp. 52–53.

This points out that a model is a *limited,* or *selective,* representation of reality. In this sense, *no model is more than an approximation of reality.*[3] Because no model is reality itself, it is a logical necessity that anomalies will be found in all models. The question should not be whether or not a model is correct — for, as I repeat, no model is reality. The question is merely *how long* it will take for the discovery of valid anomalies, and the subsequent extension of the old model into a new, "updated" one that explains whatever is known up to the present, including those anomalous observations.

In the context of efficient-market models, the anomalies are called *distortions,* or *inefficiencies.* What I have just said is that inefficiencies must always exist. Traders seek to exploit inefficiencies systematically. In so doing, by one of the properties of markets they make those inefficiencies disappear (though new ones may appear). Thus inefficiencies are temporary and it is the traders who drive them away and make the markets efficient. From the real-world point of view, an efficient market is not one that is in every respect efficient in the sense of the theoretic model. It is one with many keen competing investors, exploiting perceived inefficiencies, and it is therefore a market that is dynamically *in the process* of eliminating some inefficiencies while others appear. The concept of efficiency is approximated via this process.

Traders seek to find inefficiencies because it is a way to obtain systematic (risk-adjusted) excess returns. Any trader who claims to produce systematic (as opposed to haphazardly lucky) excess returns must at least implicitly be claiming to be exploiting an inefficiency.

The problem for the investment manager's client (for example, the pension-plan sponsor) is that those wonderful, potentially profitable inefficiencies cannot be absolutely proven until they have been exploited away. In other words, by the time convincing objective evidence has been compiled on the existence of some particular inefficiency it is likely that traders have already taken most of the profit out of it. Hence, of necessity, there must be an element of uncertainty, *ex ante,* in the attempt to identify and exploit inefficiency.

III. Inefficiencies, the Selection of Managers, and the "Track Record" as the Ultimate Bane of Future Success

I have just said that traders, or portfolio managers, who are really "onto something" have in fact discovered an inefficiency. What I have also said is

---

3. For an elaboration, see F. J. Gould and G. D. Eppen, *Quantitative Concepts for Management* (Englewood Cliffs, N.J.: Prentice-Hall, 1985), chap. 1.

that by the time an inefficiency can be clearly proven to exist it is too late, for by then it is almost certain that clever traders will have exploited those inefficiencies to the point of their disappearance (and I have stated that these traders' activities cause that disappearance).

But ironically many plan sponsors self-destruct by seeking the very proof that guarantees extinction. This contributes to the creation of what Charles Ellis describes as a "Losers Game."[4] Typically the "prudent (meaning conservative) sponsor" seeks as a prerequisite to employing a particular strategy a three- to five-year, live track record documenting the past success of that strategy. But by the time such a record is available those inefficiencies that were exploited as the cause of that success have probably vanished, and it is too late for the sponsor.

A typical scenario is this. An inefficiency is discovered. A small amount of capital is raised and a new investment-counseling firm is established to exploit the discovery. Early results are extraordinary. The initially small amount of money under management becomes a bundle as accounts grow and new clients come to the window. By the time the track record is three to five years old, everyone is signing on and the success of the strategy is essentially history. From here on it is doomed to languish in stastical mediocrity, and the best intentions are the source of built-in failure.

This picture is consistent with the fact that most of the dollars that plan sponsors invest with active managers just happen to earn returns quite short of the performance of the index. And of course this is why so many sponsors have turned to indexing.

Is indexing the only alternative? It may be possible for some plan sponsors to consistently earn more than the index. But such sponsors must be willing to develop their own skills beyond what is required to line up columns of numbers and compare five-year track records on a spreadsheet. They will need to make sound judgments and intrinsic evaluations concerning potentially profitable strategies. The thesis here is that in order to find enhancement, such evaluations will need to be performed *before* the real-world record is established. This is no different than looking for a good stock to invest in.

IV. What about Simulation?

An important tool in such evaluation might well be historical simulation, often referred to as "back-testing." Simulation is a powerful tool made possible only by the processing capability of the high-speed computer. That fact in itself should suggest there is something here worth looking at. But in spite of the technology, the process of back-testing is, among plan sponsors, in

---

4. C. D. Ellis, *Investment Policy* (Homewood, Ill.: Dow Jones–Irwin, 1985).

fairly wide disrepute. The reason is that this powerful tool can be so easily misused to produce results that mislead. I do not believe or mean to suggest that this misuse is widely intentional, though certainly it could be and surely in some instances that is what happens. For the most part, however, the majority of those who use simulation simply and unknowingly do not do so properly.

The proper implementation of this tool requires substantial technical background, methodological depth, and good clean and realistic data that may be expensive if not impossible to obtain. It also requires something else — extensive experience and judgment about the actual real-world phenomena being simulated, including in particular realistic assessments of quantities that may well be unknowable, such as the costs that would have been incurred in trading in a world in which the simulated strategy did not exist. The truth is that most back-testers simply do not have the required combination of skills, knowledge, prescience, and data to do the job properly. And some of the most egregious offenders have been academics with only a casual and superficial experience of the world they purport to study.

Unfortunately even the most technically trained plan sponsor is rather helpless in this situation. It is essentially impossible for him or her to verify the validity of someone else's back-tested study. With my academic, nitpicking mentality I can say that for certain. There is no practical way you can verify the simulations of others, and that is certainly an excellent reason for, if not rejecting such studies, at least not placing heavy reliance on them.

This is unfortunate because a careful and honest 10- or 15-year simulation is worth more than a five-year track record. The latter, as I've pointed out, is merely good evidence that an inefficiency has been discovered, exploited, and probably is no longer present. On the other hand, I doubt that back-testing has itself ever been responsible for the disappearance of an inefficiency.

V. Evaluating the Manager

The bottom line, it seems to me, is rather personal. If the plan sponsor has respect for the skill and intellectual honesty of the manager he or she may legitimately indulge in the luxury of giving some attention to simulated results (and of course this is only a special case of the credibility that the sponsor may wish to invest in the manager and his or her strategies). In this respect, if the plan sponsor is to win the loser's game, an important part of the job is to *evaluate the manager per se as well as the manager's strategy*. The bottom line is that, as much as strategies, the sponsor is a selector of persons. In markets, distorted asset prices are moved toward their risk-adjusted equilibrium values through the process of trading and the existence of competition. Thus prices are recidivistic, tending to achieve, in the long run, no more than their appropriate lackluster values. To the contrary, when we scrutinize the patterns of achievement of individuals, it seems that outliers exist and persist. That is, individuals who have been top performers for the past five years in their chosen endeavors, whatever they may be, tend to be top performers in the next five years, whether the endeavors be the same or different (and politics notwithstanding).

So, in summary, I believe the correct prescription is to focus the bet on the track record of individuals, rather than on the proven record of any particular strategy. This is not to say that one should race out to place the whole farm in the hands of bright achievers with novel and appealing trading strategies. Perhaps a well-conceived strategy goes something like this. "Most of our equity portfolio is indexed, because history tells us that this passive approach is very powerful, very hard to beat. But we do recognize the possibility, if not the probability, of finding inefficiency and doing better. And consequently some appropriate portion has been set aside for allocation to active managers." I know of several plan sponsors who do in fact adhere to a policy similar to this, within the guidelines of their particular asset-allocation constraints.

Since none of the above is particularly startling or profound, one wonders why the community at large behaves in what seems to be a less-than-rational fashion. In spite of the self-destruct feature, many plan sponsors select money managers to employ strategies that have outstanding five-year, live track records and consequently little hope of continued outperformance. Why does such selection occur? Is the plan sponsor irrational?

VI. The Principal-Agent Problem and the Concept of Regret

Economists have studied and are continuing to study scenarios where the representative of a firm has self-interest that is by some measures detrimental to, or in conflict with, the overall interest of the firm. In other words, the incentives of the individual differ from the best interests of the firm. This is related to what is called "the principal-agent problem."[5] The problem I have been discussing is a variation of this principal-agent phenomenon.

One interesting explanation of seemingly irrational behavior is the concept of "regret."[6] In the context of this discussion, regret can be explained as follows. Consider two scenarios:

---

5. See, for example, E. F. Fama, "Agency Problems and the Theory of the Firm," *Journal of Political Economy* 88, no. 2 (1980): 288–307.
6. M. Statman, "Investor Psychology and Market Inefficiencies," Preprint, Leavey School of Business Administration, Santa Clara University, Santa Clara, Calif.

Scenario 1 Use conventional and traditional standards and procedures to hire a money manager. Suppose the results are quite disappointing. The manager underperforms the market by 15%.

Scenario 2 You are innovative and somewhat unconventional in your selection. You say, "This makes sense to me," and explain why, to your board. You convince them that the choice makes sense, even though the manager has no substantial proven track record with this particular strategy. Now, as in Scenario 1, suppose results are disappointing.

What happens in these two cases? It is asserted that in Scenario 2 you experience more pain, due to *regret,* than in Scenario 1. The gist of the argument is that the outcome in Scenario 1 was essentially an act of God. You did things the way they are always done! You can't be blamed. You were prudent. In Scenario 2 you went out on a limb. You bore *responsibility.* If only you had not tried to be so smart! If only you had done things the usual way, you wouldn't have been in nearly so much trouble.

The model says that the individual has an aversion to regret (as well as risk) built into his or her utility function. In markets, people hire money managers to play the role of scapegoats, meant to bear the pain of regret. Plan sponsors who use the traditional self-destruct criteria are acting in a way that reduces potential regret, even though the results of their behavior may not be consistent with organizational objectives (that is, to maximize returns).

These behavioral (and organizational) issues will surely be the focus of continuing research. In concluding I will simply suggest one additional implication of the "regret model." Managers whose selection involves much responsibility will produce higher returns than those whose selection involves little responsibility. In an asset-pricing model where regret is a factor, the preference for low-regret managers should drive down their expected return. This provides another argument for reconsideration of traditional selection procedures.

The Analyst and the Investment Process
An Overview

T. Daniel Coggin, Ph.D.
Director of Research
Virginia Supplemental Retirement System
Richmond, Virginia

I. Introduction

This article presents an overview of a very broad topic: the role of the financial analyst in the investment process.[1] There are at least two reasons why this topic is worthy of attention. First, the analyst performs a critically important function as an instrument that translates information for the stock market. Second, the issue of the *evaluation* of analysts' job performance is also of great importance. Specifically, *can* analysts forecast earnings and returns, and (if so) are there *individual differences* in analysts' forecast ability?

In October 1982, I mailed out a questionnaire to which 41 (out of 75) large U.S. "buy-side" investment management firms (i.e., banks, insurance companies and investment advisors) responded. The term "buy-side" refers to non-brokerage investment management firms. Brokerage houses are often referred to as "sell-side" firms. Primarily because of the availability of information, the vast majority of studies to date have focused on sell-side analysts. There are four major differences between buy-side and sell-side analysts. Sell-side analysts (1) are fewer in number and concentrated in the

---

1. It is difficult for a summary article to do justice to such a subject. Those desiring more detail should go directly to the references cited here, including the excellent monograph by P. Brown, G. Foster, and E. Noreen, *Security Analyst Multi-Year Earnings Forecasts and the Capital Market* (Sarasota, FL: American Accounting Association, 1985).

Northeast; (2) are generally more highly compensated; (3) follow fewer companies in typically only one industry; and (4) serve as an important source of information for buy-side analysts.

The object of the survey was to gain information about the management structure and performance evaluation of financial analysts. According to that survey, the typical (large) buy-side investment management firm employed eight or more full-time equity analysts who followed 25 or more stocks in three or more industries and were responsible for both fundamental analysis and stock selection. The typical analyst in these firms did not have portfolio management responsibility and was evaluated on his ability to forecast earnings, pick stocks and communicate effectively. While these results are based on a relatively small sample, I believe they are representative of the general population of medium-to-large, buy-side investment management firms. This survey clearly suggests that the analyst is a key player in the equity investment game.

The remainder of this article is divided into three sections. Section II deals with analyst forecasts of company-level earnings. Contained in that section is a comparison of analyst forecasts to the forecasts of statistical models. In addition, there is a discussion of analyst error in forecasting earnings and the relationship between analyst earnings forecasts and stock returns. Section III looks at analyst forecasts of stock returns and the implications of existing research for the measurement of analyst job performance. Section IV examines the role of the analyst in the capital market. Included in that section is a discussion of the role of the analyst as an "information processor" for the stock market and the use of quantitative methods. The reader should note that the terms "earnings" and "EPS" (earnings per share), and "financial analyst" and "investment analyst" are used interchangeably in this article.

II. Analyst Earnings Forecasts

Analyst Forecasts versus Statistical Models

A classic book by Paul E. Meehl compared the predictive ability of trained psychologists to statistical models of personality and behavior.[2] Meehl's fascinating study found that the statistical models did a *better* job of classifying subjects than the psychologists. Thirty-five years and hundreds of studies later, his basic finding has been supported in a number of areas of human judgment; that is, well-formulated statistical models tend to outperform the judgment of trained professionals. This is largely attributed to the fact that

---

2. P.E. Meehl, *Clinical Versus Statistical Prediction* (Minneapolis, MN: University of Minnesota Press, 1954).

judgment introduces biases and other imperfections in information processing that well-formulated statistical models do not.[3]

A number of studies have looked at the time series properties of annual
earnings. While there are some rather complicated statistical issues involved,
the general finding is that (both at the firm level and most clearly at the aggregate level) the random walk statistical model provides a reasonably accurate *description* of the time series of annual earnings.[4] However, when it
comes to *predicting* annual (and quarterly) earnings, the analyst emerges as
the winner in comparison with a number of statistical models (including the
random walk model).[5] On the other hand, the analyst generally fails to outperform company management forecasts.[6]

Brown *et al.* looked at the determinants of analyst superiority relative
to univariate time-series models.[7] Their study suggests that analyst superiority is related to at least two factors. One, analysts can better utilize *existing*
information relative to simple univariate time-series models (a contempo-
raneous advantage). Two, analysts can use information that occurs *after*
the cut-off date for the time-series data but *before* the data of the analyst
forecast (a timing advantage). Another study by Brown, Richardson, and
Schwager found that financial analyst superiority is positively related to firm
size, meaning that the larger the company, the more advantage analysts have
over time-series models.[8]

While the weight of the current evidence tends to favor analysts over
statistical time-series models in predicting earnings, studies by Richards,

---

3. For a good introduction to this literature, see D. Kahneman, P. Slovic, and A. Tversky,
eds., *Judgment Under Uncertainty: Heuristics and Biases* (New York: Cambridge University
Press, 1982).
4. For a more detailed discussion, see G. Foster, *Financial Statement Analysis,* 2nd ed. (Englewood Cliffs, NJ: Prentice-Hall, 1986): Appendix 7.C.
5. See, for example, L.D. Brown and M.S. Rozeff, "The Superiority of Analyst Forecasts as
Measures of Expectations," *Journal of Finance* 33 (March 1978): 1-16; T.D. Coggin and J.E.
Hunter, "Analysts' EPS Forecasts Nearer Actual than Statistical Models," *Journal of Business Forecasting* 1 (Winter 1982–83): 20-23; M.S. Rozeff, "Predicting Long-term Earnings
Growth," *Journal of Forecasting* 2 (October-December 1983): 425–435; and P.C. O'Brien,
"Analysts' Forecasts as Earnings Expectations," *Journal of Accounting and Economics* 10 (January 1988): 53–83.
6. See J.S. Armstrong, "Relative Accuracy of Judgemental and Extrapolative Methods in
Forecasting Annual Earnings," *Journal of Forecasting* 2 (October-December 1983): 437–447;
and J. Hassell and R. Jennings, "Relative Forecast Accuracy and the Timing of Earnings Forecast Announcements," *Accounting Review* 61 (January 1986): 58-75.
7. L.D. Brown, R.L. Hagerman, P.A. Griffin and M.E. Zmijewski, "Security Analyst Superiority Relative to Univariate Time-Series Models in Forecasting Quarterly Earnings," *Journal
of Accounting and Economics* 9 (1987): 61–87.
8. L.D. Brown, G.D. Richardson, and S.J. Schwager, "An Information Interpretation of
Financial Analyst Superiority in Forecasting Earnings," *Journal of Accounting Research* 25
(Spring 1987): 49–67.

O'Brien, and Coggin and Hunter suggest that individual analysts are largely *undifferentiated* in their ability to predict EPS.[9] This finding (discussed in more detail in the next section) suggests that the *consensus* (mean) analyst forecast is generally superior to the forecasts of individual analysts. It should be noted that some recent studies suggest that there are benefits from *combining* statistical time-series and analyst forecasts.[10] Other studies have shown that more complex statistical models that include additional variables affecting earnings growth (such as leading economic indicators) can challenge the superiority of analysts in predicting earnings.[11] Thus, it may be premature to reject the generalizability to financial analysts of Meehl's finding regarding the superiority of statistical models.

Analyst Error in Forecasting Earnings

Having established that analysts generally do a better job of forecasting earnings than relatively simple, extrapolative statistical models, it now seems appropriate to examine the general characteristics of the *errors* made by analysts. Two recent studies are relevant to this question. Elton, Gruber, and Gultekin studied this issue in detail using data for the period 1976–1978.[12] One advantage of their study relative to many previous studies in this area is that they used a large database of analyst EPS forecasts (i.e., the I/B/E/S database maintained by the brokerage firm of Lynch, Jones & Ryan, Inc., New York). Earlier studies typically used very small samples of analysts or the Value Line analyst group.

---

9. See R.M. Richards, "Analysts Performance and the Accuracy of Corporate Earnings Forecasts," *Journal of Business* 49 (July 1976): 350–357; P.C. O'Brien, "Forecast Accuracy of Individual Analysts in Nine Industries," Working Paper No. 1940-87, Sloan School of Management, MIT, May 1988; and T.D. Coggin and J.E. Hunter, "Analyst Forecasts of EPS and EPS Growth: Decomposition of Error, Relative Accuracy and Relation to Return," Working Paper, Virginia Supplemental Retirement System, Richmond, VA, 1989.

10. See R. Conroy and R. Harris, "Consensus Forecasts of Corporate Earnings: Analysts' Forecasts and Time Series Methods," *Management Science* 33 (June 1987): 725–738; L.D. Brown, R.L. Hagerman, P.A. Griffin and M.E. Zmijewski, "An Evaluation of Alternative Proxies for the Market's Assessment of Unexpected Earnings," *Journal of Accounting and Economics* 9 (July 1987): 159–193; and J.B. Guerard, Jr., "Combining Time-Series Model Forecasts and Analysts' Forecasts for Superior Forecasts of Annual Earnings," *Financial Analysts Journal* 45 (January-February 1989): 69–71.

11. See P.D. Chant, "On the Predictability of Corporate Earnings Per Share Behavior," *Journal of Finance* 35 (March 1980): 13–21; and J.E. Hunter and T.D. Coggin, "Analyst Judgment: The Efficient Market Hypothesis Versus a Psychological Theory of Human Judgment," *Organizational Behavior and Human Decision Processes* 42 (December 1988): 284–302.

12. E.J. Elton, M.J. Gruber, and M.N. Gultekin, "Professional Expectations: Accuracy and Diagnosis of Errors," *Journal of Financial and Quantitative Analysis* 19 (December 1984): 351–363.

Elton, Gruber, and Gultekin found that (1) analyst errors in forecasting annual EPS (revised monthly) declined monotonically as the end of the fiscal year approached; (2) analysts were reasonably accurate in forecasting aggregate-level EPS for the entire economy; (3) analysts were better at forecasting industry-level EPS than company-level EPS; (4) analysts had a tendency to overestimate EPS growth for companies they believed would do well and underestimate EPS growth for companies they believed would do poorly; (5) analysts had more difficulty forecasting EPS for some companies relative to others (specifically, if analysts had large errors for a company in one year, they tended to have large errors the next year); (6) analyst divergence of opinion about EPS growth for a company tended to be at its greatest during the first four months of the year; and (7) analyst divergence of opinion about EPS growth for a company was positively related to the magnitude of the EPS growth forecast error for that company.

A recent study by Coggin and Hunter examined the errors made by analysts in forecasting year-ahead EPS and 5-year EPS growth over the period 1978–1985.[13] Their study used both the I/B/E/S database and the ICARUS database (maintained by Zacks Investment Research, Inc., Chicago). Using a variance decomposition theorem from the analysis of variance, they derived an equation for the total mean squared error (MSE) in individual analysts' forecasts for a company:

$$E(EPS_A - EPS_j)^2 = (EPS_A - C)^2 + E(C - EPS_j)^2, \qquad (1)$$

where $E( )$ is the standard expected value operator, EPS_A is the actual earnings for the company, EPS_j is the forecast of the jth analyst and C is the consensus (mean) analyst forecast for the company.

In words, this equation says that the total MSE in individual analysts' forecasts has two components: the squared error in the consensus forecast and the mean squared deviation from the consensus forecast. That is, the total MSE in individual forecasts is the sum of the squared consensus error plus the mean squared idiosyncratic error. This decomposition shows that the total MSE for randomly chosen individual analysts is always greater than the squared consensus error by an amount equal to the *variance* of the individual forecasts. This result is formally derived in the appendix to their paper. Thus, only if it were possible to predict *a priori* which analyst would be more accurate than the consensus would it be possible to improve on the consensus forecast. Current research on individual differences in analyst forecasts suggests this is not possible.

The Coggin and Hunter study had three basic findings. First, for both the 1-year and the 5-year forecast data, the squared consensus error component

---

13. T.D. Coggin and J.E. Hunter, "Analyst Forecasts of EPS and EPS Growth."

of total MSE was much larger than the mean squared idiosyncratic error component, indicating relatively small differences among analysts' earnings forecasts for a given company. They suggested at least four reasons for the relatively low level of diversity among individual analysts' forecasts. One, there could be significant communication among analysts with respect to EPS forecasts. They noted that their experience in dealing with Wall Street and regional financial analysts led them to believe that there is minimal *direct* communication of EPS forecasts among analysts. However, analysts do read many of the same industry reports and journals containing short- and long-term forecasts of industry activity. This is a form of *indirect* communication that could standardize the assumptions analysts make and thus reduce the level of idiosyncracy in individual company forecasts.

Two, they noted that analysts often talk with company management concerning the outlook for a company. This is another source of "common information" available to analysts that could serve to further reduce the level of idiosyncratic error. Three, many analysts use similar financial models in deriving their forecasts. The relative uniformity of generally accepted techniques of financial analysis could help lower idiosyncratic error. A discussion of the techniques of financial analysis is beyond the scope of this paper. A good summary is given in Cohen, Zinbarg, and Zeikel.[14] Common factors considered by analysts in valuing a company are discussed here in a later section on the valuation process. Four, they noted that their sample of companies was somewhat skewed toward larger, more well-known companies. It is possible that analysts tend to be in greater agreement concerning the future prospects for these firms.

The second major finding of the Coggin and Hunter study was that positive consensus errors (analogous to "earnings surprises") were associated with higher returns for the forecast period, while negative consensus errors (analogous to "earnings disappointments") were associated with lower returns for the forecast period. Specifically, they found that by the end of the fiscal year, the market had already begun to adjust return on a stock to the fact that actual earnings for the year were either less than or in excess of expectations. This finding extends previous research that used a statistical model to generate expected earnings and supports results reported in Brown, Foster, and Noreen.[15]

14. J.B. Cohen, E.D. Zinbarg and A. Zeikel, *Investment Analysis and Portfolio Management,* 5th ed. (Homewood, IL: Richard D. Irwin, 1987), Part 4.
15. See, for example, R. Ball and P. Brown, "An Empirical Evaluation of Accounting Income Numbers," *Journal of Accounting Research* 6 (Autumn 1968): 159–178; and P. Brown, G. Foster, and E. Noreen, *Security Analyst Multi-Year Earnings Forecasts and the Capital Market,* Chapter 4.

Finally, they found that the variance of the analysts' 5-year growth estimates (the idiosyncratic error component) was *negatively* correlated with return for forecast periods of 1 through 5 years. This finding does not support the use of the variance of analysts' 5-year growth estimates as a measure of systematic investment risk advocated by Malkiel and others.[16] This leads us to a more complete discussion of the general topic of the relationship between analyst earnings forecasts and stock returns.

Analyst EPS Forecasts and Stock Returns

The major reason analysts are asked to perform fundamental analysis and forecast earnings is because there is an implied link between EPS forecasts and stock returns. Indeed, it is a fundamental tenet of financial theory that expectations for earnings for a company be related to return to stockholders. And indeed they are. In one of the earlier studies of this relationship, Niederhoffer and Regan verified that stock prices were strongly dependent on earnings changes — both in terms of absolute change and change relative to analysts' estimates — in data for 1970.[17] Later studies by Elton, Gruber, and Gultekin; Hawkins, Chamberlin, and Daniel; and van Dijk used larger samples of analysts' expectational data (from the I/B/E/S database) to further refine our understanding of this relationship.[18] These studies showed that *current* expectations for earnings (as represented by the mean of the analysts' current forecasts) are incorporated into *current* stock prices. Furthermore, they showed that *revisions* in the consensus (i.e., mean) forecast for year-ahead earnings are *predictive* of future stock returns.

Specifically, these studies presented three key findings. First, as mentioned above, any information contained in the current consensus forecast by itself is largely reflected in the current stock price. Hence, a policy of buying stocks solely on the basis of large consensus growth estimates is generally unrewarded. Second, excess returns are available to those who can predict those stocks for which analysts will *underestimate* earnings, and even larger excess returns are possible if one can predict which stocks will experience the largest positive earnings estimate *revisions*. The phrase "excess returns" here

---

16. B.G. Malkiel, "Risk and Return: A New Look," Working Paper No. 700, National Bureau of Economic Research, Cambridge, MA, 1981.

17. V. Niederhoffer and P.J. Regan, "Earnings Changes, Analysts' Forecasts and Stock Prices," *Financial Analysts Journal* 28 (May-June 1972): 65–71.

18. E.J. Elton, M.J. Gruber, and M. Gultekin, "Expectations and Share Prices," *Management Science* 27 (September 1981): 975–987; E.H. Hawkins, S.C. Chamberlin, and W.F. Daniel, "Earnings Expectations and Security Prices," *Financial Analysts Journal* 40 (September-October 1984): 24–38; and D. van Dijk, *Almost Everything You Ever Wanted to Know about Consensus Earnings Revisions,* unpublished MBA thesis, Baruch College–CUNY, June 1986.

refers to returns in excess of those required by the capital asset pricing model (CAPM). (Some authors use the phrase "abnormal returns.") The results reported in this section are generally robust to the substitution of raw, "unadjusted" returns.

Third, revisions in the consensus estimate for earnings tend to have *momentum;* that is, an increase in the consensus forecast in one month is often followed by another increase in the next month. The availability of excess returns on stocks that experience sizable increases in the consensus earnings forecast has been measured to last for holding periods of from 2 to 12 months. It has been argued by some that this finding is inconsistent with the existence of an "efficient market."[19] The stock market does not "instantaneously" react to changes in the consensus forecast and allows excess returns to a strategy that takes advantage of that fact. This topic will be briefly discussed in the concluding section.

In summary, as several authors have noted, Lord Keynes appears to have been correct when he compared professional investing to participating in a contest to pick which 6 contestants out of 100 in a photo-beauty contest will be chosen by the rest of the judges. In Keynes's words "... each competitor has to pick, not those whose faces which he himself finds prettiest, but those which he thinks likeliest to catch the fancy of other competitors, all of whom are looking at the contest from the same point of view."[20]

III. Analyst Return Forecasts

As we have seen, a key responsibility of investment analysts is forecasting stock returns. In most cases, the analyst forecasts company-level returns directly. However, in some cases, the analyst provides input (i.e., forecasts of earnings, dividends, and growth rates) to a valuation model (such as a dividend discount model), which, in turn, forecasts returns. In either case, the analyst is central to the process of generating expected returns. These forecasts are usually in the form of "Buy," "Hold," and "Sell" recommendations. The portfolio manager uses these recommendations, in conjunction with other quantitative and nonquantitative aspects of evaluating a company, to construct stock portfolios for clients.

The Valuation Process

In a survey of 1,000 members of the Financial Analysts Federation (170 responded), Chugh and Meador studied the process by which financial analysts

---

19. See, for example, D. Givoly and J. Lakonishok, "Financial Analysts' Forecasts of Earnings: Their Value to Investors," *Journal of Banking and Finance* 4 (September 1980): 221–233.
20. J.M. Keynes, *The General Theory of Employment, Interest and Money* (New York: Harcourt, Brace & Company, 1936): 156.

evaluate common stocks.[21] They found that analysts consistently emphasize the long term over the short term. Key variables for the long term were expected change in EPS, expected return on equity (ROE), and industry outlook. Key variables for the short term were industry outlook, expected change in EPS, and general economic conditions. Other important factors mentioned by the analysts were quality and depth of management, market dominance, and "strategic credibility" (ability to achieve stated goals). According to their survey, expected growth in earnings and ROE appeared to be the most significant aspects of the valuation process. The primary sources of information for the analysts were presentations by top management, annual reports, and Form 10-K reports.

The Quality of Return Forecasts

Each quarter Zacks Investment Research, Inc. tracks the performance of stocks recommended by analysts at 10 major brokerage houses and reports the results in the *Wall Street Journal*. Table 1 presents a summary of the results as of 12/30/88. For the 12 months ending 12/30/88, 6 of the 10 brokerage house Recommended Lists outperformed the S&P 500 stock index. For the 30 months ended 12/30/88, 5 of the 10 outperformed the S&P 500.

A number of other studies have examined the value of analysts' forecasts of stock returns. The majority of these studies have also focused on the forecasts of sell-side analysts. While there is some disagreement in this area,[22] the general finding is that there is economically valuable information in analysts' buy/sell recommendations. Specifically, recent studies of U.S., Canadian and U.K. analysts have shown that excess returns are available to investors who follow the published recommendations of analysts employed by brokerage houses.[23]

---

21. L.C. Chugh and J.W. Meador, "The Stock Valuation Process: The Analysts' View," *Financial Analysts Journal* 40 (November-December 1984): 41–48. This study expands and updates an earlier study by R.A. Bing, "Survey of Practitioners' Stock Evaluation Methods," *Financial Analysts Journal* 27 (May-June 1971): 55–60.

22. See, for example, R.E. Diefenbach, "How Good is Institutional Brokerage Research?" *Financial Analysts Journal* 28 (January-February 1972): 54–60; C.M. Bidwell, III, "How Good is Institutional Brokerage Research?" and L. Shepard, "How Good is Investment Advice for Individuals?" *Journal of Portfolio Management* 3 (Winter 1977).

23. See P.L. Davies and M. Canes, "Stock Prices and the Publication of Second-Hand Information," *Journal of Business* 51 (January 1978): 43–56; L. Stanley, W.G. Lewellen and G.G. Schlarbaum, "Further Evidence on the Value of Professional Investment Research," *Journal of Financial Research* 4 (Spring 1981): 1–9; J.H. Bjerring, J. Lakonishok, and T. Vermaelen, "Stock Prices and Financial Analysts' Recommendations," *Journal of Finance* 38 (March 1983): 187–204; E. Dimson and P. Marsh, "An Analysis of Brokers' and Analysts' Unpublished Forecasts of UK Stock Returns," *Journal of Finance* 39 (December 1984): 1257–1292; and E.J. Elton, M.J. Gruber, and S. Grossman, "Discrete Expectational Data and Portfolio Performance," *Journal of Finance* 41 (July 1986): 699–714.

TABLE 1. *How the Big Brokerage Houses' Favorite Stocks Performed in Periods Ending 12/30/88.*[a]

Brokerage House	3 Months	12 Months	30 Months
A.G. Edwards	3.4%	27.5%	19.9%
PaineWebber	3.6	22.7	19.6
Smith Barney	1.8	20.8	21.1
Shearson	0.4	20.3	25.5
Dean Witter	1.0	18.1	8.0
Prudential-Bache	3.2	17.6	14.9
Kidder Peabody	2.3	16.5	15.6
Merrill Lynch	0.4	14.6	10.9
Drexel Burnham	3.2	14.3	12.4
Thomson McKinnon	1.5	6.5	24.5
Average Broker	2.1	17.9	17.2
Comparison Yardsticks			
Dow Jones 30 Index	3.6	16.2	21.5
S&P 500 Index	3.0	16.6	19.0
Average Stock[b]	−0.6	20.3	5.8

a. Source: *Wall Street Journal,* 2/3/89 and Zacks Investment Research, Inc. All figures are price change plus dividends. Broker portfolios are equal-weighted and rebalanced monthly (with no transaction costs) to reflect changing recommendations.
b. Equal-weighted average of 3,000 stocks followed by the 10 brokerage houses.

Put in the current jargon, these studies show that analysts' stock recommendations have a "positive IC" (information coefficient). The IC is defined as the correlation between predicted and actual stock returns. Some researchers have argued that analysts are "worth their keep" if and only if it can be shown that they can forecast earnings and returns. The evidence to date supports the hypotheses that they can (1) outperform simple statistical models in forecasting earnings and (2) provide economically valuable information in forecasting returns.

Evaluating Analyst Job Performance

Having now established the fact that analysts are indeed a valuable component of the investment process, it seems logical to discuss how they themselves are evaluated. My 1982 survey indicated that analysts are evaluated on their ability to forecast earnings and returns, and on how well they communicate investment ideas and information.

A number of investment organizations have established quantitative rating systems to evaluate their analysts. My 1982 survey indicated that 71% had done so. Several articles have been written on the topic of evaluating financial analysts.[24] These papers have focused overwhelmingly on the ability of analysts to forecast return, while other "relatively minor" issues such as ability to communicate investment information received little or no attention. My 1982 survey found that the most common elements of an analyst rating system are: accuracy of stock performance forecasts, accuracy of estimate information (e.g., earnings, dividends, and growth rates), and ability to communicate investment information to portfolio managers. It would then seem that ability to forecast stock return is a key (if not *the* key) element of an analyst's job description.

Three recent studies are relevant to this issue. Coggin and Hunter examined a fundamental question: Are there individual differences in analysts' abilities to forecast stock returns?[25] Using a statistical technique called *meta-analysis,* they analyzed the ICs for analysts at a regional trust company over the period 1979–1981, and for a larger sample of analysts nationwide in 1982. Meta-analysis showed that all apparent differences in analysts' ICs were attributable to *sampling error.* Hence, in their data, there were no real individual differences in analysts' abilities to forecast return. Dimson and Marsh replicated the Coggin and Hunter analysis on a sample of British brokers and analysts over the period 1980–1981 and got the same basic result.[26] Elton, Gruber, and Grossman found no evidence of one U.S. brokerage firm being consistently better than another in recommending stocks over the period 1981–1983.[27]

It was previously noted that research suggests minimal differences in analysts' abilities to forecast earnings. We now have evidence that there are no differences in analysts' abilities to forecast returns. Thus the combined evidence suggests that rating schemes that base an individual analyst's salary and bonus on differential ability to forecast earnings and returns amount to holding a *lottery* for that award!

24. See W.S. Gray, "Measuring the Analyst's Performance," *Financial Analysts Journal* 22 (March-April 1966): 56–63; A. Barnea and D. E. Logue, "Evaluating the Forecasts of a Security Analyst," *Financial Management* 2 (Summer 1973): 38–45; F. Mastrapasqua and S. Bolten, "A Note of Financial Analyst Evaluation," *Journal of Finance* 28 (June 1973): 707–712; and B.C. Korschot, "Quantitative Evaluation of Investment Research Analysts," *Financial Analysts Journal* 34 (July-August 1978): 41–46.
25. T.D. Coggin and J.E. Hunter, "Problems in Measuring the Quality of Investment Information: The Perils of the Information Coefficient," *Financial Analysts Journal* 39 (May-June 1983): 25–33.
26. E. Dimson and P. Marsh, "An Analysis of Brokers' and Analysts' Unpublished Forecasts of UK Stock Returns."
27. E.J. Elton, M.J. Gruber, and S. Grossman, "Discrete Expectational Data and Portfolio Performance."

It is important to emphasize that the existing evidence does *not* suggest that analysts can't forecast return. Indeed, there is previously cited evidence that they *can*. The mean analyst IC is *not* zero; rather, it is about 0.10. The point here is that the existing data suggest there are no real *between-analyst differences* in ability to forecast return.

In an effort to accommodate this finding, the regional trust company mentioned above designed an analyst evaluation system that rates the analysts as a *group* on the return prediction dimension. At this firm, the analysts supply estimates of earnings, dividends, and growth rates to a three-phase dividend discount model, which then calculates expected returns for a reference list of stocks. The IC is measured for the entire reference list of stocks followed by the group of analysts. If that IC is significantly positive, the analysts (as a group) are rated favorably on that dimension. Other specific criteria are then rated on an analyst-by-analyst basis, such as ability to communicate investment information and analyses in both verbal and written form.

IV. Analysts and the Capital Market

The Analyst as Information Processor

As O'Brien has noted, accounting and finance researchers (and practitioners) are increasingly relying on analysts' forecasts as proxies for the "unobservable market expectation" for future earnings.[28] The empirical evidence that financial analysts are, in general, superior to univariate time-series models in forecasting earnings and the increasing availability of analyst forecast data (from sources like Lynch, Jones & Ryan, Inc. and Zacks Investment Research, Inc., cited above) have fostered this tendency. The idea that the information content of analysts' forecasts for earnings and returns is relevant to the theory and practice of accounting and finance is well established.

In a totally efficient capital market, analysts' forecasts for earnings and returns would not matter. Every market participant (both analysts and investors) would have exactly the same information at exactly the same time; hence, no one would have an "informational advantage" over anyone else. However, there is mounting evidence that the stock market is not totally efficient. While the weight of the evidence suggests that analysts are generally undifferentiated in their ability to predict earnings and returns, those predictions *can* be profitably employed by investors in the stock market.

This article has noted evidence that the ability to forecast *changes* in the consensus analyst earnings forecast for a company yields excess returns in the stock market. Some studies have examined the *timing* and *speed* at

---

28. P.C. O'Brien, "Analysts' Forecasts as Earnings Expectations."

which analyst forecast information is disseminated to stock market investors.[29] This is an important area of research that will likely yield insights into just how that information is translated into excess returns. Evidence was also discussed that supports the hypothesis that analysts' buy/sell recommendations can be used to earn excess returns in the stock market. Other research has shown that the dividend discount model of expected stock returns (driven by analyst forecast data) is an economically valuable tool in predicting actual stock returns.[30]

Quantitative Methods

Recent studies have shown that a majority of investment management firms do not use quantitative methods to value common stocks. A survey reported in *Pensions & Investment Age* (November 10, 1986) reported that only 8% of respondents use quantitative methods to manage stocks; a survey conducted by Arthur D. Little, Inc., in March 1987 reported that only 30% of respondents indicated intensive use of quantitative methods in their overall money management effort.[31] This small minority of quantitative managers spans a continuum from using analysts to provide input to quantitative models to using *no* analysts at all, relying instead on computers and "artificial intelligence" to process information and select and trade stocks. Hence, 20 years after the "quantitative revolution" of the late 1960s, most money managers apparently continue to rely on conventional (i.e., nonquantitative) methods of investment management. In the case of stocks, this generally means that financial analysts perform fundamental security analysis and make recommendations to portfolio managers about which stocks to buy and sell. A relatively large subjective component is then applied to the final investment decision. No doubt, this process has been successful (and will continue to be successful) for *some* investment management firms. A discussion of the fact that most investment managers continue to *underperform* the stock market (i.e., the S&P 500 stock index) is beyond the scope of this article.[32]

---

29. See P. Brown, G. Foster, and E. Noreen, *Security Analyst Multi-Year Forecasts and the Capital Market,* Chapter 4, and Appendixes A.1, A.2.; and P.C. O'Brien, "Analysts' Forecasts as Earnings Expectations."
30. See E.H. Sorensen and D.A. Williamson, "Some Evidence of the Value of Dividend Discount Models," *Financial Analysts Journal* 41 (November-December 1985): 60–69; and T.D. Coggin, "The Dividend Discount Model and the Stock Selection Process," in D.E. Logue, ed., *Handbook of Modern Finance, 1986 Update* (Boston: Warren, Gorham & Lamont, 1986).
31. *Quantitative Methods and Information Technologies for Investment Advising,* Arthur D. Little, Inc., Cambridge, MA, April 1987.
32. See T.D. Coggin, "Active Equity Management," in F.J. Fabozzi, ed., *Portfolio and Investment Management* (Chicago: Probus Publishing Company, 1989) for a discussion.

The fact remains that analysts provide a valuable information processing service to the vast majority of *active* stock market investors. There is another form of stock market investing called *passive* investing, which includes the growing index fund business. Passive investment management assumes that securities are efficiently priced and does *not* involve the use of analysts' estimates in an effort to "beat the market."[33] Currently, however, the vast majority of money invested in the stock market is actively managed. As long as active stock market investing remains popular, analysts will be a vital component of the investment process.

---

33. For more detail on "active" versus "passive" investment management, see W.F. Sharpe, *Investments,* 3rd ed. (Englewood Cliffs: Prentice-Hall, 1985), Chapter 20.

Benchmark Portfolios and the Manager/Plan Sponsor Relationship

Jeffery V. Bailey, CFA
Vice President
Richards & Tierney, Inc.

Thomas M. Richards, CFA
Principal
Richards & Tierney, Inc.

David E. Tierney, Ph.D.
Principal
Richards & Tierney, Inc.

I. Introduction

Large U.S. pension plans typically invest their funds across a wide range of asset classes and money managers. The complexity of these investment management programs raises a number of intriguing questions. We examine two particular issues:

- First, can the diverse components of multiple-manager pension plans be brought together to achieve the plans' investment objectives?
- Second, can the contributions of the various components of the plans' investment results be identified and evaluated?

We believe that the answer to these two questions is "yes," provided appropriate benchmarks are employed in the design and control of the plans' investment programs.

Consider the example of VAM Associates, an institutional common stock manager. Consultants usually classify VAM as a "growth" stock manager. VAM has several distinguishing portfolio characteristics, including a practically permanent zero exposure to utility stocks. Also VAM's portfolio exhibits consistently large positions in technology stocks. These persistent under and overweightings relative to the market reflect a long-run business decision on the part of VAM, rather than a short-run investment valuation judgment.

TABLE 1. *VAM Associates, Portfolio and Market Data.*

	1982	1984
Rate of Return Data		
S&P 500 Return	21.1%	6.1%
VAM Associates Return	36.5	−2.9
Technology Sector Return	45.2	−2.9
Utility Sector Return	21.1	25.4
Portfolio Composition Data		
VAM's Technology Weight	40.0%	30.0%
VAM's Utility Weight	0.0	0.0

As shown in Table 1, the S&P 500 produced a 21.2% return during 1982, while VAM's portfolio returned 36.5%. Not coincidentally, the technology sector, which comprised over 40% of VAM's portfolio, generated a 45.2% return. In contrast, the S&P 500 returned 6.1% and VAM's portfolio experienced a −2.9% return in 1984. Utility stocks, which had zero representation in VAM's portfolio, returned 25.4% during that year.

Daralyn, a thoughtful performance evaluator, has been reviewing VAM's investment results. She does not presume that VAM's strong performance relative to the market in 1982 demonstrates positive value in VAM's active management decisions. Neither does she assume that VAM's weak relative performance in 1984 reflects negative active management contributions. Daralyn knows that without appropriate benchmarks, investment skill is obscured and performance evaluation conclusions are more error prone.

Multi Corporation employs VAM Associates and 14 other managers to invest the common stock segment of its pension plan's investment portfolio. The large majority of these other managers pursue a "growth" style similar to that of VAM. In 1982, the aggregate return for Multi Corporation's common stock managers was 35.6% versus 21.2% for the S&P 500. In 1984, the managers' aggregate portfolio return was 1.7%, versus 6.1% for the S&P 500.

The trustees of Multi Corporation's pension plan might inquire of Daralyn, "Were the plan's common stock investment objectives achieved in either 1982 or 1984? Moreover, did the allocation of funds among the managers add value to the plan's investment program?" Again, Daralyn would emphasize that without appropriate benchmarks, she could not offer meaningful answers.

We believe that benchmarks offer pension plans an effective means of addressing two difficult investment policy issues:

- Distinguishing active management skill from random results.
- Effectively combining money managers within a total investment program.

Despite growing interest in the subject, remarkably few organizations have attempted to integrate truly appropriate benchmarks into their investment management operations. We hope to increase the awareness among plan sponsors and money managers of the importance and value of investment benchmarks. To this end, we first present a conceptual discussion of benchmarks. We then consider several prominent issues involved in manager benchmark portfolio construction. Finally, we develop a case study that illustrates the utility of benchmarks in the context of manager performance evaluation. The scope of this article does not permit us to discuss how managers may be more efficiently aligned within a pension plan's investment program by using benchmarks.

II. Investment Benchmark Concepts

Webster's Dictionary defines a benchmark as a "standard or point of reference in measuring or judging quality, value, etc." Applying this general definition to money management, we view an investment benchmark as a passive representation of a manager's investment process. In this sense, it represents the prominent financial characteristics that the manager's portfolio would exhibit in the *absence* of active investment judgments.

An alternative definition expresses an investment benchmark as encompassing the manager's "area" of expertise. Just as a fisherman has his favorite fishing hole, the manager also has distinct preferences for certain types of securities from which to make portfolio selections. These preferences reflect the foundations upon which the manager's investment process is applied.

A little algebra succinctly conveys these concepts. Begin with the simple identity of an investment manager's portfolio:

$$P = P. \tag{1}$$

Now, consider an appropriately selected benchmark portfolio, B. Adding and subtracting B from the right-hand side of equation (1) results in:

$$P = B + (P - B). \tag{2}$$

Define the manager's active investment judgments, A, as being the difference between the manager's portfolio, P, and the benchmark, B, so that $A = (P - B)$. Equation (2) becomes:

$$P = B + A. \tag{3}$$

Equation (3) states that two components comprise a manager's portfolio. One component represents the manager's benchmark and the other represents the manager's active management decisions.

We extend the discussion by introducing a market index, M. Adding and subtracting M from the right-hand side of equation (3) gives:

$$P = M + (B - M) + A. \tag{4}$$

We interpret the difference between the manager's benchmark portfolio and the market index, $(B - M)$, as the manager's investment style or fundamental investment biases. Defining $S = (B - M)$, equation (4) becomes:

$$P = M + S + A. \tag{5}$$

There are several interesting applications of equation (5). First, note that if the manager runs an index fund, then $S = (B - M) = 0$ (i.e., no style or biases) and $A = (P - B) = 0$ (i.e., no active management). Consequently, equation (5) reduces to $P = M$. The manager's portfolio is equivalent to the market index.

Second, if we define the manager's benchmark portfolio as the market index (i.e., $S = (B - M) = 0$, or no style), then equation (5) reduces to equation (3), and substituting M for B gives:

$$P = M + A. \tag{6}$$

Many money managers and plan sponsors have been willing to define a manager's benchmark as a broad market index. Equation (6) demonstrates that in these situations both parties implicitly believe that the manager has no distinct investment style. Yet most practitioners would agree that today the large majority of money managers pursue very specific investment styles. Indeed, many managers are retained by plan sponsors for precisely this reason. How does this contradiction affect plan sponsors?

The example of VAM Associates and Multi Corporation illustrated the ambiguity created by inappropriate benchmarks. In general, the lack of proper benchmarks for money managers presents the plan sponsor with two problems:

- Difficulty distinguishing active management skill from random results.
- Uncertainty concerning the most efficient combination of managers.

With respect to the first issue, active management results inherently exhibit a high degree of variability. Investment skill is difficult to detect even under ideal conditions. The lack of valid benchmarks seriously compounds this problem. Benchmarks facilitate the performance evaluation process by providing an accurate reference point by which to judge the value of active management.

Regarding the second issue, responsibility for allocating funds among the plan's managers falls to the plan sponsor. Through this allocation process, the plan sponsor attempts to achieve complete coverage of the various market segments within each asset class, consistent with the plan's investment objectives. Just as VAM Associates persistently holds no utility stocks, Multi Corporation's equity managers, in aggregate, may fail to cover certain sectors of the common stock market, while they may overemphasize other sectors. Unless this under- or overemphasis is desired by Multi Corporation, an unproductive form of risk has been introduced into its investment program. Benchmarks permit the plan sponsor to identify and correct undesired "gaps" in the coverage of asset class segments resulting from the aggregate investment styles of the plan's management team.

III. A Simple Benchmark Design

In order to introduce several important features of benchmark portfolios, consider a "typical" emerging growth stock manager. Suppose we could induce selective amnesia on this manager. In particular, while the manager retains his fondness for emerging growth stocks, he suddenly has no strong beliefs concerning the future course of the economy and stock market, or the relative value of specific securities within the emerging growth sector. What kind of portfolio would our amnesic manager own?

Rather than holding a broadly diversified portfolio of securities resembling the entire stock market, we expect the manager to select a portfolio of common stocks concentrated in immature companies that exhibit significant growth potential. As a matter of policy, the manager has stated that these stocks represent his "fishing hole," or area of expertise. Within this distinct group of stocks his portfolio would be diversified, with no significantly different emphasis on any one issue, except possibly for liquidity considerations. Further, the manager may hold some reserve cash representing temporarily uninvested funds resulting from trading or income flows.

This collection of stocks and cash would comprise the emerging growth stock manager's benchmark portfolio. Let us now fully restore the manager's memory. We anticipate that he would immediately invoke his recovered active investment judgment, creating a portfolio whose holdings differed from those of the benchmark portfolio, both in terms of specific names and weights. For example, the manager might believe several companies within the emerging growth sector are significantly undervalued. They would be held in his portfolio in percentages exceeding those of the benchmark portfolio. Alternatively, the manager might find other stocks in the benchmark to be currently unattractive and totally exclude them. He might even temporarily hold securities not included in the benchmark. All of these deviations from the benchmark represent active bets; it is the process by which the manager adds value to the passive investment results of the benchmark. Nevertheless, the benchmark portfolio is the appropriate representation of the manager's expected risk posture and the proper standard for evaluating the effectiveness of the manager's active management decisions.

IV. Benchmark Portfolio Properties

While in practice a "correct" benchmark portfolio is simply one that both the manager and his clients agree fairly represents the manager's investment process, we believe there are several basic characteristics possessed by any useful benchmark.

- *Unambiguous*. The names and weights of securities comprising the benchmark are clearly delineated.
- *Investable*. The option is available to forego active management and simply hold the benchmark.
- *Measurable*. It is possible to readily calculate the benchmark's own return on a reasonably frequent basis.
- *Appropriate*. The benchmark is consistent with the manager's investment style or biases.
- *Reflective of current investment opinions*. The manager has current investment knowledge (be it positive, negative, or neutral) of the securities which make up the benchmark.
- *Specified in advance*. The benchmark is constructed prior to the start of an evaluation period.

The failure of a benchmark to possess any of these properties compromises its utility as an effective investment management tool. From this perspective, a number of commonly used benchmarks are seriously flawed. An example of one such flawed benchmark highlights the importance of these desirable benchmark properties.

Consultants and plan sponsors frequently use the median manager from a broad universe of common stock managers as a benchmark to evaluate the performance of other common stock managers. Yet this median manager benchmark, with the exception of being measurable, cannot lay claim to any other desirable benchmark properties.

Most critically, the median manager benchmark is not specified in advance. Compilers of peer groups identify the median manager only on an *ex post facto* basis. Before an evaluation period, we have no knowledge of the future median manager. The median manager benchmark also is uninvestable. Neither the manager being evaluated nor his clients has the option to invest in the median manager's portfolio. Further, the median manager benchmark is ambiguous in that the composition of the median manager's portfolio is unavailable for inspection, either before or after the evaluation period. In addition, the median manager's portfolio undoubtedly contains many securities for which the manager being evaluated has no current investment opinion. Finally, the median manager benchmark is unlikely to be appropriate because of the high probability that the median manager's investment style differs from that of the manager being evaluated.

Why are these deficiencies of concern? From the perspective of performance evaluation, the multitude of investment styles present in most manager universes produces an "apples and oranges" comparison problem. It begs the question, "To *what* is the manager expected to add value?" Without a valid reference point, investment skill remains an elusive notion. Conversely, a benchmark representing the manager's area of expertise explicitly ties the manager's performance to the manager's investment process. The value of active management stands out as a measurable and understandable concept.

With respect to the implementation of a multiple-manager investment program, the median manager benchmark is totally irrelevant. The lack of advance specification and ambiguity of composition make this benchmark useless to the plan sponsor desiring to understand the aggregate investment style of its particular manager alignment. On the other hand, a properly constructed benchmark portfolio clearly specifies a manager's investment process. Combining the benchmarks of a plan's managers allows the plan sponsor to design a management team consistent with the plan's investment objectives.

V. Building Benchmark Portfolios

Plan sponsors and managers interested in building benchmark portfolios usually have two initial questions. The first is "Who should build a manager's benchmark portfolio?" Essentially, there are three possible sources: the plan sponsor who hires the manager, a consultant hired by the manager or plan sponsor, or the manager. We strongly believe that a money management firm is best positioned to design its own benchmark. Benchmarks designed by "outsiders" represent second-best solutions. Although at times the manager may require technical assistance, only the decision-makers within the manager firm possess a detailed knowledge of the many subtle aspects of the firm's investment process.

The second question is "What is the 'right' way to build a benchmark portfolio?" We do not believe that a single "correct" construction technique exists. We do know, however, that most current construction methods are preferable to simply using the market portfolio as a manager benchmark.

Research into benchmark design has accelerated in recent years.[1] With growing interest in the subject, we expect new approaches to be continually developing. Nevertheless, without attempting to prescribe a rigid formula for building a benchmark portfolio, our experience suggests that several logical steps enhance the quality of benchmark design:

- Identify prominent aspects of the manager's investment process.
- Select securities consistent with that investment process.
- Devise a weighting scheme for the benchmark securities, including a cash position.
- Review the preliminary benchmark portfolio and make modifications.
- Rebalance the benchmark portfolio on a predetermined schedule.

An analysis of the manager's past portfolios often identifies prominent aspects of the manager's investment process. Care must be taken, however, to avoid a blind reliance on statistical averages of past portfolio characteristics. These characteristics are contaminated with active investment decisions. Recall equation (3) whereby $P = B + A$. The manager's benchmark *and* active bets compose the manager's portfolio. Over time, active bets cancel out, revealing persistent portfolio characteristics that represent the manager's investment process. But that time period may far exceed the horizon over which historical data is available. As a result, the benchmark builder complements the examination of past portfolios by extensively reviewing the investment process with decision-makers in the manager's organization.

The selection of benchmark portfolio securities requires both a broad universe of potential candidates and a set of screening criteria consistent with the manager's investment process. Commonly applied criteria include market capitalization, various financial ratios (e.g., price-to-book, price-to-earnings, dividend yield), and factors from fundamental risk models (e.g., exposure to growth risk or market variability). The manager modifies this screened security list by adding (deleting) securities for which the firm has (does not have) an informed investment opinion, be it positive or negative.

With respect to security weights, many managers' portfolios give the appearance of equal weighting as opposed to capitalization weighting. Appearances may be deceiving, however. Depending on the manager's investment process, certain portions of the capitalization spectrum will often re-

---

1. Barr Rosenberg, "The Capital Asset Pricing Model and the Market Model," *Journal of Portfolio Management* (Winter 1981), and Martin L. Leibowitz, *Total Return Management*, Salomon Brothers, 1979, present basic benchmark portfolio concepts. Walter Good, "Measuring Performance," *Financial Analysts Journal* (May/June, 1983), and "Accountability for Pension Fund Performance," *Financial Analysts Journal* (January/February, 1984), discusses applications of benchmark portfolios by plan sponsors. Mark Kritzman, "How to Build a Normal Portfolio in Three Easy Steps," *Journal of Portfolio Management* (Summer, 1987), presents a benchmark portfolio building process.

ceive consistently higher or lower representations in the manager's portfolio than other portions. A valid benchmark reflects these features, as well as any specific weight constraints which, for example, might result from client restrictions on holding particular securities.

The security selection and weighting steps produce a preliminary benchmark portfolio. Bearing in mind that the manager's active management decisions will be judged relative to this benchmark, at this point the firm's decision-makers review its composition and make any desired final modifications. By our experience, this final review, along with the previous construction steps, benefits the firm by offering formal insights into its investment process that may never have been fully contemplated before.

Keeping the benchmark portfolio current with the manager's investment process necessitates rebalancing the benchmark at regularly scheduled intervals (for example, quarterly). This rebalancing involves updating the benchmark for changes in the characteristics of benchmark securities or the manager's group of informed investment opinions.

Despite the apparent simplicity of these benchmark construction procedures, we do not mean to understate the complexity of the task. Conceptually, the problem is to determine, in advance, a benchmark design that does not "invade" the manager's active management. A proper benchmark walks a fine line between the manager's "normal" or policy investment decisions and the manager's active investment judgments.

Furthermore, the logistics of actually constructing and maintaining a benchmark portfolio require considerable resources, including: a security database containing fundamental investment characteristics on all possible investment candidates; an efficient computer screening capability; a flexible security weighting system; and a means to maintain the integrity of the benchmark over time.

VI. A Case Study

We now present a case study which highlights the value of investment benchmarks in performance evaluation. Specifically, we evaluate the performance of two equity managers over the period January 1, 1979 through June 30, 1983. We also consider a subsequent time period of July 1, 1983 to June 30, 1985 as a follow-up to the original study. We first apply four "traditional" approaches, all of which arrive at the same conclusion. We then show how a benchmark portfolio approach produces a completely different answer.

The Horse Race   Table 2 presents annualized returns for the two managers over the initial four-and-one-half year period. Simply comparing the two managers' returns against each other is one means of evaluating their relative investment skills. In fact, many plan sponsors make hire/fire decisions

---

TABLE 2. *Manager*
Portfolio Returns
(Annualized Returns,
1/1/79 – 6/30/83).

Manager A	35.2%
Manager B	19.6
S&P 500	19.3
T-bills	12.2

---

based on such limited information. A casual inspection of the performance data tempts one to conclude that the return spread between Managers A and B is so great that Manager A must be the superior investor.

Peer Groups We do have additional information, however. Peer group comparisons are frequently used to evaluate manager performance. Using data collected by SEI Corporation, Figure 1 (a favorite of marketers) and Table 3 compare the cumulative returns of Managers A and B to a broad sample of other equity portfolios over four time periods. The results of these comparisons place Manager A in the first quartile for all four periods, while Manager B lies consistently in the third and fourth quartiles. Based on this

---

FIGURE 1. *Equity Funds (Cumulative Returns to June 30, 1983).*

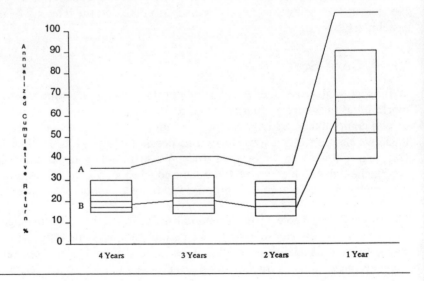

TABLE 3. *Equity Funds (Annualized Cumulative Returns to June 30, 1983).*

	4 Years	3 Years	2 Years	1 Year
5th Percentile	30.0%	32.3%	29.4%	88.4%
25th Percentile	22.9	24.9	23.9	66.5
Median	19.9	21.5	20.7	58.0
75th Percentile	17.2	18.2	17.5	51.6
95th Percentile	15.0	14.4	13.0	39.7
Manager A	35.0	41.1	35.1	103.9
Manager B	19.3	20.5	15.0	57.2
S&P 500	19.1	19.7	19.3	60.9

Source: SEI Corporation.

peer group comparison, Manager A's investment skills appear far superior to those of Manager B.

Reward-to-Variability   Other analytical methods incorporate risk into the evaluation process. One such method relates a portfolio's excess returns to its standard deviation of returns. Figure 2 plots the returns and standard deviations of returns of the two managers and the S&P 500 over the period of analysis. The slope of a line extending from the risk-free rate to a particular

FIGURE 2. *Equity Funds (Reward-to-Variability, 1/1/79 – 6/30/83).*

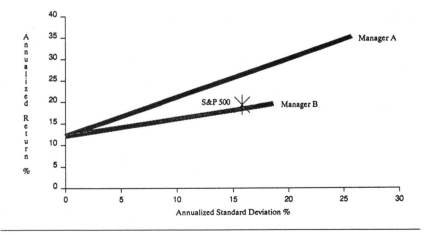

TABLE 4. *Multiple-Factor Model, Performance Attribution Analysis (Benchmark = S&P 500).*

	Manager A	Manager B
Market Timing	1.6%	0.1%
Market Sector Emphasis	7.1	3.9
Industry Exposure	0.2	−1.9
Unexplained	4.0	−1.7
Performance Increment	13.4%	0.3%

Source: BARRA.

portfolio's risk-return location, commonly known as the Sharpe measure, indicates the portfolio's excess return per unit of total risk. Although the the standard deviation of Manager A's return is larger than that of Manager B's, Manager A's excess return is considerably larger than Manager B's. The Sharpe measure therefore indicates superior performance on the part of Manager A relative to Manager B.

Multiple Factor Risk Analysis An alternative risk-adjusted performance measure utilizes a multiple-factor risk model. The model, developed by BARRA, incorporates financial factors identified as common to security returns, which in addition to the market factor include market capitalization, dividend yield, price-earnings ratio, price-book ratio, industries, and others. Table 4 lists the return contributions associated with the two managers' exposures to these common factors.

Table 4 shows that market sector exposures (for example, exposure to small or large capitalization stocks) account for the largest portion of the incremental returns for both portfolios. However, Manager A also has a significantly large return that cannot be explained by the multiple-factor model. Based on this large positive residual return, the model rates Manager A's performance superior to that of Manager B's.

These four traditional performance evaluation approaches fail to take into account some very important information. Crucial insights into the success of the two managers' active management decisions is gained by considering their respective areas of expertise: their benchmark portfolios. Manager A consistently selects from a universe of small capitalization stocks, primarily in the consumer and technology industries. Manager B selects from a quite different universe composed of larger capitalization stocks, principally in the basic industry and capital goods sectors. Table 5 presents the investment returns of the two managers and their respective benchmarks over the performance evaluation period.

TABLE 5. *Benchmark Analysis (Initial Evaluation Period, 1/1/79 – 6/30/83).*

	1979	1980	1981	1982	6 Months 1983	Annualized Return
Manager A	32.6%	37.7%	11.0%	38.9%	37.8%	35.2%
Benchmark A	38.1	43.4	15.5	44.8	40.8	40.8
Value of Active Management	– 5.5%	– 5.7%	– 4.5%	– 5.9%	– 3.0%	– 5.6%
Manager B	24.5%	26.1%	0.7%	12.5%	25.7%	19.6%
Benchmark B	19.6	21.5	– 3.5	8.4	23.5	15.0
Value of Active Management	4.9%	4.6%	4.2%	4.1%	2.2%	4.6%
S&P 500	18.6%	32.4%	– 4.9%	21.1%	22.2%	19.3%

Table 5 shows that Manager B significantly outperformed its benchmark, while Manager A underperformed its benchmark. This evaluation strongly suggests that through active management, Manager B was able to add value within his area of expertise, while Manager A's active judgments were not fruitful.

Why did the benchmark portfolio performance evaluation produce a different answer than the traditional approaches? In this situation, the answer lies in the strikingly different "fishing holes" from which the two managers select their portfolios.

Managers' portfolio returns are strongly influenced by the performance of their respective investment styles. Yet the returns to various investment styles fluctuate relative to one another. Over time, these relative returns will not persist in any particular direction. Conversely, truly skillful active managers will consistently add value to their investment styles. This case study provides a vivid example of the need to accurately represent managers' "fishing holes" when evaluating performance.

During the period of analysis, small capitalization, consumer and technology stocks performed extremely well relative to the market. Basic industry and capital goods stocks performed poorly. Manager A's portfolio benefited from these market conditions while Manager B's did not. Because the manager's returns are dominated by their respective styles, an accurate assessment of their active management capabilities cannot be made until we account for the effects of the managers' styles. The benchmark analysis deals specifically with this problem.

We note that the ability to identify the best performing investment style far outweighs the benefits of selecting superior managers. However, few, if

TABLE 6. *Benchmark Analysis (Subsequent Evaluation Period, 7/1/83 – 6/30/85).*

	Next 6 Months Ending 12/83	Next 12 Months Ending 6/84	Next 18 Months Ending 12/84*	Next 24 Months Ending 6/85*
Manager A	− 9.4%	− 18.5%	− 8.5%	3.4%
Benchmark A	− 7.6	− 15.2	− 4.9	7.6
Value of Active Management	− 1.8%	− 3.3%	− 3.6%	− 4.2%
Manager B	2.8%	− 1.7%	4.1%	13.7%
Benchmark B	0.8	− 5.5	0.1	9.4
Value of Active Management	2.0%	3.8%	4.0%	4.3%
S&P 500	0.1%	− 4.8%	4.1%	11.5%

*Annualized.

any, plan sponsors have demonstrated this investment management ability. We believe that plan sponsors' efforts are more productively focused on retaining managers who can consistently add value to their investment styles through their active investment judgments.

Given the initial results of the benchmark analysis, how do the two managers perform over a subsequent time period? Table 6 shows the performance of the two managers' actual portfolios and their benchmarks over the two-year period ending June 30, 1985. Once again Manager B has outperformed its benchmark, while Manager A underperformed its benchmark. This time, however, Manager A's benchmark performed poorly relative to both Manager B's and to the market. In fact, a plan sponsor enamored by Manager A's apparently strong relative performance over the initial four-and-one-half year period would have experienced an opportunity cost of almost 22% during the subsequent two years by hiring Manager A over Manager B.

Benchmark performance evaluation frequently produces results consistent with traditional approaches. Our case study presents an extreme, although quite plausible, example. Nevertheless, the moral of the story is clear: Performance evaluation not directly related to a manager's investment process runs the risk of being "fooled" by the results of the manager's style. Performance evaluation using an appropriate benchmark focuses on the value of the manager's active investment judgments, rather than the short-run performance of the manager's style.

VII. Conclusion

The use of benchmarks by plan sponsors and managers will continue to grow. To date, plan sponsors and consultants have taken the lead in developing benchmark portfolios for their managers. However, managers have a vital business stake in seeing that benchmark portfolios accurately reflect their investment processes. Therefore, we expect that more managers will begin to construct their own benchmarks and supply them to clients.

What are the implications of increased benchmark use? Most importantly, we expect plan sponsors will develop a more formal understanding of the relationship between their investment objectives and their investment management structures. Instead of hiring a group of managers within various asset classes with little apparent rhyme or reason, plan sponsors will allocate funds to asset classes and managers with specific objectives in mind. Results will be compared to realistic expectations, with a concomitant enhanced understanding of the value added to (or subtracted from) the investment programs by the various components of the plans' management structures. Modifications in those structures, if deemed necessary, will be carried out within orderly and internally consistent frameworks.

Managers should also benefit from the increased use of benchmarks. Through constructing benchmark portfolios, they gain greater insight into their investment processes. Inconsistencies and inefficiencies in those processes will be readily apparent. Perhaps more importantly, we expect there will be less "manager bashing" by plan sponsors as performance is evaluated relative to appropriate benchmarks. Skillful managers will be better able to consistently demonstrate their talents, regardless of whether their investment styles are in or out of favor.

Appropriate benchmark portfolios provide a framework around which the plan sponsor can develop a more effective investment program. Benchmark portfolios facilitate both the assessment of active management skill and the efficient allocation of funds among money managers within the plan's total portfolio. Benchmark portfolios are essential investment tools for the plan sponsor concerned with passing the value of active management down to the plan's bottom line.

Stock Index Futures
Mechanics, Pricing, and Hedging

Frank J. Fabozzi, Ph.D., CFA
Visiting Professor of Finance, Sloan School of Management
Massachusetts Institute of Technology
and
Editor, *The Journal of Portfolio Management*

Bruce M. Collins, Ph.D.*
Vice President, The First Boston Corporation

Edgar E. Peters
Portfolio Manager, Structured Investment Products Division
The Boston Company, Inc.

I. Introduction

Stock index futures have constructively and dramatically changed the equity investment process. Since the inception of stock index futures in February 1982, trading activity has grown rapidly. Currently, there are four broad-based stock index futures traded in the United States: The Standard & Poor's 500 Composite Index, the New York Stock Exchange Composite Index, the Major Market Index, and the Value Line Index.

The great popularity of stock index futures contracts may be explained by many factors, most of which are embodied in the principle of risk management. First, there is enormous interest in the equity markets. Furthermore, investors perceive themselves as having a correct opinion on the probable direction of the market more often than they are certain about which stocks to buy or sell. Stock index futures contracts have become a viable alternative means of taking positions based on the direction of market moves. Second, the economic, financial and political information that tends to affect stock market prices is widely disseminated by the news media daily, and the general public normally feels in a good position to evaluate general market

---

*This article was written while Dr. Collins was Manager of Index Products Research at Shearson Lehman Hutton, Inc.

conditions. Third, institutions and individuals holding large stock portfolios can use stock index futures as a timing device to either protect their cash values, accelerate market entry, or enhance returns. Fourth, professional arbitrageurs often use the stock index futures contracts to create synthetic stock and money-market positions that, depending on relative price levels, profit from market inefficiencies. Fifth, futures contracts are leveraged investments, which involve high financial risks; however, the potential profitability, to a futures position, could be very rewarding on a leveraged basis.

The purpose of this article is to describe the fundamental investment characteristics of these contracts, trading mechanics, pricing, and hedging strategies.

II. Stock Index Futures Contracts

A futures contract is a firm legal agreement between two parties: a buyer or a seller and an established exchange or clearinghouse. In this contract the parties agree to take or make delivery of a commodity at a specific price and at a specified time and place. A stock index futures contract is an agreement to pay or receive some dollar amount ($500 for New York Futures Exchange [NYFE] contract and the S&P 500 contract, $250 for the Major Market Index [XMI]) times the difference between the purchase price and the sale price. The value of a stock index futures contract at any time is equal to the product of the multiple for the contract and the current futures price.

Stock index futures differ from traditional commodity futures contracts (such as agricultural futures or interest rate futures contracts) in that there is no claim on an underlying deliverable asset. The claim is on the value of the contract and settlement is in cash. Stock index futures are therefore referred to as *cash settlement* contracts.

All futures contract positions are adjusted on a daily basis (that is, they are marked-to-the-market). At the end of each trading day, the current futures price is compared to the previous day's closing price, and if the futures price has risen (fallen), the long (short) investor receives from the short (long) investor the amount of the increase (decrease). Although this procedure is accomplished through an exchange, the investor's account is adjusted daily. Settlement is made by an exchange of money determined by the difference between the value of the contract at the final settlement and the previous day's closing price.

Margin

There are two concepts of margin that relate to futures contracts. The first is the traditional margin requirements regulated by the exchanges. A second concept of margin refers to variation margin and essentially represents the daily adjustment to changes in contract value. This section focuses on traditional margin requirements and the leverage it provides for investors in stock index futures. The sections that follow elaborate on the concept of variation margin and illustrate the daily cash flows associated with a futures position.

Margin requirements for futures contracts are similar in concept to stock margin requirements — both serve to provide brokers with protection from trading losses and foster investor confidence in the financial markets. Margin requirements for futures contracts, however, differ from stock margin in significant ways. Stock margin is essentially a down payment toward the purchase of a property where ownership changes hands on its receipt. In contrast, futures margin is a performance bond or good-faith payment that acknowledges that the contractual obligations will be honored.

Margin requirements include initial margin and maintenance margin and are specified differently for speculators, hedgers, and spreaders. The differential is intended to reflect the risk associated with the intent of the investor. Initial margin is the minimum amount that a customer must provide before a transaction can be executed. Maintenance margin represents the minimum level of equity that must be preserved in an account to maintain a position.

The size of the initial and maintenance margin for futures contracts is regulated by the commodity exchange where the contract trades. Stock margin is regulated by the Federal Reserve Board, the Securities and Exchange Commission, and the exchange where the stock is traded. In addition, brokerage firms have the discretion to set their own margin requirements but must satisfy the minimum margin requirements set by the exchanges.

The daily settlement feature of futures contracts yields daily changes in the customer account balance. The daily cash flows, or variation margin, are debited or credited to the account. A reduction in the account balance from adverse price movements may require that the customer post additional margin. Unlike futures contracts, the gains or losses from stock price movements are not realized until the stock is sold. In addition, when the futures account balance falls below the required maintenance margin level, enough additional margin must be posted to satisfy the initial margin requirement, which is not true for stock. After a stock is purchased and the initial margin has been posted, only the maintenance margin requirement must then be satisfied.

III. Mechanics of Trading Stock Index Futures

In this section we will discuss the mechanics of stock index futures trading. It is absolutely essential to understand these mechanics if one intends to employ these contracts in an investment strategy.

Taking and Liquidating a Position

When a trader takes a position in the market by buying a futures contract, the trader is said to be in a *long position*. If the trader's opening position is the sale of a futures contract the trader is said to be in a *short position*.

The trader can liquidate a position prior to the final settlement date by taking an offsetting position. For a long position, this means selling an identical number of contracts; for a short position, it means buying an identical number of contracts. Or the trader can wait until the final settlement day and liquidate his or her position by cash settlement.

The broker is required to provide confirmation of the execution of an order as soon as possible. The confirmation form that is filled out when a position is taken indicates all the essential information about the trade. When the order involves the liquidation of a position, the confirmation form shows the profit or loss on the position and the commission costs.

It is not uncommon to purchase a security through one brokerage firm and sell it through another. However, this is usually not done with futures contracts. The brokerage firm that executes the order to establish the initial position also executes the order to liquidate the position.

When a trader takes a position in the market, another party is taking the opposite position and agreeing to satisfy the commitment set forth in the contract. What if the party defaults on the obligation? Is the trader's only recourse to sue the defaulting party? Does that mean a trader must be concerned with who the other party is before taking a position in the futures market? Moreover, if the trader wants to liquidate a position before the final settlement date, must the trader do so only with that party?

The trader need not worry about the financial strength and integrity of the other party to the contract. Once the order is executed, the direct relationship between the two parties is severed. A clearing corporation associated with each exchange interposes itself as the buyer to every sale and the seller to every purchase. Thus, each of the parties to the contract is free to liquidate his position without being concerned about the other party.

Margin Requirements

The various margin requirements for trading stock index futures contracts can be illustrated through a stock replacement strategy used by some institutional index fund managers who are indifferent between holding the stocks or holding futures. An index fund will sell its stocks, replace them with a dollar equivalent of futures contracts and place the proceeds in Treasury bills.[1] This strategy was available in the third week of April 1988, using the June 1988 S&P 500 futures contract.

---

1. The example applies to an institutional account where the stock position is replaced with a futures position and Treasury bills. The Treasury bill account usually is not touched and varia-

TABLE 1. *Assumed Futures Position and Value of Contracts for Margin Requirement Illustration.*

Day	Trade Price	Value of 193 Contracts ($)*
1	$259.00	$259.00 × 500 × 193 = $24,993,500

Trading Days 2 through 10

Day	Settlement Price	Value of 193 Contracts
2	$258.60	$24,954,900
3	259.25	25,017,625
4	257.30	24,829,450
5	257.90	24,887,350
6	256.20	24,723,300
7	261.85	25,268,525
8	263.85	25,461,525
9	264.80	25,553,200
10	264.00	25,476,000

*The contract value is $500 times the futures price. Since there are 193 contracts, the per contract value is multiplied by 193.

Suppose that an index fund invested $25,052,888 in S&P June 1988 futures contracts to replace an equivalent amount of stock on April 14, 1988.[2] The closing futures price that day was 259.0 and the closing cash index was 259.75. The number of contracts required to satisfy the dollar value of the portfolio is 193 ($25,052,088/[500 × 259.75]). The futures position is viewed as as a hedge against cash, and therefore the initial margin requirement is $10,000 times 193 or $1,930,000. The investor's cash position can be used to satisfy the initial margin. The maintenance margin for this transaction is the same as the initial margin.

Table 1 presents the closing settlement price of the S&P 500 June 1988 futures contract for nine days following April 14, 1988. The variation margin

tion margin is satisfied each day in cash. Index funds are discussed in Bruce M. Collins and Frank J. Fabozzi, "Creating and Managing an Index Fund Using Stock Index Futures," the next article in this book.

2. The correct calculation to determine the number of futures contracts to be sold is (dollar value/[500 × cash index]). This number, as a rule of thumb, should come within .10 of a round number of futures contracts which is equivalent to $9,650 on 193 contracts, or .1 × 500 × 193. This represents an approximate $25 million position adjusted to account for the necessity of using a round number of futures contracts.

TABLE 2. *Margin Requirements and Account Equity for the Purchase of 193 S&P 500 Contracts.*

Initial margin per S&P 500 contract = $10,000
Initial margin for 193 S&P 500 contracts = $1,930,000 (193 × $10,000)
Maintenance margin per S&P 500 contract = $10,000
Maintenance margin for 193 S&P 500 contracts = $1,930,000

Day	Settlement Price	Value for 193 Contracts	Equity in Account	Variation Margin
1	$259.00	$24,993,500	$1,930,000	—
2	258.60	24,954,900	1,891,400	$(38,600)
3	259.25	25,017,625	1,992,725*	62,725
4	257.30	24,829,450	1,804,550	(188,175)
5	257.90	24,887,350	1,987,900	57,900
6	256.20	24,723,300	1,823,850	(164,050)
7	261.85	25,268,525	2,475,225	545,225
8	263.85	25,461,525	2,668,225	193,000
9	264.80	24,553,200	2,759,900	91,675
10	264.00	25,476,000	2,682,700	(77,200)

*Accounts have 24 hours to satisfy negative variation margin. Margin calls are satisfied the next day. Thus, $1,992,725 = $1,930,000 + $62,725.

from the account is examined on a day-to-day basis below and is summarized in Table 2. We assume that daily variation margin is reflected by the equity in the account. In practice, institutional investors post the initial margin in Treasury bills while satisfying the negative variation margin with cash (which is required). They withdraw positive variation margin and maintain only the minimum required. In our example, we relax this assumption.

Day 2 The futures price declined from 259.00 to 258.60 or .40 index points. The decrease in the contract value is subtracted from the investor's account. This is what is meant by marked-to-the-market. The equity in the investor's account is the initial margin less $38,600. The investor must now transfer the entire amount, $38,600, into the account to satisfy the maintenance margin. If the maintenance margin is below the initial margin, as is the case with speculators, no additional margin would be required. The initial margin for speculators is $3,667,000 (193 × $19,000). In this case, $1,737,000 would have to be lost before the maintenance margin requirement is violated. In practice, when the equity in the account is near the maintenance margin level, additional cash may be added to the account in anticipation of a decline in futures prices. The additional amount provides a cushion and may prevent a margin call. This is particularly important when there is a differential between initial margin and maintenance margin.

Day 3 The futures price increased from 258.60 to 259.25, or .65 index points. The contract value of the position is increased by $62,725. Notice that the equity in the account is $62,725 above the margin requirements because the account had previously been restored to the maintenance margin level.

Day 4 The futures price declined by 1.95 index points settling at 257.30. This reduces the equity in the account by $188,175. The loss pushes the equity in the account below the required maintenance margin and the investor must raise additional cash to satisfy the margin.

Day 5 A .60 index point increase in the futures price to 257.90 increases the equity in the account by $57,900. Because the equity in the account was restored on the previous day to the maintenance margin level, the account balance is $1,987,900.

Day 6 A significant decline of 1.7 index points in the futures price yields a $164,050 reduction to the equity in the account. The investor has 24 hours to satisfy the maintenance margin requirement.

Day 7 A dramatic increase in the futures price to 261.85 adds $545,225 to the equity in the account. The value of the account is now $2,475,225. Thus, the futures price can fall by 4.16 index points or 1.59% before the margin requirements are violated.

Day 8 An increase in the futures price to 263.85 increases the equity in the account by $193,000. This adds to the surplus in the account. The investor may choose to withdraw the cash for alternative investments, as is often the practice of institutional investors.

Day 9 A .95 index point rise in the futures price increases the equity in the account by $91,675. If we assume the investor does not withdraw cash from the account, there is sufficient equity in the account to satisfy margin requirements should the futures price fall 6.27 points at some time in the future.

Day 10 On the final day of our analysis the futures price has fallen to 264.00. There is a $77,200 reduction to the equity in the account. Because there is a surplus of equity in the account, no margin call is required.

In our illustration we have assumed that the index fund deposited cash to meet the initial and variation margins. As an alternative, Treasury bills or letters of credit may be used for initial margin. Variation margin *must* be satisfied with cash.

Commissions

Like the commissions on common stock transactions, the commissions on executions of stock index futures contracts are fully negotiable. The commissions charged on stock index futures contracts are based on a round trip. For individual investors, these commissions range from $40 to $100 per contract at full service brokerage firms. For institutional investors, the typical commission per contract is under $15. Assuming a round-trip commission of $50 per contract, the cost of transacting is typically less than 0.1% (0.001) of the contract value. A round-trip commission for a portfolio consisting of the underlying stocks would be roughly 1% of the value of the stocks.

IV. The Theoretical Futures Price

In theory, the price of any futures contract should be equivalent to the cost of buying and holding the underlying cash instrument from today until contract settlement. Therefore, based on arbitrage arguments, the equilibrium price for any futures contract can be determined based on the following information:

1. The price of the instrument in the cash market.
2. The cash yield on the cash market instrument.
3. The interest rate for borrowing and lending until the settlement date.

The borrowing and lending rate is referred to as the *financing rate*. The *cost of carry* is defined as the difference between the financing cost and the yield that can be earned on the cash instrument.

The theoretical (or equilibrium) futures price can be shown to be equal to:

Theoretical futures price = Cash price × (1 + Cost of carry).

The difference between the cash price and the futures price is called the *basis*. To the extent that the actual basis differs from the theoretical basis (cash price minus theoretical futures price), arbitrage opportunities exist.

In the case of stock index futures, the cash instrument is the cash index that is the underlying instrument for the contract. The cash yield is the dividend yield of the index. In the price formula, then:

Cost of carry = (Financing rate − Annualized dividend yield)

× (Days to settlement/365).

To illustrate the pricing formula, assume:

Cash index = 275
Financing rate = 6.50% (.065)

Annualized dividend yield = 2.00% (.02)
Days to settlement = 60

Then

$$\text{Cost of carry} = (.065 - .02) \times (60/365)$$
$$= .007397.$$

$$\text{Theoretical futures price} = 275 \times (1 + .007397)$$
$$= 277.03.$$

A Closer Look at the Theoretical Futures Prices

To derive the theoretical futures price using the artibrage argument, several assumptions have to be made. The implications of these assumptions for the divergence between the actual futures price and the theoretical futures price are discussed below.

Interim Cash Flows No interim cash flows due to variation margin or coupon interest payments are assumed. However, we know that interim cash flows can occur for both of these reasons. Because we assumed no variation margin, the theoretical futures price is technically the theoretical price of a forward contract because a forward contract is not marked to market at the end of each trading day.

The Financing Rate In deriving the theoretical futures price it is assumed that the borrowing rate and lending rate are equal. The financing rate generally used in practice is the riskless interest rate for investments equal to the number of days of the settlement contract. For example, if the stock index futures contract has six months to settlement, the financing rate is the six-month Treasury bill rate. In reality, however, the borrowing rate is not equal to the lending rate. Therefore, there is not one theoretical futures price that will not allow arbitrage opportunities, but instead a theoretical band around the theoretical futures price that reflects the borrowing and lending rates.

Uncertainty about Dividend Yield The development of the theoretical futures price assumes that (1) the dividends that will be received are known with certainty and (2) the timing of receipt of the dividends from each stock in the index is known with certainty. Because neither condition is met in practice, the actual futures price may diverge from the theoretical futures price.

Buying and Selling the Index The arbitrage model assumes that if the actual futures price diverges from the theoretical futures price, arbitrageurs will drive the actual toward the theoretical futures price. The difficulty faced by arbitrageurs is that it is too costly to purchase all the stocks in the index. Instead, arbitrageurs will buy or sell only a subset of stocks in the index. However, the subset of stocks is selected so that they will mirror the index. Because of the transaction costs associated with constructing the subset of stocks to be bought or sold, there is a theoretical band rather than a single theoretical futures price that reflects transaction costs.

V. Overview of Hedging

The major economic function of futures markets is to transfer price risk from hedgers to speculators. Hedging is the employment of futures as a substitute for a transaction to be made in the cash market. The hedge position locks in the current value of the cash position. If cash and futures prices move together, any loss realized by the hedger on one position (whether cash or futures) will be offset by a profit on the other position. When the profit and loss are equal, the hedge is called a *perfect hedge*. In the stock index futures market, a perfect hedge returns the risk-free rate.

In practice, hedging is not that simple. When hedging with stock index futures, a perfect hedge can only be obtained if the return of the portfolio being hedged is identical to the futures contract. Since it is likely that both the stock portfolio and the futures contract have nonmarket components of return, a perfect hedge will rarely, if ever, happen.

The effectiveness of a hedge on an equity portfolio is determined by:

1. The relationship between the portfolio and the index underlying the futures contract.
2. The relationship between the cash price and futures price when a hedge is placed and when it is lifted.

As we stated earlier, the difference between the cash price and the futures price is called the *basis*. Consequently, hedging involves the substitution of basis risk for price risk.

A stock index future uses a stock index as its underlying commodity. Since the portfolio to be hedged will have different characteristics than the underlying stock index (unless it is a stock index fund), there will be a difference in the return pattern of the hedged portfolio and the futures contract. This practice—hedging with a futures contract that is different than the commodity being hedged—is called a *cross-hedge*. In the physical and commodities markets, this occurs, for example, when an okra farmer hedges a crop using corn futures. Corn is the commodity with a traded futures contract that may have the strongest price relationship to okra. In the equity markets, the hedger must choose the stock index, or combination of stock indexes with futures contracts, that best tracks the equity portfolio.

Consequently, cross-hedging adds another dimension to basis risk. The non-index related component of return in an equity portfolio will not be hedged by a stock index futures position.

Cross-hedging is the name of the game in portfolio management. There are no futures contracts on specific common stock shares. The only futures traded that are related to the equity markets have specific stock indexes as the underlying commodity. How well the price of a portfolio of common stocks tracks an index and the behavior of the basis will determine the success of a hedge.

The foregoing points will be made clearer in the illustrations presented in the remainder of this article.

Short Hedge and Long Hedge

In portfolio management, the short hedge is more commonly practiced. Long hedges are generally used in asset allocation strategies. However, it is the short hedge that is referred to as hedging in the marketplace.

A *short hedge* is used by a hedger to protect against a decline in the future cash price of a commodity or a financial instrument. To execute a short hedge, the hedger sells a futures contract (agrees to make delivery of the underlying commodity or financial instrument). Consequently, a short hedge is also known as a *sell hedge*. By establishing a short hedge, the hedger has fixed the future cash price and transferred the price risk of ownership to the buyer of the contract. Three examples of who may want to use a short hedge follow.

1. A corn farmer will sell his product in three months. The price of corn, like the price of any commodity, will fluctuate in the open market. The corn farmer wants to lock in a price at which he can deliver his corn in three months.

2. A corporate treasurer plans to sell bonds in two months to raise $85 million in capital. The cost of the bond issue to the corporation will depend on interest rates at the time the bond issue is sold. The corporate manager is uncertain of the interest rates that will prevail two months from now and wants to lock in a rate today.

3. A pension fund manager knows that the beneficiaries of the fund must be paid a total of $3 million four months from now. This will necessitate liquidating a portion of the fund's common stock portfolio. Should the value of the shares that he intends to liquidate in order to satisfy the benefits to be paid be lower in value four months from now, a larger portion of the portfolio would have to be liquidated. The pension fund manager would like to lock in the price of the shares that will be liquidated.

A *long hedge* is undertaken to protect against the purchase of a commodity or financial instrument in the cash market at some future time. In a long hedge, the hedger buys a futures contract (agrees to accept delivery of the underlying commodity or financial instrument). A long hedge is also known as a *buy hedge*. The following three examples are instances where a party may use a long hedge.

1. A food processing company projects that in three months it must purchase 30,000 bushels of corn. The management of the company does not want to take a chance that the price of corn may increase by the time the company must make its acquisition. It wants to lock in a price for corn today.
2. A bond portfolio manager knows that in two months $10 million of his portfolio will mature and must be reinvested. Prevailing interest rates are high but may decline substantially by the time the funds are to be reinvested. The portfolio manager wants to lock in a reinvestment rate today.
3. A pension fund manager expects a substantial contribution from participants four months from now. The contributions will be invested in the common stock of various companies. The pension fund manager expects the market price of the stocks in which she will invest the contributions to be higher in four months. She therefore wants to lock in the price of those stocks.

Hedging Illustrations

Before illustrating the nuances associated with hedging with stock index futures, we first present several numerical illustrations from the commodities area.

Assume that a corn farmer expects to sell 30,000 bushels of corn three months from now. Assume further that the management of a food processing company plans to purchase 30,000 bushels of corn three months from now. Both the corn farmer and the management of the food processing company want to lock in today's price. That is, they want to eliminate the price risk associated with corn three months from now. The cash or spot price for corn is currently $2.75 per bushel. The futures price for corn is currently $3.20 per bushel. Each futures contract is for 5,000 bushels of corn.

Since the corn farmer seeks protection against a decline in the price of corn three months from now, he will place a short, or sell, hedge. That is, he will promise to make delivery of corn at the current futures price. He will sell six futures contracts since each contract calls for the delivery of 5,000 bushels of corn.

The management of the food processing company seeks protection against an increase in the price of corn three months from now. Consequently, it will place a buy, or long, hedge. That is, it will agree to accept delivery of corn at the current futures price. Since it is seeking protection against a price increase for 30,000 bushels of corn, it will buy six contracts.

Let's look at what happens under various scenarios for the cash price and the futures price of corn three months from now, when the hedge is lifted.

Suppose that, when the hedge is lifted, the cash price declines to $2.00 and the futures price declines to $2.45. Notice what has happened to the basis under this scenario. At the time the hedge was placed, the basis is −$.45 ($2.75 − $3.20). When the hedge is lifted, the basis is still −$.45 ($2.00 − $2.45).

The corn farmer, at the time the hedge was placed, wanted to lock in a price of $2.75 per bushel of corn, or $82,500 for 30,000 bushels. He sold six futures contracts at a price of $3.20 per bushel, or $96,000 for 30,000 bushels. When the hedge is lifted, the value of the farmer's corn is $60,000 ($2.00 × 30,000). The corn farmer realizes a decline in the cash market in the value of his corn of $22,500. However, the futures price declines to $2.45, so the cost to the corn farmer to liquidate his futures position is only $73,500 ($2.45 × 30,000). The corn farmer realizes a gain in the futures market of $22,500. The net result is that the gain in the futures market matches the loss in the cash market. Consequently, the corn farmer does not realize an overall gain or loss. When this occurs, the hedge is said to be a *perfect* or *textbook* hedge.

Because there was a decline in the cash price, the food processing company would realize a gain in the cash market of $22,500 but would realize a loss in the futures market of the same amount. Therefore, this buy or long hedge is also a *perfect* or *textbook* hedge.

This scenario illustrates two important points. First, for both participants there was no overall gain or loss. The reason for this result was that we assumed the basis did not change when the hedge was lifted. Thus, if the basis does not change, a perfect hedge will be achieved. Second, notice that the management of the food processing company would have been better off if it had not hedged. The cost of corn would have been $22,500 less in the cash market three months later. This, however, should not be interpreted as a sign of poor planning by management. Management is not in the business of speculating on the price of corn in the future. Hedging is a standard practice to protect against an increase in the cost of doing business in the future.

Suppose that the cash price of corn when the hedge is lifted increases to $3.55 and that the futures price increases to $4.00. Notice that the basis is unchanged at −$.45. Since the basis is unchanged, the cash and futures price we have assumed in this scenario will produce a perfect hedge.

The corn farmer will gain in the cash market since the value of 30,000 bushels of corn is $106,500 ($3.55 × 30,000). This represents a $24,000 gain, compared to the cash value at the time the hedge was placed. However, the corn farmer must liquidate his position in the futures market by buying six futures contracts at a total cost of $120,000, which is $24,000 more than when the contracts were sold. The loss in the futures market offsets the gain in the cash market and we have a perfect hedge. The food processing company would realize a gain in the futures market of $24,000 but would have to pay $24,000 more in the cash market to acquire 30,000 bushels of corn.

Notice that the management of the food processing company under this scenario saved $24,000 in the cost of corn by employing a hedge. The corn farmer, though, would have been better off if he had not used a hedging strategy and simply sold his product on the market three months later. However, it must be emphasized that the corn farmer, just like the management of the food processing company, employed a hedge to protect against unforeseen adverse price changes in the cash market.

In the previous two scenarios we have assumed that the basis does not change when the hedge is lifted. In the real world, the basis does, in fact, change between the time a hedge is placed and when it is lifted. Now we shall illustrate what happens when the basis changes.

Assume that the cash price of corn decreases to $2.00, just as in the first scenario; however, assume also that the futures price decreases to $2.70 rather than $2.45. The basis has now widened from −$.45 to −$.70 ($2.00 − $2.70). For the short (sell) hedge, the loss in the cash market of $22,500 is only partially offset by a $15,000 gain realized in the futures market. Consequently, the hedge resulted in an overall loss of $7,500.

There are two points to note here. First, if the corn farmer had not employed the hedge, the loss would have been $22,500, since the value of his 30,000 bushels of corn is $60,000, compared to $82,500 three months earlier. Although the hedge is not a perfect hedge because the basis widened, the loss of $7,500 is less than the loss of $22,500 if no hedge had been placed. This is what we meant earlier in the article when we said that hedging substitutes basis risk for price risk. Second, the management of the food processing company faces the same problem from an opposite perspective. An unexpected gain for either participant results in an unexpected loss of equal dollar value for the other. That is, the participants face a "zero-sum game." Consequently, the food processing company would realize an overall gain of $7,500 from its long (buy) hedge. This gain represents a gain of $22,500 in the cash market and a realized loss of $15,000 in the futures market.

The results of this scenario demonstrate that when *(a)* the future price is greater than the cash price at the time the hedge is placed, *(b)* the cash price declines, and *(c)* the basis widens, then: *the short (sell) hedger will realize an overall loss from the hedge, and the long (buy) hedger will realize an overall gain from the hedge.*

Table 3 summarizes the impact of a change in the basis on the overall profit or loss of a hedge when the futures price is greater than the cash price at the time the hedge is placed.

TABLE 3. *Summary of Basis Relationships for a Hedge.*

Price		Absolute Change in Basis	Overall Gain (+) or Loss (−) When at Time Hedge is Placed Cash Price is Less than Futures Price	
Cash	Futures		Short Hedge	Long Hedge
Decreases	Decreases by same amount	No change	0	0
Decreases	Decreases by a smaller amount	Widens	−	+
Decreases	Decreases by a greater amount	Narrows	+	−
Increases	Increases by same amount	No change	0	0
Increases	Increases by a smaller amount	Narrows	+	−
Increases	Increases by a greater amount	Widens	−	+

Cross-Hedging Illustrations

Not all commodities have a futures market. Consequently, if a hedger wants to protect against the price risk of a commodity in which a futures contract is not traded, the hedger may use a commodity that he believes has a close price relationship to the one he seeks to hedge. This adds another dimension of risk when hedging. The cash market price relationship between the commodity to be hedged and the commodity used to hedge may change.

Since hedging financial instruments using futures frequently involves cross-hedging, we will first illustrate the key elements associated with a cross-hedge for a commodity.

Suppose that an okra farmer plans to sell 37,500 bushels of okra three months from now and that a food processing company plans to purchase the same amount of okra three months from now. Both parties want to hedge against price risk. However, okra futures contracts are not traded. Both parties believe that there is a close price relationship between okra and corn. Specifically, both parties believe that the cash price of okra will be 80% of the cash price of corn. The cash price of okra is currently $2.20 per bushel and the cash price of corn is currently $2.75 per bushel. The futures price of corn is currently $3.20 per bushel.

Let's examine various scenarios to see how effective the cross-hedge will be. In each scenario, the difference between the cash price of corn and the futures price of corn at the time the cross-hedge is placed and at the time it is lifted will be assumed to be unchanged at −$.45. This is done so we may focus on the importance of the relationship between the two cash prices at the two points in time.

We must first determine how many corn futures contracts must be used in the cross-hedge. The cash value of 37,500 bushels of okra at the cash price of $2.20 per bushel is $82,500. To protect a value of $82,500 using corn futures with a current cash price of $2.75, the value of 30,000 bushels of corn ($82,500/$2.75) must be hedged. Since each corn futures contract involves 5,000 bushels, six corn futures contracts will be used.

Suppose that the cash price of okra and corn decrease to $1.60 and $2.00 per bushel, respectively, and the futures price of corn decreases to $2.45 per bushel. The relationship between the cash price for okra and corn assumed when the cross-hedge was placed holds at the time the cross-hedge is lifted. That is, the cash price of okra is 80% of the cash price of corn. The basis for the cash price of corn and the futures price of corn is still −$.45 at the time the cross-hedge is lifted.

The short cross-hedge produces a gain in the futures market of $22,500 and an exact offset loss in the cash market. The opposite occurs for the long cross-hedge. There is neither an overall gain nor a loss from the cross-hedge in this case. That is, we have a perfect cross-hedge. The same would occur if we assume that the cash price of both commodities increases by the same percentage and the basis does not change.

Suppose that the cash price of both commodities decreases but the cash price of okra falls by a greater percentage than the cash price of corn. For example, suppose that the cash price of okra falls to $1.30 per bushel while the cash price of corn falls to $2.00 per bushel. The futures price of corn falls to $2.45 so that the basis is not changed. The cash price of okra at the time the cross-hedge is lifted is 65% of the cash price of corn, rather than 80% as assumed when the cross-hedge was constructed.

For the short cross-hedge the loss in the cash market exceeds the realized loss in the futures market by $11,200. For the long cross-hedge the opposite is true. There is an overall gain from the cross-hedge of $11,200. Had the cash price of okra fallen by less than the decline in the cash price of corn, the short cross-hedge would have produced an overall gain while the long cross-hedge would have generated an overall loss. We refer to the risk that the cash price of the commodity to be hedged does not change as predicted relative to the cash price of the commodity used for hedging as *cross-hedge price risk*.

VI. Hedging with Stock Index Futures

We have demonstrated in this article that a successful hedge strategy will depend on what happens to the basis between the time the hedge is placed and the time the hedge is lifted. When hedging with stock index futures, however, a *perfect* or *textbook* short hedge will return the risk-free rate of interest, not zero. Therefore, an S&P 500 index fund (with no tracking error) fully hedged with S&P 500 futures selling at fair-value will return the risk-free rate. It will be the equivalent of selling the stock and placing the proceeds in a cash equivalent investment. This point is crucial to any equity hedging strategy. The cost of carry is the theoretical basis of a stock index futures contract. If the basis were always equal to the cost of carry, there would be little basis risk since the cost of carry can be estimated with a fair degree of accuracy.

Mispricing, then, is the major portion of basis risk. It can be defined as the difference between the actual futures price and its theoretical price according to the cost-of-carry model defined earlier. The Treasury bill rate is used as the financing rate in the model. We will see later that mispricing is random, and is therefore the major source of basis risk.

We have also seen in Section V that when cross-hedging, the price risk of a portfolio of common stocks will depend on the pricing of the futures relative to the underlying cash or spot index. Since a stock index futures contract will often be used to hedge a portfolio that is not identical in composition to the underlying stock index, any hedge employing stock index futures is a cross-hedge. Therefore, a relationship between the value of the stock index and the stock portfolio must be estimated.

Finally, the relationship between the stock index futures contract and its underlying index will also be important. The return of the two instruments can vary significantly due to speculative mispricing. So in implementing a cross-hedge, it should be recognized that the relationship between the common stock portfolio and the underlying stock index must be adjusted for the imperfect relationship between the index and the stock index futures contract. This is a particularly important point when determining the appropriate hedge ratio for implementing a cross-hedge using stock index futures.

The Minimum Risk Hedge Ratio

It is tempting to use the portfolio beta as a hedge ratio because it is an indicator of the sensitivity of the portfolio returns to the stock index return. It appears, then, to be an ideal sensitivity adjustment. However, applying beta relative to a stock index as a sensitivity adjustment to a stock index futures contract assumes that the index and the futures contract have the same volatility. If futures always sold at their fair price, this would be a reasonable assumption. However, mispricing is an extra element of volatility in an index futures contract. One study has shown that mispricing adds 20% to the volatility of the futures contract.[3] Since the futures contract is more volatile than the underlying index, using a portfolio beta as a sensitivity adjustment would result in a portfolio being over-hedged.[4]

---

3. Ed Peters, "Hedged Equity Portfolios: Components of Risk and Return," *Advances in Futures and Options Research*, 1B (1986), pp. 75–92.
4. When a hedge is held until expiration, or if the hedger has the luxury of waiting until the futures contract is fairly priced, the return to mispricing is no longer an unknown factor. Using beta as a hedge ratio locks in the mispricing as an element of return. Strategies known as synthetic cash or cash-and-carry arbitrage use this relationship to achieve incremental returns

The most accurate sensitivity adjustment would be the beta of the portfolio relative to the futures contract. However, there are a number of operational problems in this adjustment. First, futures contracts have an element of "seasonality" to them that make beta estimates for individual stocks highly unstable. Second, the calculation of these beta estimates adds an additional computational burden on the hedger.

A recent study has shown that the beta of the portfolio relative to the futures contract is equivalent to the product of the beta of the portfolio relative to the underlying index and the beta of the index relative to the futures contract.[5] For widely used indexes, such as the S&P 500 and the NYSE Composite Index, the former is readily available. The latter number can be easily computed.

Therefore, the minimum risk hedge ratio (h) can be expressed as:

$$h = B_{PI} B_{IF},$$

where

h = the minimum risk hedge ratio
B_{PI} = the beta of the portfolio relative to the index, and
B_{IF} = the beta of the index relative to the futures contract.

While the beta of the index relative to the futures contract may still be unstable, it will be significantly more stable than the beta of individual stocks relative to futures contracts.

This minimum risk hedge ratio plays the same role in hedging a stock portfolio that the relations between the cash price of okra and the cash price of corn did in our cross-hedging example earlier in the article. The coefficient of determination will indicate how good the relationship is and will allow the hedger to assess the likelihood of success of the hedge.

Examples of Hedging Using Stock Index Futures

To demonstrate how stock index futures can be used to hedge the market risk of a portfolio of common stocks, actual cases will be used.

Suppose the investor had $1 million in an S&P 500 index fund on July 1, 1986 and wished to hedge against a possible market decline. The account was to be hedged for July 1, 1986 through August 31, 1986. To hedge against an adverse market move during the period, the investor decides to enter into a short hedge by selling S&P 500 futures contracts.

The first thing the investor has to do is to determine how many contracts to sell. This depends on the portfolio's beta (B_{PI}), the beta of the

---

above the risk-free rate. However, if the duration of the hedge is unknown, then the return due to mispricing is also unknown, making it an extra element of risk. Then beta is not an appropriate hedge ratio.
5. Peters, "Hedged Equity Portfolios."

index relative to the futures contract (B_{IF}), and on the dollar value of a S&P 500 futures contract. The steps for determining the number of contracts are as follows:

Step 1 Determine the "equivalent market index units" of the market by dividing the market value of the portfolio by the current index price of the futures contract:

$$\text{Equivalent market index units} = \frac{\text{Market value of the portfolio}}{\text{Current index value of the futures}}.$$

Step 2 Multiply the equivalent market index units by the two-beta hedge ratio to obtain the "beta-adjusted equivalent market index units":

$$\text{Beta-adjusted equivalent market index units} = B_{PI} \times B_{IF} \times \text{Equivalent market index units}.$$

Step 3 Divide the beta-adjusted equivalent market index units by the multiple specified by the futures contract. For S&P 500 contracts the multiple is $500:

$$\text{Number of contracts} = \frac{\text{Beta-adjusted equivalent market index units}}{\$500}.$$

In our illustration, the September 1986 S&P 500 contract was selling at 250.01 on July 1, 1986, the day the hedge was to be initiated. The beta (B_{PI}) of the S&P 500 is, of course, 1.00. The beta relative to the futures contract was estimated by a regression analysis to be 0.745. Therefore, the number of contracts needed to hedge a $1 million S&P 500 index is computed as follows.

Step 1

$$\text{Equivalent market index units} = \frac{\$1,000,000}{253.95}$$

$$= \$3,937.78.$$

Step 2

$$\text{Beta-adjusted equivalent market index units} = 1.00 \times .745 \times \$3,937.78$$

$$= \$2,933.648.$$

Step 3

$$\text{Number of contracts} = \frac{\$2,933.648}{\$500}$$

$$= 5.87.$$

TABLE 4. *Hedging a $1 Million S&P Fund Using S&P 500 Futures.*

Situation

Own $1 million in a S&P 500 Index Fund on 7/1/86.
Need to hedge against an adverse market move.
Time the hedge is held is unknown at the start.
Hedge is lifted 8/31/86.

Facts

	7/1/86	8/31/86
Cash price of S&P 500	252.04	234.91
Price of 9/86 S&P 500 futures	253.95	233.15

Beta of the portfolio relative to the index = 1.000
Beta of the index relative to the futures = 0.745
Minimum risk hedge ratio = 1.000 × 0.745 = 0.745

Outcome

Cash Market	Futures Market	Cost of Carry	Mispricing
7/1/86 — Time hedge is placed			
Own $1,000,000 portfolio	Sell 6 9/86 S&P 500 futures contracts at 253.95	+1.26	+0.65
8/31/86 — Time hedge is lifted			
Own $942,034.60	Buy 6 9/86 S&P 500 futures contracts at 233.15	+0.43	−2.19
Loss in cash market = $67,965.40	Gain in futures market = $62,400		
Overall loss = $5,565.40			

This number will be rounded up to six contracts. This means that the futures position was equal to $761,850 (6 × 500 × 253.95). On August 31, 1986, the hedge was removed. The S&P 500 index fund returned −6.80% or a loss of $67,965.40. The futures contract was selling at 233.15 for a gain of 8.19% or $62,400, resulting in a trivial loss of $5,565.40. This short hedge is summarized in Table 4.

Let us analyze this hedge to determine why it was successful. As explained earlier, in hedging we exchange basis risk for price risk. Consider the basis risk. At the time the hedge was placed, the index was at 252.04. The September 1986 S&P futures contract was selling at 253.95. The basis was equal to 253.95 − 252.04 = 1.91. The cost of carry was equal to 1.26 index units, thus, mispricing equaled 0.65 index units.

When the hedge was removed at the close on August 31, 1986, the index stood at 234.91. The futures contract was selling at 233.15, or a discount of

1.76 units. The basis had changed by 3.67 index units alone or $1,835 per contract. This means that the basis alone returned $11,010 ($1,835 × 6 contracts). The index dropped 17.13 index units for a gain of $8,565 per contract or $51,390.

Thus, the futures position returned $11,010 due to basis change, and $51,390 due to the change in the index. Combined, this comes out to the $62,400 gain in the futures position. Since the index fund suffered a loss of $67,965.40 for the period, the net position lost $5,565.40 or −0.56%.

In this example, the two-beta hedge ratio minimized the effect of the basis which swung 3.67 index units. If B_{PI} had been used rather than the two-beta hedge ratio, the number of contracts for hedging would have been calculated to be eight rather than six. This would have resulted in a 1.5% gain in the position. While it is usually preferable to have a gain rather than a 0.56% loss, the purpose of hedging is to neutralize the equity exposure. The two-beta hedge ratio gave a return much closer to zero.

In this example, we examined basis risk. Since we were hedging a S&P 500 Index Fund with S&P 500 futures, there was no cross-hedge price risk. However, most portfolios are not S&P 500 funds. When hedging those portfolios with S&P 500 futures, we are cross-hedging. As we have discussed, cross-hedging entails cross-hedge price risk when the portfolio being hedged does not behave as predicted by its beta.

Suppose you owned the Dow Jones Industrials and hedged that portfolio from July 1, 1986 to August 31, 1986. The Dow Jones in a regression analysis is shown to have a beta relative to the S&P 500 of 1.05% and an R^2 (coefficient of determination) equal to 93.3%. We follow the same procedure to calculate the number of contracts needed for a $1 million portfolio:

Step 1
$$\text{Equivalent market index units} = \frac{\$1,000,000}{253.95}$$
$$= \$3,937.78.$$

Step 2
$$\text{Beta-adjusted equivalent market index units} = 1.05 \times .745 \times 3937.78$$
$$= \$3,080.328.$$

Step 3
$$\text{Number of contracts} = \frac{\$3,080.328}{\$500}$$
$$= 6.16.$$

Again, this would be rounded to six contracts. This means that the futures position would return $62,400, as in the previous example.

According to the market model, the Dow Jones should have returned −7.14% as predicted by its beta [1.05 × (−6.80)]. However, the Dow actually returned −7.35% for a loss of $73,500. This means that the hedge position returned −1.11%, or a loss of $11,100. If this had been a perfect hedge, the portfolio would have lost $71,400. The hedge would have lost $9,000, or 0.99%. Overall, the hedge worked well, losing 0.2% due to cross-hedge price risk. Table 5 summarizes this hedge.

In both illustrations, the transaction costs would have been a trivial $150, or $25 per contract round trip.

TABLE 5. *Hedge a $1 Million Dow Jones Industrial Index Fund Using S&P 500 Futures.*

Situation

Own $1 million worth of Dow Jones Industrial stocks on 7/1/86.
Need to hedge against an adverse market move.
Time the hedge is held is unknown at the start.
Hedge is lifted 8/31/86.

Facts

	7/1/86	8/31/86
Value of portfolio	$1,000,000	$927,500
Cash price of S&P 500	252.04	234.91
Price of 9/86 S&P 500 futures	253.95	233.15

Beta of the portfolio relative to the S&P 500 = 1.05
Beta of the index relative to the futures = 0.745
Minimum risk hedge ratio = 1.05 × 0.745 = 0.782
Coefficient of determination (R^2) = 93.3%

Outcome

Cash Market	Futures Market	Cost of Carry	Mispricing
7/1/86 — Time hedge is placed			
Own $1,000,000 portfolio	Sell 6 9/86 S&P 500 futures contracts at 253.95	+1.26	+0.65
8/31/86 — Time hedge is lifted			
Own $927,500 portfolio	Buy 6 9/86 S&P 500 futures contracts at 233.15	+0.43	−2.19
Loss in cash market = $73,500	Gain in futures market = $62,400		
Overall loss = $11,100			

VII. Conclusion

The introduction of stock index futures has provided investment managers with an effective means of risk management. These instruments allow investors to reduce or increase equity exposure quickly at modest cost. Furthermore, stock index futures can be used to preserve gains or enhance returns. This can be accomplished because the market for stock index futures is large and liquid and there is an effective arbitrage mechanism which assures that investors will obtain a fair futures price. Over $10 billion in value per day is traded in the S&P 500 futures markets.

The intent of this article is to familiarize the reader with stock index futures, including their application to hedging.

Creating and Managing an Index Fund Using Stock-Index Futures

Bruce M. Collins, Ph.D.*
Vice President
The First Boston Corporation

Frank J. Fabozzi, Ph.D., CFA
Visiting Professor of Finance, Sloan School of Management
Massachusetts Institute of Technology
and
Editor, *The Journal of Portfolio Management*

I. Introduction

Index funds represent a passive-equity approach to portfolio management. The manager of the portfolio does not attempt to identify under- or over-valued stock issues based on fundamental security analysis. Nor does he attempt to forecast general movements in the stock market and to structure the portfolio so as to take advantage of those movements. Instead, index funds are designed to track the total-return performance of a visible market index of stocks.

The indexing approach to portfolio management began with studies of the efficiency of the equity market in the late 1960s and early 1970s. It was reinforced in the late 1970s and 1980s by studies showing the persistent underperformance of active money managers versus performance benchmarks like the S&P 500.

If these findings are accepted, then the costs associated with active-equity portfolio management may not enhance the return on a portfolio. These costs consist of the research costs associated with uncovering mispriced stocks, the transaction costs of buying and selling stocks to take advantage

*This article was written while Dr. Collins was Manager of Index Products Research at Shearson Lehman Hutton, Inc.

of mispricing, and the transaction costs incurred in trying to time the market. Consequently, a passive approach to equity portfolio management may be more appropriate for the typical sponsor of a fund. About 55% of the benefit assets of the 200 largest pension funds were indexed as of December 1988, with 36% of all index fund investments internally managed. Approximately two-thirds of those pension funds with index funds use stock-index futures as a management tool.[1]

Due to the transaction costs of rebalancing, however, passive management has also fallen short. The introduction of products derived from indexes has provided managers with tools that, correctly used, can enhance the returns to an index fund. The replacement of stocks with undervalued futures contracts can add 50 to 100 basis points to an indexed portfolio's annualized return without incurring additional risk. In addition to incremental return, the portfolio itself can be tilted or biased toward a specific characteristic, such as overweighting in a particular sector, or tilted in favor of a performance factor, such as dividend yield or a price/earnings ratio. The creation of tilted index portfolios is a way of preserving a relationship with the benchmark while pursuing an active strategy.

In this article we focus on investment management of index funds, with emphasis on the use of stock-index futures.

II. Using Stock-Index Futures and Treasury Bills to Construct an Index Fund

As we explained in the previous article, the price of an index-futures contract should be equivalent to the cost of buying and holding the underlying cash index (i.e., the stocks that comprise the index) from today until contract settlement. Holders of stocks incur financing costs while earning dividends. The difference between the two is called the *cost of carry,* as shown below:

$$\text{Theoretical futures price} = (\text{Cash index}) \times (1 + \text{Cost of carry}),$$

where

$$\text{Cost of carry} = (\text{Financing rate} - \text{Annualized dividend yield})$$
$$\times (\text{Days to settlement}/365).$$

The difference between the cash price and the futures price is called the *basis.*

If stock-index–futures contracts are priced according to their theoretical value, a portfolio consisting of a long position in stock-index futures and Treasury bills will produce the same return as that of a portfolio of common stocks constructed to replicate the underlying index. To see this,

---

1. *Pension and Investment Age,* January 23, 1989, p. 14.

suppose that a fund manager wishes to index $90 million to the S&P 500 index. Also assume the following:

1. The S&P 500 is currently 300.
2. The S&P 500–futures index with six months to settlement is currently selling for 303.
3. The expected annualized dividend yield is 4%.
4. The annualized yield of six-month Treasury bills currently is 6%.

Using the yield on six-month Treasury bills as the financing rate and the fraction (Days to settlement/365) as 0.5, the cost of carry is

$$\text{Cost of carry} = (.06 - .04) \times (0.5)$$
$$= .01.$$

The theoretical futures price is

$$\text{Theoretical futures price} = \text{Cash index} (1 + \text{Cost of carry})$$
$$= 300 (1 + .01)$$
$$= 303.$$

Thus, the actual futures price is equal to its theoretical futures price. Alternatively, in dollar terms, the cost of carry is −3. The basis for this six-month S&P 500 futures contract is

$$\text{Basis} = \text{Cash index} - \text{Futures price}$$
$$= 300 - 303 = -3.$$

Thus the difference between the cash index and the futures price is equal to the cost of carry (in dollars).

Let us now see why a portfolio consisting of S&P 500–futures contracts and six-month Treasury bills will replicate the performance of the S&P 500 cash index over six months. First, however, we must determine the number of futures contracts to purchase. Since each contract is 500 times the value of the current index, the purchase of 600 contracts will obtain $90 million of equivalent equity. Consequently, the two strategies that the fund manager may select are:

Strategy 1: Direct purchase of $90 million of equity to replicate the performance of the S&P 500.
Strategy 2: Buy 600 S&P 500–futures contracts with a settlement six months from now at 303 and buy $90 million of six-month Treasury bills.[2]

We can now examine the portfolio value for each strategy under various scenarios for the price of the index when the contracts settle six months

---

2. In this illustration, margin requirements are ignored. The T-bills can be used for initial margin as explained in the previous article.

TABLE 1. *Comparison of Portfolio Values from Purchasing Stocks to Replicate an Index and from a Futures/T-Bill Strategy When There Is No Mispricing and the Market Increases.*

Assumptions

1. Amount to be invested = $90 million
2. Current value of S&P 500 = 300
3. Value of the S&P 500 at settlement (six months later) = 330
4. Current value of S&P futures contract = 303
5. Expected annualized dividend yield = 4%
6. Annualized yield on six-month Treasury bills = 6%

Strategy 1: Direct Purchase of Stocks

Increase in value of index = 330/300 − 1 = 0.10

Market value of portfolio that mirrors the index

$$= 1.10 \times \$90,000,000 = \$\ 99,000,000$$
$$\text{Dividends} = 0.02 \times \$90,000,000 = \$\ \ 1,800,000$$
$$\text{Value of portfolio} = \$100,800,000$$
$$\text{Dollar return} = \$\ 10,800,000$$

Strategy 2: Futures/T-Bill Portfolio

Number of S&P 500 contracts to be purchased = 600

Gain from sale of one contract

Purchased for	303
Sold for	330
Gain per contract	27

$$\text{Gain from 600 contracts} = 600 \times \$500 \times 27 = \$\ \ 8,100,000$$
$$\text{Value of Treasury bills} = \$90,000,000 \times 1.03 = \$\ 92,700,000$$
$$\text{Value of portfolio} = \$100,800,000$$
$$\text{Dollar return} = \$\ 10,800,000$$

from now. We will investigate three scenarios: the S&P 500 increases to 330, remains unchanged at 300, and declines to 270. At settlement the futures price converges to the value of the index. Tables 1 through 3 show the value of the portfolio for both strategies for each of the three scenarios. For a given scenario, Strategy 1 (long position in the stock portfolio) and Strategy 2 will produce the same value for the portfolio.

Several points are worth noting. First, in Strategy 1 the ability of the portfolio to replicate the S&P 500 depends on how well the portfolio is constructed to track the index. On the other hand, assuming that expected dividends are realized, the futures–T-bill portfolio (Strategy 2) will mirror the performance of the S&P 500 exactly. Second, the cost of transacting is less for Strategy 2. For example, if the cost of one S&P contract were $12.50, then the transaction costs for Strategy 2 would be $7,500 (600 contracts multiplied by $12.50 per contract). This would be considerably less than

TABLE 2. *Comparison of Portfolio Values from Purchasing Stocks to Replicate an Index and from a Futures/T-Bill Strategy When There Is No Mispricing and the Market Does Not Change.*

Assumptions
1. Amount to be invested = $90 million
2. Current value of S&P 500 = 300
3. Value of the S&P 500 at settlement (six months later) = 300
4. Current value of S&P futures contract = 303
5. Expected annualized dividend yield = 4%
6. Annualized yield on six-month Treasury bills = 6%

Strategy 1: Direct Purchase of Stocks
Change in value of index = 300/300 − 1 = 0
Market value of portfolio that mirrors the index
= 1.00 × $90,000,000 = $90,000,000
Dividends = 0.02 × $90,000,000 = $ 1,800,000
Value of portfolio = $91,800,000
Dollar return = $ 1,800,000

Strategy 2: Futures/T-Bill Portfolio
Number of S&P 500 contracts to be purchased = 600

Loss from sale of one contract
Purchased for   303
Sold for   300
Loss per contract   3

Loss from 600 contracts = 600 × $500 × 3 = $ (900,000)
Value of Treasury bills = $90,000,000 × 1.03 = $92,700,000
Value of portfolio = $91,800,000
Dollar return = $ 1,800,000

the transaction costs associated with the acquisition of a broadly diversified equity portfolio constructed to replicate the S&P 500. Finally, the analysis of the performance of each strategy gives the dollar value of the portfolio at the end of the six-month period in the absence of taxes. With Strategy 1, no taxes will be due if the securities are not sold, though taxes will be due on dividends. With Strategy 2, taxes must be paid on the interest from the Treasury bills, and on any gain either from the disposal of the futures contract or due to the inability to postpone any gain at the end of a tax year because of the unique tax treatment of futures contracts.[3] Because of this complication,

3. Cornell and French argue that it is this tax option that causes futures to trade at a discount to their theoretical value. See Bradford Cornell and Kenneth French, "Taxes and the Pricing of Stock Index Futures," *Journal of Finance* (June 1983): 675–94.

TABLE 3. *Comparison of Portfolio Values from Purchasing Stocks to Replicate an Index and from a Futures/T-Bill Strategy When There Is No Mispricing and the Market Declines.*

Assumptions
1. Amount to be invested = $90 million
2. Current value of S&P 500 = 300
3. Value of the S&P 500 at settlement (six months later) = 270
4. Current value of S&P futures contract = 303
5. Expected annualized dividend yield = 4%
6. Annualized yield on six-month Treasury bills = 6%

Strategy 1: Direct Purchase of Stocks
Decrease in value of index = 270/300 − 1 = −0.10
Market value of portfolio that mirrors the index
= 0.90 × $90,000,000 = $81,000,000
Dividends = 0.02 × $90,000,000 = $ 1,800,000
Value of portfolio = $82,800,000
Dollar return = $ (7,200,000)

Strategy 2: Futures/T-Bill Portfolio
Number of S&P 500 contracts to be purchased = 600

Loss from sale of one contract
Purchased for 303
Sold for 270
Loss per contract 33

Loss from 600 contracts = 600 × 500 × $33 = $ (9,900,000)
Value of Treasury bills = $90,000,000 × 1.03 = $92,700,000
Value of portfolio = $82,800,000
Dollar return = $ (7,200,000)

---

the use of the futures–T-bill strategy would be more appropriate for funds not subject to taxation.

III. Creating an Index Fund

The first step in creating an index fund is to select a bogey or performance benchmark. The choice of a benchmark may assume a multiple function. The fund performance may be measured against the market or a subset or sector of the market. For example, the fund may be intended to match the performance of an industry sector or by capitalization.[4] Once established,

---

4. For a discussion of the considerations in selecting a small capitalization index, see Bruce M. Collins and Frank J. Fabozzi, "Considerations in Selecting a Small Capitalization Benchmark," *Financial Analysts Journal* (forthcoming).

this performance is measured against the market. A pure index fund, however, by definition, is intended to perfectly replicate the market portfolio. In reality, the market portfolio is not known with certainty. Nonetheless, the S&P 500 has served as the consensus representative of the market portfolio. Recently, the Wilshire 5000 and the Russell indexes have served as benchmarks for some index funds.

As an alternative to holding the underlying equities that make up the index, as illustrated earlier, an index fund can be created by purchasing futures contracts and Treasury bills. The two alternative methods will generate the same returns. Furthermore, the choice of a benchmark with a liquid futures contract is attractive because it makes a stock-replacement program possible. Among the indexes with futures contracts are the S&P 500 Index, the Major Market Index, the Value Line Index, and the NYSE Composite Index.

The advantages and disadvantages of creating a synthetic index fund by holding long-stock index futures and Treasuries, versus holding a long-stock portfolio, are listed below.

Index Fund	Advantages	Disadvantages
Long Stocks	Receive stock dividends	High initial transaction costs
	Restructurings often yield positive returns	Market impact costs
	Special dividends	Tracking error
	Stock replacement	Custodial costs
Synthetic	Low transaction costs	Variation-margin risk
	No tracking error	Price risk
	No custodial costs	
	No cash drag from reinvesting dividends	

The index fund using the long-stocks approach has advantages related to special events, such as stock dividends. Otherwise, the decision to create the index fund using the underlying stocks must be measured against the disadvantages of the synthetic index fund. There are two risks relating to holding futures contracts. First is the risk that the futures will be overpriced when purchased. That is, because stock index futures expire quarterly, the position may need to be rolled out to the next contract. The risk is that the spread is overpriced. Both circumstances have a negative impact on the performance of the index fund; consequently, its objective of matching the performance of the bogey may not be achieved.

The second factor that may influence the performance of a synthetic index fund is variation margin. Because futures are marked-to-the-market there are daily cash flows (referred to as *variation margin*) into or out of an account. Consequently, the futures position will outperform the index in an up market and underperform in a down market. This means the total dollar value of the investment may change due to variation margin. An under-hedging technique is used to minimize the risk of misperformance due to variation margin. This involves purchasing fewer futures contracts to neutralize the trade-off between sustaining smaller losses in the futures position in a down market and an increased cash position from satisfying the variation margin.[5]

A stock-replacement strategy is an alternative to holding the index or a synthetic index fund. It involves the replacement of a long equity position with an equivalent exposure in the futures market and investing the proceeds from the stock sale in Treasury bills. By swapping between the portfolio of stocks that replicate an index and a combination of futures and Treasury bills when the futures are undervalued, an investor should be assured of equaling the market return and have a good chance of exceeding it. In 1987, for example, index-fund managers employing this strategy would have been able to outperform the S&P 500 index by as much as 150 basis points.

IV. Considerations for Constructing a Replicating Portfolio or Basket

The objectives in basket construction are two-fold: (1) to minimize the cost incurred when trading in some of the smaller capitalized issues while (2) retaining the basket's ability to track the index. Designing the optimal replicating portfolio may involve holding all the stocks in the index or a subset. The size of the basket affects transaction costs, but holding fewer stocks than contained in the index generates tracking error. Tracking error represents the risk that the replicating portfolio or basket will perform differently than the benchmark. Statistically, it is the standard deviation of the actual returns from the expected return.

The trade-off between basket size and tracking error is shown in Figure 1. The returns from a basket of 250 stocks, for example, may mistrack the S&P 500 by 0.6%. This means that there is a 68% probability that the returns from the portfolio will fall within 0.6% of the returns from the S&P 500 on an annualized basis.

It is next to impossible for a portfolio's returns to exactly match the return on the index. Even if a portfolio is designed to exactly replicate an index, tracking error will result.[6] There are several reasons for this. First,

---

5. The adjustment process is explained in Bruce M. Collins, "Index Fund Investment Management," in *Portfolio & Investment Management,* ed. Frank J. Fabozzi (Chicago: Probus Publishing, 1989), Chapter 10.
6. Positive tracking error holding all 500 stocks is a consequence of using historical returns in the estimation process and due to the changing composition of the index.

FIGURE 1. *S&P 500 Stock Index — Tracking Error versus Size.*

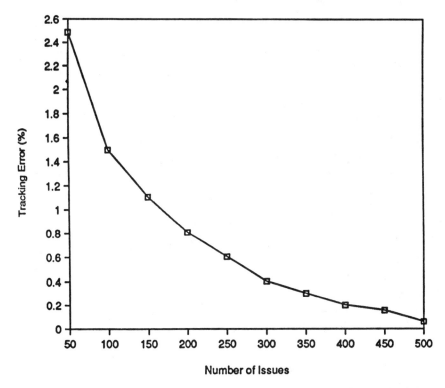

because odd-lot purchases are cumbersome, index funds usually comprise round lots; the number of shares of each stock in the basket is rounded off to the nearest hundred from the exact number of shares indicated by the basket-building algorithm. This rounding may affect the ability of smaller baskets (less than $25 million) to accurately track the index.

Second and more importantly, composing a stock index is a dynamic process; because most indexes are capitalization-weighted (with the notable exception of the Major Market Index and the Value Line), the relative weights of individual issues are constantly changing. In addition, the list of stocks comprising the index often changes. Thus, the cost of continually adjusting the portfolio, as well as timing differences, hinders a portfolio's ability to accurately track an index. The former problem is eliminated by holding all stocks in the index. The portfolio is then self-replicating, which simply means the weights are self-adjusting. If, however, the basket contains fewer stocks than the index, the weights are not self-adjusting and may require periodic rebalancing. Rebalancing is discussed in more detail in Section VII below.

The construction of a basket determines the weightings. Two issues must be addressed: the method of averaging and the method of weighting. In practice, there are two methods of averaging used in the calculation of popular indexes: arithmetic and geometric. No contracts based on a geometric average are currently traded. Prior to 1988, the Value Line contract was based on geometric averaging.

There are three basic ways to weight stocks: market value of capitalization, price, and equal-dollar weighting. The market-value weight of a single stock in an index is determined by the proportion of its value to the total market value of all stocks in the index. Typical price weighting assumes equal shares invested in each stock; the price serves as the weight. Equal-dollar weighting requires investing the same dollar amount in each stock. With capitalization weighting, the largest companies naturally have the greatest influence over the index value. Consequently, under- or over-weighting of a large capitalization stock can lead to substantial mistracking. Also, these stocks tend to be the most liquid. Price weighting endows the stock with the highest price with the greatest influence on the index value. Equal-dollar weighting does the opposite. In this case, the lowest priced stocks have the greatest potential to move the index for a given change in stock price, such as one-eighth. It is important to understand these properties when constructing an index fund.

An arithmetic index is simply the weighted average of all stocks that comprise the index where the weights are determined by one of the weighting schemes mentioned:

$$\text{Index} = \text{constant} \times \text{sum (weight} \times \text{price)}$$

The constant represents an arbitrary number used to initialize the value of the index.

Table 4 illustrates the distinction between the three weighting schemes by presenting a hypothetical index using all three. Exxon will have the greatest influence on the index value of a capitalization-weighted index because it has the largest market value, whereas 3M has the greatest influence in the price-weighted index. Notice that total shares are the same for each stock with a price-weighted index, whereas their weights are the same with the equal dollar-weighted index. The performance of one index versus another depends on the relative performance of the individual stocks that comprise the index. The price-weighted index will outperform the capitalization-weighted index should Merck and 3M outperform the other stocks simply as a matter of weightings. Furthermore, the same outcome would occur should Exxon and GE underperform the other stocks. The key to understanding relative index performance, therefore, is to understand the relative weights of the stocks.

TABLE 4. *Basket Size: $1,000,000 — July 27, 1988.*

	7/27	Total Shares (MM)	Total Cap ($MM)	S&P 500 Weight (%)	Cap Weight (%)	Cap Shares	Price Weight	Price Shares	Eq $ Weight	Eq $ Shares
AXP	26.625	420.802	11,203.85	0.61	7.61	2,858	11.54	4,334	20.00	7,512
GE	41.5	902.953	37,472.55	2.03	25.45	6,133	17.98	4,334	20.00	4,819
MMM	62.875	227.493	14,303.62	0.78	9.72	1,545	27.25	4,334	20.00	3,181
MRK	54.125	393.996	21,325.03	1.16	14.48	2,676	23.46	4,334	20.00	3,695
XON	45.625	1,379.000	62,916.88	3.41	42.74	9,367	19.77	4,334	20.00	4,384
Totals:	230.75		$147,221.93	7.99	100.00	22,579	100.00	21,670	100.00	23,591

Arithmetic market-value or price weighted indexes can be easily replicated. This means that, as the price of a stock changes, the weights auto-
matically adjust to remain consistent with the number of shares. This is
true of any arithmetic index that is not equal-dollar weighted. Although
the weights change, the share amounts do not. Consequently, no rebalancing is necessary. The implication for index funds is that holding the entire
basket reduces the need for rebalancing.

Some rebalancing may be necessary even if the entire index is held,
because changes in the weighting may occur for any of the reasons listed
below.

- Some issues may cease to exist due to mergers.
- A company may be added to or deleted from the index should it meet
  or fail to meet capitalization or liquidity requirements for inclusion in
  an index or listing on an exchange.
- A company may split its stock or issue a stock dividend.
- New stock may be issued.
- Current stock may be repurchased.

Should any of these events occur, the constant term in the index-valuation
equation may require adjustment to avoid a discontinuous jump in the index
value. The constant term is commonly known as the divisor.

In summary, the first step in creating a stock-index fund is simple but
important: The manager must choose which index to replicate. To create a
stock-replacement program, the chosen index must have an actively traded
futures contract. Furthermore, having chosen an index, the manager must
then decide how closely to replicate it. As we have shown, not all indexes
are calculated in the same way. The precise construction of the basket of
stocks is related to the averaging and weighting methods used to calculate
the index. An arithmetic index can be exactly tracked by owning all stocks
in the index in the proportions suggested by its weight in the index.

Because the number of stocks comprised in an index can be substantial
(see Table 5), the cost of initializing an indexed portfolio can be high. In addition, the exchange listing may have performance implications for a stock-
replacement program. NYSE-listed stocks can take advantage of the Designated Order Turnover (D.O.T) system, which may improve the speed and
therefore the cost of execution. As an alternative to ownership of all stocks
in the index, a set of smaller, but nevertheless efficient, portfolios are available. The selection of an indexed portfolio with fewer stocks than the index
involves several factors. First, whatever portfolio is ultimately selected, it
will be subject to residual risk. The manager must weigh the residual risk
against the transaction costs related to maintaining a portfolio of all stocks
in the index. The risk, of course, is that the portfolio will underperform the
index. Second, once the manager decides on a level of residual risk and

TABLE 5. *Index Composition Comparison (June 1988).*

	Value Line	S&P 500	Russell 2000	Russell 3000
By Names				
New York Stock Exchange	1,149	462	549	1,297
American Stock Exchange	95	9	327	363
Over-The-Counter	343	29	1,124	1,340
Toronto Stock Exchange	15	0	0	0
By Capitalization				
New York Stock Exchange	77.16%	96.93%	36.62%	85.97%
American Stock Exchange	4.66	0.68	12.41	2.34
Over-The-Counter	17.54	2.39	50.97	11.69
Toronto Stock Exchange	0.64	0.00	0.00	0.00
	100.00	100.00	100.00	100.00

transaction costs, a method is required to construct a basket that meets these criteria.

The cost of an equity transaction consists of two components; commissions and market impact. Market impact is a consequence of the stock bid/ask spread and any price concession caused by an investor's demand for liquidity. It is the price movement that is a consequence of the transaction.

At any given time, the price at which a basket of stocks can be bought or sold will differ substantially from the cash-index price, which is based on the prices at which each of the individual stocks comprising the index last traded. To sell a list of stocks at a given instant, the seller would receive the sum of the current bid prices of the individual stocks on the list (in the case of purchasing, the buyer would have to pay the current offer prices). The difference between the cash index and the cost of buying or selling a basket of stocks is a measure of market impact.

The level of market impact varies over time and depends upon several factors. Most prominent among these are the liquidity of the individual stocks in the basket and the size of the portfolio being transacted. Liquidity has a dual impact. The more liquid a security, the smaller the bid-ask spread and hence the smaller the difference in price between the last transaction and the desired one. Furthermore, the presence of buyers and sellers decreases the market impact of a large trade. Relatedly, market impact will increase as the size of the basket increases because of the unlikelihood of being able to transact all the shares at the current bid (or offering price).

One cost-management trading mechanism that developed in the equity market is program trading. Program trading involves the purchase or sale of a portfolio of stocks.

Program Trading

Program trading is a trading technique for the simultaneous purchase or sale of a list of stocks rather than the discrete purchase or sale of each of the individual stocks. The cost of executing a diversified portfolio should be less than executing each stock in the portfolio individually, just as the risk of holding a diversified portfolio is less than that of holding an individual stock. Because the initiation of an index fund expresses an investor's desire to obtain broad market exposure, the purchase of any stock in the portfolio through a program trade is informationless, and therefore should cost less than a similar aggregation of informed trades. Furthermore, program trading allows the investor to transfer execution risk to the broker, which essentially provides the investor with an insurance-protection option. The broker guarantees a price to the investor and in doing so provides the desired level of price protection. The cost of the option is negotiated with the broker. For these reasons, program trading provides a cost-effective means of initiating an index fund or rebalancing an existing portfolio.

The cost of initiating and maintaining an S&P 500 Index fund averages 10 to 15 basis points in commissions, 25 basis points in market impact, and 5 basis points in rebalancing costs.[7]

V. Methods of Constructing a Basket

Four methods are used to build a basket designed to track an index. The first method simply involves purchasing all stocks in the index in proportion to their weightings in the index. The remaining three methods all involve constructing baskets with fewer stocks than the index. The first of these is a capitalization method that calls for purchasing a number of top capitalization stocks and equally weighting the residual stock weightings across the basket. Thus, if the top 200 high-capitalization stocks in the S&P 500 are selected for the basket and they account for 85% of the total capitalization of the index, the remaining 15% is evenly apportioned among the 300 stocks.

The second method generates a stratified sample of the index, defining each stratum by industry. The objective of this technique is to reduce residual risk by diversifying the basket across industry sectors in the same proportions as in the benchmark. Stocks within each industrial sector are then selected using either capitalization ranking, valuation methods, or an optimization method.

---

7. The costs of rebalancing are directly related to turnover. Passive strategies, such as index-fund investments, usually incur less turnover than active or dynamic strategies when the benchmark is dominated by large capitalization issues. Small-capitalization-stock–index funds incur larger transaction costs because the stocks tend to be lower priced and less liquid. Historically, the average cost for small-cap portfolios is 25 basis points in commissions, 75 to 125 basis points in market impact, and, due to higher turnover, 10 basis points in annual rebalancing costs.

The final method uses a quadratic optimization procedure to generate an efficient set of portfolios. The efficient set includes minimum-variance portfolios for different levels of expected returns. The investor can select a portfolio among the set that satisfies his or her level of tolerable risk.

VI. Returns Enhancement Strategy

A stock-replacement program involves the replacement of stock with futures contracts and T-bills and is designed to enhance returns to an index fund. When a stock replacement program is contemplated, the value of a basket should be stated as a number of futures contracts. An index fund will sell its stocks, replace them with futures contracts of equivalent monetary value, and place the proceeds in a short-term investment fund. As a rule of thumb the size of a basket in dollars should correspond to a number of whole futures contracts. The calculation of an appropriate number of equivalent futures is

$$\text{Number of futures contracts} = \text{Dollar value}/(500 \times \text{Index}).$$

For a given dollar value, an algorithm generates the number of futures contracts that satisfies the tolerance level. For example, suppose a manager is interested in creating a $25 million index fund designed to replicate the S&P 500. The number of futures contracts required to match the value of the stock position when the S&P 500 index is trading at 275 is

$$\$25,000,000/(500 \times 275) = 181.81.$$

This does not satisfy our tolerance level. If $25 million represents an investment ceiling for the manager, the number of futures contracts is reduced to 181, otherwise it is rounded upward to 182. In either case, the initial value in dollars is adjusted to reflect the dollar value of the required number of futures contracts.

There is no guarantee, however, that an optimal or efficient portfolio can be constructed at that amount. This is not a significant problem at the $25 million level, but becomes a greater problem as the value of the portfolio is reduced and when the portfolio is purchased in round lots. Therefore, the basket design evolves from the need to closely replicate the index and to closely reflect a whole number of futures contracts as part of a stock-replacement program. There are programming algorithms that will satisfy these requirements and deliver the baskets that track best.

The use of stock-index futures and Treasury bills to construct an index fund that would reproduce the performance of the underlying index if the futures were priced according to their theoretical values was demonstrated in Tables 1 through 3 of Section II. However, when the actual futures price is less than its theoretical price, the index-fund manager can enhance the portfolio's return by buying the index and Treasury bills. That is, the return on the futures–T-bill portfolio will be greater than that on the underlying index when the position is held until the expiration of the futures contract.

Costs can be reduced measurably by using a return enhancement as discussed in the previous sections. Whenever the difference between the actual basis and the theoretical basis exceeds the market impact of a transaction, the aggressive manager should consider replacing stocks with futures or vice versa. Returns can be enhanced significantly through such a strategy, which literally surpasses market impact.

Once the strategy has been put into effect, several subsequent scenarios may unfold. First, should the futures become sufficiently rich relative to stocks, the futures position is sold and the stocks repurchased. Second, should the futures remain fair-valued, the position is held until expiration, when the futures settle at the spot value and the stocks are repurchased in the market at close.[8]

To illustrate a return enhancement strategy suppose that in our initial example the current futures price was 301 instead of 303; that is, the futures contract is undervalued. Table 6 shows the value of the portfolio from each strategy for each scenario. As can be seen, the value of the portfolio is $600,000 greater by buying the futures contracts and Treasury bills.[9]

Thus far our illustration has assumed that the index-fund manager initiated the fund by buying undervalued Treasury bills and buying stock-index futures. If an index-fund manager has an existing portfolio that only includes stocks, the manager should monitor the futures market to look for opportunities to enhance return through a stock-replacement strategy when the futures become sufficiently underpriced to generate excess returns after transaction costs.

If the futures are held until expiration, the annualized incremental return before transaction costs (commissions and market impact) is as follows:[10]

$$\text{Annualized dividend yield} + \frac{\text{Basis}}{\text{Cash index}} \times \frac{365}{\text{Days to settlement}}$$

Using our earlier illustration, since the basis is -1 $(300-301)$, the annualized incremental return before transaction costs, assuming (365/Days to settlement) equals 2, is

---

8. A third scenario involving calendar spreads is beyond the scope of this article.

9. In Tables 1 through 3 the gain on each contract will be $1,000 greater (two times $500) for each scenario. Since there are 600 contracts, the gain will be $600,000 greater. When there is a loss as a result of the decline in the index value at settlement, the loss is $1,000 less per contract, or $600,000 for 600 contracts.

10. Notice that if the cost of carry is equal to the basis (or, more specifically, the basis as a percentage of the cash index), the annualized incremental return is zero since there is no mispricing.

TABLE 6. *Enhancement of Portfolio Return for a Futures/T-Bill Portfolio When the Futures Contract Is Underpriced.*

Assumptions
1. Amount to be invested = $90 million
2. Current value of S&P 500 = 300
3. Current value of S&P 500 futures contract = 301
4. Expected annualized dividend yield = 4%
5. Annualized yield on six-month Treasury bills = 6%
6. Theoretical price of futures contract = 303

If Value of Index at Settlement is 330
Value of portfolio for Strategy 1 (direct purchase of stocks)
(from Table 1) = $100,800,000

Value of portfolio for Strategy 2 (futures–T-bill portfolio)
Gain per contract = 330 − 301 = 29

Gain for 600 contracts = 600 × $500 × 29 = $	8,700,000
Value of Treasury bills	$ 92,700,000
Value of portfolio	$101,400,000

If Value of Index at Settlement is 300
Value of portfolio for Strategy 1 (direct purchase of stocks)
(from Table 2) = $90,180,000

Value of portfolio for Strategy 2 (futures–T-bill portfolio)
Loss per contract = 300 − 301 = −1

Loss for 600 contracts = 600 × $500 × 1 = $	(300,000)
Value of Treasury bills	$ 92,700,000
Value of portfolio	$ 92,400,000

If Value of Index at Settlement is 270
Value of portfolio for Strategy 1 (direct purchase of stocks)
(from Table 3) = $82,800,000

Value of portfolio for Strategy 2 (futures–T-bill portfolio)
Loss per contract = 270 − 301 = 31

Loss for 600 contracts = 600 × $500 × 31 = $	(9,300,000)
Value of Treasury bills	$ 92,700,000
Value of portfolio	$ 83,400,000

$$\text{Annualized incremental return} = .06 - .04 + \frac{(-1)}{300} \times 2$$

$$= .0133 \text{ or } 1.33\%$$

Therefore, the incremental dollar return of $600,000 as a result of the underpricing of the futures contract becomes a 1.33% or 133 basis-point annualized incremental return.

Historically, there have been opportunities to enhance returns from stock-replacement strategies.

VII. Tracking Issues and Rebalancing

Once the basket is purchased for a stock-replacement program, three central issues must be managed. First, the integrity of the replication requirements must be maintained. This means monitoring the actual tracking performance of the portfolio versus the index. Recall that this is not a problem if the weights are self-adjusting. Should the basket represent a subset of the index, however, daily monitoring of the position is crucial to assure meeting the replication requirements (i.e., matching the performance of returns). A daily report should be generated that provides aggregate tracking information. Substantial mistracking will reflect imbalanced weight between the basket and the index. Consequently, the basket may not reflect the prescribed number of futures contracts, which will jeopardize the stock-replacement program. To manage this problem, periodic rebalancing is required. Because managing an index fund is a dynamic process, the manager is forced to periodically rebalance the portfolio and intuitively weigh the transaction costs associated with rebalancing against the risk of increasing levels of tracking error.

The basket may require rebalancing should one of the following conditions arise: 1) additional exposure is desired, 2) the basket mistracks the index, 3) the composition of the index changes, or 4) capitalization changes.

The decision to rebalance is related to the anticipated impact of mistracking on returns. Once the decision is made, however, an optimization procedure is utilized to realign the basket at a minimum cost. Index funds are designed to avoid issues of selection and market timing, but because the portfolio generates dividend income, and with the possibility of cash inflows, the issue of timing cannot be entirely avoided. One solution is to invest the proceeds in money-market instruments until sufficient cash can be distributed across the entire portfolio. Another possibility is to combine the timing of additional cash investments with portfolio rebalancing, which may be less costly than treating the issues separately. The weights are again determined using an optimization procedure. A new basket is created at a different dollar level using the procedure described before. The procedure generates a list of buy and sell recommendations that will bring the basket back into line with the manager's objective at an acceptable cost. Rebalancing is often executed through a program trade on the basis of a negotiated price.

VIII. Constructing a Bridge between Active and Passive Management

Index-fund management can be applied to active management through market timing (asset allocation) or risk management. Three methods are worth mentioning. The first is the construction of a biased or tilted basket designed to emphasize a particular sector of the index or a performance factor such as earnings momentum, dividend yield, or price/earnings ratios. The basket is built to maintain a strong relationship with the benchmark by minimizing tracking error while creating a bias that is intended to enhance returns. The exact nature of the bias can be determined through traditional active-management methodologies. The construction of the portfolio is designed to manage risk.

The second method exploits the fact that indexes are exposed to different factors. By combining the long basket with one or more short futures positions, factor exposure can be realized at a low cost and the potential exists for additional realized returns. By example, low-capitalization exposure can be achieved when holding a portfolio indexed to the Russell 1000 by shorting the S&P 500 futures contract. Again, the sector decision can be reached by fundamental analysis.

The last method is an asset-allocation application. This strategy involves holding indexed equity and bond portfolios and using stock-index futures and bond futures to implement the asset allocation. The index funds represent the passive side whereas the asset-allocation decision represents the active side.

Arbitrage, Program Trading, and the Tail of the Dog

Gary L. Gastineau
Vice President
Salomon Brothers Inc

I. Introduction

Ever since stock-index options and futures became active trading vehicles, investors and regulators who had come to accept stock options have questioned the desirability of the newer instruments. Even a casual reader of the business press must be impressed with reports that we are in a "new era" of highly volatile securities markets and ever growing transaction volume. The press reports domination and distortion of the markets by a small group of investors characterized in a broad sense as arbitrageurs. Arbitrageurs fall into two distinct camps. The *risk arbitrageur* attempts to profit by speculating on mergers, acquisitions, and other corporate restructuring. Risk arbitrage flourished in the merger markets of the early and mid-1980s, peaking at about the time of the Levine and Boesky scandals. The focus of this discussion, however, is on the other kind of arbitrageur, commonly known as *the program trader* or the *stock-index arbitrageur*.

The term *program trading* originally included many large-scale portfolio adjustments by institutional investors. As a result of media attention focused on index arbitrage, the original meaning is less commonly used, but remains a source of occasional confusion. Program trading in the form of index options and futures arbitrage is not primarily an option phenomenon, but its expiration effect is much like the impact attributed to stock options a few years ago. Furthermore, option-related phenomena like port-

/ **131**

folio insurance are so closely tied to the effects attributed to program trading that any regulation of index options and futures markets has broad implications.

II. Arbitrage

The classic definition of arbitrage describes the simultaneous purchase in one market and sale in another of virtually identical securities or commodities. The arbitrageur profits by exploiting the difference in price between the two markets. The arbitrage process makes the market operate more effectively by eliminating price differences. Pure arbitrage, where the items purchased and sold are identical, is rare and opportunities are infrequent. In many cases, however, similar securities or commodities either exist or can be constructed in two different markets and a pricing discrepancy can be detected and exploited. Much of the detection and exploitation turns on the availability of high-speed, on-line electronic computation and communications tools. The presence of so much sophisticated silicon and the absence of any detailed knowledge on the part of the average investor about how and why this kind of arbitrage works, has led to the widespread view that this is a largely autonomous sector of the market that serves as the tail that wags the dog. Program trading is credited or blamed for dramatic movements in stock prices, particularly on days when stock-index options and futures expire. The true relationships between stock-price behavior and the trading of index options and futures are complex, but they are not beyond the understanding of the investor who is willing to spend some time thinking about how markets work.

III. What Has Happened to the Securities Markets?

As Figures 1–3 illustrate, the securities markets have been characterized by rapidly growing volume and declining transaction costs. The volume on the New York Stock Exchange, Figure 1, has grown from 1.5 billion shares in 1965 to 27.5 billion shares in 1985, a compound growth rate of nearly 15%. The number of companies listed for trading has grown from 1,273 to 1,541 over the same period, a much more modest growth rate of less than 1% annually. Figure 2 shows that trading volume in the average company grew from less than 5,000 shares per day in 1965 to more than 70,000 shares per day in 1985.

Most participants in the securities markets will agree that anything that increases the trading volume of a security tends to reduce the average transaction cost, because greater volume tends to narrow the spread between the bid price and the asked price. The bid-asked spread, though frequently ignored in transaction-cost analysis in favor of a focus entirely on commissions, is an extremely important cost of doing business. Opportunities to

FIGURE 1. *New York Stock Exchange Reported Share Volume, 1965–1986.*

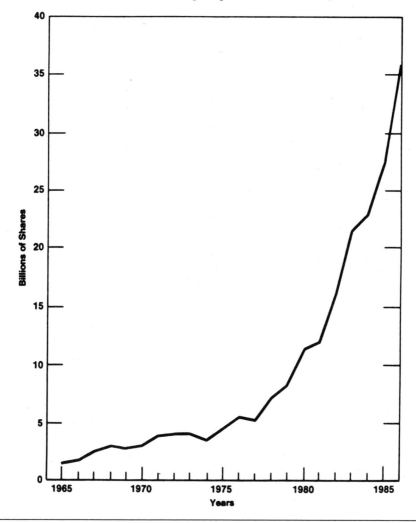

lower transaction costs by eliminating the bid-asked spread are sometimes available to institutional investors, but most market participants must buy at the asked price and sell at the bid price.

The growth in volume and the corresponding decline in the average bid-asked spread has been accompanied by a dramatic decline in institutional brokerage commissions from fixed rates 20 years ago to fully negotiated rates today. As illustrated in Figure 3, the securities industry under competitive ("third market") and Securities and Exchange Commission pressure

FIGURE 2. *New York Stock Exchange Reported Share Volume, Average Listed Company, 1965–1986.*

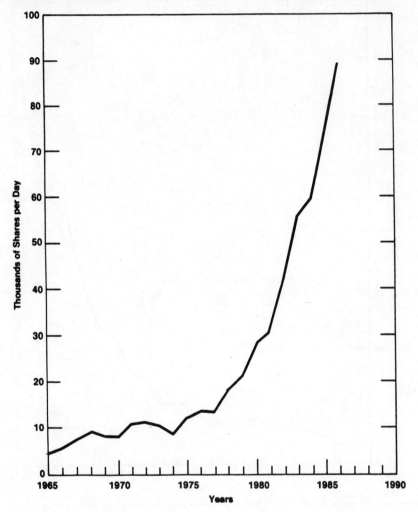

adopted the first quantity discounts in 1968. In May 1975 fully negotiable commission rates were adopted. Because the services provided in exchange for commission dollars vary so widely, an unequivocal graph of commission declines since the mid-1960s would be virtually impossible to construct. It is no secret that unbundled, pure execution commissions on listed stocks for large institutional traders can be less than five cents per share today. The pre-1968 fixed rate worked out to $.39 per share on a $40 stock.

FIGURE 3. *Commissions (cents per share).*

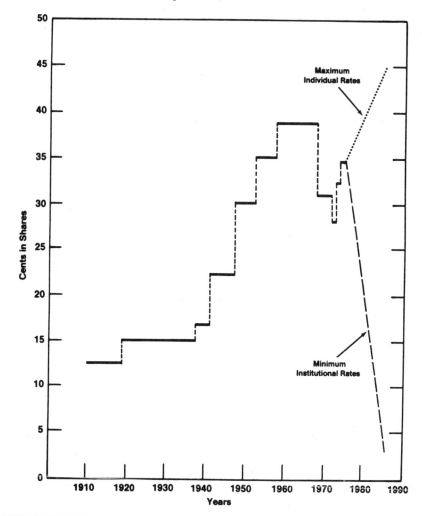

Just as the volume of common-stock trading and the cost of trading that volume have changed dramatically, there have been equally significant developments in markets for derivative securities. The growth in derivative-securities markets combined with increased trading volume and declining trading costs has led to many of the phenomena that are now perceived as shaking the foundations of an efficient securities market. Figure 4 illustrates the growth in derivative markets superimposed upon the growth of New York Stock Exchange common-stock trading.

FIGURE 4. *Volume of Common Stocks and Derivative Securities, 1965–1986.*

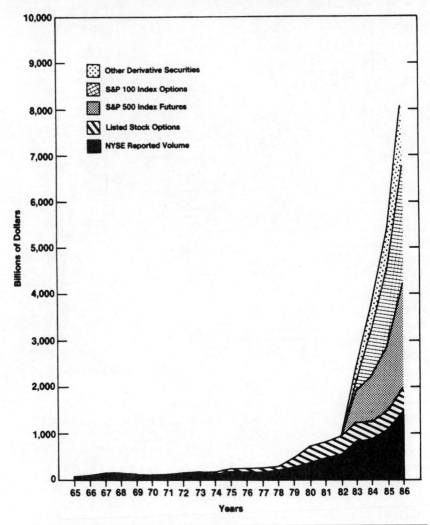

Figure 4 may exaggerate the importance of equity-derivative instruments relative to trading in the underlying stocks. First, the options are related to the underlying market by assuming that each option contract is equal in value to the face value of the underlying security or index. In addition, both options and futures contracts are outstanding for a relatively short period of time, whereas the common stocks are outstanding throughout the period. Even if we mentally reduce the apparent impact by half to compensate for these factors, the growth of the derivative markets cannot be ignored.

The dramatic growth in derivative markets, particularly the growth in index options and index-futures options, suggests several things:

1. If these markets are responsible for destabilizing the equity markets, we should expect a great deal more destabilization than we have seen.
2. Even a casual examination of bid-asked spreads and commission costs in the index futures and options markets suggests that transaction costs in these markets are *even lower than in the underlying securities markets after the cost reductions of recent years.*
3. Lower transaction costs have probably been partly responsible for the fact that institutional portfolio turnover (reflected in the growing volume figures) is much higher today than 20 years ago. Even the most conservative investor can modify a portfolio at low cost today.
4. With the very dramatic increase in volume, a great deal more must be going on than meets the untutored eye.

Before anyone goes too far in accusing the derivative markets of creating instability, it seems appropriate to examine recent patterns of stock-price fluctuations. Primarily for historic reasons, the press and the public tend to focus on movements in the Dow Jones Industrial Average as the primary indicator of what is going on in the stock market. Because the Dow and the broader averages have moved up sharply since Autumn, 1982, there has been a tendency to lose perspective on what a given point move in the Dow means. A 20-point move in the Dow was better than a 2–percentage-point change when the Dow was at 900. A 20-point move is less than a 1–percentage-point change with the Dow over 2000. The tendency to report a 10- or 20-point change as a major market move persists. The press reports dramatic swings measured in points for the Dow and rarely notes that these dramatic swings pale in comparison with earlier price changes measured in percentage terms.[1] When the Dow Jones Industrials dropped 41.91 on April 30, 1986, that was the largest one-day *point* decline on record at the time. However, that 2.3% decline had been exceeded at least 362 times over the preceding 60 years for an average of *once every two months.* Even the 4.61% decline (86.61 Dow points) of September 11, 1986, had been exceeded four times in the postwar period and numerous times before. We will have more to say about this decline in a moment.

By any standard, the extraordinarily volatile markets of October, 1987, are in a class by themselves. As this is written, these events are still surrounded by controversy. A preliminary judgment suggests that the decline was initiated by portfolio managers reacting to investment fundamentals in a time-honored manner: concern about the federal budget and trade deficits, inflation, recession, currency relationships, and interest rates led to a number of individual decisions to sell common stocks. What would have been a

---

1. *Newsweek* did make this point when calling for a 10-for-1 split in the Dow (March 2, 1987, p. 55).

moderate decline was turned into a rout when portfolio-insurance sell orders were triggered. Too many investors tried, like the biblical camel, to pass through the eye of a needle. Index arbitrage was impractical during much of this period. The absence of index arbitrage may have contributed to panic, particularly on what is now known as Black Monday.

Serious studies of market volatility, most notably one by Laslow Birinyi and Nicholas Hanson of Salomon Brothers, correctly pointed out that volatility in the stock market had *declined,* not increased, prior to the decline of late 1987.[2] Our own study of option premiums and stock-price volatility confirms this conclusion for the period since listed stock-option trading began.[3] The net effect of somewhat lower volatility when combined with rising volume and falling transaction costs had created an environment in which investors could make changes in their portfolios more easily and at less cost than ever before. Ironically, it was the ease and cheapness with which portfolio transactions could be made that led to the program trading or stock-index–arbitrage phenomenon. The efficient futures markets which index arbitrage helped create in turn made portfolio insurance feasible.

IV. Portfolio Adjustments Using Derivative Markets

Suppose a large institutional investor decides on the basis of a consultation with his fortune teller or other guru to move from a 10% cash position to 25% cash in equity portfolios. This may seem like a relatively modest change, but for many institutions this move can require the sale of securities worth several billion dollars. To put that number in perspective, the average value of securities traded daily on the New York Stock Exchange in 1985 was barely over $4 billion. Obviously the exchange can handle this investor's volume; but there may be a few other people who want to sell stocks at about the same time. This investor's decision may have a perceptible impact on the market.

The investor can accomplish this portfolio change in several ways. If the actual positions in the portfolio are liquidated on the exchange, the impact on the market is direct. Less costly ways to make this change would be to sell stock-index futures, sell index–call-option contracts, or buy index-put-options. Some institutional managers will use futures or options, but others lack the authority to trade in the derivative (options or futures) markets. These managers will do what institutional portfolio managers have done for years. They will call one of the major block trading firms and solicit bids for the securities they would like to sell to raise cash in their portfolios. At some

2. Laszlo Birinyi and H. Nicholas Hanson, *Market Volatility: Perception and Reality* (New York: Salomon Brothers, December 1985).
3. Gary L. Gastineau, *The Options Manual* (New York: McGraw-Hill, 1988), chap. 10.

risk of oversimplification, the securities firm asked to make a bid will usually lay off some risk in the index futures or options market or in the market for options on individual stocks. The methods used to arrive at a price for the securities to be sold by the institution to the block positioning firm are frequently complex. The block positioning firm may lay off only part of the risk in the derivative securities markets, or it may place some or all of the securities directly with a buyer. The securities firm is in business to make a profit, and it is safe to assume that, on average, it does so. Also given the volume in the derivative markets, it is safe to assume that many transactions initiated by someone who wants to change the market exposure of a portfolio will give rise to a series of transactions. Apart from the market impact, declining transaction costs and growing derivative markets make this kind of portfolio adjustment far less costly than it was even a few years ago. *Dramatic changes in exposure to market risk are possible at modest cost.*

An effort by one or several institutional portfolio managers to reduce equity-market exposure either simultaneously or in sequence will put downward pressure on the stock market and the derivative markets. The prices of stocks, index futures, and index call options will decline until some market participant finds it attractive to buy them.

If the primary impact of the original sale implementation is on the derivative markets, a program trader, index-fund manager, or index arbitrageur will find it attractive to buy index futures or index call options and sell some common stocks (long or short). Thus, even if the decision by the institutional manager to reduce equity-market exposure is originally implemented in the derivative markets, it eventually leads to actual sales of stocks. The uptick rule on short sales often inhibits index-arbitrage transactions, but the distortions it causes were not a problem prior to Black Monday. Index funds switching from stocks to underpriced futures and arbitrageurs closing long stock–short futures positions help mitigate the effect of the uptick restriction. Proposals to eliminate the uptick rule, entirely for index-arbitrage transactions, may eliminate this problem.

Obviously the same mechanism works in reverse when one or several portfolio managers decide to increase their exposure to the equity markets. Because these markets are related, a decision by one large participant to sell (or to buy) will lead to subsequent movement in the pricing of both the underlying securities and the derivative securities. The important point is that *it was the investment decision by the portfolio manager that created the opportunity for the program trader.* The program trader does not operate in a vacuum, and does not act in order to move the market. The reason the market moves is the original portfolio decision that only incidentally created an opportunity for the arbitrage-oriented program trader. The September 11, 1986 decline and the October 1987 decline were initiated by portfolio managers concerned about the economic outlook and anxious to reduce their commitment to equities. This initial decision to sell was amplified by another group, the *portfolio insurers*.

V. Portfolio Insurance

Portfolio insurance is another phenomenon that has been growing quietly but rapidly. Portfolio insurance is a technique whereby an institutional portfolio manager purchases an actual or synthetic put option. The synthetic put option is usually created in the index-futures market. The insurance provides a high degree of assurance that the performance of the portfolio will not fall below a certain standard over a period that can range up to several years.

There is no organized reporting of insured portfolios, but one reasonable estimate is that institutional equity portfolios worth approximately $10 billion were managed under a commitment to portfolio insurance at the end of 1985. This had grown to more than $40 billion by the end of 1986, and continued growth was probably measured in billions of dollars of new commitments per month in early 1987.

More often than not, synthetic puts for insured portfolios are created or actual puts are purchased when there has been a prior decline in the underlying equities. The idea behind portfolio insurance may seem like locking the barn door after the horse has been stolen. A better way to phrase it might be this: Accept risks early in a period as long as you are sure that a very-low-risk portfolio can earn your minimum required return over the balance of the period. If early returns are good, little of the low-risk asset need be purchased. If early returns are poor, the risk of the portfolio will need to be very low later in the period. Portfolio insurers will be major participants in the derivative securities markets only *after* a market move has occurred. If the Dow were to drop several hundred points, even over a period of three to six months, the effect on existing insurance programs plus the growth of new insurance programs would lead to systematic sales of index futures or purchases of index puts. At various times during a subsequent market rise the derivative contracts would be closed, providing the portfolios with increased exposure to the market on the upside. By the nature of portfolio insurance, puts usually will be created—that is, index futures positions will be *sold*—during and subsequent to market declines; and futures positions will be *purchased* during and subsequent to market advances. The decision to take a position in the derivative markets is determined in advance by the ground rules of the portfolio-insurance program. The general pattern used by all portfolio-insurance programs is similar: Insurance puts are purchased *after* a decline. Actual or synthetic puts are liquidated *after* an advance. The insurance is purchased or sold without much regard for any overpricing or underpricing of the derivative instrument.

Because insurance programs trigger automatic or semiautomatic futures or options transactions, there will be occasions when portfolio insurance will have an impact on *relative values* in the derivative securities markets. Through the activities of program traders, the change in relative valuation of the derivative markets will have a significant impact on the value of the underlying equity securities. In other words *portfolio insurance will tend to accentuate market advances and declines.* While insurance transactions operate directly in the derivative markets, they create the same kind of opportunities for program traders that *anyone* using the stock market or the derivative markets creates.

VI. Program Trading: A Mechanism for Market Equilibrium

As a variety of articles and books on index options and futures have noted, there is a band of prices within which index futures and options can trade relative to the value of the underlying index without giving rise to an arbitrage opportunity. The uncertainty associated with using a basket of securities rather than the entire index, the cost of undertaking a variety of transactions, and several other factors combine to make program trading an occasional rather than an ongoing practice. Program traders exist to take advantage of pricing discrepancies. They iron out the discrepancies that other market participants create between the derivative markets and the underlying equities markets. Some index funds also act as program traders, switching between stocks and index futures to take advantage of pricing discrepancies. Whereas the typical program trader is trying to create a synthetic Treasury bill with a greater yield than a Treasury bill, the index-fund arbitrageur is trying to create an index fund with a better return than the index.

It is useful to divide the major participants in the equity derivative markets into two categories. The division is based upon the effect their market participation has on the equilibrium between the derivative markets and the underlying securities markets. It is difficult to come up with a name for each category without implying that either or both are somehow doing something inappropriate. Investors who use these derivative markets to adjust the overall equity exposure of a portfolio have found a quick way to increase or reduce equity market exposure in a short period of time. They might be called "price acceptors." They accept the price the market offers. The portfolio insurer is also a price acceptor. The portfolio insurance operational algorithm calls for a futures or options market transaction in response to certain behavior in the portfolio or in the index. Many of these price acceptors are aware of valuation issues and valuation discrepancies, but in the overall context of the business they are trying to run, they cannot afford to let valuation discrepancies keep them from avoiding greater risks, such as the risks associated with having too much or too little stock market exposure. Other things being equal, they tend to push prices out of equilibrium.

The term "price setters" might suggest something illegal, so let us call the program traders, arbitrageurs, index funds, and valuation enthusiasts, "equilibrators." Equilibrators take advantage of the opportunities created by the price acceptors and bring the underlying equities and their derivative markets back into equilibrium. They are, in effect, setting the prices of the derivative securities. They make possible participation of price acceptors without undue market disruption, and they keep total transaction costs modest.

VII. Some Thoughts on Regulation

A number of proposals have been made to reduce or eliminate the occasionally unsettling effects of options and futures transactions, especially close to expiration dates. The so-called triple witching hours, when a variety of contracts expire at the same time, have been the focus of considerable debate.

The nature of the factors leading to this expiration-day phenomenon suggest that this is a problem that may not go away by itself. Looked at another way, however, it is not necessarily a problem. As the Stoll and Whaley study of the expiration phenomenon correctly pointed out, the price distorting effect of program trading seems to be concentrated in a period of a few minutes immediately before expiration on the last day of the life of an option or futures contract.[4] One is led to the suspicion that more information on market orders will help reduce even this temporary instability induced by program traders. The plan to use opening rather than closing prices to arrive at option and futures settlement prices might also be helpful, but I suspect disclosure will prove more important than timing.

Theoretical analysis and empirical studies have generally concluded that the growth of derivative securities markets and falling transaction costs reduce volatility as well as increase market efficiency. The action of the market on September 11, 1986 and in October 1987 calls this conclusion into question. It is entirely possible that the ease, speed, and economy with which a market timing decision or a portfolio insurance transaction can be implemented will lead to market instability. Here too, however, other market participants have an incentive to take offsetting actions once they understand how and why the market timers and portfolio insurers are operating.

The only reasonable conclusion is that no unequivocal answer is possible until we have had more experience. One can only hope that regulators' initial efforts will focus on dissemination of information to give the market

---

4. Hans R. Stoll and Robert Whaley, "Expiration Day Effects of Index Options and Futures," New York University Graduate School of Business, New York, 1986.

mechanism a chance to work before artificial limitations are imposed on investors' freedom of action. The history of markets is full of examples where the basic market mechanism itself has provided admirable regulation. All too often the rush to regulate has destroyed a market without providing any added protection to market participants.

It is too soon after the crash of 1987, and this author's perspective is too limited, to provide perfect solutions to all the problems that have come to light. Nonetheless, an options-oriented perspective and an admitted free-market bias suggest that revisions in the market mechanism should include the following at a minimum:

1. The capacity of automatic order entry and execution systems must be far larger than anyone would have thought necessary a few years ago.
2. Information on customer limit orders and order flow now available only to exchange specialists must be totally computerized and readily available to all interested parties.
3. Option position limits must be eliminated. If position limits had been scrapped before October, 1987, and long-term puts had been available, the crash might have been much less severe.[5]
4. The requirement that short sales only be made on price upticks should be modified. It delays price equilibrium and contributes to the chaos of a selling panic.

Hopefully, these revisions will be included among the inevitable structural changes that the crash has initiated. If these changes are included, the market's capacity to provide portfolio insurance will equal the demand. The price of index puts will reflect the risk of relying on dynamic hedging. Market forces will balance supply and demand; and Adam Smith will have been proved right once again.

------

5. For extensive documentation of this point, see Gary L. Gastineau, *Eliminating Option Position Limits: A Key Structural Reform* (New York: Salomon Brothers, August 30, 1988) and Sanford J. Grossman, "Insurance Seen and Unseen: The Impact on Markets," *The Journal of Portfolio Management,* Summer 1988, pp. 5-8. At least one SEC Commissioner has recognized this point: See Joseph Grundfest, "Perestroika on Wall Street: the Future of Securities Trading," *Financial Executive,* May/June 1989, pp. 20-25.

The Revolution in Composite Assets

Donald L. Luskin
Senior Vice President
Wells Fargo Investment Advisors

I. Introduction

There is a subtle but pervasive revolution going on in the theory and practice of investment — a revolution in the most fundamental assumptions with which investors frame their notions of their investment assets. The old regime of security analysis emphasized individual assets, but over the last quarter century it has been gradually replaced by a new regime of portfolio management, with corresponding emphasis on composite assets. The new emphasis on composite assets is as revolutionary in relation to traditional investment perspectives as an Apollo astronaut's photograph of the whole Earth rising above the Sea of Tranquility is to a map of the New York City subway system.

By "composite assets" I mean diversified investment aggregates, such as portfolios of stocks or bonds, that are themselves made up of individual assets, but are nonetheless thought of globally, as indivisible units. The composite-asset perspective operates on the macrocosmic, whole-portfolio level, relegating individual assets to the role of mere building blocks.

II. Investment Strategies with Composite Assets

At this writing, approximately \$200 billion is invested on behalf of America's largest and most sophisticated corporate and public pension plans and endowments in various equity and fixed-income index funds. The phenomenal growth of index funds is only partially attributable to frustration with traditional active management. Perhaps it is explained just as well by a preference for systematic diversification, rigid investment discipline, and tight cost control made possible by a perspective that treats the benchmark index as a single composite asset.

The impact of these enormous funds, and the attitude that has made them so popular, can be seen when a new stock is added to Standard and Poor's 500, the most widely followed benchmark index. In the weeks following addition, the new stocks can be observed to noticeably outperform the market, reflecting not only buying pressure from index funds but also the enhancement of the stock's credibility and prestige resulting from membership in this exclusive composite-asset club.

Many index funds now seek not simply to mimic or reproduce published indexes but instead to offer what amount to competing alternative composite assets. Some such funds offer biases, or "tilts," in index composition or weighting in favor of particular investment attributes, such as yield or size, while still maintaining diversification and broad market exposure. Others use quantitative models to select securities thought to be underpriced, combining them in portfolios designed to track, yet still outperform, a published index. In both cases investors are still pursuing the holy grail of better-than-market performance, but they are doing so in a new composite-asset framework.

Asset-allocation strategies are born not only of the recognition that it is difficult or impossible to beat the market through stock selection but also of the belief that such a pursuit is essentially trivial. Allocation decisions between broad investment classes — that is, composite assets — are now understood to be the prime contributor to risks and returns. On the strategic level pension plans now typically retain specialized consultants to help allocate assets to meet long-term obligations while maximizing expected return. On the tactical level investment managers recommend short-term shifts between composite assets in response to models of the relative risk-adjusted attractiveness of asset classes.

Stock-index futures are arguably the most successful new products in the history of the securities industry, trading a daily value far in excess of the underlying stock market. They are used by institutions as generic proxies for composite assets — units for transferring systematic risk in all manner of hedging, positioning, and restructuring activities at the whole-portfolio level. Arbitrage between index futures and their underlying physical indexes treats the stock and futures exchanges as competing marketplaces for equivalent and interchangeable composite assets.

III. Trading in Terms of Composite Assets

Unfortunately, the futures market remains the closest current approximation to a composite-assets exchange, leaving a gross mismatch between the way investors think about their investment goals and the way they must carry them out. For investors who customarily think in terms of composite assets, a preference to trade in the same composite terms inevitably flows from important functional requirements of their investment strategies. Transactions must be made proportionately and simultaneously across all the assets comprising a composite asset, yet institutions like the New York Stock Exchange and the over-the-counter network of government bond dealers still only trade individual assets, one at a time.

To redress this deficiency, the securities-brokerage industry has improvised several ex officio exchange mechanisms of its own. In "package" trading a broker acts as an off-floor dealer/specialist to facilitate simultaneous trading of a list of assets. In equities it has been estimated that package trading now accounts for upward of 25% of daily volume on the New York Stock Exchange.

In the increasingly popular "crossing networks," brokers provide a central computerized bulletin-board facility on which investors may confidentially post lists of assets to be traded. Executions are consummated when lists, or combinations of lists, are able to be paired off via computer. Although these networks are still in their infancy, they have already begun to attract significant interest from investors; their trading volume is now reported in the millions of shares on many days.

The revolution in composite assets has caught the New York Stock Exchange in an uncomfortable, competitive position. On the one hand, in the wake of the October 1987 crash, the NYSE is seeking to strengthen its infrastructure to handle orders motivated by composite-asset strategies. Though it recently put rules in place to prohibit use of its computerized order-entry systems for index-futures arbitrage on days when the market experiences large price changes, at the same time it would like to take a leadership role in the inevitable growth of the trading of composite assets. For example, it has recently announced the creation of a specialist post for trading entire standardized portfolios of stocks all at once.

The revolution in composite assets will be complete when exchange mechanisms allow investors to trade and clear composite assets entirely in composite terms. For instance, someday investors will be able to place an order to buy a $10 million composite asset comprising a specified number of individual assets, with a specified theoretical tracking error versus a specified index, and specified levels of biases toward specified economic and risk factors. Ultimately, clearing institutions may need to evolve to accommodate transfers of wealth in units subtler than share certificates.

IV. Roots of the Composite-Asset Revolution

Like most revolutions, the revolution in composite assets has been gradual, progressing inevitably out of a complex of economic, conceptual, regulatory, and technological factors. Most fundamentally, it was necessitated by the sweeping institutionalization of markets that has occurred over the past 25 years. The vast magnitude of institutional investment funds, and the complexities of accommodating their astonishing rate of growth, are grossly out of scale with the notion of traditional analysis of individual assets. Diversification of institutional holdings into composite assets is virtually automatic, and a matching conceptual framework is functionally unavoidable.

Beyond this simple argument of necessity, there are other, subtler reasons why institutional investors have come to prefer to think and act in terms of composite assets. First, the regulatory environment has developed in ways that increasingly mandate it. For example, the Employee Retirement Income Security Act of 1974 (ERISA) judges the prudence of individual investment opportunities in their whole-portfolio context, explicitly acknowledging the axiom that uncorrelated, risky individual assets can be combined into less risky composite assets. Thus traditional investment decisions on the individual-asset level take a back seat to considerations of how they will affect the overall composite assets of which they are but components. As another example, Financial Accounting Standards Board (FASB) Statement 87 is forcing corporations to account for the values of their pension plans as the surplus of assets over liabilities. FASB 87 mandates that the surplus itself be thought of as a single asset (or liability) owned by the corporation, a super-composite-asset perspective not only beyond individual assets but even beyond individual asset classes as well.

Second, institutional investors have increasingly come to be measured by unforgiving standards of performance, denominated by indexes that are themselves composite assets. There has even evolved a new consulting business in designing custom-made measurement indexes, called normals, geared to creating benchmarks of particular management styles. When the measure of success—and thus compensation, as well—is denominated in composite terms, even traditional investors whose thinking is dominated by analysis of individual assets are subtly induced to adopt the composite-assets perspective.

Third, institutional investors are drawn to perceived cost benefits of the composite-asset perspective. Management fees for computer-driven composite-asset strategies such as indexing generally are much lower than those for labor-intensive strategies dependent on active individual-asset analysis. Furthermore, many believe that composite-asset–trading techniques such as package trading reduce the explicit and implicit costs of transacting. Because a composite asset can be thought of as a single trade, much larger than any of its components taken individually, by packaging the transaction in a single conceptual unit the trader should be entitled to a quantity discount resulting in lower unit commissions. Potentially more significant, the percentage bid/ offer spread is thought to be lower for relatively informationless composite assets than it would be for individual assets, because they are presumably less risky for the marketplace to facilitate.

Whatever the economic or regulatory stimuli, the revolution in composite assets would not have been possible without the development of a constellation of new concepts and processes of quantitative analysis. As Graham and Dodd's *Security Analysis* drew for a generation of investors a map of the world dominated by individual assets,[1] Markowitz's *Portfolio Selection* introduced a new generation to "Modern Portfolio Theory," the language of composite assets.[2] In the 25 years since Markowitz's theoretical work was first published, his basic insights have been extended to a complex of implementation-oriented tools that give portfolio managers the conceptual framework in which assets can be described, measured, and manipulated as composites.

Modern Portfolio Theory (MPT) might have remained nothing more than an academic artifact had it not been for the parallel development of inexpensive high-speed computers capable of putting MPT's insights at the practical disposal of portfolio managers. With the data-processing tools available 25 years ago, merely constructing a census-index fund was a prohibitively laborious exercise. Today's microcomputers, on the other hand, have allowed MPT to be brought to a point of refinement where huge portfolios can be constructed and optimized instantaneously, creating the capability to make and implement the most complex portfolio-level decisions in a micro-timing context appropriate even for day-trading.

V. Afterword

Like mountaineers who scale the peak one step at a time, only to be startled when they look back down their path and realize just how high they have climbed, many observers are made uncomfortable by the revolution in composite assets. Have today's computer-driven, composite-asset–oriented in-

---

1. Benjamin Graham and David Dodd, *Security Analysis* (New York: McGraw-Hill, 1962).
2. Harry M. Markowitz, *Portfolio Selection* (New York: John Wiley, 1959).

vestment processes somehow grown too far and too fast, forgetting that the individual assets that make them possible are the life blood of real corporations and governments?

For some, the stock market crash of October 1987 was the long-awaited proof that the composite-assets revolution has spun out of control. The truth is exactly the opposite. Thinking and trading in composite assets has, in fact, given investors an unprecedented degree of control over their investments. It was this very control that allowed investors to almost instantly effect a drastic negative revaluation of equities that, in the past, would have taken months to accomplish. As technologies of all types, from the automobile to the telephone, have accelerated almost every aspect of contemporary life, thinking and trading in terms of composite assets has similarly accelerated the investment process. If markets are, primarily, mechanisms for the expression of opinions in the form of prices, our society should endorse technologies that make such expressions more efficient and more free.

Measuring and Interpreting Volatility

Joanne M. Hill, Ph.D.
Vice President
PaineWebber

I. Introduction

The measurement of historical volatility is an important component in the evaluation of options and option strategies. Historical volatility is commonly compared to the volatility implied in option prices to assess whether options are trading "cheap" or "rich." Volatility measured over different historical time periods also often serves as a basis for developing forecasts of volatility for option valuation or strategy analysis. Applications of option valuation include determining the cost of portfolio insurance and the value of options attached to or embedded in fixed-income instruments such as callable bonds, putable bonds, and mortgage-backed securities.

The estimation of volatility from a series of price data is not as straightforward as it may seem. It is not unusual to see different annualized historical volatility estimates for the same time period from different sources. In most instances, different "acceptable" calculation methods explain these discrepancies in the measurement of historical volatility. This article reviews several methodological issues in the calculation of an annualized volatility estimate from historical price data. These issues include the measure used for the rate of return, the number of degrees of freedom and mean (sample or population) used in the calculation, and the method for annualizing the "periodic" standard deviation estimate. Specific recommendations are made with regard to the appropriate methodology for the volatility estimation, depending on the circumstances at hand. A method for converting volatility measures to expected price ranges is also suggested. These price ranges, which are anticipated with a given probability over a specific time interval, can be useful benchmarks for comparison with actual changes in price over the same time interval.

Standard deviation is used to measure historical volatility. The formula for the standard deviation or volatility measure over a sample of N observations of a variable R is calculated as follows:

$$\text{Volatility} = SD = \left[\sum_{i=1}^{N} \left(\frac{(R_i - \bar{R})^2}{N-1} \right) \right]^{1/2}, \tag{1}$$

where

R_i = observation i on variable R;
$\bar{R}$ = the average of R_i, $i = 1, 2, ..., N$; and
N = the number of observations in the sample.

This article evaluates some alternative methods for applying this formula in calculating the historical volatility from a time series of prices. The method chosen can significantly influence the level of the historical volatility measure.

II. Return Calculation and Return Distribution Assumptions

Two measures of return are commonly used:

1. Percentage changes in daily prices
2. Natural logarithm of price relatives

Both percentage price changes and the natural logarithm of price relatives are acceptable as return measures. Percentage price changes are often used with daily price data. These returns are typically assumed to follow a normal probability distribution (see Figure 1a).

Another acceptable return measure is the natural logarithm (ln) of price relatives (P_t/P_{t-1}) between date t and $t-1$, that is, $\ln(P_t/P_{t-1})$. This term is equivalent to $1 + R$, where R is the continuously compounded return over interval t or e^{Rt}; that is, $\ln(P_t/P_{t-1})$ is equivalent to $1 + e^{Rt}$. When the return interval is short, such as a day in length, the difference in terms of the annualized measure between continuous compounding of gains and losses and daily compounding is very small. (The use of daily percentage price changes is consistent with a process of daily compounding.)

Both percentage price changes and the natural logarithms of price relatives are normally distributed variables if price changes are independent of

FIGURE 1. *Normal and Lognormal Density Functions.*

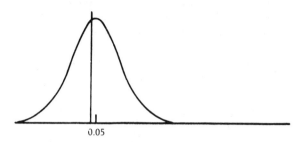

0.05

a) Normal Density Function
(Mean: .05 or 5%, Standard Deviation: .30 or 30%)

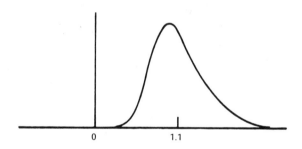

0   1.1

b) Lognormal Density Function
(Mean: 1.10, Standard Deviation: .34)

Source: J.C. Cox and M. Rubinstein, *Options Markets* (New York: Prentice Hall, Inc., 1985), p. 202.

one another.[1] The standard deviation formula in equation (1) can be used as a measure of the volatility of a distribution when the underlying variable is distributed normally. Note that the Black–Scholes model assumes that prices are lognormally distributed, as shown in Figure 1b. A lognormal distribution

1. This conclusion follows from the central limit theorem of probability theory, assuming price changes are independent of one another and distributed identically. This assumption has an interesting implication. If price changes are independent of one another, there should be no pattern in the sequence of price changes, that is, price changes should follow a random walk. The use of historical volatility measures determined by equation (1) is, therefore, inconsistent

of prices is the equivalent of a normal distribution of the logarithm of those prices. Since the logarithm of a variable is a measure of its continuous rate of change, the assumption that continuous (or directly measured) rates of change (return) are normally distributed is consistent with lognormality in prices. Note also that assuming price relatives, or P_t/P_{t-1}, are lognormally distributed is identical to assuming $\ln(P_t/P_{t-1})$ or $\ln(1+R)$ is normally distributed. Therefore, either measure of return can be used in volatility calculation, depending on convenience.

III. The Calculation of Daily Standard Deviation from Daily Return Data

Divisor or Degrees of Freedom

When using sample data that include the sample mean to calculate a variance or standard deviation, the sum of the squared deviations about the sample mean should be divided by the number of those observations (N) minus 1, that is, by $N-1$. The divisor of $N-1$ rather than N is appropriate because the mean is calculated from a sample, thereby reducing the degrees of freedom by 1.

The @ STD function in Lotus 1-2-3 divides by N and therefore understates the sample volatility estimate.[2] The effect of using N rather than $N-1$ is a decreasing function of N; that is, for very large N, the difference is trivial; however, for small N (for example twenty observations or less), the effect can be significant. Table 1 contains historical volatility estimates for the March 1986 Treasury bond futures contract using 10, 20, and 30 days of price data. These volatility estimates are calculated using both N and $N-1$ to illustrate the effect of calculating a population volatility measure where a sample measure is appropriate. Note that the 10-day annualized volatility estimates based on N and $N-1$ differ by .50%. The 20-day volatility estimates differ by .35%, and the 30-day volatility estimates by .20%.

---

with the validity of technical analysis based on a pattern or trend in price changes. Any pattern or trend in prices would produce serially related price changes. In the presence of serial correlation, the formula for standard deviation should be adjusted to take into account the dependence (or serial correlation) of price changes on one another. The adjustment required is to multiply the standard deviation by the square root of $(1+S)/(1-S)$, where $S =$ the serial correlation between daily returns. See also note 5.

2. On page 292 of the Lotus 1-2-3 manual, the following formula for a sample standard deviation is provided:

Sample STD = @ SQRT (@ COUNT (list)/(@ COUNT (list) − 1)) *@STD (list)

where (list) = the range of cells over which the calculation is to be done.

TABLE 1. *Historical Volatility Estimates Using Different Calculation Methods.*[a]

| | Basis for Annualizing Volatility | | |
	250 days	260 days	365 days
10-day Volatility Estimates			
% price changes			
$N = 10$	8.61%	8.78%	10.41%
$N = 9$	9.08	9.26	10.97
Ln(price relatives)			
$N = 10$	8.59	8.76	10.38
$N = 9$	9.05	9.23	10.94
20-day Volatility Estimates			
% price changes			
$N = 20$	13.54%	13.81%	16.36%
$N = 19$	13.89	14.16	16.78
Ln(price relatives)			
$N = 20$	13.57	13.84	16.40
$N = 19$	13.93	14.20	16.83
30-day Volatility Estimates			
% price change			
$N = 30$	12.12%	12.36%	14.65%
$N = 29$	12.33	12.57	14.90
Ln(price relatives)			
$N = 30$	12.15	12.39	14.68
$N = 29$	12.36	12.60	14.93

a. Based on the closing prices of the March 1986 Treasury bond futures contract over the period from December 13, 1985, through January 27, 1986.

Use of Sample or Population Mean

It is, in fact, correct to use the population mean instead of the sample mean for calculating volatility when a theoretical basis exists for the mean of the distribution or when the mean of the population is either given by assumption or known with certainty. In most cases, however, the population mean is unknown, and the sample mean is used as the "best estimate" of this unknown value. Therefore, most volatility measurement appropriately uses $N-1$ as the divisor in equation (1). If the population mean is known or fixed by assumption, it is acceptable to divide by N.

An example of the use of a population mean is in the calculation of the standard deviation of the residual errors in a regression. These errors are by definition distributed normally with a mean of 0. Therefore, many residual standard deviations are calculated as the mean of the squared residual errors. This represents the standard deviation of residual errors around a mean of 0.

Another application of the use of a population mean would be if a return or price change series is expected to have a mean significantly different from the sample mean. This expected mean may have been derived as an average of a series of returns measured over a very long period. That is, the best prediction of next period's price is the current period's price multiplied by one plus the expected rate of price appreciation. For example, the sample mean over very short time periods, say less than 30 days, may be unsustainably high or low given the range of returns typically observed for the instrument. Therefore, the standard deviation can be measured with respect to the expected return or population mean. To reiterate, in the rare circumstance when a population mean assumption is used rather than the sample mean, it is correct to use N as a divisor.

IV. The Calculation of Annualized Standard Deviation

The annualization of historical volatility from weekly or monthly percentage price changes or from price relative data is straightforward. The formula converting weekly or monthly volatility to an annualized volatility number is thus:

$$\text{Annualized Volatility} = \text{Monthly Volatility} \times \sqrt{12}; \qquad (2)$$
$$= \text{Weekly Volatility} \times \sqrt{52}. \qquad (3)$$

When the sample consists of daily data, however, the situation becomes more complicated. There are 365 days in a non-leap year and 366 in a leap year. Annualizing using a 365-day basis implicitly assumes that volatility on non-trading days is equal to that on trading days. Most academic evidence, on the other hand, suggests that returns are generated from a process that is closer to one based on trading days than one based on calendar days. If returns followed a calendar time process, volatility on Mondays would be three times that of other weekdays. However, empirical tests have shown Monday volatility is only modestly (10 to 20%) above that of other weekdays, which supports the trading time model.[3]

Therefore, the number of trading days in a typical year is the appropriate number for annualization. Since the typical year is 52 weeks and 1 day, there should be at least 110 (52 × 2) weekend days, leaving 255 trading days. The stock and commodity exchanges usually observe seven additional holi-

---

3. See, for example, D.W. French, "The Weekend Effect on the Distribution of Stock Prices," *Journal of Financial Economics* 13 (1984): 547–59 or other references cited therein.

days resulting in 247 trading days per year.[4] Banks and U.S. government bond dealers may also have several (three or four) additional holidays.

Multipliers of 250 or 260 are often used for annualizing trading-day volatility calculated from daily data.[5] The volatility estimates based on a 260 trading-day year, as shown in Table 1, are roughly 0.25% higher than those found using a 250-day year. Using a 365-day calendar basis for annualizing volatility produces estimates between 1% and 3% higher than does a 260-day basis. Obviously, the higher the level of daily volatility, the larger the difference between trading and calendar-day volatility estimates. We recommend using a 250 trading-day year:

$$\text{Annualized Volatility} = \text{Daily Volatility} \times \sqrt{250}. \qquad (4)$$

V. Interpretation of Volatility Estimates

When observing price changes in the instrument underlying an option, the question arises of whether an observed price move is consistent with the volatility implied in the option price or with a historical volatility estimate. For example, after selling a call option at a price reflecting an implied volatility of 15%, would a change in price of 2 points in 10 days be consistent with the 15% implied volatility?

One approach is to measure historical volatility over the time frame of the price move, comparing it to the implied volatility at the time the option position was opened. This method is imperfect, however, because the level of volatility over 10 days will reflect the extent of price movement on days within that period as well as the movement from the beginning to end point. A more useful approach is to find the range of prices around the initial price that is consistent with the original volatility estimate. If price movement is regularly at the extremes of this range or outside of the range, it is a positive

---

4. Stock Exchange holidays include New Year's Day, Washington's Birthday, Good Friday, Memorial Day, Independence Day, Thanksgiving, and Christmas. Banking holidays also include Martin Luther King Day (in some states), Columbus Day, and Veteran's Day, but exclude Good Friday. If Christmas and New Year's fall on a weekend day, exchange officials decide whether a holiday is given.

5. These volatility annualization formulas implicitly assume return observations are independent of one another; that is, there is no serial correlation in the return series. Results are not significantly affected by minor violations of this assumption. However, there are circumstances in which serial return correlation can be a problem. For example, a broad-based index may require two trading periods to react completely to economic information, with actively trading securities responding first and others later. Therefore, one may wish to adjust the historic volatility for the level of serial correlation in the returns when estimating volatilities of very broad indexes such as the NYSE or the Value Line Index or bond indexes. An adjustment of this type would involve applying a first order auto-regressive correction such as described in note 1 to the return or price relative series.

indication that volatility is rising. If price movements are well within the price range based on one unit of volatility, chances are that volatility is declining.

The interpretation of historical volatility as estimated by the standard deviation is the range of daily returns (or daily price relatives) around the mean in which approximately two-thirds (68.3%) of the possible future outcomes are expected to fall. In other words, for the case of 10% volatility based on percentage price changes, there is a 68.3% probability (or roughly two chances out of three) that the next day's price will be within a plus or minus 10% annualized percentage change of today's price. In terms of price relatives, this would mean there are two out of three chances that the next day's price will be between 99.37 and 100.63% of today's price or between 90 and 110% of today's price on an annualized basis; 10% annualized volatility converted to a daily volatility equals 0.63%, or $(10\%/\sqrt{250})$. Therefore, in this situation, one would expect a range of 99.37 to 100.63 on a security priced at 100 with a probability of 0.683, or 68.3%. Two standard deviations encompass roughly 95% of all possible values, or a range of 98.74 [100 − $(2 \times .63)$] to 101.26 [100 + $(2 \times .63)$]. The probabilities associated with different units of volatility for a normal distribution are shown in Table 2.

The annualized volatility measure can, therefore, easily be converted into a price range expected with a given probability over a particular time interval. First, the annualized volatility is transformed to a number applicable to the time interval involved. Second, the current price is multiplied by 1 plus or minus the periodic volatility times the units of volatility associated with the probability.

For example, the price range expected with a 95.4% probability over the next week, consistent with a 15% annualized probability and assuming the current price is equal to 100, would be given as:

Weekly Volatility $.0208 = .15/\sqrt{52}$
95.4% = 2 units of volatility
Price Range: $100 \times (1 + (.0208 \times 2)) = 104.16$;
$100 \times (1 − (.0208 \times 2)) = 95.84$.

TABLE 2.

Units of Volatility (Standard Deviation)	Probability of Observing Price in the Range of Units × Volatility
−½ to +½	.3830
−1 to +1	.6826
−1½ to +1½	.8664
−2 to +2	.9544
−2½ to +2½	.9876
−3 to +3	.9974

TABLE 3.

Initial Price = 100   Annualized Volatility = 15%
Time = 1 Month   Monthly Volatility = 4.33%

Units of Volatility (Standard Deviation)	Price Range	Chance of Observing Price Outside of Range
−½ to +½	97.83–102.16	.617
−1 to +1	95.67–104.33	.317
−1½ to +1½	93.50–106.49	.134
−2 to +2	91.34–108.66	.045

Therefore, a price range of from 95.84 to 104.10 over a period of one week can be expected with a 95.4% probability, consistent with our annualized volatility estimate of 15%.

For a given volatility, it is also possible to calculate a range of prices outside of which a price is expected to fall with a given probability. As an example, consider the case above, in which a security (or future) is priced at 100 with a 15% annualized volatility. The probabilities associated with different price ranges over a period of one month (that is, the chance of observing a price outside that range), given the 15% volatility, are shown in Table 3.

It is also possible to construct a table of price ranges for varying time periods that are associated with a particular number of volatility units. Assume one wants to know the range of prices for each of the next 8 weeks beginning today that are consistent with a 15% annualized volatility and a chance of 0.317 of being outside the range (0.683 of being within the range). Since these probabilities represent one standard deviation, simply find the appropriate standard deviation for 1, 2, ..., 8 weeks of time and multiply 1 plus this number and 1 minus this number by the current price of 100 as shown in Table 4.

TABLE 4.

Beginning Price = 100   Annualized Volatility = 15%
Initial Volatility = Annual Volatility/$\sqrt{52N}$ (N = Number of weeks)
Chance of Observing Prices Outside of Range = .317

Time In Weeks	Price Range
1	97.92–102.08
2	97.06–102.94
3	96.39–103.60
4	95.84–104.16
5	95.35–104.65
6	94.90–105.09
7	94.48–105.50
8	94.11–105.88

Note that the range expands at a much greater rate in the first 4 weeks than in the second 4 weeks. The potential upside range for one standard deviation increases by 2.08 points, from 102.08 to 104.16, between the end of the first and fourth weeks. However, the upside range increases by only 1.23 points, from 104.65 to 105.88, between the end of the fifth and eighth weeks. This is the effect of the nonlinearity of the function that converts short-term to longer term volatility.

Intuitively, these results imply that volatility increases over time, but at a decreasing rate, such that monthly volatility is considerably less than four times weekly volatility. A large price move over a short period does not necessarily mean that volatility is increasing. The price move should be evaluated in the context of this type of analysis to see whether it lies significantly outside the range of likely prices for this short period.

VI. Conclusion

The differences in volatility estimates for 10, 20, and 30 observations as shown in Table 1 confirm the methodological effects suggested by the above discussion. In summary: (1) There is little difference between volatility estimates based on the natural logarithm of price relatives versus percentage price changes over periods as short as a day, both of which should satisfy the normal distribution assumption; (2) when using a sample mean in the standard deviation formula, it is important to use the number of observations minus 1 as the divisor, especially for small return samples; (3) the annualization of a daily volatility estimate should take into account the number of trading days rather than calendar days in a year; that is, the annual volatility is estimated by multiplying the daily volatility by the square root of 250; and (4) it is possible to convert volatility measures to expected price ranges. These price ranges can be very useful as reference points for detecting changes in volatility from short-term price moves.

PART II

Fixed Income Portfolio Management

Portfolio Objectives and Management Policies for Fixed-Income Investors

Richard W. McEnally, Ph.D., CFA
Meade H. Willis, Sr., Professor of Investment Banking
University of North Carolina–Chapel Hill

I. Introduction

On the face of it, fixed-income securities are not very attractive investment media. They require that the investor surrender money up front in return for a *promise* of uneven quality to receive a stream of future cash benefits, usually spread out over the far distant future, with the certain knowledge that if the security is held for its entire life the benefits will never exceed those initially promised and may be less.[1,2] Given this limitation, it is worthwhile to inquire about the conditions under which an investor might reasonably invest in fixed-income securities.

Fixed-income investment appears to make sense under three different sets of portfolio objectives: seeking current income, attempting to accumulate value over time, and going for holding-period returns.

---

1. In speaking with student groups about bonds I often call their attention to the fact that thirty- and forty-year bonds are routinely issued, and ask them to contemplate how old they will be and what year it will be when the initial investment is paid back at maturity. This approach is not entirely fair, because (as the concept of duration has taught us) the payoff at maturity is a comparatively unimportant component of the bond's value. But it is sobering nonetheless.

2. In practice many fixed-income securities contain prepayment options, such as the right of the issuer to refund early, but these nearly always work to the benefit of the issuer rather than the investor.

II. Investing for Current Income

The traditional, conventional basis for investing in bonds has always been to provide a reasonably steady, high, and highly reliable stream of spendable income, where *income* is equated with coupon receipts. This goal is typified by the portfolio of an eleemosynary institution from which only the cash income can be spent, or by the portfolio of an income-beneficiary-remainderman trust where priority attaches to the income objective. Fixed-income securities are a classic investment medium for such portfolios. Provided the portfolio is well diversified with respect to both issues and maturities, the income stream can virtually be counted on in the senses that the cash *will* come in and it will come in at a level that changes only slowly as interest rates vary through time. Moreover, the income will be larger than other investment media can provide, at least initially. The notion of bonds as a "widows and orphans" investment is as reasonable as it is commonplace.

When the objective shifts to some combination of income plus growth of income and/or principal, the case for bonds is not compelling. The dividend stream of a diversified portfolio of common stocks is also highly reliable and relatively insensitive to interest rate fluctuations,[3] and it will almost surely grow over time along with the value of the underlying principal.[4]

With respect to portfolio-management practices, investment for current income is undemanding — indeed, the real dangers are that the portfolio will be totally ignored on the one hand, or managed more aggressively than it should be on the other! Clearly, the monitoring and control of credit risk is paramount. Maturity management designed to minimize fluctuations in income and avoid the risk of rolling over large quantities of maturing bonds in low interest-rate environments is important, and for this reason the traditional "laddered" maturity structure — in which approximately equal quantities of

---

3. For example, a review of data for the Standard & Poor's 500 reveals that over the period 1926 through 1981 there were only nine years when these common stocks showed an absolute year-to-year decrease in dividends, with the maximum decrease of 38.1% occurring in 1933; since World War II there have been only four years of dividend decrease, with the largest of these, a decrease of 4.1%, occurring in 1952.

4. Over the years 1926–1981 the dividends paid on the Standard & Poor's 500 grew at an average annual rate of 2.4%. Over a surprisingly long span in this period — from 1926 through 1958 — the S&P 500 dividend yield actually exceeded the yield on Moody's Aaa corporate bonds. Since 1958 this relationship has been reversed, but even so, through 1976, dividend growth was such that money initially invested in the stocks would have been earning more cash income than money invested in bonds after eight years, on average. (In fairness, it should be noted that for funds invested in stocks at the beginning of three years prior to 1976 — 1969, 1972, and 1973 — the dividend return as of the end of 1985 had still not caught up with the bond yield that would have resulted from investing in bonds at the beginning of these years, and because of the high yields on bonds compared to stocks since 1976 money invested in stocks at the beginning of any of these years would still be earning less.)

bonds mature at fairly regular intervals—certainly makes sense (unless the manager can forecast interest-rate highs years in advance, which seems unlikely). For similar reasons bond refunding can be a problem, especially because the temptation in managing for current income is to go for high coupon issues, and thus call risk should be watched carefully. The primary opportunity for active management probably lies in the area of swapping, both among broad sectors of the bond market or among substantially identical securities, to take advantage of what are viewed as transient yield aberrations.

III. Investing for Accumulation of Value

A second portfolio objective that rationally leads to fixed-income–securities investment is to accumulate value over time, especially when the time horizon is not extremely long or the tolerance for uncertainty is low. References to this as a "funding" portfolio objective capture its nature very well. In this context all intermediate cash throw-offs of the portfolio are reinvested. No substantive distinction is made between value that accumulates from coupon flows, from the reinvestment of intermediate flows, or from appreciation of the built-in variety resulting from discounted securities converging on their redemption prices. The goal is simply to have a portfolio value at the end of the investment horizon that equals or exceeds some target expectation. Although in practice there may be a *schedule* of horizons and target expectations, these are easily accommodated within the accumulation scheme, provided withdrawals are unrelated to coupon receipts or changes in value over short intervals.

A typical example of such an accumulating portfolio results from the occasional practice in pension management of identifying a group of retired beneficiaries and setting aside a package of assets to fund their projected benefits. Another representative example arises when a municipality floats a bond issue to fund a specific project and invests the proceeds in a portfolio designed to generate just enough cash to meet progress payments as they become due. Both these examples represent liquidating portfolios of a short-run nature. IRA accounts and employee benefit plans at the stage where contributions exceed benefit payments are also accumulating portfolios, but ones where the horizon is longer and greater uncertainty regarding future value is usually tolerated in return for an expectation of higher future value.

Because of the highly reliable nature of their flows (or perfectly reliable nature, in the case of U.S. Treasury issues), fixed-income securities are an ideal investment medium for accumulating portfolios when the horizon is short or risk-aversion is high. By proper choice of specific securities it is often possible to assemble a portfolio whose actual flows just match the pattern of needed funds, and thus there is no reinvestment and no reinvestment-rate risk, nor is there any price risk. This approach has come to be known as *portfolio dedication.*

The bad music begins when it is infeasible or excessively expensive in terms of foregone returns to match the built-in flows from portfolio securities with funds needs. Under these circumstances, the other flows—those flows that result from reinvesting intermediate cash flows, from selling bonds, from called bonds, and the like—become important, and these flows are anything but highly predictable. By holding bonds of sufficiently short maturity it is usually possible to finesse price uncertainty, but reinvestment of intermediate flows is another matter. Such reinvestment and the rate at which reinvestment occurs, or *reinvestment-rate risk,* are critical in portfolios that are accumulating value over the long run.

An alternative approach to managing reinvestment-rate risk is to match the duration of the portfolio assets and the investment horizon in the operation known as *portfolio immunization.*[5] In this approach, the portfolio is structured so that reinvestment-rate risk and price risk should just offset each other, causing the realized return to just equal the yield at which the portfolio was originally immunized, regardless of subsequent interest-rate movements. Aside from implementational issues, the big problems with immunization are the highly defensive nature of the operation and the lack of fixed-income securities with durations as long as the investment horizons that are routinely encountered. The implication of the former problem is that immunization may not be the most desirable portfolio-management practice from the perspective of returns foregone for risk avoided, whereas the latter suggests that securities other than fixed-income securities may be appropriate investments.

Despite the recent popularity of dedication and immunization, it is probably fair to say that most accumulating portfolios—and certainly most *long-run* accumulating portfolios—are not managed in a manner that formally deals with reinvestment rate risk. Instead, either by ignorance or design, it is implicitly assumed that reinvestment considerations will average out over time. At the one extreme the portfolio may be managed in an essentially passive manner, with heavy emphasis on long-term securities and portfolio composition that is fairly consistent with regard to quality, sector allocation, and the like. At the other extreme it may be run in an aggressive manner, with bets on interest-rate movements via maturity-structure shifts or on other dimensions of the portfolio. In this way the portfolio may gradually become one managed for holding-period returns, as discussed below. But what typifies all such portfolios is greater tolerance for risk, including reinvestment-rate risk, than under the highly defensive strategies.

---

5. A useful review of immunization is provided by G. O. Bierwag, George C. Kaufman, and Alden Toevs, "Duration: Its Development and Use in Bond Portfolio Management," *Financial Analysts Journal* (July/August 1983): 15–35.

If the time horizon is reasonably long *and* risk tolerances are not extremely low, then investment media other than bonds may be more suitable for accumulating portfolios. It is well known that common stocks have had higher geometric-mean periodic rates of return than bonds over long runs of history, and most observers feel that this will be the experience in the future. Moreover, common stocks with growing streams of dividends tend to have greater durations than coupon bonds. It follows, therefore, that investment in common stock will result in greater accumulation of value than will fixed-income securities over the long run, and it may allay reinvestment-rate risk better as well.[6,7]

With respect to portfolio management, appropriate techniques depend upon the level of aggressiveness that is tolerable. For defensive dedicated or immunized portfolios, about the only opportunity to add value through management is to engage in swaps to exploit temporary security or sector mispricing in a manner that does not change the basic dimensions of the portfolio. Cash-flow shocks such as those that might result from an unexpected call are especially troublesome, and exposure to this type of disruption should be monitored closely. The range of options is wide for less defensive portfolios. Many will be managed in an essentially passive manner using indexing or what amounts to indexing. Such a strategy, with its implied laddering of maturities, has the effect of minimizing reinvestment-rate shocks by exposing funds for reinvestment to a wide variety of interest-rate environments. Substitution and sector swapping is consistent with such a strategy. With increasing aggressiveness, the sky is the limit. In particular, large bets on interest rates, quality sectors, and the like may be justified provided the manager is believed to have the touch and the portfolio can bear the risk. But even at this level of aggressiveness, reinvestment considerations

---

6. For further discussion of the geometric mean and value accumulation, see my treatment in "Latane's Bequest: The Best of Portfolio Models," *The Journal of Portfolio Management* (Winter 1986): 21–30. With respect to the obvious question of what constitutes the "long run," using the Ibbotson–Sinquefeld data to examine the period 1926–1981, one finds only thirteen out of fifty-two possible five-year periods in which high corporate bonds (Moody's Aaa corporates) had greater total returns than common stocks (Standard & Poor's 500); for U.S. Treasury bonds, there are also only thirteen such periods. If the horizon is lengthened to ten years, common stocks dominated corporate bonds in thirty-six out of forty-seven possible periods, and dominated Treasury issues in forty of the possible periods. Over this span of years, the longest period over which someone who bought stocks would be behind someone who invested in corporate bonds was twenty-one years, with the holding period beginning in 1930. The longest equivalent period with Treasuries was sixteen years, beginning in the same year. See Roger G. Ibbotson and Rex A. Sinquefeld, *Stocks, Bonds, Bills, and Inflation: The Past and the Future* (Charlottesville, Virginia: The Financial Analysts Research Foundation, 1982), Exhibits B-1, B-5, and B-6.

7. The relevance of the long durations of common stocks to investing for the long run is discussed by Peter L. Bernstein in a superb but unpublished speech delivered to the Institutional Investor Annual Pension Fund Conference in New York City on February 19, 1984, entitled "What Does Long-Term Investing Really Mean?"

and the factors that enter into them—such as exposure to refunding calls—are critical.

A particular technique for dealing with accumulating portfolios, "contingent immunization," is of interest not so much for the technique itself as for the message it conveys about reinvestment-rate risk.[8] In contingent immunization, the portfolio is managed actively, so long as the combination of its value and prevailing interest rates are such that if immunized its terminal value would exceed some predetermined accumulation goal. If a point is reached at which its immunized terminal value would only just attain the goal, then active management is supposed to cease and the portfolio is to be immunized. Obviously this is nothing more than active management accompanied by a resolution to cease active management if it does not pay off. What is interesting about the technique is that it calls attention in a forceful way to reinvestment considerations. With contingent immunization the portfolio value can have substantially increased, but if the rollover rate of interest (akin to the reinvestment rate) has sufficiently dropped, the portfolio will not be adequate to reach the accumulation objective; the portfolio can have depreciated, but if the rollover rate has risen sufficiently, the accumulation outlook will have improved. The message is that, with accumulation portfolios, enhancement of value is not enough. The manager should always worry about reinvestment rates, and always concentrate on the value to which the portfolio will accumulate.

IV. Investing for Holding-Period Returns

The holding-period return, or total return, is simply the ending value of the portfolio plus cash received from investments during the holding period, all divided by the beginning-of-period value of the portfolio. In investing for holding-period returns, the objective is to maximize the return that is achieved in each period commensurate with the risk that is assumed.

Fixed-income portfolios are often managed for holding-period returns, and sometimes this emphasis is justified. But in some circumstances the targeted holding-period return is not really appropriate even though it is the objective for which the portfolio is managed, and in many circumstances it is not really *the* objective for which the portfolio is managed even though it is the *nominal* objective.

Investing for holding-period returns would appear to make the most sense under two obvious conditions: first, no legal or institutional differentiation exists between return from cash receipts and return from appreciation

---

8. Contingent immunization is a product of Salomon Brothers, Inc. For a detailed exposition see Martin L. Leibowitz and Alfred Weinberger, "The Uses of Contingent Immunization," *Journal of Portfolio Management* (Fall 1981): 51–55.

in price; and second, no particular intention exists to reinvest cash thrown off by the portfolio in fixed-income securities or even to remain invested in those securities.[9] Therefore, for example, an aggressive investor might place funds in bonds in the anticipation that interest rates will decline, with the expectation that these funds would be moved to another investment medium, such as common stocks, after the decline occurs. Under these circumstances the targeted holding-period return and fixed-income investment appear to be entirely compatible. Some fixed-income investment may also be appropriate to diversify portfolios of other types of assets that are properly managed for holding-period returns, such as *balanced* closed-end or mutual funds.[10]

In other circumstances the compatibility may not be so great. Publicly marketed bond funds and the fixed-income component of employee benefit funds are two prime examples of portfolios that are nominally managed for holding-period returns. The total rate of return is certainly the criterion by which performance of the portfolio is usually evaluated, and seems to be the objective with which most managers of such portfolios are preoccupied. However, undue emphasis on the holding-period–return objective, especially in the short run, can lead to decisions that the owners, beneficiaries, or sponsors of such portfolios might not view with approval if they knew all the facts.

Consider the position of many managers of bond-fund portfolios over the years 1982–1986, a period of dramatically declining interest rates. If the manager had anticipated any of this decline, the purely total return–oriented portfolio would have consisted of long bonds of low coupon. However, many managers of such portfolios were hesitant to shift into low-coupon issues during this interval because of the income portfolios would have foregone in the interim. In 1986, when the future outlook for interest rates appeared grim, many managers of these portfolios would have liked to shorten their maturities. However, doing so would realize heretofore unrealized capital gains and roll the money over into lower yielding securities, thereby adversely affecting the income stream once again. For this reason many managers

---

9. Differential taxation of capital gains and ordinary income, such as existed prior to the Tax Reform Act of 1986, does not constitute an institutional difference in the first sense; such differentiation would simply underscore the need to look at *after-tax* holding-period returns. The point in the text is intended to refer to situations where the differentiation alters spending or consumption decisions.

10. A number of authors have dealt with the portfolio-diversification implications of different types of fixed-income securities. See, e.g., my piece "Portfolio-Relevant Characteristics of Long Term Marketable Securities," *Journal of Financial and Quantitative Analysis* Volume 8 (September 1973): 565–585; Gordon J. Alexander, "Mixed Security Testing of Alternative Portfolio Selection Models," *Journal of Financial and Quantitative Analysis* Volume 12 (December 1977): 817–832; or William F. Sharpe, *Investments,* Third Edition (Englewood Cliffs, New Jersey: Prentice-Hall, 1985), p. 346.

resisted wholesale restructuring. They realized that even though holding-period returns may be the nominal objective of such funds, many of the investors were actually in them for income they generate. Therefore they were willing to compromise on the holding-period–return objective in return for the spendable income objective.

A similar situation is arising in pension portfolios, which are probably best viewed as accumulating portfolios even though they too are often nominally managed for holding-period returns. Because of lower borrowing costs and the fact that the Internal Revenue Service effectively subsidizes the retirement of debt via cash tender offers, many corporations are now making tender offers for their high-coupon debt that is not currently refundable.[11] Since such offers are made at prices above the current market price of the bonds, they have the effect of enhancing the holding-period return of the portfolio that holds them if the tender offer is accepted. However, some pension-fund managers are examining their reinvestment alternatives and concluding that the fund will be better off over the long run if the tenders are *not* accepted.

The point, therefore, is that there are relatively few fixed-income portfolios for which total returns should be the overriding objective, including two types that are often offered as examples of portfolios with this objective. The more common case is one in which holding-period returns can be thought of as a secondary objective, one that should be pursued as long as it is not incompatible with the primary objective of the portfolio. The incompatibility appears to be least for accumulating portfolios. Over any given horizon, value in such portfolios must necessarily accumulate at a *rate* equal to the geometric mean of the holding-period returns that are realized within that interval. As long as future holding-period returns are not sacrificed for future returns, there is no problem. (Accumulation of dollar value is another matter; if cash additions to the portfolio are being made over time, it is better for the holding-period returns to be loaded toward the end of the horizon.) Given the general movement of interest rates, which of course is beyond the control of the portfolio manager, the objective of seeking holding-period returns is a reasonable one.[12]

---

11. For a discussion of the economics of such tendering operations and the implications for investors, see Andy J. Kalotay, "Refunding Considerations for High-Coupon Debt," in *CFA Readings in Fixed Income Securities* (Charlottesville, Virginia: The Institute of Chartered Financial Analysts, 1985), pp. 136–144.

12. In "Rethinking Our Thinking About Interest Rates," *Financial Analysts Journal* (March/April 1985): 62–67, I argue that declines in interest rates are generally counterproductive from the viewpoint of the accumulating investor because of the implications for reinvestment. However, I also observe that managers should seek to increase value or avoid loss as much as possible given the interest-rate environment that exists, and conclude that holding-period returns offer a valid means of evaluating the portfolio manager.

Investing for holding-period returns is straightforward in principle even though it may be difficult in practice. The goal is simply to construct the portfolio that will show the largest appreciation over the holding period considering both the market's expectations regarding future bond prices or rates *and* the existing structure of bond prices or rates. In other words, the emphasis should be on identifying mispricing in the marketplace. Interest-rate plays, which have come to dominate total-return investing, illustrate the relevance of these considerations. The manager may have a certain expectation regarding future interest rates, and this expectation may suggest a portfolio composition whose maturity, coupon, and the like are appropriate to exploit the move towards the expected rates. But first it is necessary to check the pricing of these characteristics in the marketplace. It may be that the manager's expectations are so commonly held that the anticipated future pricing is already built in to the existing structure of yields and prices — and in fixed-income investing, as in equity investing, the largest rewards will go to the manager who can identify and exploit errors in the consensus expectation of the future.

Mispricing may also be identifiable in other large ways — bond quality, type of security, call protection, or other measurable characteristic of fixed-income securities for example — or in small ways, such as differing yields on substantially identical securities. *Scenario* or "what if" analysis should clearly play a large role in investing for holding-period returns, as should constant attention to patterns of pricing in the marketplace. If the manager's strength of conviction is sufficiently great, then the result should be portfolios that are structured with *bullet* maturities and equivalent concentration along other security characteristic dimensions.

A Framework for Analyzing Bonds
Horizon Return, Duration, and Convexity

Ravi E. Dattatreya, Ph.D.
Senior Vice President
Sumitomo Bank Capital Markets, Inc.

Frank J. Fabozzi, Ph.D., CFA
Visiting Professor of Finance, Sloan School of Management
Massachusetts Institute of Technology
and
Editor, *The Journal of Portfolio Management*

I. Introduction

Bond portfolio management requires an understanding of three attributes of a bond or bond portfolio: horizon (or total) return, duration, and convexity. In this article we explain these three attributes. We begin with a discussion of the price/yield relationship for an option-free bond.

II. Price/Yield Relationship of an Option-Free Bond

The price of a bond is equal to the present value of the cash flow expected from the bond. The cash flow is not always simple to project. In the case of noncallable bonds, barring default, the cash flow pattern is known. For bonds with embedded options such as callable bonds and mortgage-backed securities, the cash flow pattern is not known with certainty. The required rate that should be used to compute the present value of the expected cash flow will equal the yield on comparable Treasury securities plus a premium for risk plus the value of any options granted to the issuer minus an adjustment for any options the issuer grants to the bondholder.

Let's begin with the price/yield relationship for an option-free bond, that is, a bond that does not have an embedded option. (Later in this chapter we shall discuss the price/yield relationship for bonds with embedded options.)

TABLE 1. *Price/Yield Relationship for a 20-Year 10% Coupon Bond.*

Required Yield	Price (Par = 100)
7.00%	132.02
8.00	119.79
9.00	109.20
9.50	104.44
9.90	100.86
9.99	100.09
10.00	100.00
10.01	99.91
10.10	99.15
10.50	95.85
11.00	91.98
12.00	84.95
13.00	78.78

The price of an option-free bond moves in the opposite direction of a change in yield. The reason is that since the price is the present value of the cash flow, a higher (lower) yield will decrease (increase) the present value of the cash flow and therefore its price. Table 1 illustrates this for a 20-year, 10% coupon bond.

If the price/yield relationship for this bond is graphed, it would have the bowed shape shown in Figure 1. This shape is referred to as *convex* and

FIGURE 1. *Graph of Price/Yield Relationship.*

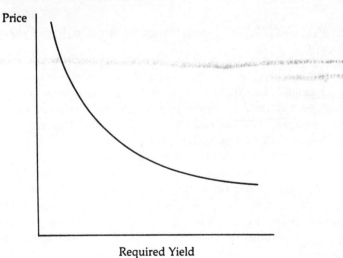

it is not unique to our hypothetical bond. The price/yield relationship for any option-free bond will have a convex shape.

While the relationship between price and yield shown in Table 1 and Figure 1 is for an instantaneous change in yield, over time three factors will change the price of a bond. First, as yields in the market change, the price of a bond will change. Second, the price of a bond selling at a discount or premium will change as it approaches maturity even if market yields do not change. More specifically, the price of a discount bond will increase while that of a premium bond will decrease. Third, as the perceived credit risk changes, the price of a bond will change.

III. Price Volatility for an Option-Free Bond

Table 2 shows the percentage change in the price of our hypothetical 20-year, 10% coupon bond for various yield changes assuming (1) the initial yield is 10% and (2) the yield change is instantaneous.

From Table 2 we can see that for small changes in required yield such as 10 basis points,[1] the percentage price increase is the same as the percentage price decrease. However, for larger changes in the required yield, this is no longer true. In fact, the percentage price increase is greater than the percentage price decrease. One implication is that, if an investor owns a bond, the price appreciation that will be realized if the required yield decreases is greater than the capital loss that will be realized if the required yield increases by the same number of basis points.

---

1. A basis point is equal to .01% (.0001). 100 basis points equals 1%.

TABLE 2. *Percentage Price Change for a 20-Year 10% Coupon Bond Selling at Par to Yield 10%.*

	Increase in Required Yield					
Required yield	10.01%	10.10%	10.50%	11.00%	12.00%	13.00%
Change in basis points	1	10	50	100	200	300
% Change in price	−0.09	−0.85	−4.15	−8.02	−15.05	−21.22
	Decrease in Required Yield					
Required yield	9.99%	9.90%	9.50%	9.00%	8.00%	7.00%
Change in basis points	−1	−10	−50	−100	−200	−300
% Change in price	0.09	0.86	4.44	9.20	19.79	32.03

These properties of an option-free bond, which are due to the convex shape of the price/yield relationship, can be summarized as follows:

Property 1: Price changes are approximately symmetric for small changes in yield.
Property 2: Price changes are not symmetric for large changes in yield.
Property 3: Percentage price increases are greater than percentage price decreases for the same change in yield.

While all option-free bonds exhibit the price/yield and bond price volatility characteristics just described, all bonds do not change by the same percentage for a given change in basis points. There are two characteristics of a bond that will determine its price volatility: coupon and maturity. The impact of these two characteristics on a bond's price volatility are summarized below:

Characteristic 1: Holding maturity and yield constant, the price volatility of a bond is greater the lower the coupon rate.
Characteristic 2: Holding the coupon rate and yield constant, the price volatility of a bond is greater the longer the maturity.[2]

Measuring Bond Price Volatility

In addition to knowing how the coupon rate and maturity of a bond will influence its price volatility, a measure that quantifies the combined impact of coupon rate and maturity is also needed to implement portfolio strategies. Such a measure is Macaulay duration,[3] which is defined below for a semiannual pay bond whose next cash flow is exactly six months from now:[4]

$$\text{Macaulay duration (in years)} = \frac{\dfrac{1\,CF_1}{(1+y/2)^1} + \dfrac{2\,CF_2}{(1+y/2)^2} + \cdots + \dfrac{n\,CF_n}{(1+y/2)^n}}{2\,\text{Price}}, \qquad (1)$$

where

---

2. Some deep discount coupon bonds are exceptions.
3. Frederick R. Macaulay, *Some Theoretical Problems Suggested by the Movements of Interest Rates, Bond Yields and Stock Prices in the United States Since 1865* (National Bureau of Economic Research, 1938).
4. For a semiannual pay bond between coupon dates, the formula for Macaulay duration must be adjusted as follows. First, instead of multiplying the cash flows by the time period $(t = 1, 2, ..., n)$, they are multipled by:

$$\text{time period} + \frac{\text{time (in days) remaining to the next cash flow}}{\text{total time (in days) between cash flows}} - 1. \qquad (2)$$

Second, the above expression is used in the present value formula rather than the time period to compute the present value of each cash flow. Third, the numerator is divided by price plus accrued interest not just price.

CF_t = cash flow in period t,
  y = yield (annual and in decimal form), and
  n = number of six-month periods.

Macaulay duration for a zero-coupon bond is equal to its maturity.

Table 3 shows how to compute the Macaulay duration for the 20-year, 10% coupon bond selling at par (100) to yield 10%.

The link between Macaulay duration and percentage price change is:

$$\text{percentage price change} = -\frac{\text{Macaulay duration}}{(1+y/2)} \times \text{Yield change} \times 100. \qquad (3)$$

The Macaulay duration divided by $(1+y/2)$ is called modified duration; that is,

$$\text{Modified duration} = \frac{\text{Macaulay duration}}{(1+y/2)}. \qquad (4)$$

Using modified duration, the percentage price change can be expressed as:

$$\text{percentage price change} = -\text{Modified duration} \times \text{Yield change} \times 100. \qquad (5)$$

For the 20-year, 10% coupon bond selling at par to yield 10%, modified duration is:

$$\text{modified duration} = \frac{9.01}{(1+.10/2)} = 8.58. \qquad (6)$$

Table 4 shows the percentage price change based on duration for our hypothetical bond and compares it to the actual price change as shown in Table 2. Note the following three points. First, for small changes in yield, Macaulay duration (modified duration) does a good job approximating the actual percentage price change. Second, for a large change in yield, the approximation is off. The error is greater the larger the change in yield. Finally, the percentage price change based on duration is less than the actual percentage price change when yields decline but greater when yields increase. This implies that the estimated price based on duration will always be less than the actual price.

For a 100 basis point change in yield (that is, a yield change of 0.01), the percentage price change based on duration will be:

$$\text{percentage price change} = -\text{Modified duration} \times (.01) \times 100$$
$$= -\text{Modified duration}. \qquad (7)$$

Thus, modified duration is the percentage price change for a 100 basis point change in yield.

While we have focused on the percentage price change, the properties discussed earlier are also applicable to the dollar price change. The relationship between the dollar price change of a bond and modified duration is:

TABLE 3. *Calculation of Macaulay Duration for a*
20-Year 10% Coupon Bond Selling at Par to Yield 10%.

Period	Cash Flow*	PV of $1 at 5%	PV of CF	Period ×PV
1	5	0.952380	4.76190	4.761
2	5	0.907029	4.53514	9.070
3	5	0.863837	4.31918	12.957
4	5	0.822702	4.11351	16.454
5	5	0.783526	3.91763	19.588
6	5	0.746215	3.73107	22.386
7	5	0.710681	3.55340	24.873
8	5	0.676839	3.38419	27.073
9	5	0.644608	3.22304	29.007
10	5	0.613913	3.06956	30.695
11	5	0.584679	2.92339	32.157
12	5	0.556837	2.78418	33.410
13	5	0.530321	2.65160	34.470
14	5	0.505067	2.52533	35.354
15	5	0.481017	2.40508	36.076
16	5	0.458111	2.29055	36.648
17	5	0.436296	2.18148	37.085
18	5	0.415520	2.07760	37.396
19	5	0.395733	1.97866	37.594
20	5	0.376889	1.88444	37.688
21	5	0.358942	1.79471	37.688
22	5	0.341849	1.70924	37.603
23	5	0.325571	1.62785	37.440
24	5	0.310067	1.55033	37.208
25	5	0.295302	1.47651	36.912
26	5	0.281240	1.40620	36.561
27	5	0.267848	1.33924	36.159
28	5	0.255093	1.27546	35.713
29	5	0.242946	1.21473	35.227
30	5	0.231377	1.15688	34.706
31	5	0.220359	1.10179	34.155
32	5	0.209866	1.04933	33.578
33	5	0.199872	0.99936	32.978
34	5	0.190354	0.95177	32.360
35	5	0.181290	0.90645	31.725
36	5	0.172657	0.86328	31.078
37	5	0.164435	0.82217	30.420
38	5	0.156605	0.78302	29.755
39	5	0.149147	0.74573	29.083
40	105	0.142045	14.91479	596.591
			Total	1801.704

Macaulay duration = $1801.704/2(100) = 9.01$

*Per $100 par.

TABLE 4. *Estimated Percentage Change in Price Using Modified Duration for a 20-Year 10% Coupon Bond Selling at Par to Yield 10%.*

			Increase in Required Yield			
Required yield	10.01%	10.10%	10.50%	11.00%	12.00%	13.00%
Change in basis points	1	10	50	100	200	300
Estimated % change	−0.09	−0.86	−4.29	−8.58	−17.16	−25.74
Actual % change	−0.09	−0.85	−4.15	−8.02	−15.05	−21.22
			Decrease in Required Yield			
Required yield	9.99%	9.90%	9.50%	9.00%	8.00%	7.00%
Change in basis points	−1	−10	−50	−100	−200	−300
Estimated % change	0.09	0.86	4.29	8.58	17.16	25.74
Actual % change	0.09	0.86	4.44	9.20	19.79	32.03

*Modified duration = 8.58.

$$\text{Dollar price change} = -\text{Price} \times \text{Modified duration}$$
$$\times \text{Yield Change} \times 100. \qquad (8)$$

The product of the price and modified duration is called *dollar duration*. That is,

$$\text{Dollar duration} = \text{Price} \times \text{Modified duration}. \qquad (9)$$

Therefore the dollar price change can be expressed as:

$$\text{Dollar price change} = -\text{Dollar duration} \times \text{Yield change} \times 100. \qquad (10)$$

We now know that duration (Macaulay, modified, dollar) provides a good approximation of the change in a bond's price for small changes in yield but not for large changes. We've also seen that by using duration the new price of a bond will be understated. To see why, let's take a closer look at the graph of the price/yield relationship for the 20-year, 10% coupon bond.

Figure 2 is the same graph as Figure 1 except that there is a tangent line drawn at a yield of 10%, the yield we assume this bond is offering. The tangent line is used to estimate what the new price will be if yield changes. Take note of three things. First, for small changes in yield the tangent line deviates little from the price/yield curve. Thus, for small changes in yield the tangent line does a good job of approximating the new price. Second, for large changes in yield the tangent line departs much more from the price/yield

FIGURE 2. *Convex Curve with Tangent Line.*

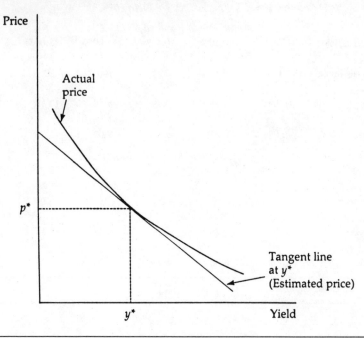

curve. In fact, as we move further and further from the 10% yield, the difference between the price estimated from the tangent line and the actual price as given by the price/yield curve increases. Third, regardless of whether the yield increases or decreases, the tangent line is below the price/yield curve. Thus, the estimated price will be less than the actual price.

What does the tangent line represent? The slope of the tangent line represents the dollar duration of a bond. Thus, our earlier observations concerning the use of duration to approximate price or percentage price change are due to the convex shape of the price/yield curve.

Convexity

Let's examine what happens to the tangent line when yield changes. As the yield increases, the slope of the tangent line flattens (becomes smaller). The slope of the tangent line steepens (becomes larger) when yield decreases. Because the slope of the tangent line represents dollar duration, this means that when yield increases, dollar duration gets smaller and when yield decreases, dollar duration gets larger. For an investor who is long a bond, an increase in dollar duration when yield decreases and a decrease in dollar duration when yield increases is an attractive investment feature.

While all option-free bonds share this feature, the rate at which dollar duration increases when yield decreases and decreases when yield increases differs for each bond. It is possible to measure the rate of change of dollar duration. The measure is popularly known as *convexity* and is measured as follows for a semiannual pay bond whose next coupon payment is exactly six months from now:[5]

$$\text{Convexity (in years)} = \frac{\dfrac{(1)^1 CF_1}{(1+y/2)^1} + \dfrac{(2)^2 CF_2}{(1+y/2)^2} + \cdots + \dfrac{(n)^2 CF_n}{(1+y/2)^n}}{4\,\text{Price}}. \tag{11}$$

Table 5 illustrates the calculation of convexity for our 20-year, 10% coupon bond selling at par to yield 10%.

Given the convexity of a bond, modified convexity and dollar convexity are computed as follows:

$$\text{Modified convexity} = \frac{\text{Convexity}}{(1+y/2)^2} \tag{12}$$

and

$$\text{Dollar convexity} = \text{Modified convexity} \times \text{Price}. \tag{13}$$

The percentage price change of bond due to convexity can be estimated using the following equation:

$$\begin{aligned}\text{percentage price change due to convexity} &= \tfrac{1}{2} \times \text{Modified convexity} \\ &\quad \times (\text{Yield change})^2 \times (100)^2.\end{aligned} \tag{14}$$

Table 6 shows the percentage price change due to convexity for our hypothetical bond.

Combining the price change due to duration and the price change due to convexity gives a considerably better approximation to the percentage change in price. This can be seen in Table 6.

The properties of convexity are summarized below without proof:

Property 1: As the yield increases (decreases) the dollar duration of a bond decreases (increases).
Property 2: For a given yield and maturity, the lower the coupon rate, the greater the convexity of a bond.
Property 3: For a given yield and modified duration, the lower the coupon rate the smaller the convexity.

---

5. Technically, the formula for convexity is:

$$\text{Convexity (in years)} = \frac{\dfrac{1(2)\,CF_1}{(1+y/2)^1} + \dfrac{2\,(3)\,CF_2}{(1+y/2)^2} + \cdots + \dfrac{n(n+1)\,CF_n}{(1+y/2)^n}}{4\,\text{Price}}. \tag{15}$$

However, the formula in the text provides almost identical values.

TABLE 5. *Calculation of Convexity for a 20-Year 10% Coupon Bond Selling at Par to Yield 10%.*

Period	Cash Flow*	PV of $1 at 5%	PV of CF	Period^2 ×PV
1	5	0.952380	4.76190	4.761
2	5	0.907029	4.53514	8.140
3	5	0.863837	4.31918	8.872
4	5	0.822702	4.11351	5.816
5	5	0.783526	3.91763	7.940
6	5	0.746215	3.73107	134.318
7	5	0.710681	3.55340	174.116
8	5	0.676839	3.38419	216.588
9	5	0.644608	3.22304	261.066
10	5	0.613913	3.06956	306.956
11	5	0.584679	2.92339	353.730
12	5	0.556837	2.78418	400.922
13	5	0.530321	2.65160	448.121
14	5	0.505067	2.52533	494.966
15	5	0.481017	2.40508	541.144
16	5	0.458111	2.29055	586.382
17	5	0.436296	2.18148	630.448
18	5	0.415520	2.07760	673.143
19	5	0.395733	1.97866	714.299
20	5	0.376889	1.88444	753.778
21	5	0.358942	1.79471	791.467
22	5	0.341849	1.70924	827.276
23	5	0.325571	1.62785	861.136
24	5	0.310067	1.55033	892.995
25	5	0.295302	1.47651	922.821
26	5	0.281240	1.40620	950.593
27	5	0.267848	1.33924	976.307
28	5	0.255093	1.27546	999.967
29	5	0.242946	1.21473	1021.589
30	5	0.231377	1.15688	1041.198
31	5	0.220359	1.10179	1058.827
32	5	0.209866	1.04933	1074.514
33	5	0.199872	0.99936	1088.305
34	5	0.190354	0.95177	1100.250
35	5	0.181290	0.90645	1110.402
36	5	0.172657	0.86328	1118.820
37	5	0.164435	0.82217	1125.561
38	5	0.156605	0.78302	1130.690
39	5	0.149147	0.74573	1134.270
40	105	0.142045	14.91479	23863.670
			Total	50006.190

Convexity = 50,006.190/4(100) = 125.02

*Per $100 par.

TABLE 6. *Percentage Price Change Using Modified Duration and Convexity for a 20-Year 10% Coupon Bond Selling at Par to Yield 10%.**

	Increase in Required Yield					
Required yield	10.01%	10.10%	10.50%	11.00%	12.00%	13.00%
Change in basis points	1	10	50	100	200	300
Estimated %						
Duration	−0.09	−0.86	−4.29	−8.58	−17.16	−25.74
Convexity	0.00	0.01	0.14	0.57	2.27	5.10
Total	−0.09	−0.85	−4.15	−8.01	−14.89	−20.64
Actual % change	−0.09	−0.85	−4.15	−8.02	−15.05	−21.22
	Decrease in Required Yield					
Required yield	9.99%	9.90%	9.50%	9.00%	8.00%	7.00%
Change in basis points	−1	−10	−50	−100	−200	−300
Estimated %						
Duration	0.09	0.86	4.29	8.58	17.16	25.74
Convexity	0.00	0.01	0.14	0.57	2.27	5.10
Total	0.09	0.87	4.43	9.15	19.43	30.84
Actual % change	0.09	0.86	4.44	9.20	19.79	32.03

*Modified duration = 8.58; modified convexity = 125.002.

Property 4: The convexity of a bond increases at an increasing rate as duration increases.

Property 2 implies that a zero-coupon bond will have greater convexity than a coupon bond with the same maturity. However, Property 3 implies that a zero-coupon bond will have lower convexity than a coupon bond with the same duration.

IV. Horizon Return

There are two yield measures that are commonly used in the bond market — yield to maturity and yield to call. The yield to maturity of a bond is the interest rate that will make the present value of its cash flow to maturity equal to its price (plus accrued interest). The yield to call is the interest rate that will make the present value of its cash flow to call equal to its price (plus accrued interest).

These yield measures are often used to assess the relative value of bonds. Unfortunately, it is only under very limited circumstances that these measures offer any insight into the relative attractiveness of bonds.

There are two drawbacks to these measures. First, yield to maturity assumes that the bond will be held to maturity. In the case of yield to call, the assumption is that the bond will be held to the call date and will be called then. Since an active bond portfolio manager may sell a bond prior to maturity or call, this assumption is not realistic. Second, the yield to maturity will only produce a return at the maturity date equal to the yield to maturity if all coupon payments can be reinvested at an interest rate equal to the yield to maturity. For the yield to call all coupon payments must be reinvested at an interest rate equal to the yield to call. The risk that coupon payments may be reinvested at an interest rate below the required interest rate is called *reinvestment risk*. How important is this risk? For some bonds, the interest income that must be generated to produce the accumulated value necessary to realize the yield to maturity (or yield to call) may constitute as much as 80% of the bond's total dollar return.

Because of the limitations of yield to maturity and yield to call for assessing the performance of a bond in a portfolio and the relative value of bonds, an alternative measure must be developed. The measure must take into consideration the three sources of dollar return from holding a bond over some investment horizon: (1) coupon interest, (2) interest from reinvesting coupon interest over the investment horizon, and (3) any capital gain or loss. This requires that a portfolio manager specify: (1) the investment horizon, (2) an interest rate that the coupon payments can be reinvested, and (3) the price that the bond can be sold at the end of the investment horizon. The last assumption is effectively equivalent to projecting what the required yield on the bond will be at the end of the investment horizon.

The rate of return computed using this framework is called the *horizon return*. Other names used for horizon return are *total return, realized compound yield,* and *effective yield.* Horizon return when the cash flows are semiannual is calculated as follows:

$$\left[\frac{\begin{array}{c} \text{Total coupon} \\ \text{payments} \end{array} + \begin{array}{c} \text{Reinvestment} \\ \text{income} \end{array} + \begin{array}{c} \text{Price at end of} \\ \text{investment horizon} \end{array}}{\text{Initial price plus accrued interest}} \right]^{2/h} - 1. \quad (16)$$

Of course, the horizon return will depend on the investment horizon and the underlying assumptions. A portfolio manager will want to investigate the sensitivity of these assumptions on a bond's horizon return. For short-term investment horizons, the horizon return is not sensitive to changes in the reinvestment rate. However, it will be sensitive to the assumed yield at the end of the horizon.

V. Application: Dumbbell-Bullet Analysis

A *dumbbell* is a combination or a portfolio of two bonds. In our application we select the bonds and their holdings such that the duration of the dumbbell is equal to that of a third bond, known as the *bullet*. We want to compare the relative attractiveness of the dumbbell and the bullet.

There are two unknowns in the creation of a dumbbell: the par holdings of each of the two bonds that comprise the dumbbell. We need two conditions to determine these two unknowns. The first condition is that the total dollar duration of the dumbbell equals that of the bullet. By equating the dollar durations, we equate the interest rate risk of the two positions. A common second condition is to equate the total market value of the dumbbell to that of the bullet. This ensures that the proceeds from the sale of the bullet (or dumbbell) can be used to purchase the dumbbell (bullet) with no cash left over after the transaction.

A comparison of the yield to maturity of the bullet to the weighted average yield to maturity of the dumbbell to determine whether a portfolio manager can enhance portfolio performance poses several problems. First, the yield for a portfolio is not simply the weighted average of the yields of the bonds in the portfolio. Instead, it is the internal rate of return of the cash flow of the portfolio. Second, as we explained in the previous section, yield to maturity is a poor measure of relative value because it assumes that the bonds will be held to maturity and that the coupon payments will be reinvested at the yield to maturity. Finally, bond price performance depends not only on duration but convexity. The following illustration demonstrates these points.[6]

Table 7 compares a dumbbell consisting of a 5-year, 8.5% bond and a 20-year, 9.5% bond blended in the ratio of 50.2% and 49.8% to a bullet of 10-year maturity and 9.25% coupon. All bonds are initially priced at par.

The yield to maturity of the bullet is 9.25%. The weighted average yield to maturity of the dumbbell is 9%. A naive analysis would suggest that there is a yield pickup of 0.25% or 25 basis points by buying the bullet and selling the dumbbell. However, while the dollar duration for the bullet and dumbbell is equal, the dollar convexity of the two is not. The dumbbell has higher dollar convexity. Thus, while there is a yield to maturity pickup by investing in the bullet, there is a convexity giveup by investing in the bullet. The yield giveup can be viewed as the cost of improving convexity.

However, if the yield on the dumbbell is properly computed based on the cash flow from the two bonds, there is a much smaller yield pickup by investing in the bullet (6.3 basis points).

We're not finished with this story. We still have not properly assessed whether the bullet or dumbbell is more attractive because the yield—whether computed as a weighted-average yield or cash flow yield—is not a meaningful

---

6. The illustrations in this section are adapted from Ravi E. Dattatreya and Frank J. Fabozzi, *Active Total Return Management of Fixed Income Portfolios* (Chicago: Probus Publishing, 1989).

TABLE 7. *Dumbbell–Bullet Analysis.*

Three bonds used in analysis:

Bond	Coupon	Maturity (Years)	Price Plus Accrued	Dollar Yield	Dollar Duration	Convexity
A	8.50	5	100	8.50%	4.00544	19.8164
B	9.50	20	100	9.50%	8.88151	124.1702
C	9.25	10	100	9.25%	6.43409	55.4506

Bullet: Bond C

Dumbbell: Bonds A and B

Composition of dumbbell: 50.2% of Bond A; 49.8% of Bond B

Dollar duration of dumbell =
$.502 \times 4.00544 + .498 \times 8.88151 = 6.434$

Average yield of dumbbell =
$.502 \times 8.50 + .498 \times 9.5 = 8.998$

Strategy: Sell the dumbbell and buy the bullet

Analysis based on average yield

Yield pickup = Yield on bullet − Average yield of dumbbell
$= 9.25 - 8.998 = .252$ or 25.2 basis points

Analysis based on duration, convexity and average yield

Dollar convexity of dumbbell =
$.502 \times 19.8164 + .498 \times 124.1702 = 71.7846$

Yield pickup = Yield on bullet − Average yield of dumbbell
$= 9.25 - 8.998 = .252$ or 25.2 basis points

Convexity giveup = Convexity of dumbbell − Convexity of bullet
$= 71.7846 - 55.4506 = 16.334$

Analysis based on duration, convexity and cash flow yield

Cash flow yield of dumbbell* =
$$\frac{(8.5 \times .502 \times 4.00544) + (9.5 \times .498 \times 8.88151)}{6.434} = 9.187$$

Yield pickup = Yield on bullet − Cash flow yield
$= 9.25 - 9.187 = .063$ or 6.3 basis points

Convexity giveup = Convexity of dumbbell − Convexity of bullet
$= 71.7846 - 55.4506 = 16.334$

---

*The calculation shown is actually a dollar-duration-weighted yield, a very close approximation to cash flow yield.

measure of potential return. To assess relative value, a horizon return must be computed over some holding period.

Table 8 shows the horizon return for the performance of the bullet and dumbbell over a six-month horizon for a parallel shift in the yield curve (i.e., the yield for all maturities changes by an equal number of basis points). The first column of the exhibit shows the change in yield. Since the strategy under consideration is to sell the dumbbell and buy the bullet, the second column shows the difference in the total dollars at the end of six months. The third column provides the same information based on horizon return rather than total dollars.

Our horizon analysis suggests that if yields change by more than 100 basis points, the dumbbell will outperform the bullet. This would generate a loss if we pursued a strategy of buying the bullet and selling the dumbbell. In contrast, a gain would be produced if yields change by 100 basis points or less. The better performance of the dumbbell for large changes in yield is due to its better convexity.

While we have restricted our analysis thus far to a parallel shift in the yield curve, Table 8 also shows the relative performance for nonparallel shifts. In the fourth and fifth columns, we assumed that if the yield on Bond C (the intermediate-term bond) changes, Bond A (the short-term bond) will increase by 25 basis points while Bond B (the long-term bond) will decrease by 25 basis points. Under this scenario, the dumbbell will always outperform the bullet. In the last two columns, the nonparallel shift assumes that for a change in Bond C's yield, the yield on Bond A will decrease by 25 basis points while that on Bond B will increase by 25 basis points. In this case, the bullet would outperform the dumbbell only if the yield on Bond C does not rise by more than 250 basis points or fall by more than 325 basis points.

Thus, horizon analysis tells us that by looking at measures such as yield (yield to maturity, average-weighted yield or cash flow yield), duration and convexity can be misleading because the performance of a security or a portfolio of securities depends on the magnitude of the change in yields over some investment horizon and how the yield curve changes.

VI. Extending the Analysis to Callable Securities

Most corporate bonds are callable prior to the maturity date at the option of the issuer. Mortgage pass-through securities may be repaid in whole or part by the homeowner prior to the maturity of the mortgage loan. Thus, mortgage pass-through securities will exhibit price/yield characteristics similar to callable corporate bonds. We will focus our attention on callable corporate bonds.

Figure 3 shows the price/yield relationship for both a noncallable bond and the same bond if it is callable. The convex curve a–a' is the price/yield

TABLE 8. *Dumbbell–Bullet Analysis Based on Horizon Analysis: Bullet Minus Dumbbell.*

Yield Change	Parallel Shift		Nonparallel Shift*		Nonparallel Shift**	
	Dollar Value	Horizon Return	Dollar Value	Horizon Return	Dollar Value	Horizon Return
−5.000	−3.59613	−7.19	−5.34489	−10.69	−1.94264	−3.89
−4.750	−3.13782	−6.28	−4.80478	−9.61	−1.56223	−3.12
−4.500	−2.72030	−5.44	−4.30917	−8.62	−1.21906	−2.44
−4.250	−2.34103	−4.68	−3.85538	−7.71	−0.91076	−1.82
−4.000	−1.99764	−4.00	−3.44084	−6.88	−0.63511	−1.27
−3.750	−1.68787	−3.38	−3.06316	−6.13	−0.39002	−0.78
−3.500	−1.40960	−2.82	−2.72005	−5.44	−0.17349	−0.35
−3.250	−1.16081	−2.32	−2.40937	−4.82	0.01635	0.03
−3.000	−0.93962	−1.88	−2.12906	−4.26	0.18126	0.36
−2.750	−0.74421	−1.49	−1.87721	−3.75	0.32293	0.65
−2.500	−0.57291	−1.15	−1.65201	−3.30	0.44291	0.89
−2.250	−0.42410	−0.85	−1.45173	−2.90	0.54271	1.09
−2.000	−0.29628	−0.59	−1.27475	−2.55	0.62373	1.25
−1.750	−0.18802	−0.38	−1.11954	−2.24	0.68729	1.37
−1.500	−0.09798	−0.20	−0.98465	−1.97	0.73464	1.47
−1.250	−0.02489	−0.05	−0.86872	−1.74	0.76695	1.53
−1.000	0.03245	0.06	−0.77046	−1.54	0.78534	1.57
−0.750	0.07518	0.15	−0.68864	−1.38	0.79086	1.58
−0.500	0.10434	0.21	−0.62213	−1.24	0.78448	1.57
−0.250	0.12095	0.24	−0.56984	−1.14	0.76714	1.53
0.000	0.12596	0.25	−0.53074	−1.06	0.73970	1.48
0.250	0.12025	0.24	−0.50387	−1.01	0.70300	1.41
0.500	0.10466	0.21	−0.48834	−0.98	0.65780	1.32
0.750	0.07999	0.16	−0.48327	−0.97	0.60484	1.21
1.000	0.04698	0.09	−0.48786	−0.98	0.54479	1.09
1.250	0.00632	0.01	−0.50136	−1.00	0.47830	0.96
1.500	−0.04132	−0.08	−0.52305	−1.05	0.40598	0.81
1.750	−0.09533	−0.19	−0.55225	−1.10	0.32839	0.66
2.000	−0.15512	−0.31	−0.58834	−1.18	0.24606	0.49
2.250	−0.22015	−0.44	−0.63071	−1.26	0.15949	0.32
2.500	−0.28991	−0.58	−0.67881	−1.36	0.06916	0.14
2.750	−0.36391	−0.73	−0.73212	−1.46	−0.02450	−0.05
3.000	−0.44169	−0.88	−0.79012	−1.58	−0.12109	−0.24
3.250	−0.52285	−1.05	−0.85237	−1.70	−0.22020	−0.44
3.500	−0.60698	−1.21	−0.91843	−1.84	−0.32149	−0.64
3.750	−0.69370	−1.39	−0.98788	−1.98	−0.42462	−0.85
4.000	−0.78268	−1.57	−1.06035	−2.12	−0.52927	−1.06
4.250	−0.87358	−1.75	−1.13548	−2.27	−0.63515	−1.27
4.500	−0.96611	−1.93	−1.21292	−2.43	−0.74198	−1.48
4.750	−1.05997	−2.12	−1.29237	−2.58	−0.84952	−1.70
5.000	−1.15491	−2.31	−1.37352	−2.75	−0.95752	−1.92

FIGURE 3. *Option-Free and Callable Bond Price/Yield Relationship.*

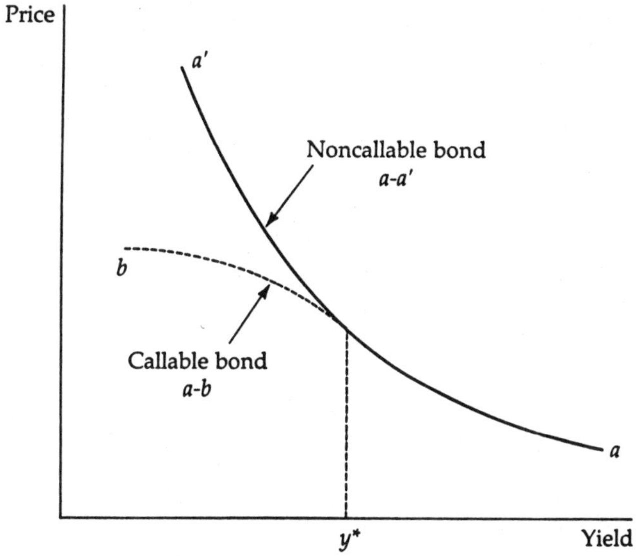

relationship for the noncallable (option-free) bond. The unusual shaped curve denoted by *a–b* is the price/yield relationship for the callable bond.

The reason for the shape of the price/yield relationship for the callable bond is as follows. When the prevailing market yield for comparable bonds is higher than the coupon interest on the bond, it is unlikely that the corporate issuer will call the bond. For example, if the coupon rate on a bond is 8% and the prevailing yield on comparable bonds is 16%, it is highly improbable that the corporate issuer will call in an 8% bond so that it can issue a 16% bond. In option terminology, the call option is deep out of the money. Since the bond is unlikely to be called when it is deep out of the money, a callable bond will have the same price/yield relationship as a noncallable bond. However, even when the option is near the money (the coupon rate is just below the market yield) investors may not pay the same price for the

Notes to Table 8
  *Change in yield for Bond C. Nonparallel shift as follows:
   yield change bond A = yield change bond C + 25 basis points
   yield change bond B = yield change bond C − 25 basis points
 **Change in yield for Bond C. Nonparallel shift as follows:
   yield change bond A = yield change bond C − 25 basis points
   yield change bond B = yield change bond C + 25 basis points

bond if it is callable because there is still the chance the market yield may drop further, making it beneficial for the issuer to call the bond.

As yields in the market decline, the likelihood increases that yields will decline further so that the issuer will benefit from calling the bond. We may not know the exact yield level at which investors begin to view the issue likely to be called, but we do know that there is some level. In Figure 3, at yield levels below y^*, the price/yield relationship for the callable bond departs from the price/yield relationship for the noncallable bond. Suppose, for example, the market yield is such that a noncallable bond would be selling for 109, but since it is callable it would be called at 104 — investors would not pay 109. If they did and the bond is called, investors would receive 104 (the call price) for a bond they purchased for 109. Notice that for a range of yields below y^*, there is price compression — that is, there is limited price appreciation as yields decline.

To develop an analytical framework for assessing relative value and evaluating the potential performance of callable bonds over some investment horizon, it is necessary to understand the components of the bond. A callable corporate bond is a bond in which the bondholder has sold the issuing corporation a call option that allows the issuer to repurchase the bond from the time the bond is first callable until the maturity date.

Effectively, the owner of a corporate callable bond is entering into two separate transactions. First he buys a corporate noncallable bond from the issuer, for which he pays some price. Then he sells the issuer a call option for which he receives the option price from the issuer. Therefore, we can summarize the position of a corporate callable bondholder as follows:

$$\text{long a callable bond} = \text{long a noncallable bond}$$
$$+ \text{short position in call} \qquad (17)$$

or equivalently,

$$\text{callable bond} = \text{noncallable bond} - \text{call option.} \qquad (18)$$

The minus sign in front of the call option means that the bondholder has sold (written) the call option.

In terms of price, the price of a callable corporate bond is therefore equal to the price of the two component parts. That is,

$$\text{callable bond price} = \text{noncallable bond price}$$
$$- \text{call option price.} \qquad (19)$$

The call option price is subtracted from the price of the noncallable bond. The reason is that when the bondholder sells a call option, he receives the option price. Graphically this can be seen in Figure 3. The difference between the price of the noncallable bond and the callable bond is the price of the embedded call option.

The price of a call option increases when the expected price volatility of the underlying instrument increases. Since the price of a call option on a bond depends on its interest rate, the price of a callable bond will depend on expected interest rate volatility.

Call-Adjusted Yield

Given the above relationship for the callable bond, a portfolio manager wants to know if the noncallable bond is correctly priced in the sense that he is being adequately rewarded for the call risk associated with owning the bond. The price that the noncallable bond should sell for can be computed as follows:

$$\text{noncallable bond price} = \text{callable bond price}$$
$$+ \text{call option price.} \qquad (20)$$

The price of the callable bond can be observed in the market. The price of the call option can be estimated using an option pricing model. Adding the two prices gives the implied price of the noncallable bond.

Given the implied price of the noncallable bond, it is then simple to compute the yield on this bond. The yield computed is referred to as the *call-adjusted yield*. The call-adjusted yield is the implied yield on the noncallable bond.

A noncallable bond is priced fairly if the call-adjusted yield for a callable bond is the proper yield for a noncallable bond with the same features and of the same issuer. A bond is rich or overvalued if the call-adjusted yield is less; it is cheap or undervalued if the call-adjusted yield is more.

Bond Price Volatility of a Callable Bond

As explained earlier, the two parameters of a bond that determine price volatility are duration and convexity. The duration of a callable bond, after adjusting for the call option, is commonly referred to as the *call-adjusted (modified) duration*.[7] It depends on three factors: (1) the duration of the underlying noncallable bond; (2) the ratio of the price of the noncallable bond to the callable bond; and (3) the sensitivity of the price of the call option to the change in the price of the underlying noncallable bond. The last factor is commonly referred to as the *delta* of an option and measures how the option price will change if the price of the underlying noncallable bond changes by $1.

For a callable bond in which the coupon rate is substantially above the current market rate, its call-adjusted duration will be close to 0. By contrast,

---

7. The formula for the call-adjusted duration is given in Chapter 13 of Frank J. Fabozzi, *Fixed Income Mathematics* (Chicago: Probus Publishing, 1988).

for a callable bond in which the coupon rate is substantially lower than the current market rate, its call-adjusted duration will be the same as the duration of the noncallable bond. Thus, the call-adjusted duration for a callable bond will range between 0 and the duration of the noncallable bond.

The call-adjusted convexity of a bond can also be computed. It will depend on the same three factors that determine call-adjusted duration plus (1) the convexity of the noncallable bond and (2) the convexity of the call option.

Recall that convexity measures the rate of change of dollar duration. For an option-free bond, the convexity measure is always positive. Dollar duration, which is the slope of the tangent to the price/yield relationship, increases when yield decreases and decreases when yield increases. As can be seen in Figure 3, the slope of the tangent line to the price/yield relationship for a callable bond would flatten when yield decreases. Thus, dollar duration gets smaller as yield decreases. This feature of a callable bond is referred to as *negative convexity* and causes the price compression that we referred to earlier.[8]

Horizon Return for a Callable Bond

The call-adjusted yield suffers from the same drawbacks as the yield to maturity: it assumes that the bond will be held to the maturity date and the coupon payments can be reinvested at an interest rate equal to the call-adjusted yield. Instead, the horizon return framework should be employed. The assumptions necessary to compute the horizon return for a callable bond over some investment horizon are the same as those necessary to compute the horizon return for a noncallable bond. However, to compute the price of the callable bond at the end of the investment horizon it is necessary to project both the yield on a noncallable bond and the value of the embedded call option. The latter, in turn, depends on the expected interest rate volatility at the end of the investment horizon.

For a mortgage pass-through security, two additional assumptions are required. First, the prepayment rate between the time of purchase and the end of the investment horizon must be projected in order to obtain the cash flow from the mortgage pass-through security. Because the cash flow includes coupon interest and principal repayment (scheduled and prepayments) and the payments are received monthly, the reinvestment assumption becomes more critical than for a Treasury or corporate bond. The second assumption is the prepayment rate that is expected at the end of the investment horizon.

---

8. A call-adjusted convexity can be computed for a callable bond. See Fabozzi, *Fixed Income Mathematics*, Chapter 13.

The assumed prepayment rate will determine the cash flow of the mortgage pass-through security and therefore its price.

VII. Summary

In this article we reviewed the attributes of both option-free bonds and bonds with an embedded call option (i.e., callable corporate bonds and mortgage pass-through securities) that determine their price performance. These attributes are the bond's duration and convexity.

Conventional yield measures such as yield to maturity and yield to call do not provide insight as to the potential return from owning a bond over some predetermined investment horizon, nor the relative value of bonds. Instead, because it takes into account all sources of potential dollar return expected to be realized from investing in a bond over some investment horiozon, the horizon return framework should be used.

Stochastic Valuation of Debt Securities with Application to Callable Corporate Bonds

Lakhbir S. Hayre, D. Phil.
Vice-President & Head of Mortgage Research
Financial Strategies Group
Prudential-Bache Capital Funding

Kenneth Lauterbach
Senior Associate, Financial Strategies Group
Prudential-Bache Capital Funding

I. Introduction

The proper valuation of debt securities is generally recognized as one of the central problems in quantitative financial analysis. Proper valuation is particularly important for securities with interest-rate dependent cash flows, such as floating-rate instruments, callable corporate bonds and mortgage-backed securities (MBSs). The dramatic growth over the last few years in the size and diversity of the bond market and an increase in volatility and competitiveness have forced portfolio managers to focus more closely on the investment characteristics of such securities and to estimate their relative value within the spectrum of fixed-income securities.

This article describes stochastic analysis, a general and consistent valuation methodology that can be used to compare debt securities with widely differing cash-flow patterns. It differs from traditional bond valuation in two major ways. First, instead of using constant discount rates to calculate the present values of cash flows, it uses discount rates derived from the term

Copyright © 1988 Prudential-Bache Capital Funding.
The authors would like to thank Robert Samuel for his assistance with the section on corporate bonds; Cyrus Mohebbi for his assistance with the statistical analysis; Gladys Cardona for preparation of this article; David Audley and Vincent Pica for their helpful comments; and Lisa Pendergast, Joseph Reel, and Efren Alba for their editorial assistance.

structure of interest rates. Second, instead of assuming that interest rates remain at their current levels over the life of the security, the methodology evaluates a security based on the full range of interest-rate environments that could occur over the life of the security.

Interest-rate movements are described by means of a probabilistic model. There are several different mathematical means for describing and evaluating the effects of interest-rate changes; the approach used here is a statistical "Monte Carlo" simulation by means of computer-generated random numbers.[1] Monte Carlo simulation generates a large number of random paths for interest rates in a way that is consistent with both the term structure of interest rates and their historical behavior. A security's cash flows are then obtained along each path. A value of the security for each interest-rate path is obtained by calculating the present value of its cash flows using discount rates based on that path. The distribution of these security values gives a risk/reward profile for the security.

A key output of the analysis is a spread, usually referred to as the *option-adjusted spread* (OAS), which represents an incremental return over the Treasury curve. The probability model used to generate the interest-rate paths is calibrated so that all on-the-run Treasuries have an OAS of zero. In effect, this assumes that on-the-run Treasuries are efficiently priced. All other securities are valued and compared to each other by means of their OASs, or extra returns relative to on-the-run Treasuries; if on-the-run Treasuries give a "riskless" rate of return, then the OAS is a security's implied risk premium. The OAS provides a return measure adjusted for interest-rate volatility and for the effects of embedded options, and thus allows the comparison of widely differing securities.

The methodology was initially developed for evaluating the impact of the embedded options in MBSs and callable corporate bonds,[2] and hence is often referred to as *option-adjusted analysis* (OAA). However, it can be applied to any security, regardless of cash-flow structure or uncertainty,[3] and hence can be a very powerful tool in the valuation of fixed-income securities. The terms OAA and OAS are used in this article, as they are now well known and accepted by the industry. However, it should be kept in mind that:

> *OAA is a general stochastic, term-structure–driven, valuation methodology applicable to securities with or without embedded options, whereas*

---

1. The other main approaches are continuous time-diffusion processes, which lead to differential equations (this was the approach in Kenneth B. Dunn and John J. McConnell, "Valuation of GNMA Mortgage-Backed Securities," *Journal of Finance* (December 1981)); and binomial lattices (used in Thomas S.Y. Ho and Sang-Bin Lee, "Term Structure Movements and Pricing Interest-Rate Contingent Claims," *Journal of Finance* (June 1986)). Our model uses statistical simulation since this seems to provide the most flexibility in dealing with complex cash flows such as derivative MBSs, which may depend on several correlated interest rates.
2. See Dunn and McConnell, "Valuation of GNMA Mortgage-Backed Securities."
3. Ho and Lee, "Term Structure Movements and Pricing Interest-Rate Contingent Claims."

the OAS is an incremental return over Treasuries, again applicable to any security.

Section II describes the basic steps in OAA. It illustrates the concept of an incremental return over the Treasury curve, discusses the modeling of interest-rate variation, and describes calibration of the interest-rate distribution against the Treasury curve. Section II analyzes callable corporate bonds. OAA is used to estimate the impact of call provisions on a bond's performance. It is also used to estimate effective durations and convexities for callables, and to obtain projected prices if interest rates change. Application of OAA to mortgage pass-through securities, collateralized mortgage obligation (CMO) bonds and CMO residuals is presented elsewhere.[4]

II. Valuation of a Stream of Cash Flows

Traditional Methods

The standard method for valuing a security is to find the present value of its expected future cash flows using a chosen discount rate. The discount rate that equates the present value of the security to its market price is the *yield-to-maturity* (YTM). A security's extra return relative to Treasuries is obtained by comparing the security's YTM to the yield of a Treasury with a similar maturity. The difference in yields is the security's spread over the comparable Treasury. Interest-rate volatility is generally ignored in traditional analysis; securities are evaluated based on current interest-rate levels, or in some cases by assuming a specified change in rates.

There are several problems in using traditional analysis to evaluate a security:

- In calculating the YTM, the same discount rate is used to calculate the present values of cash flows received at different times. This ignores the term structure of interest rates (exemplified, say, by the Treasury yield curve), which implies that the market assigns different discount rates to cash flows of differing maturities. In essence, the YTM is an averaged discount rate that does not fully utilize the information provided by the term structure about the market values of cash flows of different maturities.
- The choice of a comparable benchmark Treasury with which the security's yield is compared can be arbitrary and even misleading. For example, both a zero-coupon ten-year bond and a coupon-paying ten-year bullet bond would be compared with the ten-year Treasury, although the cash-flow patterns of the two securities are very different.

---

4. See Lakhbir Hayre and Kenneth Lauterbach, "Stochastic Valuation of Debt Securities," in *Managing Institutional Assets,* ed. Frank J. Fabozzi (New York: Ballinger, 1990).

This problem is especially acute for securities with cash flows contingent on interest rates, such as MBSs and callable corporate bonds, whose maturity may depend on the future course of interest rates.

■ The effect of interest-rate volatility on securities with cash flows contingent on interest rates can obviously be critical; however, interest-rate volatility can also be an important consideration for straight securities with fixed cash flows. For example, suppose a five-year bond is bought at par, with a coupon and YTM equal to 10%. If interest rates increase to 15%, the bond is worth less than what was paid for it; if interest rates decrease to 5%, the bond is worth more than what was paid for it. In other words, the value of the bond investment is determined to a large extent by future changes in interest rates. Hence, the risks and rewards of an investment in even a straight bond are dependent on interest-rate volatility, indicating that it should not be ignored in the analysis of such bonds.[5]

The valuation methodology described in this article, and generally described as option-adjusted analysis (OAA), attempts to deal with the drawbacks of traditional analysis described above. It differs from traditional fixed-income analysis in two fundamental ways:

■ OAA introduces interest-rate volatility. Instead of assuming that interest rates remain at their current levels over the life of the security, OAA evaluates securities under the more realistic assumption that interest rates are likely to vary in an unpredictable manner over the life of the security.

■ In OAA, each cash flow from the security is individually compared to a corresponding Treasury cash flow, and the security's higher return is expressed as an incremental spread over the Treasury curve. Since this incremental spread is an integral part of OAA, we start by discussing this concept in the special case of zero volatility.

Incremental Spread over Treasury Curve

A key concept in OAA is that instead of assuming a constant discount rate, discount rates are derived from the term structure of interest rates, so that cash flows at different times are discounted by different rates. In the zero-volatility case considered here, these discount rates generally are termed the *implied short-term Treasury forward rates*. In the general case of non-zero volatility, the random short-rate paths are, in a rough sense, centered around the implied forward rates.

---

5. For bonds with fixed cash flows, the effects of increases and decreases in rates tend to cancel each other to some extent. However, the effects on price of equal increases and decreases in interest rates are not symmetric and hence do not cancel one another exactly. Also, rates may be thought to have a greater chance of increasing, for example, if the yield curve is upward sloping.

TABLE 1. *Calculation of Implied Six-Month Forward Rate.*

Yield of six-month Treasury bill: 6%
Yield of one-year Treasury bill: 7%

The implied six-month forward rate (*FR*) at month 6 is given by

$$\left(1+\frac{6}{200}\right)\left(1+\frac{FR}{200}\right)=\left(1+\frac{7}{200}\right)^2.$$

Solution: $FR = 8.005\%$

In this article, the Treasury-yield curve is used as a proxy for the term structure of interest rates. Suppose that the six-month Treasury bill yields 6% while the one-year Treasury bill yields 7%. In other words, for Treasury cash flows, the market is assigning a discount rate of 6% to a cash flow six months in the future, and a discount rate of 7% to a cash flow at month 12. Let us call the six-month rate the short-term Treasury discount rate. What short-term Treasury discount rate for the period from month 6 to month 12 is implied by the present yields on the six-month and one-year Treasury bills? The answer, as shown in Table 1, is approximately 8%. This is called the *implied six-month forward rate*. If the cash flow one year from now is discounted by the current six-month rate of 6% for the first six months and the the implied six-month forward rate of 8% for the next six months, then its present value is the same as discounting by the one-year rate of 7%.

By using Treasuries of longer maturities, we can obtain implied short-term Treasury discount rates for up to thirty years in the future. If the cash flows from any on-the-run Treasury are discounted by the implied short-term discount rates, then the present value of the cash flows will equal the current price of the security. The set of discount rates for different maturities obtained by this procedure is sometimes called the *implied forward curve*.

Interpretation of Implied Forward Rates It is important to note that using the implied discount rate does not necessarily constitute an opinion on the direction of interest-rate moves.

In the example in Table 1, using a six-month discount rate of 8% for the period from month six to month 12 does not necessarily mean that the six-month Treasury bill yield is expected to be 8% at month six. However, to be consistent with the current market pricing of six-month and one-year Treasury bills, a discount rate of 8% must be used for that period. In addition to expectations of interest-rate moves, there are various possible reasons for the market dictating this implied forward rate. These reasons include liquidity, the current preferences or needs of major buyers of securities of differing maturities (the *market segmentation* hypothesis), and the risk-averse nature of most market players; collectively, these reasons are often labeled *term premia.*[6]

Calculation of Incremental Spread   As an illustration, consider a one-year security priced at $94.50, with two cash flows: $50 at month 6 and $50 at month 12. If these cash flows are discounted by the short-term Treasury rates shown in Table 1 (i.e., 6% for the first six months, and the implied rate of 8% for the next six months), the security's present value is

$$PV = \frac{\$50}{(1+6/200)} + \frac{\$50}{(1+6/200)(1+8/200)} = \$95.26.$$

Thus, if the security were a Treasury, it would be priced at $95.26. However, it is not a Treasury, and it is priced lower, at $94.50. What spread over Treasury yields is implied by this lower price? Table 2 illustrates the calculation of this incremental spread.

For a specified spread, the first cash flow at month 6 is discounted by the six-month–Treasury-bill rate plus the spread, whereas the cash flow at month 12 is discounted by the six-month rate plus the spread for the first six

6. For a good discussion of this topic, see Richard W. McEnally, "The Term Structure of Interest Rates," in *The Handbook of Fixed Income Securities,* ed. Frank J. Fabozzi and Irving M. Pollack (Homewood, Ill.: Dow Jones–Irwin, 1987), Chapter 53.

TABLE 2. *Incremental Return over Treasuries.*

Security Price: $94.50
Cash Flows: $50 at month six, $50 at month 12

Present value of cash flows at various spreads over six-month Treasury rate (6%) and implied forward six-month rate (8%):

Spread = 100 bp:

$$\frac{\$50}{(1+[6+1.00]/200)} + \frac{\$50}{(1+[6+1.00]/200)(1+[8+1.00]/200)} = \$94.53$$

Spread = 105 bp:

$$\frac{\$50}{(1+[6+1.05]/200)} + \frac{\$50}{(1+[6+1.05]/200)(1+[8+1.05]/200)} = \$94.50$$

Spread = 110 bp:

$$\frac{\$50}{(1+[6+1.10]/200)} + \frac{\$50}{(1+[6+1.10]/200)(1+[8+1.10]/200)} = \$94.47$$

Incremental return over Treasuries, or the spread that makes present value equal to market price: 105 basis points

months and the implied forward discount rate of 8% plus the spread for the next six months.

The incremental return of the security over Treasuries is the spread over the short-term discount rates that makes the present value of its cash flows equal to its market price. From Table 2, if the cash flows are discounted by the short-term rates plus 105 basis points, the present value is equal to the price of the security. The incremental return over Treasuries is thus 105 basis points.

This example, although simplified and lacking any interest-rate or cash-flow uncertainty, describes the basic concept behind what is generally termed the *option-adjusted spread* (OAS). It is an averaged incremental return over short-term Treasury rates. Since these short-term rates are generated using the current term structure of Treasury rates, one could alternatively say that the OAS represents an incremental return or spread over the Treasury curve; in other words, it is the incremental return over a portfolio of Treasuries that replicates the security's cash flows. Thus, in the above example, the security's cash flows, which cost $94.50, can be replicated using Treasuries at a cost of $95.22. The lower price of the security translates into an incremental spread of 105 basis points over short-term Treasury rates, whereas a hypothetical on-the-run Treasury with the same cash flows would have a spread of zero.

Calculation of Theoretical Value   The calculation described above for finding the incremental spread over Treasuries implied by a given price can be reversed to find the theoretical fair value implied by a specified spread. For example, if the security was a Treasury, then using a spread of zero gives a value of $95.22 for the security.

In general, OAA can be used to find the theoretical value of a security by using a spread similar to the OASs of comparable securities. For example, suppose that, in the case of the security in Table 2, the OASs of other comparable securities are about 80 basis points. Using an incremental spread of 80 basis points (i.e., discounting the security's cash flows by the implied Treasury rates plus 80 basis points) gives a value for the security of

$$PV = \frac{\$50}{(1+[6+0.80]/200)} + \frac{\$50}{(1+[6+0.80]/200)(1+[8+0.80]/200)}$$
$$= \$94.88.$$

Since the actual price of the security is $94.50, the security is cheap relative to comparable securities. (This conclusion is also implied, of course, by the fact that its OAS is 105 basis points compared with 80 basis points for comparable securities. In one case, we obtain the relative richness or cheapness in spread terms, and in the other case we obtain this relationship in price terms.)

Interest-Rate and Cash-Flow Uncertainty

The examples in Table 1 and Table 2 illustrate the basic elements of the option-adjusted methodology in the special case of zero interest-rate volatility. The steps involved in stochastic OAA in the general case of non-zero interest-rate volatility may be summarized as follows:

1. Model the fluctuations in interest rates over the life of the security in a manner that is consistent with both the term structure of interest rates and historical behavior of interest rates.
2. Obtain cash flows for the security along each interest-rate path.
3. For a chosen incremental spread over Treasuries, obtain present values for the cash flows along each possible interest-rate path by discounting by the short-term Treasury rates along the path plus the spread. The average of these present values over all possible interest-rate paths is the theoretical security value corresponding to the given spread.
4. Calculate the incremental spread over Treasuries implied by the market price of the security. This is the *option-adjusted spread*.

Figure 1 gives a schematic representation of this process. A mathematical formulation appears in the Appendix.

Modeling Interest-Rate Fluctuations As is common in modeling interest-rate movements, we assume that percentage changes in interest rates have a bell-shaped or normal frequency curve.[7] Computer-generated random numbers are used to obtain paths of interest rates, with the random numbers scaled so that the volatility displayed by the simulated interest-rate movements matches observed market volatilities. The number of possible interest-rate paths that could occur over the term of the security is theoretically infinite. Hence, a sufficient number of paths are randomly chosen so as to obtain an adequate statistical representation of the whole universe of possible paths.

Fluctuations in short-term Treasury discount rates should be modeled in a manner that is consistent with the term structure. In this article, consistency with term structure means that all on-the-run Treasuries have a zero incremental spread over the Treasury curve (i.e., over the short-term-forward-rate paths), when averaged across possible interest-rate paths. In other words, the average present value of an on-the-run Treasury, obtained by discounting its cash flows by the short-term rates and then averaging across interest-rate paths, is equal to the market price of the security. Note that this

---

7. The interest rate is said to be *lognormal*. A *mean reversion* process is applied to stop the rates from going to abnormally high or low levels. The Appendix gives a more detailed description of the interest-rate generation process.

FIGURE 1. *Option-Adjusted Valuation of a Security.*

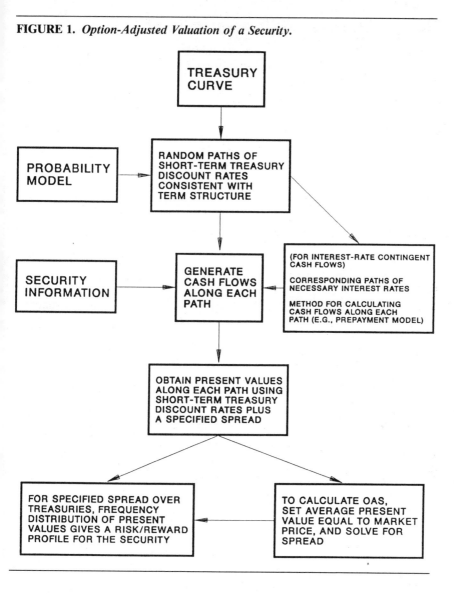

is a direct extension of the "no interest-rate uncertainty" case described in the previous section; if there is zero interest-rate volatility, this method is identical to that shown in Table 1.

This technique of calibrating interest-rate movements against the Treasury curve appears in Figures 2 and 3, which show frequency distributions of the present values of the cash flows from two-year, ten-year, and 30-year

FIGURE 2. *Distribution of Present Values of Treasury Cash Flows with No Drifts in Short-Term Rates.*

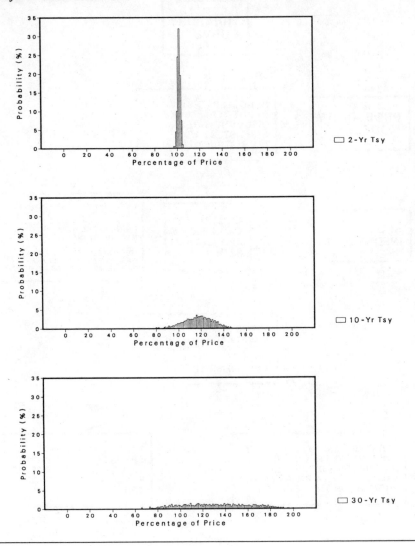

Treasuries. These present values are obtained by discounting each Treasury's cash flows by the short-term rates along each path; thus, each randomly generated path gives a present value for the security. The frequency distributions in Figures 2 and 3 are the outcomes of 2,000 random interest-rate paths.

The distributions in Figure 2 are obtained by assuming no trend in short-term Treasury rates. An initial rate of 5.50% is assumed (this is an extrapo-

FIGURE 3. *Distribution of Present Values of Treasury Cash Flows with Implied Drifts in Short-Term Rates.*

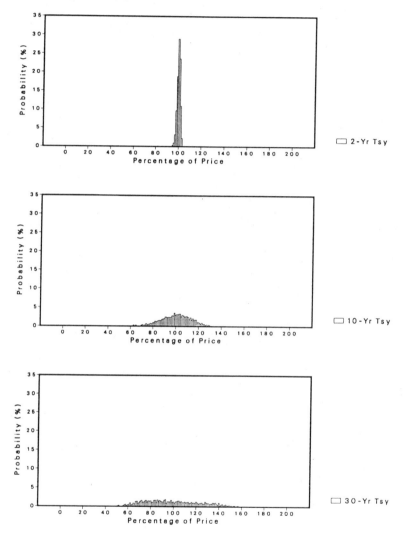

lated one-month rate from the current three-month and six-month rates of 5.77% and 6.11%, respectively). Because the longer Treasuries have higher coupons (or YTMs), the centers of their distributions are higher, that is, the average or expected present values are greater. On the other hand, the dispersion of present values is also greater for longer maturities. The market pricing of these Treasuries (all three being priced close to par) in some sense reflects the market's balancing of the greater average present values of the longer Treasuries with their greater variability in values, and may reflect other factors, such as expectations of interest-rate changes, as well.

Figure 3 shows the distributions of present values after trends or drifts have been introduced into the paths of short-term rates.[8] These drifts are chosen so that all on-the-run Treasuries, including the ones shown in Figure 2, have average present values equal to their current market prices. The drifts normalize the analysis, with the on-the-run Treasuries as a baseline. All on-the-run Treasuries have an OAS of zero; thus, it is assumed that the on-the-run Treasuries are priced efficiently and accurately reflect the values that the market assigns to riskless cash flows of differing maturities. Other securities are then valued relative to on-the-run Treasuries; the on-the-runs, which perhaps are the most liquid and desirable of securities (for a given price), are used as the benchmark for the relative valuation of securities.[9]

Cash Flows on Interest-Rate Paths For straight securities, such as non-callable Treasuries, agencies, or corporates, the cash flows are the same on all interest-rate paths. For cash flows contingent on interest rates, such as MBSs or callable bonds, a method is needed for generating cash flows as a function of the interest-rate path, for example, a prepayment model. See Section II for details on callable corporate bonds.

Present Values on Interest-Rate Paths For a chosen spread, the cash flows on each interest-rate path are discounted to the present using the short-term discount rates along the path plus the spread. If this spread is considered a fair spread over Treasuries for the security, then the present value on a path can be considered to be the fair or theoretical price for the security, *given this particular realization of interest rates*. Some interest-rate paths will positively affect the value of the security, whereas other interest-rate paths will adversely affect the present value of the security. The average of these present values can be considered the fair price corresponding to this particular spread over Treasuries.

---

8. To avoid the connotation that interest rates are expected to trend upward or downward, the drifts can be viewed simply as discounting adjustments made to bring the prices from the model into line with market prices.

9. In principle, the probability distribution can be calibrated against any reference group of securities. For example, if attention is restricted to a particular sector of the corporate market, a set of benchmark bonds in this sector can be chosen as the reference set. However, the on-the-run Treasuries seem to be the most logical reference set for a general valuation method. This process of calibration is sometimes said to ensure that the model is "arbitrage-free," because the objective theoretically is to ensure that the securities in the reference group are fairly priced relative to each other, that is, the model does not indicate arbitrage opportunities between these securities.

FIGURE 4. *Distribution of Present Values for the FNMA 9.35% Debenture of February 12, 1996.*

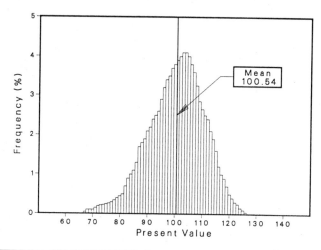

As an illustration, Figure 4 shows the distribution of present values for an agency security with an incremental spread of 50 basis points; in other words, for each interest-rate path, the cash flows from the agency are discounted by the short-term rates on the path plus 50 basis points. Short-term-rate volatility of 15% per year is assumed. The agency is the FNMA 9.35% debenture maturing on February 12, 1996. It is non-callable, hence its cash flows are fixed. Thus, variation in present values is caused by variation in the short-term Treasury discount rates. Because the coupon on the agency is fixed, low interest-rate paths lead to high present values for the security, while high interest-rate paths lead to low present values.

Also shown in Figure 4 is the average of the present values. For a spread of 50 basis points, the average is 100.54; this is the fair price if 50 basis points is considered to be a fair spread over Treasuries for this agency debenture.

Implied Spread for a Given Price   We can also calculate the incremental spread over Treasuries implied by a given price. This requires finding the spread that makes the average present value equal to the specified price.[10] In particular, the spread corresponding to the current market price of the security is the *option-adjusted spread.*

---

10. The spread is calculated by a process of iteration. An initial guess for the spread is chosen, then the average present value is calculated for this spread and compared with the specified price. The spread is then adjusted up or down repeatedly until the average present value is equal to the specified price.

As an example, the FNMA 9.35% debenture of February 1996 discussed above has a current market price of 101.1875. From Figure 4, use of an incremental spread of 50 basis points gives an average present value of 100.54, which is lower than the current market price, so that the OAS is less than 50 basis points. An iterative-solution method gives an OAS equal to 38 basis points; in other words, if a spread of 38 basis points is added to the short-term Treasury discount rates, the average of the resulting present values for the agency's cash flows is equal to 101.1875, the current price of the security.

Differences between the OAS and the Traditional Yield Spread

To summarize, the OAS differs from the traditional spread over Treasuries in two ways:

- The traditional spread is a spread off a single point on the current Treasury curve. The OAS can be viewed as an average spread over the whole Treasury curve.[11]
- Interest-rate volatility is factored into the calculation by allowing random fluctuations in discount rates and, for cash flows contingent on interest rates, calculating the security cash flows separately for each interest-rate path. This explains the term *option-adjusted* spread, since by considering the likely cash flows over the spectrum of possible interest-rate paths, we are averaging out, or adjusting for, the effects of embedded options on security cash flows.

The differences between the OAS and the traditional yield spread is illustrated in Figure 5 in the simplified case of zero interest-rate volatility.

From Figure 5, one can see that in OAA the discount rates used are the implied short-term rates obtained from the current Treasury curve, plus a spread. The OAS is the spread that makes the present value equal to the market price of the security. The discount rates hence are different for different periods. In traditional analysis, a constant discount rate is used to calculate the present value of the cash flows, with the YTM being the constant discount rate that equates the present value to the market price.

Even for securities with fixed cash flows (for which the effect of discount-rate volatility can be minor due to the offsetting effects of interest-rate moves in opposite directions), the OAS is, as discussed previously, arguably superior to the traditional spread as an indicator of relative value against Treasuries. For example, for the agency considered in Figure 4, the traditional spread is the difference between the yield of the agency and the interpolated

---

11. Although it is calculated as a spread over short-term Treasury discount rates, these rates are derived using the current Treasury curve, allowing the OAS to be interpreted as a spread over the whole curve.

FIGURE 5. *Traditional Yield Spread and OAS in the Zero-Volatility Case.*

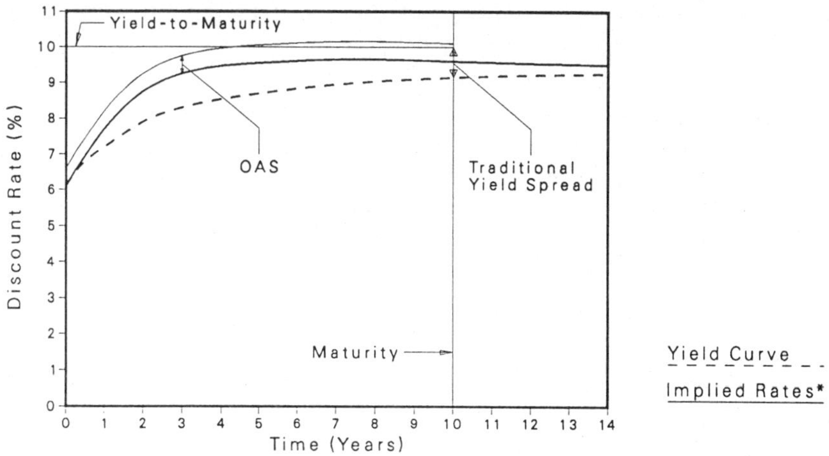

* Refers to implied short-term forward rates.

7.8-year (the maturity of the agency) Treasury yield. By contrast, the OAS is calculated by comparing each cash flow against the appropriate point on the Treasury curve; in other words, the agency is compared not against the 7.8-year Treasury but against a hypothetical portfolio of Treasuries that replicate the agency's cash flows. The OAS thus allows a more meaningful comparison of similar-maturity securities with different cash-flow patterns, such as two ten-year agencies with coupons of, say, 5% and 10%.

III. Callable Corporate Bonds

Most corporate bonds have some sort of call provision, allowing the issuer to redeem the bonds at stated times at specified prices. Corporate bonds typically have a period of call protection, after which they become callable at any time. For example, a ten-year bond may have five years of call protection, and then be callable at par from year five onward. In some cases, there may be a call premium in the form of above-par call prices in the earlier part of the callable period; for example, a 15-year bond may have seven years of call protection, and then be callable at a call price that starts at 105 at year seven and declines to par by year ten and is par from year ten onward.

The issuer's decision whether or not to exercise a call is largely (but not completely) driven by interest rates. This makes the cash flows of a callable bond interest-rate contingent in the sense that the termination of the bond's cash flows depends on future movements in interest rates.

Traditional analysis of callable bonds has tended to ignore the interest-rate-dependent nature of their investment characteristics. Typically, a YTM (assuming no call) and a yield-to-call (assuming the bond is called at the earliest call date) are calculated. The lesser of these values is often termed the yield-to-worst. Although these numbers provide some information, they tend to misstate the bond's value and do not permit an accurate determination of the effective duration of the bond.

In this section, the methodology described in Section II is applied to the analysis of callable corporate bonds. Section III also includes calculation of the OAS of a corporate bond and description of a method for calculating the effective duration of the bond. The methodology also allows us to obtain projected price paths if interest rates change.

Bond Cash Flows on Interest-Rate Paths   Although a corporation's decision to call a bond is largely interest-rate driven, the call option is not typically exercised efficiently. Transaction costs may mean that the bonds are not called until they are "in the money" by at least some minimum amount. Non-economic considerations, such as the desire to preserve investor goodwill, may also inhibit the exercise of the call. Conversely, the desire to retire unwanted debt may encourage the exercise of the call. A distinction must also be made between callability and refundability; while a bond may be callable after, say, five years, it may not be refundable until after, say, seven years. Calling the bond before the first refundable date would imply a *cash call,* that is, the corporation would retire the debt without issuing new debt to cover the cost. In many cases, restrictions on refunding will tend to discourage the corporation from calling the bond.

The approach used here is to use a refunding analysis to determine whether the bond should be called on a particular date. This leads to an interest-rate-dependent *probability-of-call* function, similar to a prepayment model for mortgage securities. The function used here calls the bond if the present value of the cash flows remaining to maturity exceeds the call price by some *Issuer Premium*."[12]

The Issuer Premium is the "cost" that the issuer would incur by redeeming the bond. It incorporates the factors discussed above, such as the cost of reissuing the debt if it is a refunding, the current ability of the corporation to raise new funds, the cost of lost investor goodwill if the bonds are retired prior to maturity, the opportunity cost of not being able to wait for a more favorable market environment if the option is of the American type, the effect of a declining call-price schedule, the transaction cost of retiring the bonds, and so on.

---

12. In a refunding context, this is basically equivalent to calling the bond if the savings in interest expenses exceed the Issuer Premium.

Obviously, there are a several issues associated with modeling this premium, many of which are specific to the issuer, but some of which can be treated generally. A fuller discussion of the issues involved in developing a corporate prepayment model is beyond the scope of this article.[13] The call-decision rule used here, though a relatively simple (compared to mortgage-prepayment models) version of a corporate probability-of-call model, which uses market data to estimate Issuer Premiums, gives results that are consistent with empirical experience.

Option-Adjusted Spreads

As discussed in Section I, the OAS for a callable bond can be interpreted as the effective spread over Treasury rates after interest-rate volatility and the effect of the bond's call provisions have been factored out. Table 3 shows OASs for three callable bonds.

Table 3 shows that the call provisions affect the bonds to different degrees, depending on various factors. The ITT bond has a call that is already in the money and has less than one remaining year of call protection; hence it is significantly affected by the call option. The Marriott and the GMAC bonds are affected to somewhat similar degrees by their call provisions. The Mariott has about four and one-half remaining years of call protection; the GMAC has no remaining call protection, but it has a lower coupon and a call premium in the form of a call price that is greater than par.

An interesting point is illustrated by the fact that the OAS of the ITT bond declines as volatility increases. The ITT bond, having a coupon of 10.80%, is likely to be called at the first call date (July 1, 1989) unless interest rates substantially increase. Hence, at first glance, it might be supposed that because a higher volatility decreases the chances of the bond being called,[14] the bond would benefit from a higher volatility. However, the interest-rate

---

13. Though many of the considerations involved in modeling mortgage prepayments also apply to corporates, it is worth noting that an important difference between mortgages and callable corporates is that prepayments on a mortgage security represent the actions of a large number of homeowners, whereas the decision to call a corporate bond typically is an all-or-nothing decision made by a single entity, namely, the corporation. Given information on interest rates and mortgage characteristics, it is possible to use statistical methods to predict the rate of prepayments on a large pool of mortgages with a fair degree of accuracy. On the other hand, because the decision of a corporation to call a bond or not will be made by one or two people (e.g., the CFO and the CEO), there will always be a degree of unpredictability about the call decision. Fortunately, however, though this is an important consideration in analysis for a single interest-rate realization, averaging a large number of interest-rate realizations (as is done in OAA) reduces the importance of this problem.

14. The *average life* of the bond, defined as the average over all interest-rate paths to the time until the bond is called, is 1.25 years at 10% volatility, 1.41 years at 15% volatility, and 1.50 years at 20% volatility.

TABLE 3. *OASs for Callable Corporate Bonds.*

Issuer	S&P Rating	Mtry.	Next Call Date	Next Call Price	Curr. Price	Cpn. (%)	YTM	Trsy. Yield Spread	OAS at Volatility of:		
									10%	15%	20%
ITT FIN.	A	07/01/92	07/01/89	100.00	101.58	10.800	10.27	168	57	30	-4
MARRIOTT	A−	02/01/96	02/01/93	100.00	99.59	9.625	9.70	85	65	50	37
GMAC	AA−	07/15/07	Callable Now	104.00	84.19	8.000	9.86	82	71	54	41

Note: Based on closing prices and Treasury rates on September 20, 1988.

realizations on which the bond will not be called are paths with high interest rates, so that the cash flows, being discounted by higher rates, will have lower present values. In other words, although a higher volatility may reduce the call risk in some cases, it also increases the interest-rate risk, that is, the chance of a reduction in the fixed-coupon bond's value due to higher interest rates is increased by higher volatility.

As would be expected when dealing with embedded options, volatility is generally a major determinant of the bonds' OASs. The next section discusses a precise method of measuring the cost of embedded options.

Cost of the Embedded Option

The cost of a bond's call provisions to the investor can be determined from OAA. In effect, this values the call option that the investor has granted to the issuer.

The option cost is found by considering a non-callable bond that is otherwise identical to the callable bond. A simple (and frequently used) technique is to calculate the YTM of the non-callable bond, find the spread over a Treasury of similar maturity, and call the difference between this spread and the OAS of the callable bond the *option cost*. However, this method ignores the fact that the regular spread and the OAS are not directly comparable. A more meaningful approach is to value callable and non-callable bonds in a consistent way, and then consider the difference.

The approach is illustrated in Table 4 for two of the bonds shown in Table 3. The OAS of the callable bond is calculated first; this OAS is then used as the spread for finding the value of the non-callable bond. The difference between the values of the non-callable and callable bonds can be

TABLE 4. *Cost of Embedded Options.*

Volatility (%)	Callable OAS (bps)	Implied Non-Callable Price	Option Cost ($)	Non-Callable OAS (bps)	Option Cost (bps)
ITT: Price = 101.58, Coupon = 10.80%, Maturity 7/1/92, 1st Call Date 7/1/89					
10	57	105.06	3.48	167	110
15	30	105.94	4.36	167	137
20	−4	107.07	5.49	167	171
GMAC: Price = 84.19, Coupon = 8.000%, Maturity 7/15/07, Callable Now, Current Call Price 104, Par in 2002					
10	71	84.99	0.80	82	11
15	54	86.33	2.14	82	28
20	41	87.35	3.16	82	41

considered to be the option cost in price terms. Similarly, if the OAS of the non-callable bond is calculated using the callable bond's price, we obtain an option cost in spread terms.

The ITT bond has a coupon of 10.80%, which is 200 to 300 basis points above current refunding rates, making it likely that the bond will be called next year unless rates substantially rise. Hence the option cost is high, even at a 10% volatility. The GMAC, on the other hand, is a deep-discounted bond with an "out-of-the-money" option; hence, its option cost is relatively low at a 10% volatility but increases at higher volatilities, which increase the value of the embedded option.

Comparison with an Option-Pricing Approach   As the above analysis indicates, it is possible to view a callable bond as a combination of a long position in a straight non-callable bond and a short position in a call option. This approach has been used to obtain the value of callable bonds.[15] The non-callable bond is valued using standard techniques, and the price of the option is calculated by means of an option-pricing model. The value of the option is then subtracted from the value of the non-callable bond to obtain the value of the callable bond. However, the results from this option-pricing approach must be interpreted carefully, and do not coincide in general with OAA, which values the callable bond directly. There are several reasons for this:

- OAA values the non-callable bond in the same way that it values the callable bond, so that a direct comparison of the two prices is possible. In contrast, the option-pricing approach often values the non-callable cash flows using traditional deterministic methods, while using a stochastic model to price the option.
- OAA uses discount rates derived from the term structure of interest rates. Standard option-pricing models typically use a constant discount rate.
- As discussed previously, issuers do not generally exercise their option efficiently. This means that the cost of the option to the investor typically is less than that implied by standard option-pricing models.

These considerations indicate some of the pitfalls in trying to apply standard option-pricing techniques to bonds with embedded options. Great care should be taken in using such techniques to value callable corporate bonds.

Price Behavior and Effective Duration

An important objective for the portfolio manager in evaluating any security is to determine its likely price behavior as interest rates change. In par-

---

15. This approach is discussed on pages 187–193 of the previous article.

ticular, it is necessary to estimate the duration of the security. The usual duration measures (Macaulay or modified) can be inaccurate for cash flows contingent on interest rates such as mortgage securities or callable corporates.

OAA can be used to calculate a measure of effective duration for callable corporate bonds. Such a measure takes into account the effect of interest-rate changes on the bonds' cash flows.[16] The effective duration is calculated by assuming that the OAS remains constant, and by moving the initial value of the short-term Treasury rate up and down by a small amount (50 basis points in this case) and calculating the new implied prices. These new prices also allow us to estimate convexity.

Table 5 shows effective durations and convexities for the bonds discussed in Tables 3 and 4, as well as for non-callable but otherwise identical bonds. For non-callables, the effective duration is essentially the same as modified duration, but is calculated in the same way as the callable bonds' durations.

The effect of a bond's call provision on its duration depends on a number of factors. One is the length of the remaining call-free period; the greater this period, the less the reduction in the bond's duration due to the call features. Another important variable is whether the embedded option is in the money or out of the money. The GMAC bond, for example, is a deep discount, and even though it is immediately callable, the reduction in the duration due to the call is minor. The ITT bond has an option that is significantly in the money and its duration consequently is substantially reduced because of the call.

The technique used for estimating effective duration can also be used for obtaining projected price paths as interest rates change. In other words, we calculate the OAS using the current price of the bond and current interest-rate levels, and then assume that the OAS stays constant as interest rates change. This allows us to calculate an implied price for each new level of interest rates.

Figure 6 shows projected price paths for the Marriott issue and for a non-callable but otherwise identical bond. Because the Marriott bond has four and one-half remaining years of call protection, there is relatively little difference in the two price paths at current-rate levels, but the difference increases as interest rates decline.

Figure 7 shows projected price paths for the ITT bond and an identical non-callable bond. The projected price path shows that the ITT bond has a high degree of negative convexity because of its call features and premium

---

16. An effective duration measure for MBSs was developed in Lakhbir S. Hayre and Cyrus Mohebbi, "Mortgage Pass-Through Securities," in this book.

TABLE 5. *Effective Duration and Convexity for Callable Corporate Bonds.*

Bond	Maturity	Next Call Date	Price	Effective Duration		Convexity	
				Callable	Non-Callable	Callable	Non-Callable
ITT FIN.	07/01/92	07/01/89	101.58	1.1	3.0	−0.3258	0.1872
MARRIOTT	02/02/96	02/01/93	99.59	4.6	5.1	0.2135	0.5683
GMAC	07/15/07	Callable Now	84.19	8.1	8.4	0.5328	1.6818

Note: Volatility assumption is 15% per annum.

FIGURE 6. *Projected Price Paths for the Mariott Bond.*

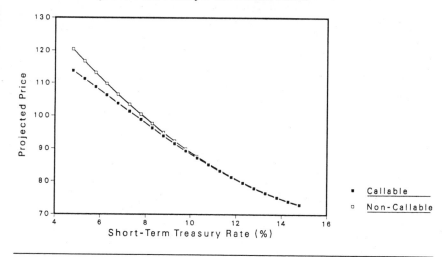

FIGURE 7. *Projected Price Paths for the ITT Bond.*

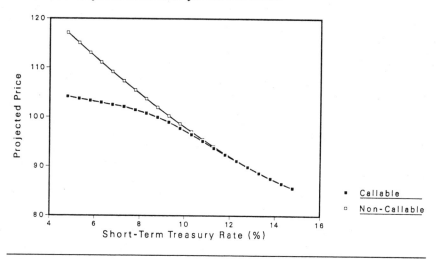

price. As interest rates decline, the price continues to increase (due to the high coupon and the remaining nine months of call protection), but there is substantial price compression, because low interest rates mean that the bond investor is only likely to receive the coupon interest until the first call date. Therefore, the rate of price increase, or duration, is declining; in other words,

FIGURE 8. *Effective Durations for the ITT Bond.*

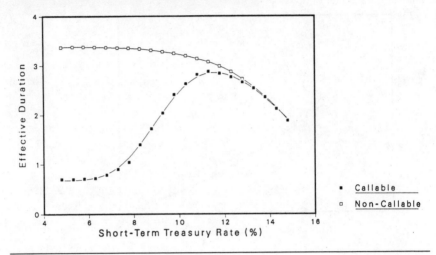

the price path has negative convexity. This relationship is illustrated in Figure 8, which shows the effective duration for the ITT bond as interest rates change, along with the effective duration of a hypothetical non-callable but otherwise identical bond.

The effective duration of the ITT bond decreases as rates decline, in contrast with the hypothetical non-callable bond, whose duration continues to increase. As interest rates continue declining, the effective duration of the callable bond bottoms out; the callable bond is then basically the same as a 10.80% bond maturing on the first call date, because it is very likely to be called at the first call date. Figure 8 makes it emphatically clear that traditional deterministic analysis can be very inappropriate for callable securities.

IV. Summary

The bond markets have undergone a major transformation in the last decade. Volatility has dramatically increased, increasing both the risks and rewards for bond investors. This has been accompanied by a tremendous expansion in the size and diversity of the market. Large sectors of the market now consist of securities, such as floating-rate instruments; MBSs; and callable corporates, which often have complex cash flows dependent on interest rates. These factors have combined to make it more difficult for the professional portfolio manager to identify value in the bond markets and assess the risk of a particular security.

Traditional bond-valuation methods can be inadequate and even misleading, especially when applied to cash flows contingent on interest rates. This article has described stochastic analysis, a bond-valuation methodology that attempts to improve upon traditional methods. It utilizes the term structure of interest rates in calculating the present values of cash flows, and it introduces interest-rate volatility into the analysis. All securities are valued relative to a base reference group, which in this article has been on-the-run Treasuries. This allows a consistent and theoretically sound comparison of different securities, including those with cash flows contingent on interest rates. Historical analysis indicates that these new valuation methods can help the portfolio manager to significantly improve returns.

It is important, however, to note the assumptions and limitations of these new valuation methods. The probabilistic model used to describe changing interest rates is consistent with historical interest-rate behavior; however, there is no guarantee that future changes of interest rates will follow historical behavior. The techniques used to obtain cash flows for a given interest-rate realization (namely, the probability-of-call function for callable corporates) are again based on historical data. Finally, differences in credit quality and liquidity between securities have not been addressed. As mentioned previously, it is possible to develop a more general stochastic-valuation model that includes credit and liquidity parameters.

Appendix: Mathematical Details

This appendix outlines the probabilistic model used to generate random interest-rate paths and the methods used to calculate theoretical values and OASs.

Probability Model

Interest rates are assumed to follow a lognormal distribution, with "mean reversion" modifications used to keep interest-rate paths within historically reasonable bounds.

Distribution of Short-Term Rates   If R_n is the value of the short-term Treasury rate at time n, then R_{n+1} is generated by means of the equation

$$\log \frac{R_{n+1}}{R_n} = \mu_n + G(R_n) + \sigma_n Z_n, \quad n \geq 0, \tag{A1}$$

where

the drifts μ_n are constants chosen so that model prices are consistent with the term structure (see equation (A2) below);

σ_n is the volatility per unit time at time n;

Z_n is a standard normal random variable; and

$G(R_n)$ is a mean reversion term given by

$$G(R_n) = \begin{cases} 0 & \text{if } L_1 \le R_n \le L_2; \\ -\gamma_0(R_n - L_2)^2 & \text{if } R_n \ge L_2; \\ \gamma_1[(L_1 - R_n)/R_n)]^2 & \text{if } R_n \le L_1; \end{cases}$$

where L_1, L_2, γ_0, and γ_1 are constants estimated using empirical behavior of interest rates.

Volatility The volatility σ_n is generally chosen to be constant, but can be a specified function of n or R_n, or else a random variable. In this latter case, a lognormal model similar to equation (A1) is used to generate the stochastic volatilities, with the drifts set equal to zero.

Other Interest Rates Given the short rates R_n, other interest rates S_n, say (e.g., mortgage rates, long-term Treasury rates), are obtained using an equation of the form

$$\log \frac{S_{n+1}}{S_n} = H(S_n)\left[\alpha\left(\log \frac{R_{n+1}}{R_n} + \delta_n\right) + \beta U_n\right],$$

where

U_n is a standard normal variable independent of Z_n;

α and β are chosen so that S_n has a specified volatility and correlation with R_n;

δ_n is the drift "differential" between R_n and S_n; and

$H(S_n)$ is a "drag" coefficient, which is equal to 1 if S_n is within specified bounds and decreases if S_n goes outside these bounds.

Relationship between Lognormal and Percentage-Rate–Change Distributions The use of a lognormal distribution to model changes in interest rates (and in stock prices) is fairly widespread, and is based on empirical results that show that percentage-rate changes tend to have an approximately bell-shaped frequency distribution. The relationship between a lognormal distribution and percentage-rate changes can be seen if we write

$$\log \frac{R_{n+1}}{R_n} = \log\left(1 + \frac{R_{n+1} - R_n}{R_n}\right) = \log\left(1 + \frac{\Delta R_n}{R_n}\right), \text{ say,}$$

$$\approx \frac{\Delta R_n}{R_n}, \text{ since for small } \epsilon, \ \log(1 + \epsilon) \approx \epsilon.$$

Hence equation (A1) can be thought of as a discrete version of the diffusion process

$$\frac{dR_t}{R_t} = \mu_t dt + G(R_t)dt + \sigma_t dW_t,$$

where W_t is a standard Wiener process.

Stochastic Valuation

For an interest-rate path or realization ω, let $R_0(\omega), R_1(\omega), R_2(\omega), \ldots$ be the values of the short-term Treasury discount rate on the path, with $R_0(\omega) \equiv R_0$, the initial rate. For a security of maturity N months, let $CF_1(\omega), CF_2(\omega), \ldots,$ $CF_N(\omega)$ be the cash flows, given this particular realization of interest rates. The basic unit of time in our model is one month, so that for securities with non-monthly cash flows, the $CF_n(\omega)$s are zero except in months with cash flows. For illustrative simplicity, in the formulae below we ignore accrued interest, partial discount periods, and so on.

Fair Value of a Security For a specified spread s, the present value of the cash flows given interest-rate path ω is defined to be

$$PV^\omega(s) = \sum_{n=1}^{N} \frac{CF_n(\omega)}{\prod\limits_{j=0}^{n-1}\left(1 + \dfrac{R_j(\omega)+s}{200}\right)^{1/6}}.$$

If s is a fair spread over Treasuries for the security, the theoretical value of the security, $PV(s)$, is assumed to be the average present value over all possible interest-rate paths. Because the number of such paths is theoretically infinite, we sample a sufficient number of paths to obtain an adequate statistical representation, and take the average of the sample as an estimate for $PV(s)$. In other words, if K is the number of interest-rate paths sampled, we estimate $PV(s)$ by

$$PV(s) = \frac{1}{K}\sum_{\omega=1}^{K} PV^\omega(s).$$

Calibration against Treasury Curve The drifts μ_n in the interest-rate process (A1) are determined so that, for all on-the-run Treasuries,

$$PV(0) = \text{Current market price.} \qquad (A2)$$

Calculation of OAS The OAS for a security is the value of s that makes $PV(s)$ equal to the current market price of the security, that is, the OAS is the solution of

$$PV(s) = \text{Current market price.}$$

Callable Corporate Bonds
Pricing and Portfolio Considerations

Andrew D. Langerman
Vice President
Drexel Burnham Lambert

William J. Gartland
Vice President
Drexel Burnham Lambert

I. Introduction

Selecting corporate bonds is a more complicated task than ever. Credit analysis, the fundamental evaluation of the incremental spread over Treasuries required to lend money in today's rapidly changing environment, has never been more difficult. Beyond this, the nominal spread received by the investor when he purchases a new issue callable bond at, say, +175 to the 30-year pays not just for credit risk, but must also compensate for the risk of early call. The investor has explicitly given the issuer certain valuable options and he must be compensated for these with extra yield.

In the low volatility interest rate environment of the 1970s (before 1979), these options were of relatively little value to the corporate issuer. Today, when rates can move down 350 basis points in a year and up 100 basis points in 6 months, these options can be worth in excess of 80 basis points on long bonds. We have developed an option pricing model to value explicitly the options embedded in corporate bonds and to separate the yield spread into the fundamental credit spread and the spread attributable to the options. Our option-adjusted spreads and call-adjusted yields allow direct comparison of bonds with different call features or different coupons.

The calls in bonds not only affect the pricing, they also strongly affect the performance of bonds when rates change. Bonds lengthen in a decline and shorten in a rally. Option-adjusted duration measures the price sensitivity of callable bonds. This measure will be of primary importance to the portfolio or asset/liability manager who wishes to target a given duration.

Some callable bonds are overvalued given their lack of call protection. Yet with spreads at historically wide levels, many callable bonds exhibit excellent value. When properly analyzed, the corporate sector can significantly contribute to portfolio performance.

There is a darker side to the rally experienced in the credit markets. The sustained surge of corporate bond tenders and redemptions is forcing portfolio managers to reinvest millions of dollars far sooner than planned to rebalance their holdings. But before we jump back into the market with this windfall, let's examine the lessons we have learned.

Lesson 1: When Rates Go Up, You Lose

In June of 1980, AT&T brought to market a 10-year issue with a coupon of 10⅜%. At +75 basis points to the 10-year Treasury, these bonds were aggressively bought by investors. However, the run-up in interest rates did not peak until mid-to-late 1981.

When AT&T issued another 10-year note in March 1981, the current coupon had risen to 13¼%, and the market value of the 10⅜ had fallen to 84.919%. Holders of the 10⅜ would be forced to realize a 15-point loss to swap into the new issue and participate in the higher yields.

Lesson 2: When Rates Go Down, You Lose

Five years after missing the opportunity to buy the 13¼, the holders of the 10⅜ had quite a different problem. By March of 1986, comparable maturity Treasury yields had fallen to about 7.35%, and the issuer's right to redeem the bonds was threatening the holders' high current income. On June 1, AT&T ended all speculation and redeemed the bonds at par, leaving the holders to reinvest at the lower market rates.

Lesson 3: When Rates Are Stable, You Win

Part of the compensation callable corporate bondholders receive is in payment for the issuer's right to redeem the bonds prior to maturity. In a stable rate environment, this right will not be exercised, and the callable bondholder will receive the premium in his coupon payments through the stated maturity of the bond. (In practice, premium call prices and, to a lesser extent, underwriting costs provide some tolerance for rate movements before bonds will be retired prior to maturity.)

Before you get the wrong idea, callable corporate bonds are still wise investments, provided you are aware of all the risks you have taken and you receive adequate compensation for these risks. In this article, we will first examine the features that impact pricing characteristics of bonds traded in the public markets and present a method for assessing the relative value of callable corporate bonds. Once the determination of value can be made, our attention will shift to the performance characteristics of the bonds, which should be considered prior to placing bonds in a portfolio.

II. Value of Corporate Bonds

In its purest form, the value of a bond is exactly equal to the present value of all its future cash flows. In this case, the cash flow schedule can be laid out with certainty (except for the risk of default), so the calculation of the bond's price is straightforward.

Cash Flow Uncertainty

While corporations do occasionally issue bonds of this type, the more general bond structures have features that introduce uncertainty in the timing of the cash flows. The issuers often reserve the right to call the bond from the bondholders at some time prior to maturity. As a result, the repayment of principal may occur sooner than anticipated if interest rates fall.

Typically, intermediates issued for 10 years are callable at par after 7 years. Seven-year issues are callable at par in 5 years, and 5-year issues are callable at par in 3 years. Telephone company issues are generally 40 years to maturity, callable after 5 years at par plus a premium that declines to zero after 35 years. Industrial and utility companies generally issue 30-year bonds that are callable at the time of issue at par plus a premium. This premium declines to zero in 25 or 29 years. These bonds are usually refunding-restricted for the first 5 or 10 years.

The refunding restriction prohibits the issuer from replacing the outstanding bonds with bonds sold at a lower interest cost. However, the company may redeem the bonds using cash generated from on-going operations, the sale of an asset or portion of the business, or the issuance of common stock. For this reason, these bonds are said to be cash callable during the refunding-restricted period.

The second major source of cash flow uncertainty is the sinking fund provisions that exist in most long industrial and utility bonds. Sinking funds provide a schedule for the orderly retirement of principal, usually at par. But the issuers often have the option to double or triple their sinking fund payments and accumulate credits that may be used to satisfy future obligations.

In the case of electric utilities, the issuers usually have an obligation to retire a fixed percentage (1%–2%) of all their outstanding debt each year at par, but they are given the option to choose the issue they retire (called a funnel sinker) or use certain credits to satisfy their obligation. As a result, holders of high coupon issues stand to lose large portions of their positions if the company funnels to that issue, or no bonds at all may be taken if the company chooses to pledge additional property in lieu of sinking bonds.

Bondholders' Risks and Rewards

The holder of a callable bond has accepted two forms of risk because of the uncertain timing of cash flows from his security. The first of these is credit risk; the incremental chance that interest and principal will not be received as scheduled due to default. The other risk is interest-rate risk. At one extreme, interest-rate risk is the chance that the issuer will exercise his call option when it is to the holders' economic disadvantage. At the other extreme it is the chance that the bondholder will be forced to hold a low-coupon bond in a rising rate environment.

Fortunately, neither of these risks is borne without compensation. To lure investors to buy corporate bonds, the issuers offer yields that exceed the yields on comparable Treasury securities. The price paid for a bond is fair when the gross spread to the Treasury yield curve adequately reflects the risks being assumed by the bondholder.

The question of creditworthiness is a complicated one based on many subjective forecasts and opinions (e.g., cash flow and profitability projections, the ability and goals of management, and opinions of accountants and analysts). For the purposes of this discussion, let us assume that the spread required for a given credit can be found. We will focus our attention on the valuation of the interest-rate risk component of the gross spread. A callable bond will be deemed fairly valued if the residual spread is adequate for the issuer's credit.

III. Determining Relative Value for Callable Bonds

There are many ways to determine the relative value of corporate bonds with embedded call options. For example, one might propose a specific interest rate scenario for the future and evaluate a selected security at several points in the future. If the bond would be called away at any of these points, a yield to that call date can be calculated and value determined. The shortcoming of this method is that it requires a fairly accurate prediction of the level of future interest rates. If one knew what rates would do in the future, there would be no uncertainty in the timing of the cash flows, and the valuation process would be identical to that of the bullet mentioned earlier.

We have chosen a volatility-based options pricing model, which explicitly calculates the value of the options. This approach subjects the callable bond to a range of interest rate scenarios determined by the perceived level of market interest rate volatility. The bond is valued at regular intervals through its stated maturity under all prevailing interest rate profiles. The results are weighted to reflect the probability of actually experiencing a particular environment.

This method does not depend on an accurate prediction of future interest rates, but merely on an assessment of the variability of the rates. On the contrary, the probabilistic approach recognizes the random nature of rate movements (sometimes up, sometimes down). The value assigned to the bond is, in a sense, a weighted average of the value for each rate scenario.

While it is useful to know how much the issuer has implicitly paid for the right to redeem his bonds, we find it most useful to express value in terms of the call-adjusted spread to the Treasury yield curve. The technique allows us to rank bonds based solely on the credit of the issuer. More importantly, if the call-adjusted spread for a particular bond exceeds the credit spread determined by the traditional analysis of creditworthiness, the bond is relatively cheap and should be an attractive buy candidate. On the other hand, if the call-adjusted spread is less than the traditionally derived credit spread, one concludes the price does not reflect the full value of the embedded calls and the bond should be sold/not bought.

IV. What is Volatility and Why Is It Important?

Volatility in the present context is the magnitude of variation in market interest rates and is measured by the standard deviation of changes in absolute yields. Just as changes in yields cause corresponding changes in bond prices, increases in interest rate volatility cause the value of the embedded options to increase, leaving less of the quoted spread to pay for the credit risk. Put simply, volatility gives time value to the options.

Throughout the 1960s and early 1970s volatility was a relatively stable 50–65 basis points per year, as shown in Figure 1. At this level of volatility, the value of the options embedded in the 30-year bonds is only about 25 basis points, depending on the specific structure (see Table 1), and the failure to recognize the options was of little consequence.

However, when the Federal Reserve stopped regulating interest rates and began focusing on the money supply in October, 1979, volatility shot up to over 200 basis points per year. It has once again stabilized somewhat. However, the new level is about 150 basis points per year. This makes the calls on long bonds worth about 120–150 basis points at this volatility. As you can see, the call premium is now a much more significant portion of the quoted yield.

FIGURE 1.

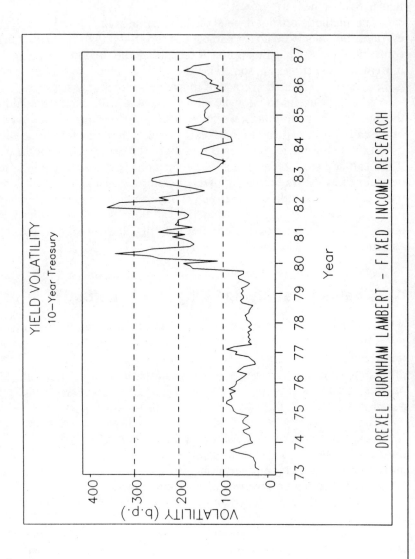

TABLE 1. *Allocation of Quoted Spread Current Coupon Bonds at Various Volatilities.*[a]

| | Yrs. to Mat. | Yrs. to Call | Quoted[a] Sprd. (bp) | Volatility | | | | | |
| | | | | 150 | | 100 | | 50 | |
				Adj. Sprd.	Opt. Prem.	Adj. Sprd.	Opt. Prem.	Adj. Sprd.	Opt. Prem.
Aa intermediate industrials	10	7	79	41	38	57	22	72	7
	7	5	86	60	26	73	13	83	3
	5	3	84	43	40	60	23	76	8
Aa intermediate utilities	10	5	84	40	44	63	20	80	3
	7	5	86	60	26	73	13	83	3
	5	3	94	53	40	70	23	86	8
Aa intermediate finance	10	7	74	36	38	52	22	66	7
	7	5	76	50	26	63	12	73	3
	5	3	84	43	40	60	23	76	8
Aa long industrials	30	10	120–125	2	119	56	65	100	21
Aa long utilities	30	5	155–165	16	147	85	78	139	23
Aa long phones	40	5	158	−12	167	68	88	129	26

a. As of October 1, 1986.

V. Portfolio Considerations

Once a bond has been identified as a buy candidate, its performance characteristics must be evaluated against the portfolio's goals. The traditional portfolio manager has always been faced with the choice of evaluating the bond to its stated maturity or recognizing that the bond may be redeemed and evaluating to the redemption date. This means choosing between radically different measures of such quantities as yield, average life, and modified duration (see Table 2).

Intuitively, it would seem that the callable bond is really a hybrid of a bond with the stated maturity and one that "matures" on the first redemption date. Then it would follow that the effective modified duration and expected life of the bond would be somewhere between these limiting cases.

The effective modified duration is computed by evaluating the price of the callable bond after a small parallel shift in the yield curve. The percentage change in the price for this small yield change is then explicitly calculated. Expected life is the weighted average time to redemption of the bonds. The weights used are the probability of being called at each evaluation point. Table 3 shows these relationships for several bonds.

The question remains, how are callable bonds perceived in the market? If the market totally ignores the embedded options, then the traditional modified duration should predict the percentage change in the bond's price for a change in market yields. The truth is that the call-adjusted modified duration is a better predictor of the price sensitivity of a callable bond.

Table 4 compares the percentage price change predicted by the two measures of modified duration with the observed change in the price of the R.J. Reynolds 11¾ of August 15, 2015. Observations were made at roughly 1-week intervals during the 3-month period from November 1, 1985 to January 31, 1986. The average magnitude of deviation from the observed change was 1.78% for the traditional MD compared with just 0.65% for the call-adjusted MD. Thus, portfolios matched on the basis of traditional duration are in reality mismatched to their corresponding liabilities, and the portfolio manager remains exposed to the interest-rate risk he sought to eliminate. In addition, such portfolios require more frequent rematching.

VI. Conclusions

A well-balanced portfolio should contain some securities that do well when rates go down, others that are best when rates rise, and still others that excel when rates fluctuate moderately around a stable level. Callable corporates will not perform as well as noncallable bonds in a significant rally, and they will lose considerable market value when rates rise significantly (unlike floating-rate instruments). Yet when rates move randomly in some moderate

TABLE 2. Bond Performance Parameters: Maturity versus Redemption.[a]

Company	Bond Description			Redemption		Measured to Maturity			Measured to Redemption		
	Coupon	Maturity	Price	Date	Price	YTM	Avg. Life	Mod. Dur.	YTC	Avg. Life	Mod. Dur.
ALUMINUM CO AMER	13.875	01/15/11	112.250	01/15/91	106.938[b]	12.28	16.04	7.39	11.46	4.27	3.16
ALABAMA PWR CO	9.375	05/01/16	98.375	05/01/91	106.380[b]	9.54	29.57	9.45	11.03	4.56	3.48
AMOCO CORP	9.875	02/01/16	104.750	02/01/96	104.387	9.39	23.62	9.70	9.40	9.31	6.01
ATLANTIC RICHFIELD	10.500	10/15/95	111.418	10/15/92	100.000	8.65	9.02	5.70	8.07	6.02	4.32
ATLANTIC RICHFIELD	11.000	04/15/13	106.792	04/15/93	106.600[b]	10.25	17.53	8.57	10.28	6.52	4.45
AMERICAN TEL & TELE	8.625	04/01/26	93.000	04/01/91	106.210	9.29	39.48	10.51	11.77	4.48	3.58
AMERICAN EXPRESS CR	10.875	05/15/13	106.606	05/15/93	105.440	10.15	26.60	8.72	10.08	6.61	4.54
BORDEN INC	8.375	04/15/16	94.250	04/15/06	100.000	8.93	28.72	10.04	9.01	19.52	8.88
BURLINGTON NORTHERN	11.625	08/15/15	111.250	08/15/95	105.760[b]	10.39	19.35	8.87	10.09	8.86	5.59
BURLINGTON NORTHERN	9.000	04/01/16	93.750	04/01/96	104.500[b]	9.64	29.48	9.79	10.34	9.48	6.16
BELL TELEPHONE CORP	8.750	04/01/26	94.500	04/01/91	107.500	9.27	39.48	10.51	11.68	4.48	3.58
CHEVRON CORP	8.750	03/01/96	100.250	03/01/93	100.000	8.71	9.40	6.27	8.70	6.40	4.79
CHEVRON CORP	9.375	06/01/16	100.250	06/01/96	104.000	9.35	22.05	9.67	9.59	9.65	6.08
CHESAPEAKE&POTO TEL	9.125	07/01/26	98.250	07/01/91	107.140	9.29	39.73	10.24	10.80	4.73	3.66
DU PONT E I DE NEMO	8.450	11/15/04	95.000	NOW	104.740	9.01	11.09	8.66	110.45	0.10	0.06
FORD MTR CO DEL	10.750	07/01/95	108.875	07/01/92	100.000	9.24	8.73	5.59	8.74	5.73	4.19
GENERAL MTRS ACCEP	10.250	06/01/90	104.640	06/01/88	100.000	8.73	3.65	2.92	7.20	1.65	1.46
GENERAL MTRS ACCEP	8.250	04/01/16	90.866	04/01/96	103.600	9.15	29.48	10.27	10.00	9.48	6.30
GENERAL MTRS CORP	7.500	08/15/93	96.363	08/15/91	100.000	8.20	6.86	5.18	8.42	4.85	3.93
HOSPITAL CORP AMER	9.000	03/15/16	94.000	03/15/96	108.250[b]	9.61	27.44	9.77	10.28	9.44	6.12

TABLE 2 *Continued*

Company	Bond Description			Redemption		Measured to Maturity			Measured to Redemption		
	Coupon	Maturity	Price	Date	Price	YTM	Avg. Life	Mod. Dur.	YTC	Avg. Life	Mod. Dur.
PENNEY J C INC	12.125	02/01/93	111.468	02/01/90	100.000	9.66	6.31	4.46	8.11	3.48	2.74
PENNEY J C INC	9.375	03/01/16	96.500	03/01/96	104.688[b]	9.74	21.33	9.60	10.27	9.40	6.04
K MART CORP	12.750	03/01/15	112.500	03/01/95	106.250[b]	11.27	18.90	8.29	10.91	8.40	5.26
MOUNTAIN STS TEL &	9.000	04/01/26	96.375	04/01/91	107.170	9.35	39.48	10.42	11.33	4.48	3.57
MARATHON OIL CO	12.500	03/01/94	100.000	03/01/87	100.000	12.49	7.40	4.68	12.35	0.40	0.38
NEW YORK TEL CO	8.625	05/15/24	93.000	05/15/91	104.520	9.30	37.61	10.10	11.39	4.60	3.54
PACIFIC BELL	11.375	08/15/24	117.500	08/15/90	108.710	9.64	37.85	9.83	7.98	3.86	3.13
PACIFIC BELL	9.250	03/01/26	97.375	03/01/91	106.060	9.50	39.40	10.18	11.12	4.40	3.48
PUBLIC SVC ELEC & G	7.500	04/01/96	94.189	04/01/91	101.700[b]	8.40	9.48	6.58	9.43	4.48	3.69
PUBLIC SVC ELEC & G	8.750	04/01/16	92.616	04/01/91	106.200[b]	9.50	29.48	9.93	12.01	4.48	3.56
REYNOLDS R J INDS I	11.350	11/01/15	110.250	11/01/95	105.675[b]	10.24	19.56	8.74	10.00	9.07	5.55
SOUTHWESTERN BELL T	11.875	10/18/21	120.375	10/18/90	109.960	9.80	35.03	9.27	8.00	4.03	3.13
TENNECO INC	12.125	05/01/05	106.331	05/01/90	105.750[b]	11.30	11.59	7.25	11.27	3.57	2.73
TENNECO INC	11.125	05/15/13	103.697	05/15/94	104.620[b]	10.70	17.11	8.37	10.80	7.60	4.91
UNION ELEC CO	8.875	05/01/96	99.750	05/01/91	108.880	8.91	9.57	6.15	9.40	4.56	3.56

a. Prices as of October 1, 1986.
b. Bond is currently cash callable.

range, the premium paid by the issuer for the embedded options gives the callable bond a considerable advantage over alternative investments. However, the investor must recognize that by accepting the additional yield, he has taken a bet on interest rate volatility.

So the callable bond investor is left with three choices:

1. Ignore the options and treat all corporate bonds alike.
2. Use a rule of thumb to value the options.
3. Use an options based method to value the options in each individual bond.

Ignorance of the options is excusable when volatility and the corresponding option values are low. But given the current level of volatility, bondholders are implicitly writing calls worth several points every time they purchase a callable bond. Ignoring the options today has a significant impact on current income. The "Rule of Thumb" approach is better, but with the multitude of corporate bond structures in existence, it is hard to believe that a few general rules will adequately cover all cases.

Systematic use of a probabilistic valuation method in the bond selection process will produce portfolios that on average provide better results than other methods. The same law of averages has made millionaires of many Las Vegas casino operators (the house always has slightly better odds). Bond valuation methods like the one discussed in this article let the investor see the true credit spread of an issue after netting out the value of the options. Inadequate compensation for credit quality cannot be hidden behind a large nominal spread that barely pays for all the calls.

Choosing callable bonds for a portfolio is, however, a two step process. Determining that sufficient compensation is being provided for all contingent risks is one part. But equally important is the need to evaluate the bond's performance characteristics in light of the embedded options. Callable bonds are viewed in the market as securities that are shorter than their stated maturities. The purchaser of a new 40-year phone bond owns a security that trades more like a 10-year Treasury in terms of its price volatility and effective modified duration. The decision to include such a bond in a portfolio should consciously reflect this fact, or the portfolio performance will not meet the expectations. Finally, investors must train themselves not to be fooled by the seemingly large spreads of some callables. The issuer's right to redeem the bonds limits their potential to appreciate during a rally. The call price becomes a ceiling. No matter how much further rates fall, the bond's price will not rise.[1]

---

1. Did someone say "negative convexity"? See Kenneth H. Sullivan and Timothy B. Kiggins, "Convexity: The Name Is New but You Always Knew What It Was," in *Institutional Investor Focus on Investment Management,* ed. Frank J. Fabozzi (Cambridge, MA: Ballinger Publishing, 1989).

TABLE 3. *Bond Performance Parameters: Traditional versus Call-Adjusted Approach.*[a]

	Bond Description			Redemption	
Company	Coupon	Maturity	Price	Date	Price
ALUMINUM CO AMER	13.875	01/15/11	112.250	01/15/91	106.938[b]
ALABAMA PWR CO	9.375	05/01/16	98.375	05/01/91	106.380[b]
AMOCO CORP	9.875	02/01/16	104.750	02/01/96	104.387
ATLANTIC RICHFIELD	10.500	10/15/95	111.418	10/15/92	100.000
ATLANTIC RICHFIELD	11.000	04/15/13	106.792	04/15/93	106.600[b]
AMERICAN TEL & TELE	8.625	04/01/26	93.000	04/01/91	106.210
AMERICAN EXPRESS CR	10.875	05/15/13	106.606	05/15/93	105.440
BORDEN INC	8.375	04/15/16	94.250	04/15/06	100.000
BURLINGTON NORTHERN	11.625	08/15/15	111.250	08/15/95	105.760[b]
BURLINGTON NORTHERN	9.000	04/01/16	93.750	04/01/96	104.500[b]
BELL TELEPHONE CORP	8.750	04/01/26	94.500	04/01/91	107.500
CHEVRON CORP	8.750	03/01/96	100.250	03/01/93	100.000
CHEVRON CORP	9.375	06/01/16	100.250	06/01/96	104.000
CHESAPEAKE&POTO TEL	9.125	07/01/26	98.250	07/01/91	107.140
DU PONT E I DE NEMO	8.450	11/15/04	95.000	NOW	104.740
FORD MTR CO DEL	10.750	07/01/95	108.875	07/01/92	100.000
GENERAL MTRS ACCEP	10.250	06/01/90	104.640	06/01/88	100.000
GENERAL MTRS ACCEP	8.250	04/01/16	90.866	04/01/96	103.600
GENERAL MTRS CORP	7.500	08/15/93	96.363	08/15/91	100.000
HOSPITAL CORP AMER	9.000	03/15/16	94.000	03/15/96	108.250[b]
PENNEY J C INC	12.125	02/01/93	111.468	02/01/90	100.000
PENNEY J C INC	9.375	03/01/16	96.500	03/01/96	104.688[b]
K MART CORP	12.750	03/01/15	112.500	03/01/95	106.250[b]
MOUNTAIN STS TEL &	9.000	04/01/26	96.375	04/01/91	107.170
MARATHON OIL CO	12.500	03/01/94	100.000	03/01/87	100.000
NEW YORK TEL CO	8.625	05/15/24	93.000	05/15/91	104.520
PACIFIC BELL	11.375	08/15/24	117.500	08/15/90	108.710
PACIFIC BELL	9.250	03/01/26	97.375	03/01/91	106.060
PUBLIC SVC ELEC & G	7.500	04/01/96	94.189	04/01/91	101.700[b]
PUBLIC SVC ELEC & G	8.750	04/01/16	92.616	04/01/91	106.200[b]
REYNOLDS R J INDS I	11.350	11/01/15	110.250	11/01/95	105.675[b]
SOUTHWESTERN BELL T	11.875	10/18/21	120.375	10/18/90	109.960
TENNECO INC	12.125	05/01/05	106.331	05/01/90	105.750[b]
TENNECO INC	11.125	05/15/13	103.697	05/15/94	104.620[b]
UNION ELEC CO	8.875	05/01/96	99.750	05/01/91	108.880[b]

a. Prices as of October 1, 1986.
b. Bond is currently cash callable.
c. Traditional measurements calculated to refunding date.

	Traditional Measures			Option-Adjusted Measures			
Yield	Avg. Life	Mod. Dur.	Spread to Dur. Matched Treas.	Option- Adj. Yield	Exp. Life	Option- Adj. Mod. Dur.	Option- Adj. Spread
11.46	4.27	3.163	468[c]	10.36	8.70	4.286	342
9.54	29.57	9.450	204	7.95	19.74	6.438	56
9.39	23.62	9.702	188	8.25	17.32	6.938	83
8.07	6.02	4.317	112[c]	7.78	7.15	4.954	63
10.25	17.53	8.568	277	9.06	12.37	5.740	176
9.29	39.48	10.505	175	7.70	27.77	6.875	28
10.08	6.61	4.542	206[c]	8.55	16.64	6.096	120
8.93	28.72	10.035	141	8.37	25.85	9.147	87
10.09	8.86	5.591	281[c]	9.29	14.37	6.321	191
9.64	29.48	9.792	212	8.54	22.68	7.456	110
9.27	39.48	10.512	173	7.66	27.55	6.850	24
8.70	6.40	4.787	160[c]	8.22	8.13	5.550	95
9.35	22.05	9.670	184	8.42	17.24	7.164	99
9.29	39.73	10.236	176	7.49	26.30	6.557	9
9.01	11.09	8.659	153	8.09	7.62	4.265	115
8.74	5.73	4.193	181[c]	8.41	6.86	4.748	132
7.20	1.65	1.458	109[c]	7.06	2.08	1.827	74
9.15	29.48	10.273	162	8.02	23.10	7.807	57
8.20	6.86	5.183	97	7.87	6.29	4.808	77
9.61	27.44	9.770	209	8.57	21.19	7.423	113
8.11	3.48	2.739	145[c]	8.07	4.13	3.174	129
9.74	21.33	9.597	223	9.00	16.94	6.977	158
10.91	8.40	5.256	367[c]	10.15	13.54	5.918	283
9.35	39.48	10.421	181	7.68	26.76	6.692	27
12.35	0.40	0.377	685[c]	10.23	2.67	1.816	391
9.30	37.61	10.104	177	7.60	25.78	6.719	19
7.98	3.86	3.129	121[c]	6.61	13.72	4.702	−47
9.50	39.40	10.177	197	7.75	25.40	6.297	38
8.40	9.48	6.579	99	7.87	7.77	5.407	61
9.50	29.48	9.931	198	8.18	21.09	6.846	76
10.00	9.07	5.547	272[c]	9.17	14.66	6.434	178
8.00	4.03	3.130	123[c]	6.69	13.58	4.656	−37
11.27	3.57	2.734	461[c]	9.80	7.66	4.285	286
10.70	17.11	8.373	323	9.79	13.06	5.990	245
8.91	9.57	6.151	156	8.25	7.93	5.318	100

TABLE 4. *Modified Duration Predicted Percentage Price Change: Traditional versus Option-Adjusted Approach.*

ISSUER: R J REYNOLDS   COUPON: 11.75   MATURITY: 08/15/15
FIRST REFUNDING DATE: 08/15/95 AT 105.875

Date	Price	YTM	YTC	Yield on Duration Matched Treasury		Modified Duration		Percentage Price Change		
								Predicted		
				Trad.	Option-Adjusted	Trad.	Option-Adjusted	Trad.	Option-Adjusted	Actual
11/01/85	101.629	11.55		10.38	10.06	8.09	6.38	—	—	—
11/08/85	102.484	11.45		10.29	9.95	8.13	6.40	0.73	0.70	0.84
11/22/85	102.918	11.40		10.16	9.85	8.13	6.40	1.06	0.64	0.42
12/13/85	105.588	11.10		9.72	9.26	8.25	6.47	3.58	3.78	2.59
12/20/85	107.907	10.85	10.77	9.01	9.12	5.62	6.50	5.86	0.91	2.20
12/27/85	108.384	10.80	10.69	8.92	9.03	5.61	6.53	0.51	0.59	0.44
01/10/86	106.059	11.05		9.83	9.46	8.21	6.46	-5.11	-2.81	-2.15
01/17/86	106.986	10.95	10.92	9.16	9.28	5.53	6.43	5.50	1.16	0.87
01/24/86	105.613	11.10		9.51	9.23	8.14	6.43	-1.94	0.32	-1.28
01/31/86	107.451	10.90	10.84	9.01	9.11	5.80	6.43	4.07	0.77	1.74

Realized Return Optimization
A Strategy for Targeted Total Return Investing in Fixed-Income Markets

Llewellyn Miller
First Vice President
Drexel Burnham Lambert

Uday Rajan
Vice President
Drexel Burnham Lambert

Prakash A. Shimpi
Vice President
Drexel Burnham Lambert

I. Introduction

The fixed-income markets have been characterized by innovation over the past several years. The mortgage sector in particular has seen the rapid growth of new and more complex products such as CMOs and MBS strips. The techniques used to value such securities have also evolved in complexity, with sophisticated models based on option pricing theory used to value option features embedded within securities. Callable bonds, for example, are analyzed as combinations of noncallable bonds and call options, with option pricing techniques used to value the latter.

The substantial increase in interest rate volatility in the early to mid 1980s is primarily responsible for the increasing emphasis on options, both embedded and explicit. One consequence of this emphasis is that recent innovations in portfolio strategy focus on hedging techniques, especially those incorporating the use of options. The basic elements involved in choosing fixed-income portfolios remain unquestioned. For example, the virtues of modified duration and convexity in controlling interest-rate risk are taken for granted.

From the viewpoint of a total return investor, conventional portfolio selection strategies do not seem to provide an answer to the problem of efficiently managing the tradeoff between risk and return. The measures typically used to quantify risk (duration mismatch) and expected return (yield

---

TABLE 1. *Advantages of RRO in Liability Funding.*
- Ensures ability to meet cash outflows
- Matches present values of assets and liabilities
- Handles cash flow uncertainty caused by option features on either the asset or liability side
- Flexible with respect to objectives and targets
  − Allows for multiple investment horizons
  − Accounts for diverse shifts in interest rates
- Identifies untenable positions well in advance
- Determines a risk-return frontier based on investor's targets
- Can incorporate margins for profit and error

---

or spread over the yield curve) have no direct bearing on the one used to evaluate historical performance (total return). This article introduces a scenario-based strategy, *realized return optimization* (RRO), that directly targets total return and is therefore an improvement over existing methods.

One of the most important applications of RRO is in the process of liability funding, that is, choosing asset portfolios to offset future cash outflows. Pension funds and insurance companies, for example, have streams of promised future cash outflows that need to be currently funded. Table 1 outlines some of the features that make RRO attractive for liability funding.

The Investor's Goal

The goal of a total return investor is to identify an appropriate balance between risk and return. In the context of liability funding, an additional requirement is that the portfolio chosen must be able to meet the liability outflows as they come due.

When measuring the performance of a portfolio, return refers to the total return earned by the portfolio over some specified period. This is measured from the cost of the original portfolio and the total market value of the portfolio at the end of the period. When purchasing assets, yield or spread over some Treasury benchmark is often used as a proxy for return. This may be misleading in some cases because the relative total returns on securities over a specific time period and under a particular interest rate scenario need not correspond to their relative yields or spreads.

Risk in the fixed-income markets refers either to credit risk or interest-rate–related risk. Credit risk is controlled through allocation among sectors distinguished by industry and quality. In this article, the focus is on interest-rate–related risk, that is, the risk of the return on an asset or portfolio deviating from what was expected due to unanticipated changes in interest rates.

Currently, the most common strategies used within the context of liability funding are immunization and portfolio insurance. Immunization typically involves matching the modified duration of the assets to that of the liabilities, sometimes ensuring that the assets have greater convexity.

Modified duration measures the sensitivity of the present value or price of a stream of cash flows to interest rates, and convexity measures the interest sensitivity of modified duration. Another version of duration that is sometimes used is Macaulay duration, which is computed for default-free and option-free bonds. It measures the horizon over which the total return on the security is "guaranteed." For example, the Macaulay duration of a Treasury strip would be equal to its term to maturity.

Portfolio insurance involves the continuous rebalancing of a risky asset and a riskless asset, depending on market moves. The riskless asset is often assumed to be an immunized portfolio. Hence, for risk management, this strategy also depends on the same parameters — modified duration and convexity — as immunization.

When duration and convexity are used as targets, interest-rate risk is measured by the difference between the durations and convexities of the assets and liabilities. Active positions on interest rates are taken by increasing or reducing the duration of the portfolio. Portfolios with lower durations do well when rates rise, since reinvestment rates are higher, while those with higher durations do well when rates fall and the price appreciation on the portfolio is high.

Is Duration a Valid Target?

The problem with using modified duration as a target is that it does not provide any information about the return that may be expected from an asset over any particular time period or change in interest rates. In other words, it does not relate to the performance measure, total return. Macaulay duration does provide information about the return on the asset over one specified time horizon. However, the measure itself loses any economic interpretation when the stream of cash flows from the asset can vary across interest rate scenarios, as is the case with all securities with option features, such as callable bonds and mortgage-backed securities.

Since the real concern is total return, why not use that as the target? The problem is that returns on fixed-income securities are generally *path dependent*. The return depends not just on interest rates at the terminal date when the security may have to be sold, but also on how they got there; that is, on the interest rate environment at each previous point in time. This is particularly true of securities with option features, where the prior exercise of an option may affect all future cash flows.

The strategy proposed here, realized return optimization, recognizes the path dependency of returns and uses it to define explicitly targets and risk measures in terms of total returns.

II. Realized Return Optimization

The key concepts in RRO are realized returns, which refers to the return earned on an asset, and required return, which defines an investor's targets.

Realized Return

The realized return (RR) on an asset refers to the total return earned on it over any specified time period. An examination of the components of realized return helps to illustrate the sources of path dependency.

1. *Initial cost:* The cost of buying the asset at the beginning of the period.
2. *Cash flows:* The cash flows received from the asset during the period, including coupons and principal, both scheduled (as on maturity) and unscheduled (e.g., prepayments). These may be path dependent.
3. *Reinvestment income:* The amount earned on reinvesting the cash flows until the end of the period. This depends on interest rates when the cash flows are realized.
4. *Terminal value:* The resale value of the asset at the end of the period. This depends on rates at the horizon date and on previous rate environments. For example, if a bond is called before the horizon, there is nothing left to sell.

The realized return over the period in question is now defined as:

$$RR = \left(\frac{\text{Cash Flows} + \text{Reinvestment Income} + \text{Terminal Value}}{\text{Initial Cost}} \right) - 1.$$

Over any past time period, the realized return on a security or portfolio can be computed easily. All the required data are available. For example, to compute the 1-year realized return on a bond purchased a year ago, the amount paid for it, the cash flows received, the amount earned on reinvestment, and what the bond could be sold for today are all known. In projecting a return over some future time period, however, the only known information is the cost of the security today. The other three values must be forecast.

Cash flows: For a noncallable bond, these are easily predicted. However, for a callable bond, a model is required to predict when the bond will be called in any given scenario. For a mortgage-backed security, a prepayment model to help predict the monthly cash flows is needed.

Reinvestment income: Given the cash flows, reinvestment income to the horizon date is computed at some expected reinvestment rate. For example, one could assume that all cash flows will be reinvested daily at the overnight funds rate. This rate would depend on the assumed scenario.

Terminal value: Particularly for securities with option features, this could be the most difficult component to project. An accurate pricing model is essential.

Sophisticated option pricing models to value the option components of callable corporate bonds and mortgage-backed securities have been developed.[1] These models permit the accurate evaluation of such securities and facilitate forecasting the price at any point in the future under any given interest rate scenario. Furthermore, a prepayment model can be used to forecast prepayment rates for the universe of actively traded and liquid mortgage-backed securities.

The explicit computation of each component of realized return allows an investor to assume a realistic or achievable reinvestment rate for cash inflows from the asset portfolio. This is an improvement over implicitly assuming that these inflows all can be reinvested at the same yield or spread of the original portfolio. Incoming cash is often reinvested at short-term rates before being used to meet cash outflows or to purchase new assets. Should the latter be necessary, the original portfolio itself may need to be rebalanced. Therefore, it may be incorrect to assume that all cash inflows are reinvested back in the original portfolio.

The computation of a 1-year realized return for a 10%, 10-year bond priced at par, in a situation of rising interest rates, is illustrated in Table 2. If

---

1. See the article by Andrew D. Langerman and William J. Gartland, "Callable Corporate Bonds: Pricing and Portfolio Considerations," in this book; and David J. Askin, Woodward C. Hoffman, and Steven D. Meyer, "The Complete Evaluation of the Option Component of Mortgage Securities," in *The Handbook of Mortgage-Backed Securities,* ed. Frank J. Fabozzi (Chicago: Probus Publishing, 1988).

TABLE 2. *Realized Return Calculation.*[a]

Initial cost (price of bond at beginning of year) = 100.00

Cash flow (coupon income over the year)	= 10.00[b]
Reinvestment income (5×0.04)	= 0.20[b]
Terminal value (price of bond at end of year)	= 95.00[b]
Total accumulated value over the year	= 105.20

Realized return = $(105.20/100.00) - 1 = 5.20\%$.

---

a. All figures are quoted as a percentage of par.
b. Projected value.

FIGURE 1. *One-Year Realized Returns.*

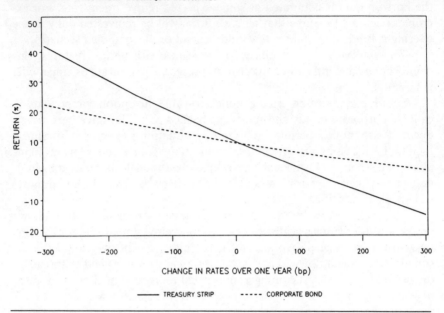

the first coupon can be reinvested at 8% until the end of the year, the rein-vestment income is $0.20 on an initial investment of $100. To project the price of the bond at the end of the horizon, a pricing model is needed.

The way in which the 1-year realized returns on a security depend on changes in interest rates over the year is illustrated in Figure 1. For simplic-ity, it is assumed throughout this article that interest rate shifts are repre-sented by parallel movements of the yield curve. The realized returns are computed for the Treasury strip maturing on 08/15/1997 and the Associates Corp. 7⅝s maturing on 04/15/1998. Over 1 year, the dominant component of the realized return is the terminal value, so that the return on both bonds is high when rates fall and low when they rise.

The 10-year realized returns on the same two bonds under various in-terest rate shifts are shown in Figure 2. The strip matures in 10 years and so has a constant return over that period. The return on the corporate bond is higher under rising rates than falling ones, because cash flow and reinvest-ment income now dominate the realized return.

For any particular time period, an expected (probability-weighted aver-age) return may be computed for each security by assigning probabilities to the scenarios considered. This measure indicates the average return that one may expect to earn on that asset across all interest rate scenarios.

FIGURE 2. *Ten-Year Realized Returns.*

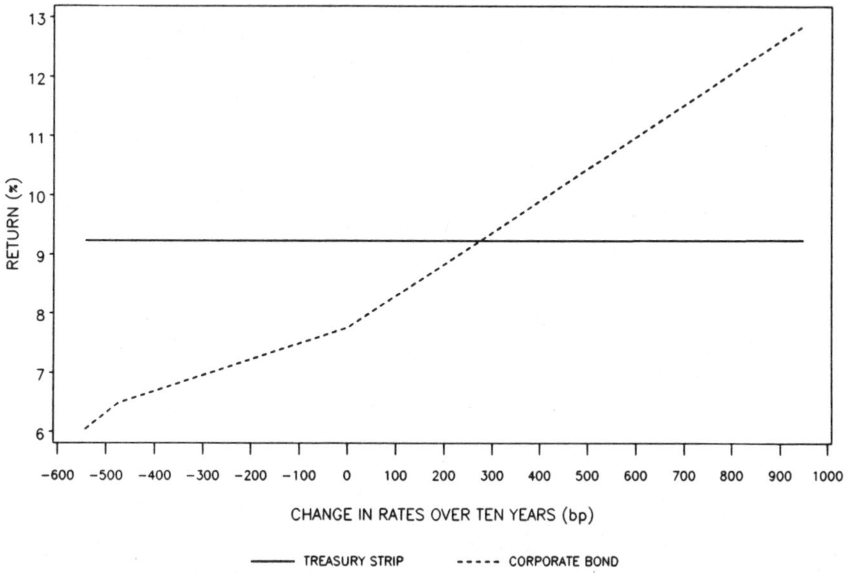

Required Return

Required return (RQ) refers to the investor's target return. Like realized return, a required return also depends on a particular scenario of interest rates and is computed for a particular period of time. An expected required return for any time period is computed in similar fashion to an expected realized return.

Required returns vary among investors, depending on needs and preferences. For pension funds and other investors funding liabilities, they are derived from the structure of the liability schedule. For active managers seeking to maximize return, they may be computed from the expected return on a benchmark portfolio such as an index. Alternatively, an investor can choose in each scenario an acceptable level of return and use that as the target.

In the context of liability funding, the required return can be computed in a manner analogous to realized return. The parallel components are listed below.

1. *Funds available:* The amount available to purchase the funding portfolio.
2. *Cash outflow:* The total cash flow to be paid out over the period.
3. *Borrowing cost:* This is the converse of reinvestment income. For convenience, any cash flows occurring during the period can be assumed

to be offset by short-term borrowing until the end of the period. This component represents the interest paid on the borrowing.

4. *Terminal amount:* This is the amount that must be available at the end of the period to fund the remaining liabilities. It may be computed as either the present value of future cash flows or the actuarially equivalent lump-sum amount.

The required return is computed as:

$$RQ = \left(\frac{\text{Cash outflow} + \text{Borrowing cost} + \text{Terminal Amount}}{\text{Funds Available}} \right) - 1.$$

Table 3 provides an example of this computation for the purpose of liability funding.

The 1-year required returns for two kinds of liabilities under different interest rate scenarios are shown in Figure 3. The first liability considered is a retired lives benefits schedule for a pension fund. In this case, the cash outflows are generally independent of interest rate movements, since the only uncertain element is the mortality rate. For this schedule, required returns vary across scenarios because of differences in the present value of the future liabilities and the borrowing rates.

The second liability shown is a Single Premium Deferred Annuity (SPDA) issued by an insurance company. In this case, the cash outflows themselves are path dependent because of the presence of several option features. The policyholder has the option to withdraw the investment at any time and the insurance company has the option to set the rate at which accounts will be credited. Such liabilities are termed interest sensitive.[2]

---

2. For a description of SPDA features, see the Drexel Burnham research report "Single Premium Deferred Annuity: Product and Risk Considerations," by Prakash A. Shimpi, March 1987.

TABLE 3. *Required Return Calculation.*

Funds available	= $100 million
Cash outflow (at end of year)	= $ 5 million[a]
Borrowing cost	= 0[a]
Terminal amount (present value of liability at end of year)	= $110 million[a]
Total estimated liability at end of year	= $115 million

Required return = ($115 million/$100 million) − 1 = 15%.

a. Projected value.

FIGURE 3. *One-Year Required Returns.*

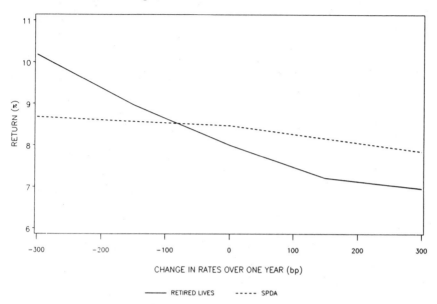

The 1-year required returns for the SPDA are high in all interest rate scenarios because the crediting rate is normally guaranteed for an initial period of up to 5 years. For the retired lives pension schedule, the required returns are high in falling rate scenarios and lower in rising ones. This is because the terminal value, measured as the present value of future benefits, is higher when rates fall and is the dominant component of the 1-year return.

The 10-year required returns for both sets of liabilities are shown in Figure 4. As with the asset returns, these returns are higher when rates rise. This is because the cash outflows are paramount in the return computation.

Specification of the Targets

The path dependency of returns requires that a scenario-based approach be used to project realized and required returns over future time periods. Since the goal is to control interest-rate risk, these scenarios are characterized in terms of future interest rate environments. Each interest rate environment is defined by the sequence of forward rates underlying the Treasury yield curve. Probabilities are assigned to each scenario to facilitate computation of averages for return and risk across all scenarios.

FIGURE 4. *Ten-Year Required Returns.*

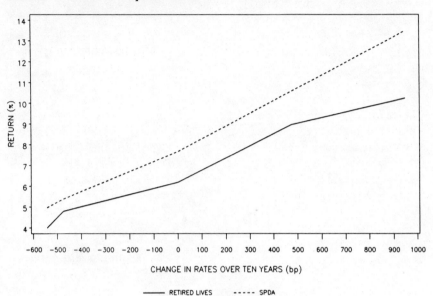

CHANGE IN RATES OVER TEN YEARS (bp)

——— RETIRED LIVES   - - - - - SPDA

The investor's targets are defined by the required returns over specified scenarios and specified periods of time. Theoretically, all possible interest rate scenarios and all possible periods of time may be of interest. As a practical matter, the number of scenarios and time periods of concern must be reduced. Some of the considerations involved in choosing scenarios and time periods are mentioned below.

Choice of Time Periods   The strategy can cater to different investment horizons on the part of the investor. For example, a pension fund with long liabilities may have a long horizon, such as over 10 years. However, the fund also may be concerned with returns over a shorter time period such as one year, possibly due to liquidity requirements.

In general, the investor should attempt to identify time periods that are risky and others that are of concern. For example, for the SPDA liabilities mentioned earlier, the high 1-year required returns imply that the first year is a risky period in rising rate environments. For most investors, a combination of a short term, an intermediate term and a long term (for example, 1, 3 and 10 years) may be adequate.

Definition of Scenarios   The scenarios considered do not necessarily have to be specified in terms of interest rates. For example, a pension fund may wish to examine the impact on its liabilities of changes in mortality rates or rates of inflation, while a taxable investor may be concerned with after-tax returns under varying tax rates.

Moreover, interest rate scenarios may be defined by the investor in any manner. For example, an interest rate scenario may be defined in terms of parallel shifts of the yield curve or in terms of a particular shape of the yield curve at the horizon date(s).

Choice of Scenarios   An investor either can use a stochastic process such as a binomial model to choose and assign probabilities to interest rate scenarios or consider particular scenarios of concern. The probability of occurrence for each scenario can be tailored to suit a particular investor's preferences. For example, an investor concerned just with rising interest rates may wish to assign a very low probability to falling rate scenarios.

As an example, scenarios over a three-stage period are indicated in Figure 5. They are generated from a binomial process that assumes at each stage that rates can go up or down by 100 basis points with equal probability. In this example, each stage is assumed to be 1 year long and the shift in rates is considered to be a parallel shift in the term structure. Figure 5 also provides an example of the implications of path dependence of returns. The interest rate environments at nodes (5) and (6) are the same, but the two points are on different paths and therefore are shown separately.

FIGURE 5. *Interest Rate Scenarios Generated Using a Binomial Process.*

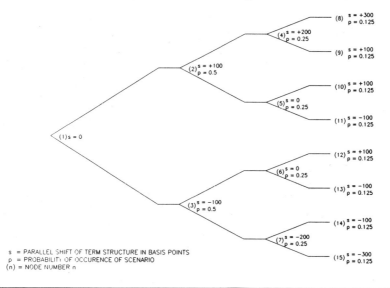

s = PARALLEL SHIFT OF TERM STRUCTURE IN BASIS POINTS
p = PROBABILITY OF OCCURENCE OF SCENARIO
(n) = NODE NUMBER n

Once the targets are defined in terms of required returns, the strategy involves choosing a portfolio that will earn realized returns as close as possible to the profile of required returns. In the most riskless case, this would involve selecting a portfolio that achieves at least the required return in every scenario and for every time period under consideration. It may not be possible to meet these strong conditions. This brings us to one of the most elegant features about RRO—the ability to quantify the risk–return tradeoff.

III. Risk Management Using RRO

Choosing the Best Measure of Risk

In trying to achieve a target, risk should refer only to the possibility of not achieving that target. Referring to Figure 6, which again shows the 1-year required returns from Figure 3, the risky situations are those in which the realized returns fall short of the required returns. Risk is incurred whenever the realized returns are projected to fall in the shaded region of the diagram, below the required return line.

For such situations, a measure of risk is needed that recognizes no risk is incurred in situations where the realized returns exceed the required returns. The risk measure proposed is the average downside deviation of the realized returns from the required returns. For comparison purposes, alternative measures of risk are examined first.

FIGURE 6. *Identifying Risk over One Year Using Projected Required Return.*

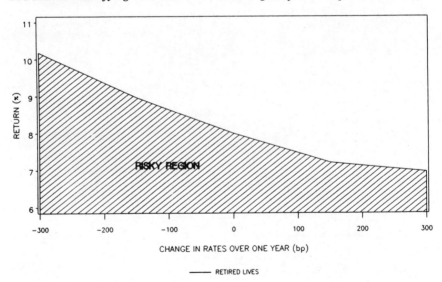

Standard Deviation about Average Return

Typically, the measure of risk used in portfolio management is the standard deviation of the returns on the portfolio about the expected or average return. This was the measure proposed by Markowitz in the context of efficient portfolio selection and the generation of risk–return frontiers.[3] Such a risk measure implies that the goal of the investor is to earn a constant return regardless of interest rate scenario. The implied required return function is the horizontal line shown in Figure 7. Using the two assets referred to earlier, along with several others, a portfolio X is chosen to minimize this risk measure for an expected return of 8.25%. Figure 8 illustrates the 1-year realized returns on this portfolio.

Total Deviation about Required Returns

Figure 7 also shows the required return function considered earlier. In this example, the required returns are also scenario dependent. To facilitate comparison, the expected required return is 8.25% in this case as well. From the figure, it is seen that a portfolio that would earn a constant 8.25% in all scenarios would have no risk in a Markowitz sense, since the average return is always earned. However, it would result in the investor missing the target in falling interest rate scenarios. This is indicated by region 1 in Figure 7.

---

3. See Harry M. Markowitz, "Portfolio Selection," *Journal of Finance* (March 1952): 77–91.

FIGURE 7. *Identifying Risk over One Year Using Implied Required Return.*

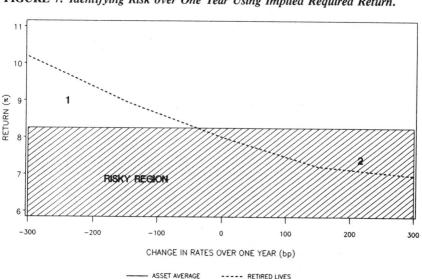

FIGURE 8. *Portfolio X Chosen to Minimize Variance of Returns.*

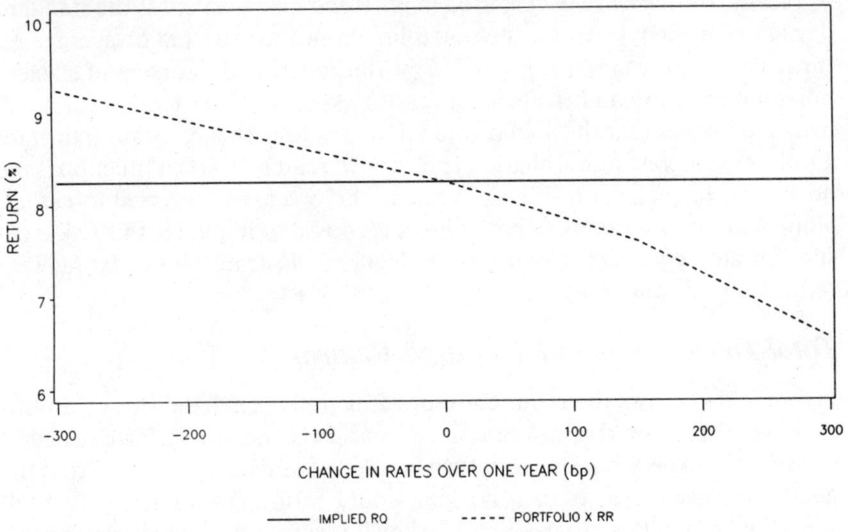

This suggests that a more appropriate measure of risk would be deviation from the required return in each scenario rather than the overall average return. Referring back to Figure 7, a portfolio manager would be willing to surrender some of the gains in the rising rate scenarios (region 2) to cover losses under falling rates (region 1). Minimizing this measure would result in a portfolio with a realized return profile closer to the required returns. Figure 9 shows the one-year realized returns on a portfolio Y, which minimizes this measure without regard to the expected return.

Downside Deviation about Required Returns

A measure that minimizes total deviation of realized returns about required returns would consider upside deviations from required returns to be as risky as downside ones. In other words, if in one scenario the required return was 8%, a portfolio that earned 10% would be considered as risky as one that earned 6%. This is inappropriate, because all risk has been removed once the target is met. A portfolio that earns a return in excess of the required return should be desired, not shunned. Therefore, the most appropriate measure of risk would be downside deviation from the required returns.

Intuitively, minimizing the total deviation about the required returns results in a portfolio that matches the required return profile as closely as possible, while using downside deviation results in a portfolio that matches or exceeds the required returns. The latter situation is preferred.

FIGURE 9. *Portfolio Y Chosen to Minimize Total Deviation of RR about RQ.*

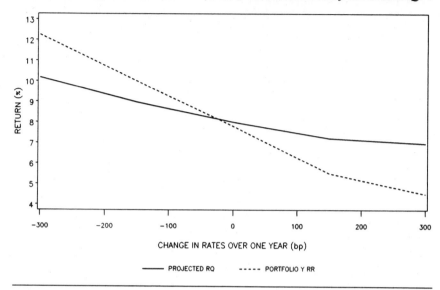

FIGURE 10. *Portfolio Z Chosen to Minimize Downside Deviation of RR about RQ.*

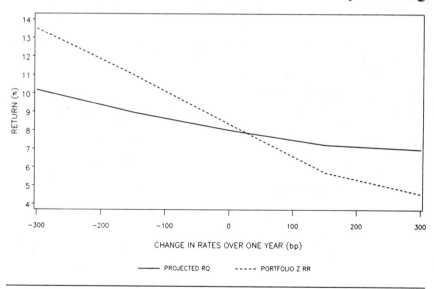

The performance over 1 year of a portfolio Z is shown in Figure 10. This portfolio minimizes the downside deviation from the required returns for all levels of expected return.

FIGURE 11. *Comparison of Portfolios X, Y and Z.*

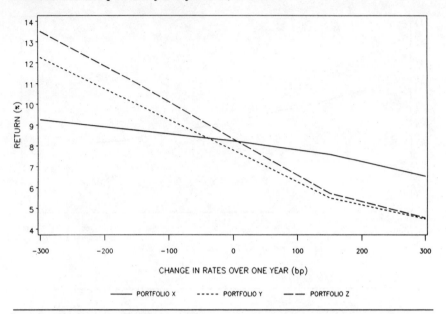

Comparison of the Three Measures

For purposes of comparison, the realized returns of the three portfolios X, Y, and Z are illustrated in Figure 11. Portfolio X earns the most stable returns across all scenarios, but does not match the required returns very well. Portfolio Z, which minimizes downside deviation from the required returns, dominates (that is, in each scenario earns higher returns than) portfolio Y, which minimizes total deviation from required returns. This need not always happen. It occurs here because minimizing total deviation penalizes both the upside and the downside equally, whereas minimizing downside deviation penalizes just the downside and allows the upside to be unrestricted. The reverse situation can never happen; that is, the portfolio minimizing total deviation will never dominate in all scenarios the portfolio that minimizes downside deviation.

The Risk–Return Frontier

Now that downside deviation from the required returns is defined as the appropriate measure of risk, the least risky portfolio for any level of expected return can be determined. This generates a risk–return frontier that defines the set of efficient portfolios. A portfolio is said to be efficient if it earns the

FIGURE 12. *Risk–Return Frontier.*

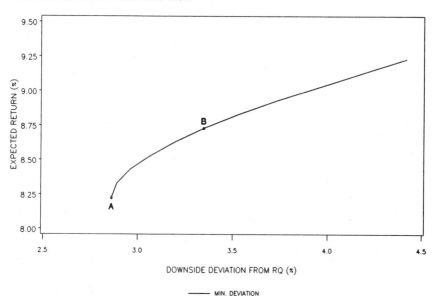

maximum return for any given level of risk. An investor wishing to avoid risk would prefer portfolios on the risk–return frontier to those within it.

A risk–return frontier is shown in Figure 12. All efficient portfolios are on the line representing the frontier. The area below the line indicates portfolios that result in unnecessary risk being incurred. No portfolio would lie in the area above the line because risk cannot be further reduced for any level of expected return. Along the frontier, the risk of not achieving the required returns increases with higher levels of expected return, as the investor trades off higher projected gains in some scenarios with higher projected losses in others.

Given a risk–return frontier for any set of required returns, the investor must choose a preferred level of expected return and find the least risky portfolio for that return from the frontier. By moving along the risk–return frontier, the investor can trade off risk for return in an efficient manner. For example, from Figure 12, portfolio A would be the least risky portfolio for all levels of expected return. An investor wishing to earn a higher return could instead choose portfolio B, which has both a higher return and a higher risk than A. This position is achieved by trading off higher returns in situations where the realized return exceeds the required return against lower returns in situations where the realized return falls short of the target.

Alternative Objectives

One of the biggest advantages of RRO is its flexibility. This adaptivity has already been mentioned in the context of choosing scenarios and time horizons. The strategy is also flexible with regard to the following goals that can be used to choose a portfolio.

1. Minimize risk across some particular scenarios (for example, just the upward sloping scenarios) rather than the entire set of scenarios.
2. Maximize expected return across either the entire set of scenarios or a chosen subset.
3. Maximize the spread earned over the required returns in some or all scenarios. This is particularly appropriate in situations where there is no risk, that is, where the required returns are met in all scenarios.

IV. Applications of RRO

Any situation where an investor wishes to maximize total return with control over risk presents a potential application of RRO. The differences in the various situations where it can be applied stem purely from the methods used to determine the required returns. Once the targets are fixed, the strategy adopted is the same.

Below, one application of RRO is presented in detail within the context of liability funding. It is compared to the previously mentioned strategies that are currently used in that context.

Liability Funding

This presents one of the most useful areas for the application of RRO. The strategies currently used — portfolio insurance and immunization — were mentioned previously.

Apart from the problems involved with using modified duration as a tool for risk control when it does not relate to the performance measure, there are other difficulties.

1. Modified duration and convexity are local measures, that is, they are valid only for small changes in interest rates. Furthermore, they are static, since they are computed at a particular point in time. Their values change daily. Continual rebalancing is required to maintain the immunized position. As a result two difficulties arise:
   (a) frequent transactions costs are incurred, and
   (b) the portfolio may not be protected against interest rate changes between rebalancings.
2. Modified duration and convexity work effectively only for parallel shifts in the yield curve. Historically, however, the term structure has often experienced changes in slope, with short-term rates being more volatile than long-term ones.

FIGURE 13. *Surplus under Immunization.*

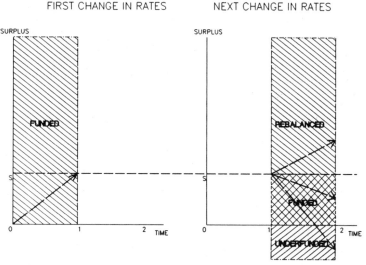

Possible changes in surplus (defined as the market value of the assets less the present value of the liabilities) when interest rates change are shown in Figure 13. Starting from an immunized position at time zero, the first change in rates results in the surplus being in the shaded region, that is, zero or positive. However, this also results in a duration mismatch between the assets and the liabilities and, if the position is not rebalanced, the next change in rates may result in a deficit. In contrast, Figure 14 shows the surplus under RRO as rates change. If times 1 and 2 both are chosen as investment horizons, the realized return will exceed the required return regardless of changes in rates, and there will not be a deficit at time 2. In the worst case, if there is some interest rate scenario under which the required return cannot be earned, that situation will be recognized in advance.

The other common funding strategy, portfolio insurance, attempts to protect the return on the portfolio over the short term. As mentioned before, it often relies on using an immunized portfolio as the riskless asset. This exposes the strategy to all the dangers inherent in immunization. Furthermore, frequent market movements can result in high transactions costs.

Interest Sensitive Liabilities

There is a large class of liabilities where immunization breaks down completely because the parameters on which it relies, modified duration and convexity, cannot be computed with sufficient precision. These liabilities are

FIGURE 14. *Surplus under RRO.*

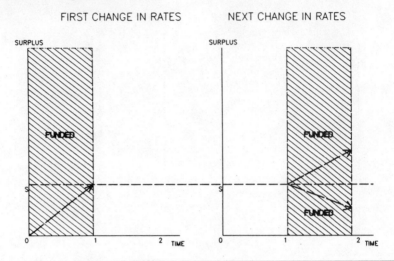

termed interest sensitive because the cash outflows depend on interest rates. They include several insurance company liabilities such as single premium deferred annuities and universal life policies.

Briefly, the estimation of parameters for these liabilities is complicated by the interplay of various option features. The insurance company has the option of choosing a crediting rate to give the policyholder each year and the policyholder has the option to withdraw the entire accumulated investment at any time for a small penalty. Furthermore, there is no market in these liabilities, so that accurate pricing is much more difficult. For such liabilities, RRO provides a very effective solution.

Evaluation of RRO

The key features of RRO that make it appealing for liability funding were introduced in Table 1 and are briefly described below.

1. It ensures that the chosen asset portfolio will be able to meet the liability cash outflows, either through cash flows received from the assets or by liquidating some of the assets. This is because the definitions of realized and required returns include both the cash flows and the present values of the assets or liabilities.
2. For the same reason, RRO ensures that, provided sufficient funds are available initially, the market value of the asset portfolio will at least equal the present value of the liabilities at the specified horizon dates, regardless of interest rate movements.

3. Since RRO is a scenario-based approach, option features on either the asset or liability side are accounted for explicitly. Under each scenario, one can determine when it is optimal to exercise any option. Moreover, when past history is available, as in the case of prepayment rates, one can also account for options being exercised when this seems suboptimal financially.
4. RRO is extremely flexible with respect to the goals and targets of the investor.
   (a) The investor can choose multiple horizons that are of concern in funding the liabilities.
   (b) The strategy allows for diverse shifts in interest rates.
5. RRO explicitly identifies the situations where risk has to be incurred, that is, the interest rate shifts and time horizons where the realized return falls short of the required return. This facilitates the design of optimal hedging strategies.
6. By using an explicit measure of risk, RRO facilitates risk–return tradeoffs, along a frontier consisting of a set of efficient portfolios. The measure of risk is based on the investor's targets, which relate directly to the measure of performance.
7. A margin for profit or error can easily be incorporated into the strategy by boosting the required returns. In situations where there is no risk, the strategy can be modified to minimize the risk related to earning a defined profit margin in each scenario.

RRO does have some potential weaknesses.

1. The set of scenarios used may not be sufficiently representative. The goal in choosing scenarios should not be to consider every possible scenario of interest rates but rather to choose a subset that accounts for the likely volatility of future rates. The scenarios should represent extreme shifts.
2. Accurate asset and liability pricing models are necessary for successful implementation, since computing the returns requires the ability to value assets and liabilities under specified interest rate scenarios at future points of time. For the assets, this is not as drastic as it may seem; the same capability is required by any scenario-based option pricing model such as the binomial model. Valuing the liabilities may be more difficult because of the absence of a liquid secondary market.

Another Application: Active Management

By explicitly quantifying the risk–return tradeoff, RRO enables the active manager to take properly evaluated positions on interest rates. An investor expecting rates to rise could, for example, choose to maximize return in rising rate scenarios, while ensuring that some floor level would be earned even if the prediction were wrong and rates were to fall instead. Using RRO, the investor could analyze the tradeoff between increasing return in rising rate scenarios and risk incurred in falling rate scenarios by constructing a customized risk–return frontier.

For active management, the required returns may be determined either solely on the basis of the investor's preferences or from the expected returns on some benchmark such as a market index.

V. Conclusion

Realized return optimization is a strategy designed to protect total return over any given horizon and under many interest rate scenarios. The key to the strategy is the ability to define the targets in the same terms as the performance measure. The flexibility afforded by the strategy makes it particularly suitable for funding liabilities – especially interest sensitive ones – and for active management.

Strategies presently used for total return maximization tend to rely on modified duration and convexity as tools for risk control. These parameters do not relate directly to the total return on an asset over any particular period of time. In addition to the theoretical difficulties mentioned earlier, it may not be possible to estimate accurately duration and convexity. Interest sensitive liabilities provide an example of such a situation.[4]

A scenario-based approach can be an improvement over conventional portfolio selection techniques because interest sensitivity can be captured explicitly, rather than summarized by two parameters. RRO goes one step further by defining the investor's targets in terms of total returns and using these targets to compute a measure of risk. This enables it to determine the most efficient manner in which to achieve the targets. It is therefore a very powerful and practical tool for risk management in total return maximization.

---

4. Detailed examples of the application of RRO are provided in "Funding SPDA Liabilities: An Application of Realized Return Optimization," by Llewellyn Miller, Prakash A. Shimpi, and Uday Rajan, and "Optimal Funding of Guaranteed Investment Contracts," by Llewellyn Miller and Nancy Roth, in *Fixed Income Portfolio Strategies,* ed. Frank J. Fabozzi (Chicago: Probus Publishing, 1989).

Mortgage Pass-Through Securities

Lakhbir S. Hayre, D.Phil.
Vice President & Head of Mortgage Research
Financial Strategies Group
Prudential-Bache Capital Funding

Cyrus Mohebbi, Ph.D.
Associate, Financial Strategies Group
Prudential-Bache Capital Funding

Few markets in recent years have experienced the rapid growth and innovations of the secondary mortgage markets. Issuance of mortgage-backed securities (MBSs) has reached record levels in recent years, with about $730 billion of new agency pass-through securities being issued from the beginning of 1986 to May 1989. The pass-through market is now comparable to the corporate market and is substantially larger than the agency market. There also has been a rapid expansion in the issuance of derivative mortgage securities, such as Collateralized Mortgage Obligations (CMOs)[1] and stripped MBSs (STRIPs), which have broadened the range of investors in MBSs. The secondary mortgage market constitutes a major segment of the fixed-income markets, and has potential for substantial continued growth; mortgage debt in the United States currently exceeds $2.6 trillion, of which only about one-third has been securitized.[2]

The mortgage market can present challenges to the investor. The typical fixed-income investor has developed valuation standards based on the relatively simple cash-flow patterns of standard bond investments, such as

Copyright © 1988 Prudential-Bache Capital Funding.
The authors would like to thank Valerie Kubisiak, Joe Reel, Gladys Cardona, Patricia Brehm, and Lisa Pendergast for their assistance.
1. For a discussion of CMOs, see Article GG.
2. Data in this article has been obtained from GNMA, FNMA, FHLMC and the *Bulletin of the Federal Reserve Board.*

Treasury or corporate securities. The cash-flow patterns of mortgage securities are more complex. Mortgage securities are self-amortizing — principal is returned gradually over the term of the security, rather than in one lump sum at maturity. A more fundamental complexity arises from the homeowner's right to prepay part or all of a mortgage at any time. Prepayment levels, which fluctuate with interest rates and a number of other economic and mortgage variables, play a major role in determining the size and timing of cash flows. In evaluating the characteristics of an MBS, it is necessary to project prepayment rates for the remaining term of the security. This introduces an element of subjectivity into MBS analysis.

Although mortgage securities are relatively complex, they should be seriously considered by fixed-income investors who seek both high credit quality and high yields. The benefits of mortgage securities include:

High Returns. The complexity and uncertainty associated with MBSs have resulted in pricing at significantly higher yields than other comparable-quality securities. Consequently, in the last 15 years passthroughs have consistently performed better than comparable Treasuries and corporates.[3] Recent yields on MBSs have been between 100 to 200 basis points higher than yields on comparable-maturity Treasuries. The recent yield spread for AAA-rated corporates over Treasuries has averaged between 30 to 90 basis points.

Wide Range of Product. The mortgage pass-through markets include 15- and 30-year securities with a wide range of coupons, as well as adjustable-rate mortgage (ARM) securities and graduated payment mortgage (GPM) securities. Recent innovations have expanded the type of MBSs that are available. CMOs have created short-, intermediate- and long-maturity securities by sequentially segmenting mortgage cash flows. STRIPs separate the interest and principal components of mortgage cash flows to create synthetic securities with a wide range of investment profiles as interest rates change.

High Credit Quality. Agency pass-throughs have a government or quasi-government guarantee as to payment of interest and principal and therefore can be considered to be of higher credit quality than corporate AAA-rated bonds. Non-agency pass-throughs typically have the same rating as the issuer.

Liquidity. There is an active and liquid market in pass-throughs. The major agency pass-through coupons are as liquid as Treasuries and more liquid than most corporates.

Monthly Income. An important consideration for the retail investor may be the regular monthly income from pass-through securities.

---

3. M. Waldman and S. Guterman, "The Historical Performance of Mortgage Securities: 1972–1985," *The Handbook of Mortgage-Backed Securities* (Frank Fabozzi, ed.) (Chicago: Probus Publishing, 1985).

This article attempts to provide a comprehensive introduction to the investment characteristics of pass-throughs.[4] Section I provides an overview of the pass-through market. Section II discusses prepayments and their effect on pass-through cash flows, and Section III discusses methods of measuring the investment life of a pass-through. Section IV describes the effect of interest rate and hence prepayment rate changes on the price and yield of a pass-through security. The final two sections cover more advanced topics. Section V discusses holding-period returns, while Section VI provides an introduction to duration and convexity and their calculation and interpretation for MBSs.

I. Overview of the Market

The Advent of the Secondary Mortgage Market

A secondary market for whole loans, or unsecuritized mortgages, existed long before the creation of mortgage pass-through securities. The secondary whole-loan market helped to reduce imbalances between lenders in capital-deficit areas and lenders in capital-surplus areas. Even though the servicing often remained with the originator of the mortgage, buyers of whole loans faced many of the legal complications and paperwork of mortgage ownership. More importantly, there was little liquidity in the whole-loan market, and buyers ran the risk of potential losses if forced to sell their mortgages quickly. The extensive details, paperwork and cost involved in these types of transactions prevented many small buyers from entering the market.

The introduction of the mortgage pass-through created a means of buying and selling mortgages that was more convenient and in many ways more efficient than the whole-loan market. Pass-through certificates are shares issued against pools of specified mortgages. The cash flows from the mortgages are "passed through," after subtraction of a service fee, to the holders of the pass-through securities on a monthly basis, typically with a delay. The payments made to the investor consist of scheduled principal and interest and any unscheduled payments of principal (resulting from prepayments and defaults) that may occur.

The great majority of pass-throughs have been issued by three agencies that were created by Congress to increase liquidity in the secondary mortgage markets and thus increase the supply of capital available for residential housing loans. The Federal National Mortgage Association (FNMA or "Fannie

---

4. The formulas for all of the mathematical concepts not presented in this article are given in the appendix to Lakhbir S. Hayre and Cyrus Mohebbi, "Mortgage Pass-Through Securities," in Frank J. Fabozzi (ed.), *Advances and Innovations in Bond and Mortgage Markets* (Chicago: Probus Publishing, 1989).

Mae"), the oldest of these agencies, was established by the federal government in 1938 to help solve some of the housing finance problems brought on by the Depression. FNMA's original mandate allowed it to buy Federal Housing Administration (FHA) and Veterans Administration (VA) loans from lenders. In 1968, Congress divided the original FNMA into two organizations: the current FNMA and the Government National Mortgage Association (GNMA or "Ginnie Mae"). GNMA remains a government agency within the Department of Housing and Urban Development (HUD), helping to finance government-assisted housing programs. FNMA became a private corporation rechartered by Congress with a mandate to establish a secondary market for conventional mortgages; that is, loans not FHA insured or VA guaranteed. Established in 1970, the Federal Home Loan Mortgage Corporation (FHLMC or "Freddie Mac") is a government-chartered corporation owned by the 12 Federal Home Loan Banks and the federally-insured savings institutions, which in turn own stock in the Federal Home Loan Banks. Like FNMA, FHLMC seeks to enhance liquidity for residential mortgage investments, primarily by assisting in the development of secondary markets for conventional mortgages.

Comparisons of GNMA, FNMA and FHLMC Pass-Throughs

Although all pass-throughs basically have the same structure—cash flows from the mortgages in the pool are passed through to the security holders after subtraction of a servicing fee—there are a number of generally minor differences among the pass-throughs issued by the three agencies. Table 1 gives basic information about the GNMA, FNMA and FHLMC pass-through programs.

Among the important features of the agency pass-through programs are:

Guarantees GNMA pass-throughs are guaranteed directly by the U.S. government as to timely payment of interest and principal. FNMA and FHLMC pass-throughs carry agency guarantees only; however, both agencies can borrow from the U.S. Treasury, and it is not likely that the U.S. government would allow the agencies to default. While FNMA guarantees the timely payment of interest and principal, FHLMC generally guarantees the timely payment of interest and the ultimate (within one year) payment of principal. From the investor's point of view, because of the guarantees, a default is essentially equivalent to a prepayment.

Payment Delay Pass-throughs pay interest after a specified delay. For example, interest for the month of August would be paid on September 15 for GNMAs (September 20 for GNMA II pass-throughs), on September 25 for

TABLE 1. *Comparison of GNMAs, FNMAs and FHLMCs.*

	GNMA	FNMA	FHLMC
Types of Mortgage	FHA/VA	Conventional (Some FHA/VA)	Conventional (Some FHA/VA)
Main Payment Types	Level Payment Graduated Payment ARM	Level Payment ARM	Level Payment ARM
Maximum Mortgage Balance	$153,100*	$168,700*	$168,700*
Age	New Origination	New or Seasoned	New or Seasoned
Term	30- and 15-Year (Some 40-Year Project Loans)	30- and 15-Year (Some 40-Year ARMs)	30- and 15-Year
Minimum Pool Size ($mm)	GNMA I: 1.0 GNMA II: 0.25	1.0	Guarantor: 1.0** Cash: 10.0 or 50.0
Number of Pools:			
Issued	GNMA I: 159,543 GNMA II: 9,043	45,811	59,730
Outstanding	GNMA I: 157,756 GNMA II: 8,853	45,549	59,593
Amount ($bb):			
Issued	405.83	149.29	283.54
Outstanding	277.91	111.44	201.04
Mortgage Coupon Allowed (%)	0.5 over Pass-Through Rate (GNMA II: 0.5-1.5 over Pass-Through Rate)	0.5-2.5 over Pass-Through Rate	0.5-2.5 over Pass-Through Rate

TABLE 1 *Continued*

	GNMA	FNMA	FHLMC
Delays (Days):			
Stated	45 (GNMA II: 50)	55	75
Actual	14 (GNMA II: 19)	24	44
Range of Coupons (%)	5.25–17.00	4.25–16.50	4.00–17.00
Denominations	$25,000 Minimum with Increments of $5,000	$25,000 Minimum	$25,000 Minimum with Increments of $5,000
Method of Payment	Multiple Monthly Checks from Issuers (GNMA II: One Check Monthly)	One Check Monthly	One Check Monthly

*Stated maximum mortgage balances are for single-family structures. Maximums are higher for multi-family dwellings, as well as for single- and multi-family structures in Alaska and Hawaii.

**Some mini-pools of $0.25 million.

FNMAs and on October 15 for FHLMCs. On these dates, the security holder would also receive any principal payments made by the mortgage holders
during the month of August. The delay is said to be 45, 55 and 75 days for
GNMAs, FNMAs and FHLMCs, respectively. However, since interest for
the month of August would be paid on September 1 if there were no delay,
the actual delays are 14, 24 and 44 days, respectively.

Pool Composition   GNMA pools consist of VA- and FHA-insured mortgages that are assumable, while FNMA and FHLMC pools generally consist
of conventional loans that are not assumable. FNMA and FHLMC pools
also tend to be much larger than GNMA pools and hence are less regionally
concentrated.

Liquidity   The growth in the size of the pass-through markets has led to
greater liquidity, with FNMAs and FHLMCs now generally as liquid as
GNMAs. Bid/ask spreads for the major coupons (currently in the 7% to
12.5% range) are generally about 1/8 of a point, which is similar to Treasuries and less than most corporates. Thus, liquidity for the major coupons is
comparable to that for Treasuries and greater than that for most corporates.

II. Prepayments and Cash-Flow Behavior

The timing and amounts of the cash flows received from a pass-through are
greatly affected by the prepayment rates of the mortgages in the underlying
pool. This makes the choice of a projected prepayment rate critical in evaluating and pricing an MBS. Prepayment rates tend to fluctuate with interest
rates and other economic variables and depend on mortgage characteristics,
such as coupon and age. There is also a strong seasonal effect on prepayment, which reflects the well-known seasonal variations in housing turnover.[5] This section addresses the prepayment conventions and models used
in pricing and trading MBSs, as well as the effect of prepayments on pass-
through cash flows.

Prepayment Models and Conventions

Twelve-Year Prepaid Life   At one time the standard approach to prepayments was 12-year prepaid life, which assumes no prepayments for the first
12 years of the pass-through's life and then full prepayment at the end of the
twelfth year. This was based on FHA data that showed that on the average

---

5. A more detailed discussion of the determinants of prepayment behavior is given in Lakhbir
S. Hayre, Kenneth Lauterbach and Cyrus Mohebbi, "Prepayment Models and Methodologies," in *Advances and Innovations in Bond and Mortgage Markets*.

mortgages terminated in their twelfth year. It is now generally realized that the 12-year prepaid life assumption can often give misleading results; prepayment rates tend to vary with interest rates and mortgage characteristics and are higher for premium coupons than for discounts. This method is now rarely used in the pricing and trading of MBSs, although quoted mortgage yields are sometimes based on it.

Constant Prepayment Rate (CPR)   A commonly used method is to assume a constant prepayment rate (CPR) for a pool of mortgages. If one thinks of the pool as consisting of a large number of $1 mortgages, then the CPR for a period is the percentage of mortgages outstanding at the beginning of the period that terminate during that period. The CPR is usually expressed on an annualized basis, while the terms *single monthly mortality (SMM)* or *constant monthly prepayment (CMP)* refer to monthly prepayment rates.

For example, if a pool of mortgages is prepaying at a constant rate of 1% per month, then 1% of the outstanding balance, after subtraction of the scheduled principal, will be prepaid in each month. Thus, if the outstanding principal balance at the beginning of the month is $100,000 and the scheduled principal payment is $1,000, then an SMM of 1% means that 1% of $99,000 (the remaining balance after the scheduled principal payment), or $990, will be prepaid that month. (Since the scheduled principal payments for a 30-year mortgage are generally small until the latter part of the mortgage term, one can, as a good approximation, multiply the outstanding balance by the SMM to obtain the amount of principal prepayment.)

The effective annual prepayment rate, or CPR, corresponding to a given monthly prepayment rate is almost, but not quite, equal to 12 times the monthly rate. For a 1% monthly rate, the CPR is 11.36%. The reason that the annual rate is less than 12% is that the monthly prepayment rate of 1% is being applied to a decreasing principal balance each month. Hence, a 1% SMM in month ten, say, means less principal prepayment in dollar terms than a 1% SMM in month one.

FHA Experience   At one time, FHA experience was a widely used prepayment model. However, it is not often used today. FHA experience projects the prepayment rate of a mortgage pool relative to the historical prepayment and default experience of FHA-insured, 30-year mortgage loans. FHA periodically publishes a table of 30 numbers that represent the annual survivorship rates of FHA-insured mortgages. The table indicates the probability for survival of a mortgage and reports the percentage of mortgages expected to terminate for any given policy year.

A mortgage pool's prepayment rates are expressed as a percentage of FHA experience. For example, if a pool of mortgages prepays at 100% FHA, then in each mortgage year the loans in the pool will terminate at the rate given by FHA statistics. A rate of 200% FHA means that the mortgages terminate twice as fast as 100% FHA experience would predict, and 50% FHA means that the mortgages terminate half as fast as 100% FHA experience would predict.

The major advantage of FHA experience over CPR is that it reflects the effect of age on prepayments and, in particular, the low prepayment levels typical of newer mortgages. Its major disadvantages are its complexity and the fact that periodic updates of the FHA data mean that the prepayment rates implied by a given percentage of FHA experience also change periodically.

Public Securities Association (PSA) Model   The current industry standard is the Public Securities Association (PSA) prepayment model, which was developed to describe mortgage prepayment behavior by combining the information in the FHA survivorship schedules with the simplicity of the CPR method. The PSA benchmark (denoted 100% PSA) assumes a series of CPRs that begin at 0.2% in the first month and increase by 0.2% thereafter, until leveling 30 months after mortgage origination, when the CPR is 6%. This is shown in Figure 1 by the kinked line denoted by "100% PSA."

Interpreting multiples of PSA is simpler than interpreting multiples of FHA. For example, a projected prepayment rate of 200% PSA means that the CPR in any month will be twice the CPR corresponding to 100% PSA; thus, for 200% PSA the CPR will be 0.4% in month one, 0.8% in month two and so on, until it levels off at 12% in month 30. Figure 1 illustrates this for 50% PSA and 150% PSA.

FIGURE 1. *PSA and Multiples of PSA.*

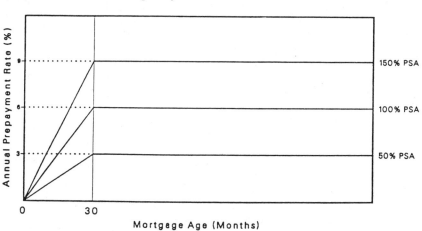

Econometric Prepayment Models   Many major Wall Street firms have developed econometric models that project prepayment rates as a function of specified economic and mortgage variables. In the most general case, an econometric prepayment model will project SMMs for each remaining month of the mortgage security. This vector of monthly prepayment rates will reflect seasonal and age variation in prepayments, as well as changing patterns of housing turnover and refinancing over time for a given pool of mortgages.

For trading and sales purposes, however, using a vector of monthly prepayments is generally impractical, since it is necessary to be able to quote a prepayment rate used in pricing or in yield calculations. Hence, the vector is usually converted to an equivalent averaged CPR or percentage of PSA. For example, the Prudential-Bache Prepayment Model calculates the PSA rate that for a given price produces the same yield as the vector of monthly prepayment rates. Using econometric models is often preferable to using recent prepayment levels as a means of choosing a projected CPR or PSA rate, since changing economic factors may have made recent prepayment levels an unreliable indicator of future prepayments.

Effect of Prepayments on Cash Flows

Figure 2 shows the cash flows generated by the pool of mortgages backing a new GNMA 9 at various prepayment rates. At a zero prepayment level, the monthly dollar cash flows from the mortgage loans are constant. Notice, however, that the composition of principal, interest and servicing that comprise each of the monthly cash flows changes as the mortgages amortize. As principal payments increase and the remaining principal balance declines, the dollar amount of interest due declines proportionally. Servicing fees, like interest payments, are calculated based on the remaining principal balance of the mortgage loan. For the GNMA 9 in Figure 2, the servicing fee is 50 basis points of interest. Pass-through investors will experience the effect of a decrease in servicing fees (as the remaining principal balance declines) in terms of slightly increasing monthly dollar cash flows.

At more realistic prepayment levels, the cash flows are more concentrated early in the pass-through term. The second diagram in Figure 2 shows the cash flows at a prepayment rate of 50% PSA—historically a slow speed for GNMA 9 prepayment levels. The principal paydowns increase for the first 2½ years, as the prepayment rate increases according to the PSA pattern until month 30. The prepayment rate then remains constant at 3% per year. Note that the total amount of principal received by the pass-through investor is fairly constant after the first two years. At an assumed prepayment rate of 50% PSA, the increase in the scheduled principal payment each period offsets the decline in prepaid principal, which is approximately a constant percentage of the remaining principal balance.

FIGURE 2. *GNMA 9 Cash Flows at Various Prepayment Rates.*

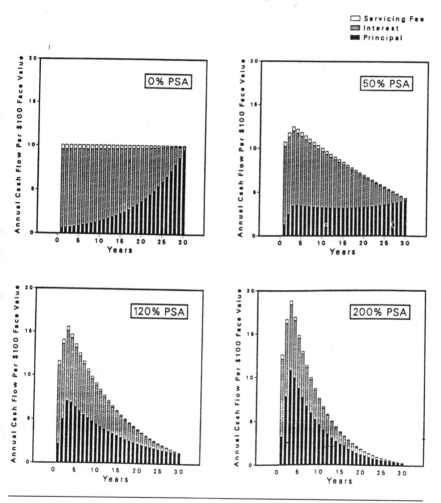

The third diagram in Figure 2 shows the cash flows at a prepayment rate of 120% PSA, which is close to recent prepayment levels. Again, the amount of principal increases for the first 2½ years, as the prepayment rate increases for 30 months before leveling off at 7.2% (1.20 × 6%) per year after month 30. The total principal payments gradually decrease after month 30, since at 120% PSA the principal balance has declined to the point at which the scheduled principal payments are much less significant than they are at 50% PSA.

FIGURE 3. *Outstanding Balances of a GNMA 9 at Various Prepayment Rates.*

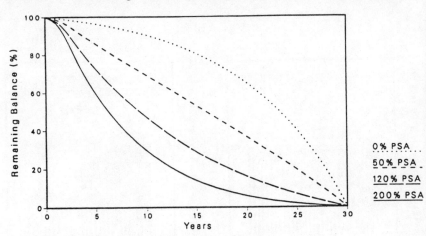

The final diagram in Figure 2 shows the cash flows at a prepayment rate of 200% PSA, which is considered to be fast by historical standards for a GNMA 9. The prepayment rate levels off at 12% per annum after month 30, and the principal paydown is concentrated in the early years.

The outstanding principal balances at 0%, 50%, 120% and 200% PSA are shown in Figure 3. These reflect the principal payment patterns shown in Figure 2.

III. Measures of Pass-Through Life

A pass-through is a self-amortizing security that returns principal throughout its term. In comparing pass-throughs (or any MBS) with other bonds, such as a Treasury that returns all its principal at maturity, it is necessary to determine some reasonable measure of the investment life of the pass-through.

The selection of a reasonable measure of mortgage life is important. Measures of investment life are used in several ways when assessing the investment's value. The measure of investment life:

- Suggests the effective span of time during which a mortgage security provides a stated yield or return.
- Suggests how to compare the mortgage security to other, more familiar bond investments—in particular, it suggests the maturity on the Treasury yield curve against which to compare a pass-through.
- Can indicate the pass-through's volatility in a shifting interest-rate environment.

TABLE 2. *Calculation of Average Life.*

Time (Years)	Principal Received ($)	Time × Principal
1	40	1 year × 40 = 40
2	30	2 years × 30 = 60
3	20	3 years × 20 = 60
4	10	4 years × 10 = 40
	100	200

$$\text{Average Life} = \frac{\text{Sum of (Time} \times \text{Principal)}}{\text{Total Principal}} = \frac{200}{100} = 2 \text{ years}$$

Average Life

Average life or weighted-average life (WAL) is defined as the weighted-average time to the return of a dollar of principal. It is calculated by multiplying each portion of principal received by the time at which it is received, then summing and dividing by the total amount of principal. For example, consider a simple annual-pay, four-year bond with a face value of $100 and principal payments as in Table 2.

As Table 2 illustrates, each time point at which principal is returned is weighted by the percentage of principal returned at that time point, so that the average life in this example could be calculated as

$$\text{Average Life} = .4 * 1 \text{ year} + .3 * 2 \text{ years} + .2 * 3 \text{ years} + .1 * 4 \text{ years}$$
$$= 2 \text{ years}. \tag{1}$$

Average life is commonly used as the measure of investment life for MBSs, and the yield of an MBS is typically compared against a Treasury with maturity close to the average life of the MBS. The average life of an MBS depends heavily on the prepayment rate.

Macaulay Duration[6]

An alternative to average life as a measure of investment life is duration. Duration, or Macaulay duration (named after Frederick Macaulay, who introduced the concept in 1938), is defined as the weighted-average time to return of a dollar of price. It is calculated by multiplying the present value of each cash flow by the time at which it is received, summing and then dividing by the price. Table 3 demonstrates the calculation of Macaulay duration for

---

6. For a more detailed discussion of duration, see the article by Dattatreya and Fabozzi in this book.

TABLE 3. *Calculation of Macaulay Duration.*

Time (Years)	Cash Flow ($)	Present Value at 10% ($)	Present Value × Time
1	30	27.27	27.27
2	30	24.79	49.58
3	30	22.54	67.62
4	30	20.49	81.96
		Price = $95.09	226.43

$$\text{Duration} = \frac{\text{Sum of (Present Values} \times \text{Time)}}{\text{Price}} = \frac{226.43}{95.09} = 2.38 \text{ years}$$

---

an annual-pay, four-year bond with cash flows of $30 each year and an assumed discount rate of 10%.

This example shows that one can obtain Macaulay duration, if, in the formula for average life, the total principal is replaced by the price and the principal payments at each point in time are replaced by the present values of the cash flows. *Thus, Macaulay duration can be thought of as the average life of a dollar of price of the security.*

Macaulay duration is often considered to be a superior measure of investment life than average life. It considers the total cash flow, not just the principal component. Thus, it can be applied to derivative MBSs, such as CPR residuals and interest-only STRIPs, that have no principal payments. It also recognizes the time value of money by giving greater weight to earlier cash flows.

Macaulay duration (or a slight variation on it called modified duration, which is defined in Section V) is often used as a measure of the volatility of price with respect to changes in yield. This is appropriate as long as the cash flows are not a function of interest rates. However, the cash flows of an MBS depend on prepayments, which are driven to a large extent by interest rates. In the case of interest-rate-dependent cash flows, great care must be taken in using Macaulay duration as a measure of price volatility. This is discussed further in Section VI.

IV. Price and Yield Behavior

This section will examine how the price and yield-to-maturity of pass-through securities vary as interest rates vary. As discussed in Section II, the cash flows from an MBS are affected by changes in interest rates, due to the resulting changes in prepayment levels. This makes the price and yield characteristics of an MBS more complex than those of a standard fixed-income security such as a Treasury.

Calculation of Yield-to-Maturity

The yield-to-maturity, or simply yield, of a security is defined as the discount rate that makes the present value of the security's cash flows equal to its current price.

For a noncallable bond, the calculation of yield is straightforward, given the price, coupon and timing of cash flows. Even for a standard callable bond, one can calculate a yield-to-call or estimate the probability of calls at different points in time. However, for an MBS there is a separate call option on each dollar of mortgage, since in general a homeowner can prepay part or all of a mortgage at any time. Furthermore, since mortgages are self-amortizing, the amount redeemed if a homeowner "exercises a call" will depend on the original term, coupon and age of the mortgage.

To calculate a yield for an MBS, a prepayment rate must be specified for each remaining month of the MBS's term. Once the prepayment rate has been chosen, cash flows can then be obtained for each month, and the yield (and other security characteristics, such as average life) can be calculated. The necessity of specifying a prepayment rate introduces an element of subjectivity into the calculation of an MBS's yield; there is generally no consensus on the projected prepayment rate of an MBS and hence no consensus on the yield.

The traditional approach to prepayments has been to assume a 12-year prepaid life, but this is generally recognized as inadequate. MBSs are now usually priced at a specified CPR or percentage of PSA. The CPR or percentage of PSA to be used for a given MBS should be chosen using relevant mortgage characteristics and economic variables.

Figure 4 shows the projected yields-to-maturity of various seasoned GNMAs plotted against average lives. These are calculated using prepayment projections from the Prudential-Bache Prepayment Model. This graph can be thought of as a GNMA yield curve. For comparison, the graph also shows the Treasury curve and an agency yield curve based on the averages of the yields of selected agencies of varying maturities. Pass-throughs have essentially the same credit quality and liquidity as agencies, so the pass-through spread over the agencies can be thought of as compensation for prepayment uncertainty and for the relative complexity of pass-throughs compared with agencies.

Mortgage Yield and Bond-Equivalent Yield   Mortgage pass-through cash flows typically are paid monthly. The yield calculated from these monthly cash flows is called the mortgage yield; it implicitly assumes monthly compounding of interest. To make the yield of an MBS comparable to semi-annual pay Treasuries or corporates, the mortgage yield must be converted to a semi-annual compounding basis, or bond-equivalent yield. The bond-equivalent yield is higher than the mortgage yield, since monthly compound-

FIGURE 4. *GNMA, Agency and Treasury Yield Curves.* *

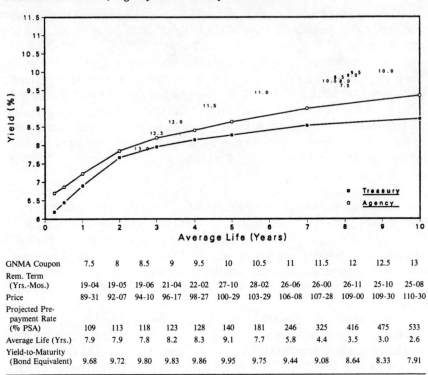

GNMA Coupon	7.5	8	8.5	9	9.5	10	10.5	11	11.5	12	12.5	13
Rem. Term (Yrs.-Mos.)	19-04	19-05	19-06	21-04	22-02	27-10	28-02	26-06	26-00	26-11	25-10	25-08
Price	89-31	92-07	94-10	96-17	98-27	100-29	103-29	106-08	107-28	109-00	109-30	110-30
Projected Pre-payment Rate (% PSA)	109	113	118	123	128	140	181	246	325	416	475	533
Average Life (Yrs.)	7.9	7.9	7.8	8.2	8.3	9.1	7.7	5.8	4.4	3.5	3.0	2.6
Yield-to-Maturity (Bond Equivalent)	9.68	9.72	9.80	9.83	9.86	9.95	9.75	9.44	9.08	8.64	8.33	7.91

*Data are based on closing prices and projected prepayments from the Prudential-Bache Pre-payment Model on August 18, 1987. The base mortgage rate is 10.34%.

ing generates a higher annual yield than semi-annual compounding. Hence, to be equivalent to the mortgage yield, the semi-annual yield must be higher.

Price Behavior as Interest Rates Vary

The prepayment of principal affects price in different ways for different coupon mortgage securities. Discount coupon securities—those with coupon rates lower than the current coupon rate—trading below par benefit from the early return of principal at par. On the other hand, premium securities trading above par experience a negative effect from early principal prepayment. As an extreme example, if a premium MBS is bought for a price of 105 and a full prepayment of principal is made the next month, 100 is received for 105 paid a month earlier.

Figure 5 shows closing prices on August 18, 1987, for seasoned GNMA, FNMA and FHLMC pass-throughs. The most striking aspect of the graph

FIGURE 5. *Prices of Pass-Through Securities.* *

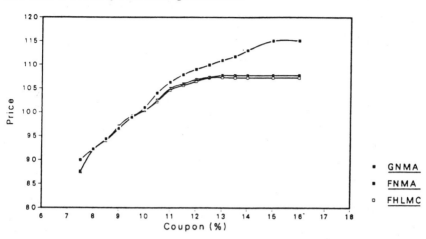

*Data are based on closing prices on August 18, 1987. The base mortgage rate is 10.34%.

is the price compression that occurs at the higher coupons. For FNMAs and FHLMCs, the prices level off and are the same for 13% and higher coupons; for GNMAs, the price compression is not as drastic, but prices still begin to level off for the higher coupons.

The price compression in premium coupon mortgage securities can be explained by the fact that prepayments tend to increase the further the coupon is above the current coupon. The higher the coupon rate on the underlying security, the greater is the likelihood that the homeowner will refinance at the lower prevailing mortgage rates. Figure 5 indicates that in the opinion of the market, the extra coupon income earned from the FNMAs and FHLMCs with coupons of 13% and higher is canceled exactly by higher expected prepayment levels.

Changes in the prevailing level of interest rates affect the prepayment rates of mortgage securities. As interest rates increase, prepayments tend to slow down, and as interest rates decrease, prepayments tend to increase. The interaction of interest-rate and prepayment-rate changes on the price of an MBS can be illustrated by looking at projected price paths if interest rates change. Figure 6 shows the projected prices of GNMA 9s and 11s as interest rates change.

As interest rates increase, the slowdown in prepayments has an adverse price effect on the GNMA 9, which is priced below par. As interest rates continue to increase, prepayments on the GNMA 9 bottom out and become relatively insensitive to interest rates, and its price behavior is similar to that

FIGURE 6. *Projected Price Paths of GNMA 9s and 11s.**

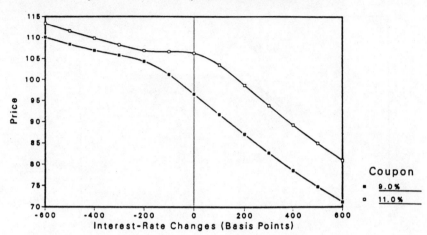

*Data are based on assumptions of a parallel shift in interest rates. Projected prices are calculated using prepayment projections from the Prudential-Bache Prepayment Model. The no-change prices are the closing prices on August 18, 1987, and the base mortgage rate is 10.34%.

of a Treasury or corporate security. For the GNMA 11, which is priced above par, the slowdown in prepayments is beneficial. It reduces the size of the price decline if rates increase 100 basis points. If rates continue to increase, any further slowdown in the prepayment rate for the GNMA 11 is minor, and the GNMA 11, like the GNMA 9, behaves like a Treasury or corporate security.

If interest rates decline, there is a sharp increase in projected prepayment rates for the GNMA 11 and consequently very little price appreciation for interest-rate declines of up to 200 basis points. However, if rates decline further, prepayments level off, and there is more price appreciation. For the GNMA 9, the drag on price appreciation does not occur unless interest rates decline by 200 or more basis points. The GNMA 9 then becomes a premium security, and there is a sharp increase in prepayments. If interest rates continue to decline, prepayments on the GNMA 9 begin to level off, and its price behavior is like that of the GNMA 11.

Yield Behavior as Interest Rates Vary

Figure 7 illustrates the effect of various interest-rate changes on the yields-to-maturity of GNMA 9s and GNMA 11s. As interest rates increase and prepayments slow down, the yield on the discount GNMA 9 decreases slightly,

FIGURE 7. *Projected Yields-to-Maturity for GNMA 9s and 11s.* *

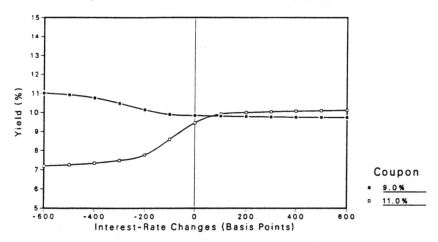

*The GNMA 9 was bought at a price of 96-17 and the GNMA 11 at a price of 106-08. Yields are calculated using projections from the Prudential-Bache Prepayment Model. The base mortgage rate is 10.34%.

while the yield on the premium GNMA 11 increases slightly. The effect is more pronounced if interest rates decline. As interest rates decrease and pre-payments accelerate, there is a sharp drop in the yield of the GNMA 11 and an appreciable rise in the yield of the GNMA 9.

Prepayment Volatility

In general, prepayment volatility is greatest for MBSs whose underlying mort-gages have coupons between 100 to 300 basis points above current mortgage rates. At the lower end of this range, a decrease in interest rates may trigger a surge in refinancings, while at the upper end, an increase in interest rates may slow down prepayments substantially. The effect of prepayments on yield will depend on the magnitude of the MBS price discount or premium; for an MBS priced at par with no payment delay, the yield-to-maturity does not depend on the level of prepayments.

V. Total Holding-Period Returns

Fixed-income securities are generally priced and traded by yield-to-maturity. However, from the investor's point of view, yield-to-maturity can be an un-satisfactory measure of the likely return from the security for two impor-tant reasons:

- The yield-to-maturity assumes that all cash flows are reinvested at a rate equal to the yield; and
- It assumes that the security is held until maturity, thus ignoring the capital gain or loss from selling the security at the end of a holding period.

The total return (or the horizon or holding-period return) measures the actual return over a specified holding period. This return is composed of three elements:

- The cash flows from the security during the holding period;
- The reinvestment income from the cash flows from the time each cash flow is received to the end of the holding period for specified levels of reinvestment rates that prevailed during the holding period; and
- The gain or loss from selling the security at the end of the period. The proceeds from the sale are equal to the price at the end of the period multiplied by the amount of principal still outstanding at the time, plus any accrued interest.

Calculation of Total Return

Table 4 illustrates the calculation of the total return from holding a three-year-old GNMA 9 for five months. The security is purchased on January 12 at a price of 96-08, i.e., $96-8/32 or $96.25 is paid for each $100 of face value, with settlement on January 20. The security is sold on June 17 for a price of 97-00, with settlement on June 20. Since the security is actually transferred between the buyer and seller and cash is exchanged on the settlement dates, these dates should be used as the beginning and end of the holding period.

The first cash flow is received on February 15 and constitutes interest and principal for the month of January. The fifth and final cash flow is received on June 15. All cash flows (including reinvestment income) are assumed to be reinvested each month at a reinvestment rate of 6%. A prepayment rate of 120% PSA is assumed.

With these assumptions, the actual return from holding the security over the five months is 4.767% or, stated as an annual rate, 11.441%. The effective annual return, with a five-month compounding frequency, is 11.825%. The corresponding bond-equivalent (semi-annual compounding) rate of return is 11.495%.

Assumptions Used in Calculating Total Returns

The calculation of a projected rate of return over a holding period requires assumptions about the values of three major determinants of the holding-period return: prepayment rates, reinvestment rates and the selling price at

TABLE 4. *Calculation of Total Return for a GNMA 9.*

Buy: $1 million face value of GNMA 9s, with a remaining term of 27 years on January 12 at 96-08. Settlement is January 20.

Amount Paid: $1MM × 96-08 = $962,500.00
+ 19 days of accrued interest = $ 4,750.00

Total $967,250.00

Cash Flows

Date	Remaining Balance	Interest	Scheduled Principal	Prepaid* Principal	Reinvest-ment** Income	Total Cash Flow
2/15	993,129.58	7,500.00	666.95	6,203.47	0.00	14,370.42
3/15	986,300.71	7,448.47	668.05	6,160.82	71.85	14,349.19
4/15	979,513.12	7,397.26	669.16	6,118.42	143.60	14,328.44
5/15	972,766.57	7,346.35	670.27	6,076.28	215.24	14,308.14
6/15	966,060.79	7,295.75	671.39	6,034.39	286.78	14,288.31
6/20	966,060.79	0.00	0.00	0.00	47.76	47.76
Totals:		36,987.83	3,345.82	30,593.38	765.23	71,692.26

Sell: Remaining $966,060.79 face value of GNMA 9s on June 17 at 97-00 for settlement on June 20.

Sale Proceeds: Remaining Balance × Price = $937,078.97
+ 19 days of accrued interest = $ 4,588.79

Total $941,667.76

Total Return over Holding Period = $\dfrac{\text{Sale Proceeds} - \text{Price Paid} + \text{Total Cash Flows}}{\text{Price Paid}}$

$$= \frac{\$941,667.76 - \$967,250.00 + 71,692.26}{\$967,250.00}$$

$$= 0.04767 \text{ or } 4.767\%.$$

Total return on an annualized basis = $4.767\% \times (12/5) = 11.441\%$.

Effective annual return with five-month compounding frequency = $(1 + \frac{.11441}{12/5})^{12/5} - 1$
$= 11.825\%$.

Total return on a semi-annual compounding basis = $2[(1 + \frac{11.825}{100})^{1/2} - 1] = 11.495\%$.

*Constant prepayment rate of 120% PSA is assumed.
**Assumed reinvestment rate is 6%.

the end of the holding period. The question of prepayment assumptions was addressed in Section III. The other two assumptions are discussed here.

Reinvestment Rates There are several approaches for determining appropriate reinvestment rates. The calculation in Table 4 uses a constant reinvestment rate of 6% with monthly roll-over of accumulated cash flows. This method is similar to assuming that all cash flows are deposited in a short-term cash or money-market account. Under this method, the money-market reinvestment rate can be allowed to change over the course of the holding period in line with projected changes in the yield level used in calculating the selling price of the security. For example, if the initial reinvestment rate is 6%, and it is assumed that yield levels will increase by 100 basis points over the holding period, then the reinvestment rate could be allowed to increase gradually to 7% over the holding period.

A second approach that is sometimes used is to reinvest each cash flow from the time it is received to the end of the holding period at a rate chosen according to the length of the reinvestment period. For example, if a cash flow is received one year before the end of the holding period, it may be reinvested at the one-year Treasury rate, rather than at a short-term money-market rate. However, this assumes that the end of the holding period is known from the start. In practice, an investor does not generally know the exact time at which the security will be sold.

A third approach is to assume that all cash flows are reinvested in securities of the same type and to assume a reinvestment rate close to the yield of the security. However, this approach raises questions about the meaning of the holding-period return, since at the end of the period some of the cash flow received is tied up in new securities.

Selling Price at End of the Holding Period   Choosing the price of an MBS at the end of the holding period is perhaps the assumption most open to question. In the example in Table 4, a known horizon selling price was assumed for illustrative simplicity. The standard approach in calculating projected returns is to assume a given change in yield levels and then calculate the price at the end of the holding period by discounting future cash flows at the assumed horizon yield. However, in projecting prepayment and reinvestment rates and in comparing the total return of an MBS with a Treasury, assumptions must be made about the relationship between changes in the yield levels of MBSs and changes in interest rates in general. A common assumption is a parallel shift in interest rates, so that short-term, MBS and Treasury yields all change by the same amount. It is important to realize that this is just an assumption, and that yield spreads of MBSs to Treasuries may widen or narrow.

As this discussion suggests, the calculation of a holding-period return requires important assumptions about reinvestment rates and the yields used to calculate the redemption value at the end of the period. This is true for all securities, not just MBSs. However, for MBSs there is the additional assumption concerning prepayment levels. These assumptions can have a large

FIGURE 8. *One-Year and Five-Year Holding-Period Returns for GNMA 9s and 11s.* *

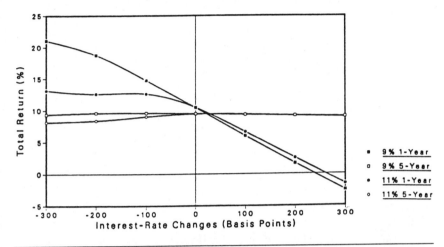

* The GNMA 9 is bought at a price of 96-08 and the GNMA 11 at a price of 105-16 with the base mortgage rate equal to 10.34%. The following assumptions are made: (1) a parallel shift in interest rates and yield spreads; (2) initial reinvestment rate is 7% with all cash flows reinvested monthly; (3) interest rates change uniformly over the year for the one-year horizon and at a rate of 100 basis points per year for the five-year horizon.

impact on the value of the projected return, so it is important that they be understood when evaluating securities on a total-return basis over a holding period.

Variation of Total Returns with Holding Period and Rate Changes

Figure 8 shows the total returns for one-year and five-year holding periods under various interest-rate changes for a GNMA 9 and a GNMA 11. A parallel shift in interest rates and the yield spreads of mortgages to Treasuries is assumed. The initial reinvestment rate is assumed to be 7% with all cash flows reinvested monthly. Interest rates are assumed to change uniformly over the year for the one-year horizon and at a rate of 100 basis points per year for the five-year horizon.

As indicated in Figure 8, the one-year returns depend on interest-rate changes to a greater degree than do the five-year returns. There are two reasons for this:

- The coupon and reinvestment income constitutes a much larger proportion of the total return over the five-year holding period, thus reducing the importance of the change in price of the security due to changes in interest rates.
- A larger proportion of the principal will pay down over the five-year period, due both to scheduled payments and prepayments. This also reduces the importance of price changes, particularly in a declining interest-rate environment when prepayments will be high.

The lackluster performance of both securities over the five-year period in the declining interest-rate scenarios is explained by the second point. The high prepayment levels result in a low remaining balance at the time of sale. This reduces the benefits from price appreciation, which in any case has become compressed by the high prepayments (as illustrated in Figure 6).

Over the one-year holding period, the GNMA 9, like other fixed-income securities, performs poorly if interest rates increase and performs well if interest rates decline (although there is some effect of price compression and high prepayments if interest rates decline by 300 basis points). The GNMA 11 does slightly better than the GNMA 9 if rates increase, due to the benefits of a slowdown in prepayments for the premium GNMA 11. In the declining interest-rate scenarios, the high prepayments and the resulting price compression cause the GNMA 11 return to level off after interest rates have declined by more than 100 basis points.

VI. Duration and Convexity

Modified and Effective Durations

In Section III, Macaulay duration was defined as a commonly used measure of maturity for MBSs. Macaulay duration, or a slightly adjusted version known as modified duration,[7] is often used as a measure of the sensitivity of price to small changes in yields. This is based on the fact that if cash flows are not dependent on interest rates, then modified duration is equal to the rate of percentage change of price with respect to changes in yield.

For an MBS, however, a key characteristic is the dependence of cash flows, via prepayments, on interest rates. This can make Macaulay or modified duration an inadequate or even misleading measure of price sensitivity. To examine the price effect for changes in interest rates, an "effective duration" is often calculated as an alternative measurement of price sensitivity.

---

7. Formally,

$$\text{Modified duration} = \frac{\text{Macaulay duration}}{1 + (y/1200)}, \qquad (2)$$

where y is the mortgage yield.

TABLE 5. *Calculation of Effective Duration for an FNMA 12.**

	Interest-Rate Change (Basis Points)		
	−25	0	25
Pricing Yield (%)	10.23	10.48	10.73
Projected Prepayment Rate (% PSA)	355	313	281
Price at 313% PSA	105.5620	104.7520	103.9547
Price at Projected Prepayment Rate	105.0172	104.7520	104.3042

Modified Duration = Price volatility assuming no change in prepayments

$$\approx \frac{-100}{\text{Price}} \times \frac{\text{Change in price}}{\text{Change in yield}} = \frac{-1}{104.7520} \times \frac{(103.9547 - 105.5620)}{0.50}$$

$$= 3.07\% \text{ per 100 b.p. change in yield}$$

Effective Duration = Price volatility assuming change in prepayments

$$\approx \frac{-100}{\text{Price}} \times \frac{\text{Change in price}}{\text{Change in yield}} = \frac{-1}{104.7520} \times \frac{(104.3042 - 105.0172)}{0.50}$$

$$= 1.36\% \text{ per 100 b.p. change in yield}$$

*Data are based on FNMA 12s priced at 104-24 on September 24, 1987. Underlying mortgage coupons were 150 to 200 basis points above prevailing mortgage rates.

Effective duration incorporates the changes in prepayment levels that may occur as a result of interest-rate changes. The formula for effective duration is:

$$\text{Effective duration} \approx \frac{-100}{\text{Price}} \times \frac{\text{Change in price}}{\text{Change in yield}}. \tag{3}$$

Table 5 illustrates the calculation of effective duration for a FNMA 12, using the closing price on September 24, 1987. The FNMA 12 had underlying mortgages with coupons 150 to 200 basis points above prevailing mortgage rates, and hence had very high prepayment volatility.

Table 5 shows that for small changes in interest rates, the change in prepayments for a high prepayment volatility premium coupon can counterbalance the effects on price of a change in yield; if interest rates increase, the resulting slowdown in prepayments will benefit the premium MBS and reduce the price decline, while if interest rates decrease, the increase in prepayment speeds will reduce the price appreciation of the security. In the example in Table 5, the FNMA 12 is projected to have an effective duration, or price volatility, of 1.36% per 100 basis points. This means that at current interest-rate levels, a one-basis-point change in yield will lead to a percentage change in price of 0.0136%. This is much lower than the price volatility of 3.07% per 100 basis points given by the traditional modified duration calculation, which does not take into account changes in prepayments.

FIGURE 9. *Modified and Effective Durations for FNMAs.* *

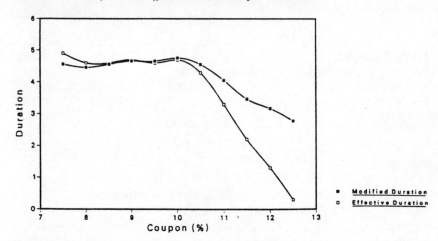

*Data are based on closing prices and prepayment projections on September 24, 1987. Effective durations are calculated using 25-basis-point moves in interest rates in each direction, with the base mortgage rate equal to 10.99%.

The example in Table 5 indicates that while the usual duration calculation may be adequate for discount or high-premium MBSs whose prepayment levels are unlikely to change much for small changes in interest rates, it can be inadequate or even misleading for low-premium coupons, which have high prepayment volatility. An effective duration calculation is more appropriate in such cases. This is borne out by historical studies that have shown that price volatilities do tend to follow the pattern suggested by effective durations.[8]

Figure 9 shows modified and effective durations for several seasoned FNMA securities. The effective durations are calculated by using 25-basis-point moves in interest rates in each direction.

Figure 9 indicates that modified duration overestimates the price volatility of low-premium coupons. This has important implications for hedging strategies. Hedge ratios based on the use of Macaulay or modified duration to estimate price volatility will fail for mortgage coupons with high prepayment volatility. (This has been a painful lesson for many participants in the MBS markets.) It is important to look at changes in both yield and

---

8. Scott M. Pinkus and Marie A. Chandoha, "The Relative Price Volatility of Mortgage Securities," in Frank Fabozzi (ed.), *Mortgage-Backed Securities: New Strategies, Applications and Research* (Chicago: Probus Publishing, 1987).

prepayment rates when calculating price volatility. Effective duration provides a means for doing this. Another useful analytic tool in this context is convexity, which measures the rate of change of price volatility.

Convexity

Considerable attention has been focused recently on the concept of convexity and in particular on the so-called "negative convexity" of MBSs. Convexity refers to the curvature of the price-yield curve. In other words, convexity is the rate of change of duration, i.e., price volatility. If one considers duration to be the speed of price changes, then convexity can be thought of as acceleration. The projected price paths shown in Figure 6 illustrate positive, zero and negative convexity.[9]

A straight line has zero convexity. Thus, since the price-yield curve of the GNMA 9 in Figure 6 is essentially a straight line at the no-change point on the horizontal axis, then the GNMA 9 has almost zero convexity at prevailing interest rates. This means that for small equal changes in interest rates the price of the GNMA 9 will increase or decrease approximately the same amount.

Discount MBSs, like Treasuries, tend to have positive convexity. Positive convexity implies that for small, equal and opposite changes in interest rates, the price increase if rates decline will be more than the price decrease if rates increase. This means that the rate of decrease in price slows down as interest rates increase, i.e., the curve has a downward "bulge" in the middle. When interest rates rise by several hundred basis points, the GNMA 9 becomes a deep-discount coupon and has positive convexity, as indicated in Figure 6.

Negative convexity means that the price/yield curve flattens as interest rates decline. This is characteristic of premium MBSs for which increasing prepayments place a drag on price increases as interest rates decline. Thus, for small equal changes in rates, the price is likely to decline more than it will increase. Referring again to Figure 6, it can be seen that at prevailing interest rates the GNMA 11 has a high degree of negative convexity, while the GNMA 9 has negative convexity if interest rates decline by between 100 to 200 basis points. If rates decline by several hundred basis points, both the GNMA 9 and the GNMA 11 become high-premium coupons and will have almost zero or even positive convexity. *Hence, negative convexity is a characteristic of low-premium MBSs.*

Calculation of Convexity Convexity can be estimated by considering small positive and negative changes in yields and calculating the changes in price in both cases. The formula for convexity is:

---

9. For a further discussion of convexity, see the article by Dattatreya and Fabozzi in this book.

TABLE 6. *Calculation of Convexity.*

	FNMA 8			FNMA 11		
Change in Rates (Basis Points)	Projected Prepayment Rate (PSA)	Yield (%)	Price	Projected Prepayment Rate (PSA)	Yield (%)	Price
−25	135%	10.32	90.35	233%	10.42	102.34
0	132	10.57	89.33	206	10.67	101.56
25	129	10.82	88.32	181	10.92	100.65

$$\text{Convexity} = \frac{100}{\text{Price}} \times \frac{\begin{array}{c}\text{Change in price} \\ \text{if rates go down}\end{array} - \begin{array}{c}\text{Change in price} \\ \text{if rates go up}\end{array}}{(\text{Change in rates})^2}$$

$$= \frac{100}{89.33} \times \frac{(90.35 - 89.33) - (89.33 - 88.32)}{(.25)^2} = 0.180 \text{ for the FNMA 8.}$$

$$= \frac{100}{101.56} \times \frac{(102.34 - 101.56) - (101.56 - 100.65)}{(.25)^2} = -2.048 \text{ for the FNMA 11.}$$

$$\text{Convexity} = \frac{100}{\text{Price}} \times \frac{\begin{array}{c}\text{Change in price} \\ \text{if rates go down}\end{array} - \begin{array}{c}\text{Change in price} \\ \text{if rates go up}\end{array}}{(\text{Change in rates})^2}. \qquad (4)$$

The prepayment rate used in calculating the new prices should reflect the changes in yield levels. Table 6 illustrates the calculation of the convexities of an FNMA 8 and an FNMA 11 using 25-basis-point changes in interest rates.

The discount FNMA 8 has positive convexity, while the low-premium FNMA 11 has negative convexity. This can be explained by considering the likely magnitudes and effects of prepayment changes for the two coupons. For the FNMA 8, prepayments do not change very much for small changes in interest rates; thus, its price behavior for small interest-rate changes is like that of a standard noncallable instrument, such as a Treasury. However, the FNMA 11 has high prepayment volatility; the increasing prepayments as interest rates decline put a drag on price increases. The benefits of a slowdown in prepayments if interest rates increase are not sufficient to offset the price compression.

Investment Implications of Convexity   Positive convexity is generally a desirable characteristic in a fixed-income security. However, this does not mean that securities with negative convexity, such as low-premium pass-throughs, should be avoided. The market may have adjusted the prices of such securities to compensate investors for the negative convexity, making their yields sufficiently high so that they offer better value than many securities with positive convexity.

Another point that should be kept in mind is that, for a given security, convexity changes with interest rates. In other words, negative convexity is a "local" property of low-premium pass-throughs; if there are substantial changes in interest rates, the low-premium pass-through will become a discount or high-premium pass-through and may then have positive convexity. This is a relevant consideration if one plans to hold the security for a year or more, when the length of the holding period makes large interest-rate changes possible. In general, securities should be evaluated and compared by calculating total holding-period returns under a range of projected interest-rate changes. The total return incorporates such factors as initial price and convexity (through the change in the price over the period) and hence will give a good indication of the value of the security.

VII. Summary

The secondary mortgage market has grown tremendously in recent years, and now constitutes a major sector of the fixed-income market, comparable in size to the corporate market and greater than the agency market. The huge amount of mortgage debt in the United States and the fact that only one-quarter of this debt has been securitized to date indicate substantial potential for growth.

This article has attempted to provide a modern treatment of mortgage-backed pass-throughs, which constitute the largest sector of the secondary mortgage markets. Pass-throughs, like all MBSs, are more complex in their investment characteristics and behavior than standard Treasury or corporate securities. Their cash flows are unpredictable; they are self-amortizing; their price/yield relationship is complicated by prepayments; and consequently, the usual interpretations of duration and convexity may be misleading.

Despite their complexity, or rather because of it, the mortgage markets provide opportunities for astute fixed-income investors seeking high yields without sacrificing high quality. The complexity of pass-throughs has resulted in pricing at significantly higher yields than comparable-quality securities. Recent yields have been between 100 to 200 basis points higher than comparable-maturity Treasuries, compared with yield spreads of 30 to 90 basis points over Treasuries for AAA-rated corporates. The credit quality of agency pass-throughs is clearly higher, however, than even AAA-rated corporates, due to U.S. government or quasi-government guarantees concerning payment of interest and principal. Historical studies have shown that, as a result of their higher yields, pass-throughs have provided consistently higher returns than Treasuries or high-quality corporates.

In sum, pass-throughs provide investors with a large and liquid market in securities that combine very high credit quality with yields that are substantially higher than other comparable-quality securities. Mortgage securities have complex investment characteristics and require a more careful analysis than a plain-vanilla Treasury or corporate security. The higher potential returns of mortgage pass-through securities, however, suggest that the extra effort may be well worthwhile for fixed-income investors.

High-Yield Mortgage Securities

Andrew S. Carron
Director
The First Boston Corporation

Eric I. Hemel
Vice President
The First Boston Corporation

I. Introduction

Over the last few years, a new market has developed for a variety of high-yield mortgage-related securities that offers both rewards and risks far greater than those offered by previously available mortgage-related instruments. Only a thorough examination of these different securities will enable an investor to take full advantage of the new opportunities that their development affords, as well as to avoid the associated hazards.

Mortgages and mortgage securities have traditionally provided yields substantially above other products of comparable credit quality. This yield differential may be attributed primarily to the recognition that mortgage cash flows are inherently uncertain.

High-yield mortgage securities are created when mortgage cash flows are divided into two or more pieces, creating at least one instrument that has a set of performance characteristics substantially different from the underlying mortgages. The defining features of these derivative securities are high yield, high credit quality, and returns that are extremely sensitive to interest rates and/or prepayment rates. At present, high-yield mortgage securities encompass residuals from CMOs and REMICs, certain stripped mortgage-backed securities, and leveraged floating-rate mortgage securities.

High-yield mortgage securities have developed out of the increasing ability of mortgage securities issuers to create derivative cash flow streams that, when viewed individually, bear little resemblance to the primary cash flows of the underlying mortgages themselves. As a result, it is now possible to construct securities based on mortgage cash flows that possess extraordinarily different risk and reward characteristics from those of the underlying mortgages. While the interest-rate risk and prepayment risk inherent in residual mortgages transfer in full to the derivative securities as a whole, different portions of those securities can be configured to meet the desires of investors with a wide array of risk/reward preferences. High-yield mortgage securities can concentrate both the risks and rewards of the underlying mortgages into instruments that require a considerably lower cash investment than that required to invest in the underlying mortgages themselves.

High-yield mortgage securities have negative attributes other than their performance risk. Due to their relatively recent introduction to the market, these securities lack the liquidity associated with the traditional mortgage pass-through market. More important, they are quite complex in comparison to traditional mortgage investments and therefore require greater effort and consideration by investors. As with other complex investments, the range in value among different high-yield mortgage securities is wide. Apparently similar instruments may have radically different performance profiles and intrinsic values. Investor success will depend upon the ability to make relevant distinctions among high-yield mortgage products.

High-Yield Mortgage Securities

Traditional fixed-income securities, including mortgage-related securities, have clearly defined principal (face value) and interest components. With a noncallable bond, the future cash flows (principal and interest) are known with certainty. Even with a traditional mortgage security, where prepayments are not fully predictable, several things are certain: Ultimately, the face value of the instrument will be repaid at par; the coupon interest payable at any time is a function of the then-remaining principal; and prepayment variations will tend to reduce the gains in a falling rate environment and accentuate the losses in a rising rate environment.

High yield mortgage securities are different. Several of these instruments — CMO residuals and interest-only (IO) strips — have little or no principal, as that term is usually understood. Leveraged floaters have a face amount of principal and a coupon, but the coupon is determined by a formula quite unlike that for traditional floating-rate securities. Principal only (PO) strips have a face amount of principal but no coupon. It is therefore useful to characterize high-yield mortgage securities as streams of cash flows rather than as packages of principal and interest. Assignment of these flows to interest income and return of principal can be made for accounting purposes, but investors should consider the economic returns — the cash flows — rather than the accounting treatment, when making investment decisions. Calculations of yield and total return depend not on the characterization of the cash, but only on the amount and the timing of the cash flow.

The lack of principal amounts for some high-yield security types requires that price quotations be based on notional principal. That is, the price is expressed as a percentage of the principal amount of the underlying collateral, even though the security itself does not include the principal. Once this pricing convention is understood, it can be used in the same manner as more traditional investments.

Reasons to Invest in High-Yield Mortgage Securities

The first reason to own these instruments is, of course, yield. Quoted yields can be substantially higher than on any other investment of comparable quality, and from 100 to 800 basis points or more over the highest yielding Treasury securities. But there are other considerations as well.

High-yield mortgage securities are more sensitive to economic conditions than other fixed-income investments. That is, the price, or present value of future cash flows, can change more in response to a given move in market interest rates and/or prepayment rates than virtually any other security in the market except options and futures. This can make some high-yield mortgage securities valuable as hedging tools.

The extent to which this risk is viewed negatively will depend on whether prospective investors evaluate the risk factors in isolation or with respect to an entire portfolio. A number of high-yield securities are high-risk investments when viewed in isolation in that they have substantial positive or negative durations and/or are highly sensitive to prepayment shifts. Nevertheless, when these instruments are added to a general mortgage portfolio in appropriate quantities, they may serve to reduce overall interest-rate risk or prepayment risk. Although many of the same risk reduction objectives can, in theory, be accomplished through the use of futures, options, and interest rate swaps, high-yield mortgage securities offer many advantages: They are available for longer terms than futures and options; they offer higher yields during the holding periods than traditional hedging instruments, which tend to reduce portfolio yield; there is no maintenance margin requirement or overcollateralization required; and they may be considered qualifying real estate investments for savings institution tax purposes. High-yield mortgage securities also provide an alternative for those investors prevented by regulation from using futures and options to hedge their portfolios.

Analysts and investors specializing in equities have long recognized that assessing the risk of an investment depends on its "portfolio effect"—that is, its effect on total portfolio risk. The potential for raising aggregate portfolio yield while reducing overall portfolio risk presents intriguing opportunities for financial institutions with significant investments in mortgages and other fixed-rate debt instruments.

II. Characteristics of High-Yield Mortgage Securities

High-yield mortgage securities offer high yield, high credit quality, and a pattern of returns unlike those of other securities in the market. The presence of high-yield mortgage securities in a portfolio can enhance returns, reduce maturity gaps, hedge mortgages and bonds, and create synthetic instruments with desirable performance profiles. These advantages can be seen most clearly when the performance of these products is compared over a range of possible economic scenarios.

Yield and Duration

As their name suggests, high-yield mortgage securities offer investors higher yields than any other security of comparable quality. Some CMO residuals, interest-only strips, and leveraged floaters have been offered at yields of 3% or more above comparable Treasury securities, based on reasonable pricing and prepayment assumptions. Yields on some CMO residuals have been as high as 25%. Moreover, payback periods can be relatively short, often 3 to 5 years (see Table 1).

To quantify price sensitivity for securities with variable cash flows, the concept of "effective duration" is more appropriate than modified duration. Effective duration is an empirically determined relationship between changes in market interest rates and the price of a security. For securities without embedded options, effective and modified duration are equal, and can be expressed as unmodified duration divided by one plus the periodic yield. For securities with embedded options, such as callable bonds or mortgages that

TABLE 1. *Characteristics of High Yield Mortgage Securities.*

Security	Average Life Range (years)	Cash Flow Duration Range (years)	Effective Duration Range (years)	Yield Spread over Treasuries (%)
CMO residuals	2–5	1–4	−15–+1	2–16
IO strips	N/M	3–7	−20–+1	0–3
PO strips	3–9	3–7	+8–+18	0–3
Leveraged floaters	3–9	3–7	−2–+14	0–3

can be prepaid, effective duration is no longer equal to modified duration. In the case of CMO residuals, the disparity is particularly great: While the modified duration of bearish residuals is 2 to 4 years, the effective duration may be in the range of -10 to -15 years.

Credit Quality

Unlike many high-yield corporate securities, the attractive returns on residuals, strips, and leveraged floaters are not a reflection of actual or perceived credit risk. Some high-yield mortgage securities such as FNMA strips carry agency guarantees. Others, such as reverse floaters and privately issued strips, are rated AAA or AA. CMO residuals are backed by collateral rated AAA or AA. The trustee structure and segregated collateral employed in structured financings provides further protection to investors. These are securities of high quality that are unlikely ever to experience downgradings, because they are fully collateralized by assets that tend to appreciate even as the debt is paying down.

Patterns of Returns

The patterns of returns depend primarily on the movement of market interest rates. Interest rate levels affect not only the discount rate but also the cash flows themselves because of the sensitivity of mortgage prepayments to interest rate changes. In CMOs with floating-rate tranches, they can also affect the coupons being paid on the bonds. Typically, much of the effect of prepayment variability on the underlying mortgages is passed through to the holder of the high-yield mortgage security.

Although variability of returns is a characteristic of all high-yield mortgage securities, the direction and pattern of movement varies. Because of the partitioning of the principal and interest components, these securities can offer investors a wide range of investment alternatives. Some perform better when interest rates rise, others when rates fall. Returns may be symmetric or asymmetric, in either up or down markets.

Each pattern of returns suggests appropriate applications for high-yield mortgage securities. For investors with a clear point of view on market direction, these instruments provide the greatest potential for value appreciation. Institutions with large portfolios of long-term fixed-rate assets may find it more advantageous to accomplish restructuring objectives through the purchase of IO strips or CMO residuals than through the sale of existing assets or the acquisition of longer term liabilities. High-yield mortgage securities may be used to hedge other instruments or to create synthetic instruments with returns superior to traditional products.

How to Analyze High-Yield Mortgage Securities

Because the performance of high-yield mortgage securities is so sensitive to economic conditions, it is not sufficient to evaluate their purchase strictly on the basis of a single quoted yield to maturity. Investors should evaluate the sensitivity of returns to changes in the financial environment. This technique is generally termed *scenario analysis*.

The amount, timing, and value of the cash flows of high-yield mortgage securities are dependent on the course of economic events. Investors must understand how the value of these instruments will vary under the most likely scenarios. Scenarios are typically characterized by a projected path of future interest rates and mortgage prepayment rates. Each of these can vary independently, although there is a strong relationship between the level of market interest rates and the prepayment rates on fixed-rate mortgages. Interest rate changes influence investor discount rates, cash flow reinvestment rates, and coupon levels on floating-rate bonds. Prepayment rate changes affect the amount of cash flow from principal paid to bondholders and the size of the remaining balance on which interest continues to accrue.

Traditional yield calculations are insufficient to describe the complex interactions among these factors and the resulting impact on the value of the investments. Scenario analysis is a technique for modeling the performance of an investment under a variety of circumstances, aggregating these forecasts, and comparing alternative strategies.

For high-yield mortgage securities, scenario analysis begins with a set of possible market interest rate movements. This may range from a small number of highly simplified events (stable rates, rates up 100 basis points, rates down 100 basis points) to a random simulation of interest rate paths that can involve thousands of trials. It is also necessary to account for the fact that interest rate changes are not uniform across maturities and sectors — a model of yield curves and yield spreads is helpful. Finally, it is necessary to forecast mortgage prepayment rates for each interest rate scenario based on the level and pattern of mortgage rates, the age of the mortgages, and other factors. A typical prepayment model is shown in Figure 1.

Models like this can provide a realistic view of the cash flows anticipated from high-yield mortgage securities. Often, probabilities are assigned to each scenario, allowing calculation of an average expected return weighted by the probabilities. This reliable method of comparing alternative investments takes into account the fact that the realized performance of most securities in the market — and high-yield mortgage securities in particular — is dependent on future market conditions.

While scenario analysis is a powerful tool that may be used to evaluate a wide variety of fixed-income investments, it is not a perfect predictor. Actual prepayment rates may diverge from the model's estimate for reasons

FIGURE 1. *Prepayment Model.*

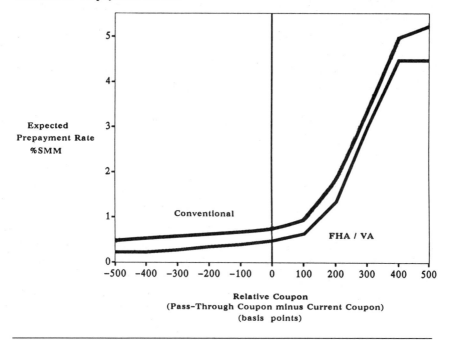

Expected
Prepayment Rate
%SMM

Conventional

FHA / VA

Relative Coupon
(Pass–Through Coupon minus Current Coupon)
(basis points)

unrelated to interest rates, mortgage age, and other factors accounted for. This variance is as likely to work to the benefit as to the detriment of the investor. Similarly, unanticipated events may cause yield spreads to narrow or widen, or yield volatility to increase or decrease. Scenario analysis nevertheless provides the best means of assembling all of the currently available market information into a structure that permits meaningful comparison among very different instruments.

III. CMO Residuals

Collateralized mortgage obligation (CMO) residuals present a relatively new investment opportunity for sophisticated investors. Previously, investments in residuals were available only to those institutions willing to issue CMOs. This required the expense and effort of creating issuing subsidiaries, filing shelf registrations with the Securities and Exchange Commission (SEC), developing or arranging for bond administration capabilities, and establishing investment banking and mortgage finance relationships. Because of several recent legal and accounting developments, investors can now purchase interests in residual cash flows directly from CMO issuers. This can involve purchasing existing residuals "off the shelf" from CMO issuers such as mortgage bankers, home builders, mortgage conduit operations, or investment banks, or it can entail the purchase of "custom tailored" residuals created by a special issuer according to the investor's specifications.

CMO residuals are the equity of the corporation or trust that issued the CMO. Generally, this equity is sold to investors on a private-placement basis, where the investor purchases common stock or Certificates of Beneficial Interest in the Owner Trust. A few CMO-issuing corporations have issued common stock to the public. Residuals may be issued as REMIC residual interests.

Residuals arise from the creation of a structured financing in which the cash flows of a pool of assets are used to fund the cash flow requirements of one or more classes of collateralized debt. For the most part, residual cash flows result from the positive spread between the cash flow generated by a pool of assets and the cash flow required to serve one or more classes of bonds collateralized by those assets. This is shown schematically in Figure 2. Indeed, the spread between the mortgage and CMO cash flows is the primary reason for issuing a CMO.

All investments in residuals assign to the investor an expected (but uncertain) stream of future cash flows. Figure 3 shows a typical pattern for residual cash flows in relation to the CMO bond cash flows. Initially, the level of cash flow is high. It begins to drop rapidly with the amortization of the assets collateralizing the bonds. As the shape of the expected cash flow in-

---

FIGURE 2. *CMO Cash Flows.*

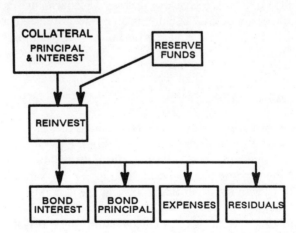

FIGURE 3. *CMO Cash Flows.*

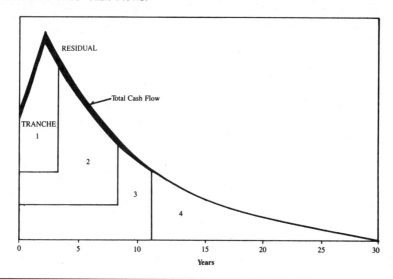

dicates, residuals typically have a final cash flow corresponding to the final maturity of the collateral, but the expected cash flow duration of the investment is very short.

Unlike most fixed-income investments, these cash flows are not explicitly divisible into principal and interest components. As CMO equity, residuals represent the ownership of the stream of excess cash flows generated by the trust—that is, the net income or "profits."

Residuals essentially represent a leveraged investment in a closed-end, match-funded bond portfolio. Economically, ownership of residuals amounts to ownership of a pool of collateral that is partially funded through a series of liabilities, generally CMOs. The economic characteristics of residuals depend on the characteristics of the assets, the characteristics of the liabilities, and how they are combined. The structural integrity required of the CMO bonds by the rating agencies ensures that the assets will always prove sufficient to support the bonds with the same degree of creditworthiness as the assets. Therefore, unlike investments in some mismatched asset/liability strategies, an investment in residuals will not produce cash shortfalls after the investment has occurred.

Components of Residual Cash Flows

Residuals are cash flows resulting from the difference between the cash generated by a pool of collateral and that required to fund bonds that are entirely supported by that collateral. Behind the seemingly complicated nature of residual cash flows are a number of basic building blocks, each of which behaves in a straightforward manner. By understanding each component individually, it becomes possible to understand how and why residuals behave the way they do. The components of residual cash flow are:

- Collateral principal payments
- Collateral interest payments
- Reinvestment interest on collateral cash flow
- Bond principal retirements
- Bond interest payments
- Bond administration expenses

The behavior of each of these components will vary depending upon the type of collateral, the types of bonds, and other details specific to the structured financing. Each of the six components of residual cash flow will respond differently to the general state of the economy and general conditions in the financial markets.

Collateral principal payments have two parts: scheduled payments and unscheduled prepayments. In fact, the majority of the principal paid from a pool of mortgages in a given period consists of unscheduled principal. Because of this, the amount of cash flow available to the residuals will vary substantially with the rate of prepayments. Generally, the slower the prepayment rate, the greater the longevity of the cash stream payable to residual holders. The exact impact of prepayment changes on residual cash flows, and thus on total performance, can vary significantly from one residual to the next.

Collateral interest payments are another major source of cash inflow in a CMO. Unlike collateral principal payments, in which only the timing of cash flows is affected by prepayments, both the timing *and* the total amount of collateral interest payments will vary with prepayments. As prepayment rates increase, the total amount of collateral interest payments that will be received decreases, and vice versa.

Reinvestment interest on collateral cash flow is the third source of residuals. All CMO structures require some delay between the receipt of collateral cash flows and the scheduled payments to bondholders. While collateral pays monthly, most CMOs pay quarterly. Therefore, there is usually some period during which collateral cash flows must be reinvested. Most, if not all, of the reinvestment interest earned on the cash flows awaiting payment to bondholders is paid to residual holders. While this is not typically a main source of residual cash flow, its effect will be greater in CMOs where the size of the residual is small in percentage terms, or where the reinvestment period is longer.

An important determinant of the amount of reinvestment interest payable to the residual holder is the actual interest rate available on the funds to be reinvested. For residual holders, this component of their cash flow will generally increase as interest rates increase, since these temporary cash balances are invested in money market instruments earning current market rates.

Bond principal retirements absorb collateral cash flow and its reinvestment interest. Most CMOs have been issued with the provision that the rate of prepayment on the collateral will determine the rate of principal retirement on the bonds. This means that rapid amortization of the bonds almost always occurs when the collateral prepays rapidly. Similarly, if the collateral prepayment slows down, so will that of the bonds. Because the size of the residual cash flows is a function of the amount of bonds outstanding, rapid retirements of CMO bond principal tend to hurt residual holders, while slow retirements tend to help them.

Bond interest payments, like bond principal retirements, absorb collateral cash flow and reinvestment interest. Increases in these interest payments always reduce the amount of cash flow available to residual holders. The amount of interest to be paid varies directly with the remaining amount of bond principal and, in the case of floating-rate tranches, with the level of the bond's index rate.

Most CMO floaters have their coupons indexed to three-month LIBOR. The cash flow to residual holders in these transactions will tend to increase as the index rate decreases and decrease as the index rate increases. The position of the floating-rate CMO residual holder is analogous to that of a financial institution that finances fixed-rate assets with floating-rate liabilities. Unlike such a financial institution, however, the residual investor is ensured that there will never be a negative spread between the collateral and the liabilities it supports.

Bond administration expenses are the last and least significant end to which collateral cash flows must be applied. To the extent that these bond expenses increase, the returns to the residual holders decrease. These fees include expenses for the Indenture Trustee, accountants, rating agencies, and legal counsel. Some of these expenses will increase over time because of inflation. Thus, bond administration expenses, as a percentage of residual cash flow, will have a tendency to rise, since the compounding effects of expense inflation occur simultaneously with the amortization of both the collateral and the bonds.

The timing of cash flows under a characteristic scenario for residuals produced by a typical CMO, the FBC Mortgage Securities Trust V, is illustrated in Table 2.

Different Types of Residual Investments

Residuals represent the differential between mortgage collateral and CMO bond cash flows; as such, they are highly sensitive to minor alterations in the

TABLE 2. *FBC Mortgage Securities Trust V, Summary of Residual Cash Flows (FHLMC 9.4% WAC Collateral, Priced at 185% PSA).*[a]

For the Year Ending January 20	Principal & Interest on FHLMC Certificates	Reinvestment Income at 6.00%	Principal & Interest on Bonds	Bond & Trust Expenses	Draws from Reserve Funds[b]	Bond Administrator Fee[c]	Distributable Cash Flow
1988	$75,964	$431	$72,049	$87	$ 0	$39	$4,220
1989	94,515	539	90,520	100	0	50	4,383
1990	83,718	477	80,257	94	0	50	3,794
1991	74,083	422	71,099	89	0	50	3,267
1992	65,523	374	62,970	84	0	50	2,793
1993	57,919	330	55,753	80	0	50	2,366
1994	51,165	292	49,350	77	0	50	1,980
1995	45,166	258	43,670	73	0	50	1,630
1996	39,838	227	38,636	70	0	50	1,309
1997	35,107	200	34,175	68	0	50	1,015
1998	30,906	176	30,219	65	0	50	748
1999	27,177	155	26,719	63	0	50	500
2000	23,867	136	23,590	62	0	50	302
2001	20,929	119	20,700	60	0	50	238
2002	18,322	105	18,126	59	0	50	191
2003	16,009	91	15,843	57	0	50	150
2004	13,958	80	13,819	56	0	50	113
2005	12,139	69	12,023	55	0	50	80

TABLE 2 *Continued*

For the Year Ending January 20	Principal & Interest on FHLMC Certificates	Reinvestment Income at 6.00%	Principal & Interest on Bonds	Bond & Trust Expenses	Draws from Reserve Funds[b]	Bond Administrator Fee[c]	Distributable Cash Flow
2006	$10,527	$60	$10,431	$54	$ 0	$50	$51
2007	9,097	52	9,020	54	0	50	25
2008	7,831	45	7,771	53	0	49	4
2009	6,710	38	6,664	52	0	32	0
2010	5,718	33	5,684	52	0	15	0
2011	4,840	28	4,817	51	2	1	0
2012	4,063	23	4,050	51	15	0	0
2013	3,377	19	3,373	51	27	0	0
2014	2,333	14	2,337	50	40	0	0
2015	1,574	9	1,582	50	48	0	0
2016	420	3	422	38	603	0	227
Total	842,799	4,804	815,668	1,858	736	1,427	29,387

a. Dollars in thousands rounded to the nearest thousand.

b. Draws from the Reserve Funds are sufficient to cover shortfalls as well as to release funds from the Bond Reserve Fund upon the retirement of the Bonds.

c. Fees due to the Bond Administrator that are not payable from funds released from the lien of the Indenture are deferred until sufficient cash flow from the Reserve Funds becomes available.

collateral or bond structures. Thus, the economic characteristics of residuals do not lend themselves to a single stereotype.

In order to demonstrate how residuals can perform differently, this section will discuss the three basic kinds of CMO residuals produced to date, which we will label as "bearish," "humped," and "stable." As new CMO structures continue to evolve, it is likely that hybrids of these residual types will emerge.

Bearish residuals increase in yield as interest rates increase, and decrease in yield as interest rates fall. The overwhelming majority of CMO residuals produced prior to the fall of 1986 were bearish residuals. This kind of residual was created by using mortgage securities as collateral for CMOs with only fixed-coupon tranches. The large negative duration of bearish residuals, comparable to shorting an ordinary bond, makes them attractive for hedging purposes. This feature can be seen in Figure 4, where a typical investment in bearish residuals is shown to yield in excess of 20% for interest rate increases in excess of 100 basis points, with a steep decline in yield for interest rate drops of more than 50 basis points. Bearish residuals are offered at wide spreads over long U.S. Treasury bonds and are especially attractive in light of their counter-cyclical performance characteristics.

FIGURE 4. *Scenario Yields on Bearish Residuals.*

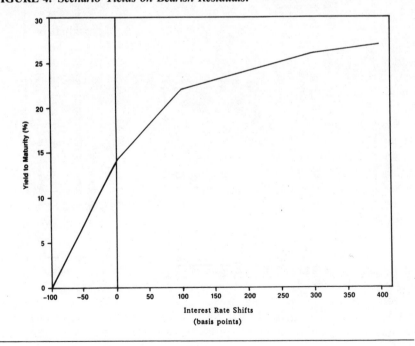

The shorter maturity tranches of a multi-class, fixed-rate CMO will have lower coupons than the longer tranches when the yield curve is positively sloped. Thus, as the underlying mortgages prepay and amortize and the shorter, lower coupon tranches pay down, the average coupon rate on the remaining bonds will rise. For example, the FBC Mortgage Securities Trust III Series A at issue had three tranches of unequal size bearing coupon rates of 8.825%, 9.70%, and 9.50%, respectively, resulting in a weighted average coupon of 9.073%. The underlying collateral has a coupon rate of 10%. Initially, therefore, the residual cash flows are approximately equal to 0.927% of the amount of the bonds outstanding: 10% received from the collateral, less 9.073% on average paid on the bonds. After the first tranche is retired, however, the weighted-average coupon of the CMO would be 9.638%. At that point, the residual cash flows would be smaller, because there are fewer bonds outstanding and because the weighted-average coupon on the remaining bonds increases. These residuals have a relatively short payback period, or "stated" duration. (Stated duration is calculated by projecting the cash flows and then determining the average amount of time until receipt of present value.) The amount of residual cash flow declines sharply over time. Stated duration on most residuals of this type ranges from 2 to 4 years. Events in the more distant future have little impact on the return to residual holders.

As a consequence, if interest rates fall and prepayments rise, rapid prepayments of the shorter classes will both reduce the coupon spread between the CMO and the mortgage collateral and shorten the longevity of the residual cash flows. Conversely, in a rising rate environment, residual holders will enjoy both a wider spread and longer lasting residual cash flows. Due to these relationships, the performance of bearish residuals will tend to be inversely related to that of most fixed-income securities. Whereas most fixed-income investments perform best in a falling rate environment, bearish residuals will perform better in a rising rate environment.

Humped residuals tend to command a higher yield than bearish residuals because their yield at pricing generally represents their best possible performance. They do not have the substantial upside of bearish residuals, nor are they "natural" hedges. Their most attractive characteristic is their current yield. These residuals exhibit extremely high returns if interest rates remain relatively stable after the CMO is issued; their performance declines if interest rates either increase or decrease dramatically. Scenario yields on humped residuals are shown in Figure 5.

Stable residuals offer lower yields than humped residuals because they have much less downside risk. Within a wide range of market rates—generally 200 basis points above and below the market level at issuance—these residuals behave like short-term money market instruments. Their yield rises and falls with market rates, but at a spread substantially above competing investments. As shown in Figure 6, under a falling interest rate environment,

FIGURE 5. *Scenario Yields on Humped Residuals.*

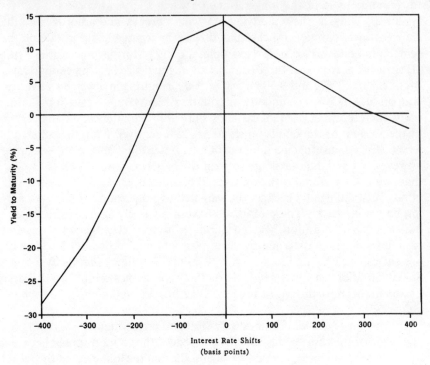

the yield drops as rates decline up to 200 basis points, and then begins to rise. Under a rising rate environment, the yield increases as interest rates increase up to 200 basis points, and then begins to decline.

Stable residuals were first created with the FBC Mortgage Securities Trust VI, the first CMO consisting primarily or exclusively of floating-rate tranches. The residual cash flows in cases like this arise from the difference between the coupon payment on fixed-rate mortgage collateral and the floating-rate payments to CMO holders.

Stable residuals, like floating-rate securities, have an expected effective duration close to zero. As interest rates change, two opposing forces affect the residual cash flows. First, changes in interest rates cause the spread between the fixed-rate assets and floating-rate liabilities to change. Lower levels of LIBOR, for example, create a greater spread between the fixed-rate collateral and the floating-rate liabilities. That is, as LIBOR declines, the size of residuals increases; conversely, as LIBOR increases, the size of residuals decreases.

FIGURE 6. *Scenario Yields on Stable Residuals.*

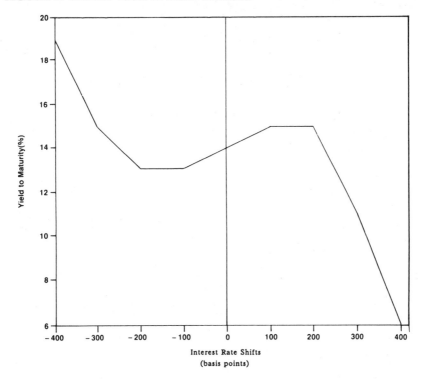

Second, changes in interest rates cause changes in prepayment speeds. Declining rates accelerate prepayments, and vice versa. Higher prepayment rates, in turn, reduce the level of residual cash flows. Conversely, lower rates of prepayment increase residual cash flows.

Figure 7 demonstrates the effect of simultaneous changes in LIBOR and prepayment rates on residual cash flows. For stable residuals, if mortgage and short-term rates go down, residual cash flows per period go up, but they are received for a shorter period of time than they otherwise would have been. Conversely, if mortgage and short-term rates go up, residual cash flows go down, but their expected longevity increases, since the underlying mortgages prepay at slower rates.

As long as mortgage rates and short rates move roughly in tandem, these two effects will offset each other to a large extent, producing fairly constant present values. The value of stable residuals can be affected, however, by divergences from the historical inverse relationship between LIBOR and prepayment rates. When spreads between mortgage rates and short-term rates

FIGURE 7. *FBC Mortgage Securities Trust X Residual Cash Flow under Alternative LIBOR and Prepayment Rates.*

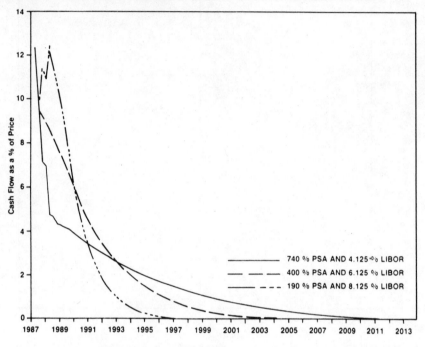

shift, investors will receive the greatest return when mortgage rates rise and short-term rates fall, that is, when the yield curve steepens. Conversely, investors will receive their poorest return when mortgage rates fall while short-term rates rise.

Bonds Taxable as REMIC Residual Interests

An alternative CMO structure eliminates non-securitized residual cash flows. Instead, the cash flow that would have gone into residuals is structured into high-coupon CMO bonds, which are publicly offered. The first appearances of this structure were the Collateralized Mortgage Securities Corporation, CMO Series J and K. In each of these transactions the traditional first tranche was stripped of some of its coupon interest, which was subsequently placed in a new second tranche with a small amount of principal. The J-2 and K-2 bonds are rated securities with face principal amounts and coupon rates. They carry high coupon rates (e.g., 100% or more) and prices (e.g., 300 or higher). Their yields tend to be lower than those for residuals sold as private placement owner trusts or limited partnerships, reflecting the fact that they constitute AAA-rated debt rather than unrated equity.

This new structure was facilitated by the 1986 tax law that created Real Estate Mortgage Investment Conduits (REMICs). While these instruments are corporate bonds, they are, for income tax purposes, REMIC residual interests. This is in contrast to the other CMO bonds, which are, for income tax purposes, REMIC regular interests. The analysis of the after-tax returns of REMIC residual interests is complicated and beyond the scope of this article.

Analyzing Residuals

Unlike most fixed-income investments, residuals are not explicitly separated into principal and interest components. They do not carry a stipulated rate of return on an identifiable notional amount. Rather, their cash flows are "contingent," depending for their ultimate size on the performance of a given pool of collateral. Market rates of interest, collateral yields, and mortgage prepayment rates all affect cash flows.

When a price is quoted, it is quoted at a certain pricing speed and discount rate, and the investor typically examines a range of internal rates of return over different shifts in interest rates and prepayment speeds. This range shows the investor how the residuals will perform in different cases and makes clear the shape of the residuals. In analyzing residuals, investors focus on yield or payback period; because the secondary market for residuals is limited, projected total rate of return is less meaningful than for other high-yield mortgage securities.

Investors can purchase residual cash flows without the expenses and encumbrances of issuing CMOs directly. With high yields and a variety of performance characteristics — characteristics that can be tailored to fit an investor's needs — CMO residuals present new opportunities for financial management.

IV. Strips

Mortgage strips are created by altering the distribution of interest and principal on a pass-through from pro rata to an unequal allocation. In the extreme case, interest only (IO) is paid to one class of investor while principal only (PO) is paid to the other class of investor. More moderate allocation can be made as well. FNMA 8s, for example, can be broken down into equal principal amounts of 5% and 11% strips.

A variant of stripped mortgage-backed securities was the forerunner of today's high-yield mortgage securities. Even before mortgage-backed securities were created, trading of whole loans took place, and often the coupon rate associated with these loans was less than that paid by the borrower. The originator, who typically continued to service the loan, would retain a portion of the coupon interest. Over time, these servicing portfolios were seen to generate cash flows in excess of the costs of servicing; hence the term "excess servicing." An active market in the trading of servicing portfolios developed. Mortgage bankers and thrifts could originate new loans at or near par, strip a portion of the coupon, and resell the loans at a discount. The stream of excess servicing, although somewhat uncertain, was expected to have a present discounted value in excess of the discount on the loans sold.

Stripped mortgage-backed securities are a refined descendant of excess servicing. A stripped mortgage-backed security is either a pass-through or a pay-through instrument with two or more different tranches. Unlike traditional serial-pay CMOs, where payments of principal are made sequentially, in the strip structure payments are usually made concurrently to all classes. Unlike traditional pass-throughs, which have a single class and where all certificate holders receive pro rata shares of principal and interest, the allocation of principal differs from the allocation of interest in a strip. For example, a security may be created with two tranches, each representing a half share in the underlying principal amount. The interest payments may be allocated differently: One-third may be allocated to one class, for example, and two-thirds to the other class. Thus, the tranches would have a coupon rate below and above that of the underlying collateral, respectively.

This process is valuable because it separates the linkage between the dollar price of the security and its prepayment rate. In the pass-through market, prices above par are associated with higher prepayment rates, and prices below par are associated with lower prepayment rates. The stripping process allows either the creation of premium securities with slow prepayment rates when discount collateral is used or discount securities with fast prepayment rates when premium collateral is used. This innovation expands the range of performance for mortgage securities, creating instruments that fit a wider variety of investor needs. Mortgage strips are typically created as agency pass-through or private-label rated pass-through securities, or as tranches of CMOs/REMICs. They therefore enjoy the same credit quality and financing ability as more traditional instruments. Like traditional pass-throughs, strips are generally considered qualifying mortgage assets for savings institutions.

The first publicly offered stripped mortgage-backed securities were issued in the second half of 1986. Premiums and discounts were created from seasoned collateral, as shown in Figures 8 and 9. The coupon on the collateral was such that the collateral itself would have been priced near par. In one transaction, the coupon of the premium tranche was raised to a super premium 600%, with most of the principal of course allocated to the discount tranche. In early 1987, the "ultimate" stripped mortgage-backed securities were issued: the interest-only/principal-only (IO/PO) structure. All of the interest and none of the principal go to one tranche, while the other

FIGURE 8. *Graphical Analysis of SMBS: Parent Is a FNMA 8%.*

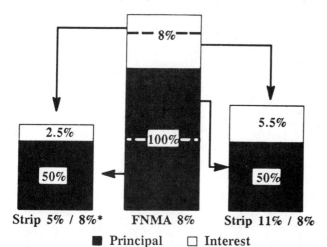

*Strip 5% / 8% means that a Synthetic 5% Coupon Security has been derived from an underlying 8% Security.

FIGURE 9. *Graphical Analysis of SMBS: Parent Is a FNMA 9%.*

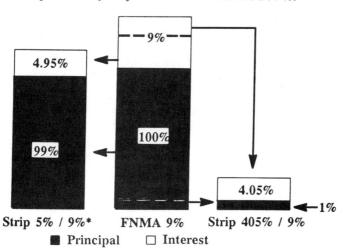

*Strip 5% / 9% means that a Synthetic 5% Coupon Security has been derived from an underlying 9% Security.

tranche is a zero-coupon instrument. Most strip offerings have been of the IO/PO variety. Generally speaking, it is the IO stripped security that will most often fit into the "high-yield" category, because its value is more likely

FIGURE 10. *Cash Flow on a FNMA 7-1/2% MBS (8% WAC, 240 Month WAM, 0.55% SMM).*

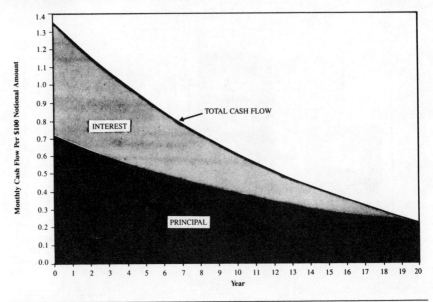

to demonstrate acute sensitivity to fluctuations in interest rates and prepayment rates. PO securities backed by higher collateral will also offer higher yields.

Determinants of Cash Flow and Yield in IO/PO Strips

The cash flows from a typical mortgage-backed security are shown in Figure 10. If the underlying pass-through were stripped to produce IO and PO classes, the holders would receive the amounts shown by the areas marked "Interest" and "Principal," respectively. PO holders receive both amortization and prepayments, while IO investors receive all of the coupon payments.

Investors in IO strips face uncertainty with respect to the timing and ultimate amount of cash that will be realized. Prepayments are the major factor that affect the timing and amount of IO cash flows. The slower the rate of prepayments on the underlying collateral, the higher the rate of return to the IO holder. Figure 11 shows the cash flows to IO investors at different prepayment rates. Because of the concentration of prepayment risk in IO securities, and the concomitant uncertainty of cash flow, investors in IO strips are compensated with higher yields than they would receive on other types of mortgage securities. The highest yields occur with collateral just above the current coupon, because those securities have the greatest potential for

FIGURE 11. *Prepayment Sensitivity: Interest Only Strip.*

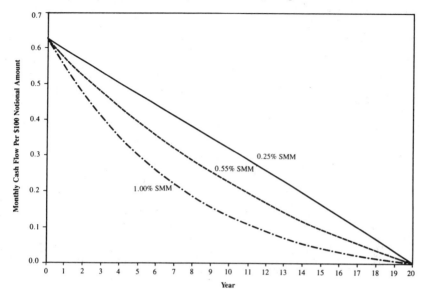

substantially faster prepayments and a consequent loss of value with modest declines in interest rates. Conversely, lower yields occur when the collateral prepayment rate remains level or slows down for small changes in market interest rates, that is, for discount or higher premium collateral.

Investors in PO strips can be certain of the amount of cash that will be realized, but not the timing of the cash flows. The faster the rates of prepay-·ments on the underlying collateral, the higher the rate of return to the PO holder. Figure 12 shows the cash flows to PO investors at different prepayment rates. Because of the defined face amount and the stabilizing effect of scheduled principal amortization, PO strips are slightly less sensitive to prepayment rates than are IO strips. Nevertheless, PO strips can still demonstrate substantial price volatility, particularly when backed by higher coupon mortgages. In such circumstances, PO strips would be offered at higher yields to compensate for the prepayment uncertainty. Higher coupon mortgages have more potential for a deceleration in cash flow than do current coupon or discount mortgages already demonstrating a low prepayment rate.

Different Types of Strips

Investors can purchase strips in a wide variety of forms. Strips are available either as direct agency securities or as securities issued by private issuers

FIGURE 12. *Prepayment Sensitivity: Principal Only Strip.*

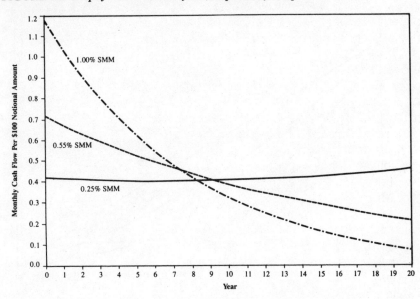

backed by agency collateral. For instance, FNMA issued its Trust 1 IO/PO Strip backed by its own mortgage pools. Similarly, First Boston Mortgage Securities Corporation issued its SPLITS™, Series B IO/PO backed by FNMA 9s.

SPLITS backed by FNMAs and FHLMCs have exactly the same collateral as synthetics issued by those agencies directly. Payments from the underlying collateral are passed to investors when received.

Privately issued strips can also be purchased in the form of CMO bonds. Some CMO tranches have been issued that do not entail sequential payment of principal. For instance, one tranche of First Boston Mortgage Securities Corporation CMO Trust XI was issued with a coupon of 100%. This gave the tranche almost exactly the same financial properties as an IO backed by GNMA 11s, which was the collateral backing the CMO. Regardless of whether a strip is a direct agency issue, a private pass-through, or a tranche of a CMO, investors should focus almost exclusively on the collateral to determine investment performance.

IO Strips and Portfolio Hedging

Strips can prove effective in hedging both bond and mortgage-based portfolios. Bearish investors can use strips and certain CMO residuals to reduce the volatility and increase the yield of a range of fixed income debt and mortgage-based portfolios.

The performance of the IO tranche will depend disproportionately on prepayments. The amount of cash received in each period is determined by the principal amount of mortgages outstanding at the beginning of the period. As the mortgages amortize and prepay, the notional principal upon which the coupon is computed will decrease. Higher rates of prepayment therefore reduce the return to the investor in IO strips. Since higher prepayments are associated with declining interest rates, the value of an IO strip will generally move inversely with those of other fixed-income debt instruments. Specifically, because IO strips perform better with lower prepayment rates, they should prove especially effective in raising the yield while reducing the prepayment sensitivity of portfolios consisting largely of current coupon and discount mortgages. IO strips may be thought of as a long put option (or short call option) on prepayments. The same is true for bearish CMO residuals.

As an example, consider a thrift institution holding $100 million in recently originated 8.5% and 9.0% mortgage securities, with an approximate market value of $102 million, yielding 7.95%. That firm could purchase $40 million notional principal amount of an IO strip backed by GNMA 11s, at an approximate cost of $12 million. The aggregate portfolio would then have a yield spread of approximately 140 basis points over short-term funding costs that is protected over a range of -100 to $+200$ basis point shifts in interest rates. In a rising rate environment, the strip position would appreciate at approximately the same rate as the mortgage portfolio declined in value. Conversely, in a 100 basis point declining rate environment, the GNMA portfolio would appreciate and the IO strip would decrease in value, but the combined market value would be stable. These results are shown schematically in Figure 13. This strategy has an advantage over other hedging techniques in that the cash flows on the IO strip decline over time, roughly matching those on the mortgage portfolio. The average life of the IO strip will lengthen and shorten approximately in lockstep with the mortgage security portfolio.

PO Strips and Synthetic Securities

Principal-only strips generally have very long effective durations. When backed by premium mortgages, they may be offered at relatively high yields. Taking advantage of these two properties, investors can combine PO strips with money market, floating-rate, or other short duration securities to form intermediate duration synthetics. These synthetics may have higher yields than comparable maturity securities found in the market.

For example, $10 million face amount in PO strips backed by FNMA 9s may be combined with $30 million of 2-year Treasuries. The combination has performance characteristics similar to a 7-year Treasury over a ±200 basis point range of yield curve shifts, but consistently provides higher total returns. Over a 1-year holding period with no change in rates, the synthetic

FIGURE 13. *GNMA plus IO Strip Portfolio.*

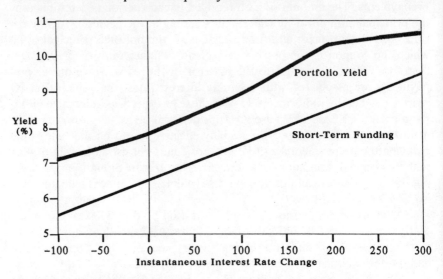

security returns 9.1% to the 7-year's 7.1%. In rising rate environments, the short maturity of the 2-year Treasury prevents the return of the synthetic from declining as sharply as the 7-year Treasury. With falling interest rates, rising prepayments on the PO strip more than offset the small appreciation of the 2-year to maintain a return advantage over the 7-year.

V. Leveraged Floaters

A third type of high-yield mortgage-backed security is the leveraged floater. A leveraged floater is a security whose interest rate varies by a multiple of a specified index or inversely with that index. Thus, unlike traditional floaters, whose hallmark is a coupon that remains close to market and a price that remains close to par, the leveraged floater will react sharply to changes in market yields.

Leveraged floating-rate mortgage-backed securities have been created as tranches of CMOs and share many of the attributes of other mortgage securities, including prepayment uncertainty. There are two basic types of leveraged floaters.

One subcategory of leveraged floaters is the "super floater": When the index rises, the coupon is reset upwards by more than the move in market rates, and when the index declines the coupon shifts downward by a multiple of the drop. The coupon rate is quoted according to a multiple of the index and a constant, such as "2 × LIBOR − 7%." The super floater is a bearish instrument, increasing in value when rates are rising and declining in value when rates are falling.

The other subcategory is the "reverse floater": When the index declines, the coupon is reset upwards, and vice versa. A simple reverse floater might have a coupon of "14% − LIBOR." Reverse floaters are bullish instruments, increasing in value when rates are falling and declining in value when rates are rising. Reverse super floaters have also been created, so that a one-point rise in the index generates more than a one-point drop in the coupon (and vice versa). Reverse floaters were introduced to the market before super floaters.

Reverse floaters were first developed in early 1986 for the corporate bond sector. These securities had relatively short maturities, but had coupons that varied inversely with market rates, thus providing investors with a means of participating in the market rally with instruments of short final maturity.

The value of a reverse floater varies inversely with interest rates as a result of two factors: the coupon and the rate of discounting. When market yields decline, the reverse floater coupon rises while the discount rate declines. Both factors increase the value of the security.

A reverse floater has an effective duration longer than its cash flow duration—longer even than its final maturity—which is to say it will be more volatile than even a zero-coupon bond of the same maturity. Figure 14 shows

FIGURE 14. *Reverse Floater Expected Yield Analysis.*

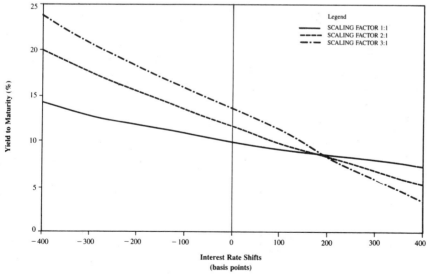

how reverse floaters with different leverage factors can be expected to perform across a range of interest rate shifts.

A mortgage-backed reverse floater has an additional characteristic not found in traditional reverse floating-rate notes. As interest rates decline, the coupon on a reverse floater will increase and the discount rate will drop, which by themselves would give a sharp boost to the value of a reverse floater. But at the same time, the rate of prepayments on the underlying collateral will increase, more quickly reducing the outstanding balance on which the coupon is earned, thereby attenuating some of the increase in value.

Conversely, in a rising rate environment, the coupon will decrease, the discount rate will rise, and prepayments will slow, all of which combined will sharply depress the value of the instrument. In the terms of fixed-income analysis, these securities have substantial negative convexity. Unlike CMO residuals and IO strips, however, leveraged floaters do have "principal" assigned to them, and a rapid acceleration of prepayments will not result in the evaporation of the security's value.

Super floaters offer investors a highly bearish security with attractive immunization properties in a rapidly rising rate environment. Because its coupon resets at a multiple of the underlying index, super floater investments provide yields higher than the cost of short-term liabilities when interest rates

FIGURE 15. *Performance of Leveraged Floaters.*

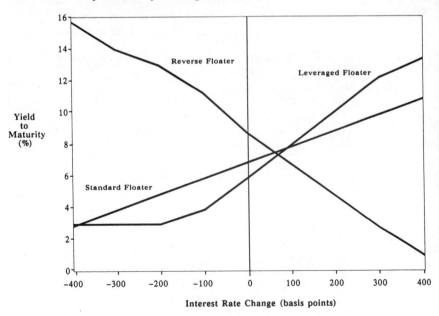

increase. Because of this property, super floaters are offered at relatively low initial yields, usually somewhat below that obtainable on a traditional floater.

Reverse floaters are offered at high initial yields. These yields will improve with any decline in rates. Because of their initially high yields, reverse floaters will generally outperform a traditional floater or a super floater until rates rise by more than 100 basis points. Figure 15 presents typical performance profiles for standard, super, and reverse floaters. The exact performance of these instruments will be specific to the issue, depending on the leverage factor, initial rate, and price.

Reverse floaters are suited either for the investor with a definite belief that market rates are stable or heading downwards, or for the sophisticated investor in the context of a portfolio of other securities. For example, they may be used to offset high-cost floating-rate liabilities, such as interest rate swaps. They may also be used with other high-yield mortgage securities to create stabilized yields in excess of what is obtainable from traditional mortgage securities. Figure 16 shows the performance of a reverse floater combined in a ratio of two to one with an IO strip. The reverse floater exhibits bullish performance, while the IO strip exhibits bearish performance. The synthetic, however, exhibits a surprising degree of stability at attractive yields.

FIGURE 16. *Performance of a Reverse Floater Combined with IOs.*

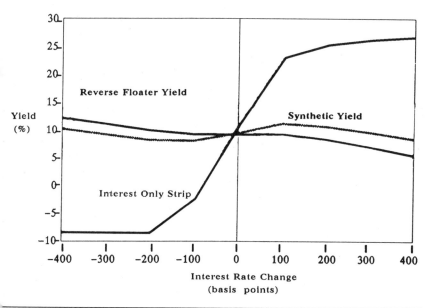

VI. Conclusions

While the evolution of high-yield, high-risk mortgage securities presents new opportunities to investors, it is not an unmixed blessing. Many forms of high-yield mortgage securities are extremely complex, and the value range is wide; investor success will require the ability to analyze and discriminate among various high-yield products. Investors who do not take the time and effort to understand the performance characteristics and qualitative differences between individual high-yield mortgage securities are not likely to enjoy maximum economic performance. For those who do, however, the rewards could prove substantial.

High-yield mortgage securities are not for all investors; they are powerful vehicles that tend to have large degrees of interest-rate risk, prepayment risk, or both. Like most new markets, the market for high-yield mortgage securities often exhibits considerable inefficiencies and can therefore offer abnormally high yield spreads, both before and after adjustment for risk. It is inevitable that these spreads will narrow over time as the high-yield mortgage market matures. In the interim, investors who are already familiar with mortgages and the associated risks may find that the effort to understand the evolving forms of high-yield mortgage securities will result in considerable benefits.

Overview of Interest Rate Risk Control Tools for Investment Management

Frank J. Fabozzi, Ph.D., CFA
Visiting Professor of Finance
Sloan School of Management
Massachusetts Institute of Technology
and
Editor, *The Journal of Portfolio Management*

I. Introduction

Since the late 1970s, the fixed income market has been characterized by substantial interest rate volatility. As a result, managers of fixed income portfolios need tools to protect against interest rate volatility. Futures contracts on fixed income instruments, first traded in 1975, offer fixed income managers the opportunity for interest rate protection. Exchange-traded options on fixed income instruments, which began trading in 1982, allow fixed income portfolio managers to protect against adverse interest rate movements. The early 1980s saw the introduction of interest rate swaps, a tool that asset/liability managers could use to protect against adverse interest rate movements. In the 1980s, dealers began writing interest rate agreements that allowed asset/liability managers to cap their interest rate costs or to place a floor on their investment returns.

The purpose of this article is to provide an overview of these interest rate risk control tools, focusing on their risk-return characteristics and how they can be employed by fixed income portfolio managers. Details of the contracts and trading mechanics are not discussed.

*The author wishes to acknowledge the helpful comments of Dessa Fabozzi, Frank Jones and Beth Krumholz.

II. Futures and Forward Contracts

Futures and *forward contracts* are agreements in which two parties, the buyer and seller, agree to transact at some predetermined future date at a price specified today. The price at which the parties agree to transact at is called the *futures price*. The seller of the contract agrees to make delivery of some designated instrument (or commodity) while the buyer agrees to accept delivery. While there are futures and forward contracts in which the "thing" to be delivered[1] is a commodity, fixed income security, foreign currency, or stock index, our focus is on contracts involving fixed income securities. Since the price of a fixed income security depends on interest rates, we refer to these contracts as *interest rate futures* or *forward contracts*.

The differences between futures and forward contracts are:

1. Futures contracts are standardized agreements as to the delivery date (or month), quality and quantity of the deliverable, and are traded on organized exchanges. A forward contract is usually nonstandardized, and secondary markets are often nonexistent or extremely thin.

2. Unlike forward contracts, there are margin requirements for futures contracts. The amount of the margin that must be posted when a futures position is opened is called initial margin. The trader's equity in a futures account will change each day as the position is *marked to market*. This means that each day the profit from the previous day is calculated and added to the trader's account balance. If there is a loss it is subtracted from the trader's account balance. The exchange specifies a minimum maintenance margin. If as a result of marking the position to market the value of the account falls below the maintenance margin, the broker will request additional margin (called variation margin). The trader can withdraw funds from the account if profits are realized. Forward contracts are not marked to market.

3. Because of the marking to market procedure, there may be interim cash flows from a futures position – additional cash might have to be added to the trader's account or might be withdrawn from the trader's account – depending on whether there are adverse or favorable price movements.

4. The parties in a forward contract are exposed to credit risk because either party may default on their obligation. In contrast, credit risk for futures contracts is minimal because the clearing corporation associated with the exchange where the futures contract is traded guarantees the other side of the transaction. That is, the clearing corporation becomes the buyer to every seller and the seller to every buyer.

---

1. Actually, some futures contracts specify cash settlement rather than physical delivery of the underlying instrument. Examples include stock index futures, Eurodollar CD futures and municipal bond index futures.

In addition, although both futures and forward contracts set forth terms of delivery, futures are not intended to be settled by delivery; in fact, generally less than 2% of outstanding contracts are delivered. In contrast, forward contracts are intended for delivery.

Since all other characteristics of futures and forward contracts are the same, we will generally refer only to futures contracts below.

Risk-Return Characteristics

When an investor takes a position in the market by buying a futures contract, the investor is said to be in a *long position* or *long futures*. If, instead, the investor's opening position is the sale of a futures contract, the investor is said to be in a *short position* or *short futures*.

The investor who is long a futures position will realize a dollar for dollar gain (loss) at the settlement date if the price of the futures contract increases (decreases). For an investor who is in a short position, the opposite is true: a dollar for dollar loss (gain) will be realized if the price of the futures contract increases (decreases). When the underlying instrument is a fixed income instrument, the price change of the futures contract will depend on the prevailing interest rate. The futures price will increase (decrease) when interest rates decline (increase).

To illustrate, suppose there is a futures contract which calls for the delivery of $100,000 par value of an 8%, 30-year Treasury bond in two months at a futures price of $100,000.[2] This means that the buyer of the contract agrees to take delivery of $100,000 par value of an 8%, 30-year Treasury bond two months from now and pay the seller (who agrees to make delivery of the same bond) a price of $100,000. Suppose that at the delivery date, the yield on 30-year Treasury bonds is 7%, 100 basis points lower than when the futures contract was entered into by the two parties. At the delivery date, the value of the bond would be $112,472. The buyer of the futures contract would therefore pay $100,000 for a Treasury bond with a market value of $112,472. Because the futures price will equal the cash price at the delivery date (a process referred to as *convergence*), the futures price would be $112,472. Thus the buyer of this futures contract would realize a profit of $12,472. The seller of the futures contract would have to sell (deliver) the bond for $100,000 but purchase it for $112,472, realizing a loss of $12,472 since by convergence the futures price would be $112,472. Suppose, instead, that interest rates increased by 100 basis points, from 8% to 9%. At the delivery date, the market value of the Treasury bond and therefore the futures price would be $89,681. The buyer of the futures contract would realize a

---

2. While no such futures contract exists, it does illustrate the principles without cluttering the illustration with unnecessary details.

loss of $10,319 while the seller of the futures contract would realize a gain of $10,319.

These risk-reward characteristics also apply when the futures contract is liquidated prior to the delivery date even though complete convergence does not occur. The payoff will depend on the futures price at the time of liquidation of the position. We can summarize the position of the two parties to a futures contract as follows:

	interest rates decrease (futures prices increase)	interest rates increase (futures prices decrease)
buy futures (long futures)	$ for $ gain	$ for $ loss
sell futures (short futures)	$ for $ loss	$ for $ gain

Applications

A futures contract can be employed to lock in the price of a fixed income security or, equivalently, lock in an interest rate. This is referred to as *hedging*. By locking in a price or rate, downside risk is eliminated. However, the cost of eliminating that risk is the sacrifice of the upside potential that could be realized if there is an advantageous movement in the price or rate. Two examples will illustrate this.

The manager of a fixed income portfolio knows that she must sell $20 million of Treasury bonds two months from now to satisfy a liability. Suppose that the manager is constrained from selling the bonds today. The manager then faces the risk that if interest rates on Treasury bonds rise in two months, the price of the bonds will decline. By selling the correct amount of futures contracts, the manager can lock in a price today.[3]

To see how, suppose that interest rates rise two months from now. The manager will realize a loss when the bonds are sold. However, the futures price will decline. Since the manager sold futures contracts and can now purchase them at a lower price to cover her position, a profit will be realized. The profit from the futures position plus the proceeds from the sale of the bonds in the cash market should equal the price the manager tried to lock in today. If interest rates fell instead of rising, the bonds will be sold at a higher price but the manager will realize a loss on the futures position. The net effect should be a price close to the price that the manager tried to lock in today. Notice that in this case, the portfolio manager lost the opportunity to benefit from a decline in interest rates.

---

3. The appropriate number of contracts is called the hedge ratio. For an explanation of how to determine the hedge ratio when hedging with interest rate futures contracts, see Mark Pitts and Frank J. Fabozzi, *Interest Rate Futures and Options* (Chicago: Probus Publishing, 1989), Chap. 9.

The strategy illustrated above is called a *sell* or *short hedge*. Effectively the manager has sold Treasury securities at a price determined today (the futures price).

Suppose that the manager of the fixed income portion of a pension fund has been told that a contribution of $10 million will be received one month from now. The manager plans to invest the proceeds in Treasury securities and believes that interest rates will decline in one month. If so, when the pension contribution is received, it will have to be invested at a lower interest rate. The manager prefers to lock in a rate today rather than risk the possibility of investing at a lower yield one month from now.

The portfolio manager can use the futures market to lock in a rate today. The objective is to offset any loss in the cash market with a gain in the futures market if interest rates fall. From our earlier discussion, we know that if interest rates decline, the buyer of a futures contract benefits. By buying the correct number of futures contracts, the portfolio manager can lock in a Treasury rate today. This strategy is called a *buy* or *long hedge*. Effectively, the portfolio manager has purchased Treasury securities today at a predetermined rate. If interest rates decline, the gain on the futures position will offset the lower interest rate that will be earned by owning the Treasury securities purchased one month hence. However, if interest rates rise, the portfolio will not benefit since there will be a loss on the futures position that will offset the higher interest rate that will be realized by buying the Treasury securities one month from now. Once again, we see that by using futures contracts to hedge a position, the hedger locks in a rate and gives up the benefit from an advantageous move in interest rates.

Hedging is a special case of controlling interest rate or price volatility for a fixed income portfolio. An active fixed income portfolio manager who wishes to change the price volatility of a portfolio can use futures to do so. By buying futures, the exposure of a fixed income portfolio to interest rate changes will increase. By selling futures, the opposite is true.

III. Options

An option is a contract in which the writer of the option grants the buyer of the option the right to purchase from or sell to the writer a designated instrument at a specified price within a specified period of time. The writer, also referred to as the seller, grants this right to the buyer in exchange for a certain sum of money called the *option premium* or *option price.*

When an option grants the buyer the right to purchase the designated instrument from the writer, it is called a *call option.* When the option buyer has the right to sell the designated instrument to the writer (seller), the option is called a *put option.* The price at which the instrument may be bought or sold is called the *exercise* or *strike price*. The date after which an option is void is called the *expiration date*. While there are options in which the instrument that may be bought or sold is a commodity, fixed income security, individual common stock, stock index, or foreign exchange, we will focus here only on options on fixed income securities. We refer to these options as interest rate or debt options.

The most liquid exchange-traded interest rate options are not options on a fixed income security, but options on interest rate futures contracts. In the case of a call option on an interest rate futures contract, exercise by the buyer results in the buyer acquiring a long futures position and the seller acquiring a corresponding short futures position. For a put option on an interest rate futures contract, exercise by the buyer results in a short position in the futures contract for the buyer and corresponding long futures position for the seller.

Risk-Return Characteristics

The buyer of an option is said to be *long the option;* the writer (seller) is said to be *short the option*. The maximum amount that an option buyer can lose is the option premium. The maximum profit that the option writer (seller) can realize is the option premium. The option buyer has substantial upside return potential while the option writer has substantial downside risk. This risk-return characteristic also holds for options on interest rate futures contracts.

One of the determinants of the option premium is the price of the underlying instrument — the option premium for a call will increase if the price of the underlying instrument rises (or equivalently, if the interest rate on the underlying fixed income security falls). The option premium for a put will move in the direction opposite to the change in the price of the underlying instrument or equivalently the same direction as the interest rate on the underlying fixed income security.

To illustrate, suppose there is a call option on $100,000 par value of a 30-year, 8% coupon Treasury bond and that if such a bond was available in the market today, its price would be $100,000. Also suppose that for this option (1) the exercise price is $100,000, (2) the option expires in two months, and (3) the option can only be exercised at the expiration date. Finally, suppose that the option premium is $1,000. This means that the buyer of this call option has the right, but not the obligation, to buy $100,000 par value of an 8% coupon, 30-year Treasury bond for a price of $100,000 in two months. To obtain this right, the buyer must pay the seller of this call option today $1,000 (the option premium). Two months from now, if interest rates have increased above 8%, the price of an 8%, 30-year Treasury bond will be less than $100,000. The call option buyer would not exercise the option, because the call option grants the buyer the right to purchase a bond with a current market value of less than $100,000 for a price of $100,000. The call option buyer would let the option expire, thereby realizing a loss equal to the option premium, $1,000. The option premium is the maximum loss that the call option buyer will realize. In contrast to the position of the option buyer, the seller or writer of our hypothetical call option realizes a maximum profit equal to the option premium of $1,000.

Suppose, instead, interest rates decreased so that the price of 8%, 30-year Treasury bonds increased in value to more than $100,000. The call option buyer would exercise the option, thereby acquiring an asset for $100,000 that has a market value in excess of that amount. The profit of the call option buyer will equal the difference between the market value of the Treasury bonds at the expiration date and $100,000, reduced by the option premium. The price of the bonds would have to increase by more than $1,000 for the call option buyer to realize a profit. By buying the call option, an investor retains all the upside potential that would be realized by owning bonds when interest rates decline but reduces that upside potential by the amount of the option premium. The flip side of this position is that of the call option writer. If interest rates fall enough so that the market value of the bonds rise by more than the option premium of $1,000, the call option writer realizes a loss. The loss is only limited to how low interest rates will decline, reduced by the option premium.

Basically, the position of the call option buyer and call option writer at the expiration date can be summarized as follows:

	interest rates decrease (price of underlying security increases)	interest rates increase (price of underlying security decreases)
buy calls (long calls)	profit if price of underlying security increases by more than option premium	maximum loss is option premium
sell calls (short calls)	loss if price of underlying security increases by more than option premium	maximum profit is option premium

Suppose instead of a call option, our hypothetical option is a put option. In this case, two months from now the put option buyer has the right, but not the obligation, to sell $100,000 of 8%, 30-year Treasury bonds to the put option writer for $100,000. The put option buyer pays the option premium of $1,000 to acquire this right. If interest rates fall below 8% in two months, the price of the Treasury bonds would rise above $100,000. It would not make any sense for the put option buyer to exercise the option because by doing so he would be selling bonds with a value in excess of $100,000 to the option writer for a price of $100,000. Therefore, if interest rates fall the put option buyer would not exercise this option, realizing a loss on the option position of $1,000 (the option premium). The put option writer realizes a profit of $1,000.

For the put option buyer to benefit, interest rates must increase enough so that the price of the Treasury bonds declines by more than $1,000. The put option buyer realizes all the upside potential associated with selling Treasury bonds short in a rising interest rate environment without incurring a risk of loss greater than the option premium. However, the upside potential is reduced by the amount of the option premium. The seller of the put option is exposed to all the downside risk, reduced by the amount of the option premium.

The position of the put option buyer and put option writer at the *expiration date* is summarized below:

	interest rates decrease (price of underlying security increases)	*interest rates increase (price of underlying security decreases)*
buy puts (long puts)	maximum loss is option premium	profit if price of underlying security falls by more than option premium
sell puts (short puts)	maximum profit is option premium	loss if price of underlying security falls by more than option premium

Contrast the option positions with the futures positions. A futures position retains all the upside potential and downside risk associated with a long or short position in a security. Option positions retain all the upside potential reduced by the amount of the option price. In exchange for the option price, the option buyer has acquired downside risk protection.

Applications

In explaining how futures can be used for hedging, we indicated that the user of futures sacrifices upside potential. The purchase of options, however, can be employed to retain upside potential and purchase downside protection, as the following examples illustrate.

Consider once again the portfolio manager who plans to sell $20 million of Treasury bonds two months from now. Earlier we assumed that she wanted to hedge the Treasury bond sale and did so by selling futures contracts. Suppose instead that she wants to hedge in such a way that if interest rates rise, a price today will be locked in; but if rates fall, the portfolio will benefit by selling the bonds at a higher price. Suppose also that to accomplish this the manager purchased put options. As explained above, if interest rates rise, the put buyer (the manager in our example) will benefit from the purchase of put options. If an appropriate number of put options are purchased, the profit from the put options can be used to offset the lower price received for the bonds when interest rates have increased. If, instead, interest rates fall, the manager can let the put options expire and can sell the bonds at a higher price. The proceeds, however, will be less than if the manager did not purchase put options. The lower proceeds reflects the cost of purchasing the option.

Let's return to the manager of the fixed income portion of a pension fund who has been told that a contribution of $10 million will be received one month from now. The manager can lock in an interest rate on the Treasury securities by buying futures. If interest rates rise, however, the manager will not benefit from the higher interest rate that can be earned on the $10 million. Suppose that instead of buying futures, the manager buys call options. If in one month interest rates decline, the manager must invest the expected proceeds at a lower interest rate. However, as explained earlier, the buyer of a call option will realize a profit when interest rates decline. By purchasing an appropriate number of call options, the profit realized by the portfolio manager will offset the lower interest rate on the bonds purchased. This will establish a minimum interest rate on the proceeds to be reinvested. Should interest rates rise rather than fall, the portfolio manager will not exercise the call option and the proceeds will be invested at the higher rate. However, because of the cost of the call options, the interest rate that will be earned will be less than if the manager did not purchase call options.

Because the buyer of an option can let the option expire, options can be employed when there is uncertainty whether a transaction that the hedger wants to protect against will ever take place. That is, options can be used to protect against asymmetric risk. This is illustrated in the following two examples.

In our earlier examples, it was assumed that the portfolio manager knew that the pension sponsor would contribute $10 million one month from now. By assuming that the portfolio manager expects but is not certain that $10 million will be received, we've altered the situation. Assume the following: (1) the manager buys futures, (2) interest rates rise, and (3) the plan sponsor contributes $4 million instead of the anticipated $10 million. As a result of the long futures position, there will be a loss when interest rates rise. This loss will offset the benefit of the higher interest rate that will be earned on the $4 million invested so as to lock in a rate on that amount. However, for the remaining $6 million that was hedged by selling futures, there will be a loss without any offsetting benefit from the higher interest rate. Using options instead of futures, the outcome is different under the assumptions we made. By buying call options, the manager can let them expire unexercised. The $4 million actually received can be reinvested at the higher interest rate. The cost of this approach is equal to the price of the call options. This cost can be thought of as (1) the cost of capitalizing on a higher rate and (2) the cost of the flexibility that permits the manager to walk away from the contract if planned proceeds are not received.

Suppose that a life insurance company has sold a guaranteed investment contract (GIC) in which it guarantees for a payment of $10 million an interest rate of 9% per year for the next five years. The contract permits the policyholder to contribute $2 million more to the policy in the next month. The risk that the life insurance company faces is that if interest rates decline below 9%, the policyholder will contribute $2 million and the company has agreed to pay 9%, a rate higher than prevailing rates. The life insurance company can lock in a rate near 9% by buying futures contracts. Should interest rates fall, it is more than likely that the policyholder will add $2 million to the GIC. The gain in the long futures position resulting from a decline in interest rates will, if the correct number of futures contracts are bought, offset the lower interest rate that will be earned by the insurance company on the $2 million. But consider what happens if interest rates rise over the next month. The policyholder will probably invest the proceeds elsewhere at an interest rate greater than 9%. The life insurance company, however, still has a long futures position which will realize a loss.

To understand the position of the life insurance company, consider what it did by allowing the policyholder to add $2 million. The company effectively gave an option to the policyholder to contribute more funds to the GIC. The policyholder benefits from this long option position if interest rates decline. Recall from our earlier discussion that a long call option position benefits from a decline in interest rates. Since the policyholder has a long call position, the life insurance company has a corresponding short call position. To protect itself in this situation, the life insurance company should purchase call options. Assume that the call options have one month to expiration. If this strategy is followed, let's look at what happens if interest rates change. If interest rates fall below 9%, the company will receive $2 million that it must invest at a lower interest rate than it guaranteed. To offset the lower interest income, the company will realize a profit on the call options it purchased. Should interest rates rise above 9%, no funds will be received by the company but it will not exercise the call options. The cost of this strategy is the price of the call options.

IV. Interest Rate Swaps

An interest rate swap is an agreement whereby two parties (called counterparties) agree to periodically exchange interest payments. The dollar amount of the interest payments exchanged is based on some predetermined dollar principal which is called the *notional principal amount*. The dollar amount each counterparty pays to the other is the product of the agreed-upon periodic interest rate times the notional principal amount. The only dollars that are exchanged between the parties are the interest payments, not the notional principal amount. In the most common type of swap, one party agrees to pay the other party fixed interest payments at designated dates for the life of the contract. This party is referred to as the *fixed rate payer*. The other party agrees to make floating interest rate payments and is referred to as the *floating rate payer*.

For example, suppose that for the next five years institution X agrees to pay institution Y 10% while institution Y agrees to pay institution X the six-month London Interbank Offered Rate (LIBOR). Furthermore, assume that the notional principal amount is $50 million and that payments are exchanged every six months for the next five years. This means that every six months, X (the fixed rate payer) will pay Y $2.5 million (.10 × $50,000,000/2). The amount Y (the floating rate payer) will pay will be: six-month LIBOR × $50,000,000/2. For example, if six-month LIBOR is 7%, Y will pay X $1.75 million (.07 × $50,000,000/2).

Risk-Return Characteristics

The value of an interest rate swap will fluctuate with market interest rates. To see how, let's consider our hypothetical swap. Suppose that interest rates change immediately after X and Y entered into the swap. First, consider what would happen if the market demanded that in any five-year swap the fixed-rate payer must pay 11% in order to receive six-month LIBOR. If institution X (the fixed-rate payer) wanted to sell its position, say to institution A, then A will benefit by only having to pay 10% (the original swap rate agreed upon) rather than 11% (the current swap rate) to receive LIBOR. X will want compensation for this benefit. Consequently, the value of X's position has increased. Thus, if interest rates increase, the fixed-rate payer will realize a profit and the floating-rate payer will realize a loss.

Next, consider what would happen if interest rates declined to, say, 6%. Now a five-year swap would require the fixed-rate payer to pay 6% rather than 10% to receive LIBOR. If institution X wanted to sell its position to institution B, the latter would demand compensation to take over the position. Thus, if interest rates decline, the fixed-rate payer will realize a loss while the floating-rate payer will realize a profit.

The risk-return profile of the two positions when interest rates change is summarized below:

	interest rates decrease	*interest rates increase*
floating-rate payer	gain	loss
fixed-rate payer	loss	gain

Contrast the position of the counterparties in an interest rate swap to the position of the long and short futures (forward) contract. The long futures position gains if interest rates decline and loses if interest rates rise — this is similar to the risk-return profile of a floating-rate payer. The risk-return profile of a fixed-rate payer is similar to that of the short futures position:

gaining if interest rates increase and losing if interest rates decrease. By taking a closer look at the interest rate swap we can understand why the risk-
return relationships are similar.

Consider X's position. X has agreed to pay 10% and receive six-month
LIBOR. More specifically, based on a $50,000,000 notional principal amount,
X has agreed to buy a commodity called "six-month LIBOR" for $2.5 mil-
lion. This is effectively a six-month forward contract whereby X agrees to
pay $2.5 million in exchange for delivery of six-month LIBOR. If interest
rates increase to 11%, the price of that commodity (six-month LIBOR) is
higher, resulting in a gain for the fixed-rate payer who is effectively long a
six-month forward contract on six-month LIBOR. The floating-rate payer is
effectively short a six-month forward contract on six-month LIBOR. There
is thus a forward contract corresponding to each exchange date. *Thus, an
interest rate swap can be viewed as a package of forward contracts.*

Now we see can why there is a similarity between the risk-return relationship for an interest rate swap and a futures/forward contract. If interest
rates increase to say 11%, the price of that commodity (six-month LIBOR)
has increased to $2.75 million (.11 × $50,000,000/2). The long forward position (the fixed-rate payer) gains and the short forward position (the floating-
rate payer) loses. If interest rates decline to say 9%, the price of our commodity has decreased to $2.25 million (.09 × $50,000,000/2). The short forward
position (the floating-rate payer) gains and the long forward position (the
fixed-rate payer) loses.

Consequently, interest rate swaps can be viewed as a package of more
basic interest rate control tools, such as futures/forwards.

Applications

Interest rate swaps can be used to change the nature of asset cash flows from
fixed to floating or from floating to fixed. This is illustrated in the following
examples.

Suppose a thrift has a portfolio consisting of long-term fixed-rate mortgages. Since the thrift acquires its funds in the short-term market, the risk it
faces is that the short-term rate will rise above the rate earned on the mortgages. The thrift's objective is to lock in an interest spread over the cost of
its funds. However, its cost of funds is variable since it borrows short term.
Depending on swap terms at the time, the thrift may be able to use an interest
rate swap to change its asset cash flows from fixed to floating. The thrift in
this case agrees to receive floating and pay fixed.

Consider a life insurance company that has guaranteed a 10% rate on a
GIC for the next five years. Suppose that the life insurance company has the
opportunity to purchase what it considers an attractive floating-rate instrument in a private placement transaction. The risk that the company faces is
that interest rates will fall so that it will not earn enough to realize the 10%

guaranteed rate plus a spread. Depending on swap terms at the time, the insurance company may be able to use interest rate swaps by paying floating and receiving fixed.

Options and Forward Contracts on Swaps

There are also options on interest rate swaps. These options are referred to as *swaptions*. The buyer of this option has the right to enter into (or exit from) an interest rate swap agreement on predetermined terms by some specified date in the future. For example, a *put swaption* is an option allowing the buyer to enter into an interest rate swap in which the buyer pays a fixed interest rate and receives a floating interest rate and the writer receives a fixed interest rate and pays a floating interest rate. A *call swaption* is an option that allows the buyer to enter into an interest rate swap in which the buyer pays a floating interest rate and receives a fixed interest rate while the writer receives a floating interest rate and pays a fixed interest rate.

There are also forward contracts on interest rate swaps. With this agreement, two parties agree to enter into an interest rate swap agreement on predetermined terms at some date in the future.

V. Interest Rate Agreements

An interest rate agreement is an agreement between two parties whereby one party, for an upfront premium, agrees to compensate the other if a designated interest rate is different from a certain level. When one party agrees to pay the other when the designated interest rate exceeds a certain level, the agreement is referred to as an *interest rate cap* or *ceiling*. An interest rate agreement is referred to as an *interest rate floor* when one party agrees to pay the other when the designated interest rate falls below a certain level.

The terms of an interest rate agreement include:

1. the underlying index
2. the strike rate which sets the ceiling or floor
3. the length of the agreement
4. the frequency of settlement
5. the notional principal amount.

For example, suppose that C buys an interest rate cap from D with the following terms:

1. the underlying index is the six-month LIBOR rate
2. the strike rate is 8%
3. the agreement is for 7 years
4. settlement is every six months
5. the notional principal amount is $20 million.

Under this agreement, every six months for the next seven years D will pay C whenever six-month LIBOR exceeds 8%. The payment will equal the dollar value of the difference between six-month LIBOR and 8%. For example, suppose six months from now six-month LIBOR is 11%, then D will pay C $(.11 - .08) \times \$20,000,000/2$, or $300,000. If six-month LIBOR is 8% or less, D does not have to pay anything to C.

As an example of an interest rate floor, assume the same terms as the interest rate cap we just illustrated. In this case, if six-month LIBOR is 11%, C receives nothing from D. However, if six-month LIBOR is less than 8%, D compensates C for the difference. For example, if six-month LIBOR is 7%, D will pay C $(.08 - .07) \times \$20,000,000/2$, or $100,000.

Interest rate caps and floors can be combined to create an *interest rate collar*. This is done by buying an interest rate cap and selling an interest rate floor.

Risk-Return Characteristics

In an interest rate agreement, the buyer pays an upfront fee, which represents the maximum amount that the buyer can lose and the maximum amount that the writer of the agreement can gain. The only party that is required to perform is the writer of the interest rate agreement. The buyer of an interest rate cap benefits if the underlying interest rate rises above the strike rate. The writer must compensate the buyer. The buyer of an interest rate floor benefits if the interest rate falls below the strike rate, the writer having to compensate the buyer.

What are the equivalents of interest rate caps and interest rate floors? These contracts are equivalent to a package of interest rate options. Since the buyer benefits if the interest rate rises above the strike rate, an interest rate cap is similar to purchasing a package of put options; the seller of an interest rate cap has effectively sold a package of put options. The buyer of an interest rate floor benefits from a decline in the interest rate below the strike rate. Therefore, the buyer of an interest rate floor has effectively bought a package of call options that were sold by the writer of the option. An interest rate collar is equivalent to buying a package of put options and selling a package of call options.

Once again, a complex contract can be viewed as a package of basic contracts, or options in the case of interest rate agreements.

Applications

To see how interest rate agreements can be used for asset/liability management, consider the problems faced by the thrift and life insurance company we used earlier to illustrate the applications of interest rate swaps.

Recall that the thrift's objective is to lock in an interest spread over the cost of its funds. However, since it borrows short term, its cost of funds is uncertain. The thrift may be able to purchase a cap such that the cap rate plus the cost of purchasing the cap is less than the rate it is earning on its long-term fixed-rate mortgages. If the cost of short-term funds declines, the thrift does not benefit from the cap. However, its cost of funds declines. Therefore, the cap allows the thrift to impose a ceiling on its cost of funds but retain the opportunity to benefit from a decline in rates. This should not be surprising since the interest rate cap is simply a package of call options.

The thrift can reduce the cost of purchasing the cap by selling a floor. By doing so, the thrift agrees to pay the buyer of the floor if the underlying rate falls below the strike rate. By selling the floor, the thrift receives a fee. However, the thrift has sold off the opportunity to benefit from a decline in rates below the strike rate. By buying a cap and selling a floor, the thrift has created a range for its cost of funds (i.e., a collar).

Recall the problem of the life insurance company that has guaranteed a 10% rate on a GIC for the next five years and is considering the purchase of an attractive floating rate instrument in a private placement transaction. The risk that the company faces is that interest rates will fall so that it will not earn enough to realize the 10% guaranteed rate plus a spread. The life insurance company may be able to purchase a floor to set a lower bound on its investment return, yet retain the opportunity to benefit should rates increase.

VI. Summary

We have highlighted the differences between the risk-return relationship for futures and options. With futures, a rate or price can be locked in, sacrificing any beneficial interest rate or price movement. With interest rate options, the option buyer for a price (the option premium) can lock in a rate or price but retain any benefit from favorable rate or price movements. Interest rate swaps and interest rate agreements are nothing more than packages of these basic contracts.

Questions

Overview of the Investment Management Process
Fabozzi and Fabozzi

1. Explain and give an example of how a financial institution's investment objectives may be determined by its liabilities.
2. In verifying the claim that the portfolio manager has outperformed the market, several adjustments to the return must be considered before the comparison can be made. What are these adjustments?
3. What is the theoretical market portfolio used for evaluating performance according to CAPM?
4. Explain how it can be possible for a portfolio manager to outperform a predetermined index on a risk-adjusted basis, but still fail to meet the portfolio's investment objectives.

The Many Dimensions of the Asset Allocation Decision
Arnott and Fabozzi

1. What are the three major asset allocation decisions?
2. Which asset allocation decision comes first, and why?
3. What primary features distinguish tactical asset allocation from dynamic asset allocation?

Pension Fund Investment Policy
Bodie

1. Explain how portfolio insurance affects the return distribution for pension plans. How does the return of the portfolio using portfolio insurance compare to the return of an uninsured portfolio?
2. Explain the Black–Dewhurst proposal with respect to pension plan investing.
3. Explain how the "pension put" effect compares to the Black–Dewhurst proposal in influencing the level of funding and the type of investment in pension plans.

The Collapse of the Efficient-Market Hypothesis
Reinganum

1. How could CAPM be used to interpret Nicholson's early results that low P/E stocks outperform high P/E stocks?
2. How can the tax-loss-selling hypothesis be used to explain the January effect?
3. What is meant by an informationally-efficient market?

Efficient Markets, Investment-Management Selection, and the Loser's Game
Gould

1. Why is it necessary that anomalies be found in all models?
2. Why does Charles Ellis describe the investment management process as a "Loser's Game"?
3. Why should a manager avoid placing heavy reliance on simulations when testing the reliability of a particular investment strategy?
4. Explain how the concept of regret may be used to explain the traditional principal/agent problem in investing.

The Analyst and the Investment Process
Coggin

1. When comparing simple extrapolative statistical models earnings forecasts to analysts earnings forecasts, which does a better job? Why?
2. Discuss the relationship between analysts' EPS forecasts and stock returns. [*Hint:* Distinguish between the importance of *current* estimates versus estimate *revisions*.]
3. Has research to date found significant differences in individual analysts' abilities to forecast earnings and returns? Discuss what this means for the task of evaluating analysts' job performance.

Benchmark Portfolios and the Manager/Plan Sponsor Relationship
Bailey, Tierney, and Richards

1. Why are traditional index benchmarks viewed as passive representatives of the manager's investment process?
2. Explain some of the problems encountered when the median manager of a group of portfolio managers is used as the benchmark for performance evaluation.
3. Identify the steps involved in defining a benchmark portfolio.
4. Why should you be cautious when analyzing statistics on past portfolio performance to evaluate current performance?
5. Why are benchmark portfolios useful in the investment management process?
6. Explain the basic characteristics of any useful benchmark.

Stock Index Futures
Fabozzi, Collins, and Peters

1. What is a futures contract?
2. Why are stock index futures contracts referred to as "cash settlement" contracts?
3. What is meant by "marked-to-market"?
4. What are the differences between initial margin, maintenance margin, and variation margin?
5. What is the theoretical price of a futures contract?
6. "There is not one theoretical futures price but a band around the theoretical price that will not permit arbitrage profits." Comment.
7. Define what is meant by a "perfect" hedge.
8. Why would an equity portfolio manager want to implement a short or sell hedge?
9. What is meant by basis risk and cross-hedge price risk?
10. What role does beta play in determining the number of futures contracts needed to hedge a stock portfolio.

Creating and Managing an Index Fund Using Stock Index Futures
Collins and Fabozzi

1. Explain the tradeoffs between using stocks versus T-bills and stock index futures contracts to create an indexed fund.
2. Explain how a stock replacement strategy can be used to enhance the returns of an indexed fund.
3. Explain the different weighting schemes that can be used in constructing an index.
4. Explain the risks in choosing a basket of a smaller number of stocks to track an index rather than including all the stocks in the index.
5. Explain the rationale behind program trading.
6. Explain the methods of creating a basket to track an index.
7. Explain the process of monitoring and rebalancing a portfolio created to track an index.
8. Explain how active management can be used within an indexed portfolio to enhance returns.

Arbitrage, Program Trading, and the Tail of the Dog
Gastineau

1. How does a risk arbitrageur attempt to make a profit in the stock market?
2. What is program trading and why is it used by institutional investors?
3. Why is program trading sometimes considered to be the tail that wagged the dog?
4. Explain how it could be said that more efficient markets made portfolio

insurance feasible, which may have magnified market movements on Black Monday.

5. Why is it suggested that portfolio insurance is "like locking the barn door after the horse is stolen"?

The Revolution in Composite Assets
Luskin

1. What is a composite asset?
2. Explain how investors can seek "better than market" performance in a composite asset framework.
3. How can stock index futures be used in asset allocation?
4. How does the dealer community facilitate trading in composite assets?

Measuring and Interpreting Volatility
Hill

1. What are the two commonly used methods for calculating volatility?
2. What is a "price relative"?
3. How should standard deviation be adjusted when using a sample mean rather than a population mean?
4. What does using annualized volatility on a 365-day basis assume about the volatility of returns on non-trading days? How can volatility be adjusted to correct for this?
5. How can annualized volatility be converted to a price range expected with a given probability in a particular time interval?
6. What is the effect of the nonlinearity of the function that converts short-term to longer term volatility mean for volatility estimates?

Portfolio Objectives and Management Policies for Fixed-Income Portfolios
McEnally

1. What portfolio objectives make sense for bond investors?
2. What is a "laddered maturity" strategy?
3. In an immunization strategy, what is the underlying theory behind matching the portfolio duration to the investment horizon when seeking to lock in a portfolio return?
4. What is contingent immunization?
5. What is meant by a dedicated portfolio?
6. What is a "holding period return"?
7. What is the goal when investing for "holding-period" returns?

A Framework for Analyzing Bonds
Dattatreya and Fabozzi

1. Is the following statement correct? "The relationship between the price of a bond and the return required by investors is a linear one." Explain.

[A "linear one" means that, on a price/yield graph, the relationship can be represented by a straight line.]

2. What characteristics of a bond affect its price volatility?
3. If a bond's yield changes as shown below, indicate the number of basis points that the yield has changed:

Initial yield	New Yield	Change in yield in basis points
8.00%	9.00%	
7.85%	8.35%	
6.25%	7.75%	
9.90%	6.30%	
7.90%	7.70%	

4. Consider the following three hypothetical option-free bonds all selling at a yield to maturity of 9%:

Bond	Coupon	Maturity
A	9%	8 years
B	7%	8 years
C	11%	6 years

(a) Which of these bonds will have the largest price volatility? Why?
(b) Which of these bonds will have the smallest price volatility? Why?
(c) Which of these bonds will have the highest Macaulay duration? Why?
(d) Which of these bonds will have the lowest Macaulay duration? Why?

5. Calculate the Macaulay duration and modified duration for an 8% coupon bond with 5 years to maturity and selling to yield 8%. (This means that the price of the bond is its par value.)
6. Calculate the Macaulay duration and modified duration for a zero-coupon bond with 5 years to maturity and selling to yield 7%.
7. If a bond has a modified duration of 6 and the required yield changes instantaneously by 50 basis points, what is the approximate percentage change in this bond's price?
8. Is the following statement correct? "Duration measures the approximate dollar price change of a bond."
9. Is the following statement correct? "Using modified duration to approximate the new price of a bond if yield changes will always overstate the new price." Explain.
10. What does the convexity measure of a bond represent?
11. Why are yield to call and yield to maturity poor measures of the relative value of bonds?
12. Is the weighted-average yield of two bonds in a portfolio a good measure of the portfolio's yield?
13. To calculate the horizon return of a bond, what information is needed?
14. What is meant by "negative" convexity? Which bonds exhibit such a property and why?

Stochastic Valuation of Debt Securities with Application to Callable Corporate Bonds
Hayre and Lauterbach

1. What is the meaning of the "implied short-term Treasury forward rate"? Does it necessarily constitute an opinion on the direction of interest rates?
2. How is Monte Carlo simulation used in stochastic analysis?
3. What is meant by the option-adjusted spread (OAS)?
4. How can OAS be used to determine the relative value of callable corporate bonds for rich/cheap analysis?
5. Describe the steps involved in calculating OAS for bonds with uncertain cash flows.
6. What is the implied spread of a bond?
7. How does OAS differ from traditional yield spread analysis?
8. Compare the OAA approach with the traditional option pricing approach used in evaluating callable bonds.
9. How can the cost of a bond's call provisions to the investor be determined from OAA?

Callable Corporate Bonds
Langerman and Gartland

1. What is the refunding restriction in callable corporate bonds?
2. What is a call-adjusted spread in a bond and how is it used to assess relative value?
3. What is the weighted average life of a bond?
4. How does volatility affect the price of callable bonds?
5. In what type of interest rate environment are callable bonds of greatest value?

Realized Return Optimization
Miller, Rajan, and Shimpi

1. Explain why using a yield or spread over a Treasury benchmark might be misleading when evaluating the potential performance of a portfolio.
2. Explain some of the problems with using modified or Macaulay duration as targets in portfolio management.
3. Why is downside deviation about required returns a more appropriate measure of risk than total deviation for a funding portfolio?
4. What are the components of realized return? Which are path dependent?
5. Explain the problems with using immunization measures in liability funding strategies and why realized return optimization may be a more appropriate tool to use.

Mortgage Pass-Through Securities
Hayre and Mohebbi

1. What is the basic structure of a pass-through security?
2. Are all pass-through securities backed by the full faith and credit of the U.S. government?
3. Why is it difficult to analyze a pass-through security?
4. What is meant by a "constant prepayment assumption" and how is it used in evaluating pass-through securities?
5. What is the relationship between the CPR and the PSA model?
6. Why is Macaulay duration an inappropriate measure of price volatility for a pass-through security?
7. Look at Figure 6 on page 276. The two GNMA securities exhibit a price/yield characteristic described in the Dattatreya/Fabozzi article. What is that characteristic?
8. What information would be needed to calculate the total return of a pass-through security?

High-Yield Mortgage Securities
Carron and Hemel

1. Why shouldn't a high-yield mortgage security be evaluated strictly on the basis of a single quoted yield to maturity?
2. What is a CMO residual and what are the components of its cash flow?
3. What is a stripped mortgage-backed security and how is it created?
4. What is an IO and a PO security?
5. How can IO strips be used for portfolio hedging?
6. What is a leveraged floater?
7. What is a reverse floater?

Overview of Interest Rate Risk Control Tools for Investment Management
Fabozzi

1. What is the difference between a forward and futures contract?
2. "Interest rate futures and option contracts are purely speculative instruments." Comment.
3. Give an example of how interest rate futures contracts can be used by a portfolio manager who anticipates an inflow of cash one month from today that will be invested but anticipates a decline in interest rates.
4. "When hedging, this contract can be used to protect against an adverse interest rate movement but still maintain the opportunity to benefit from a favorable interest rate movement." Which contract is being referred to in the quote, a futures contract or an options contract?
5. What type of contract can an asset/liability manager use to alter the cash flow characteristics of an asset from floating to fixed?

6. An institutional investor owns $50 million of a floating-rate security. This institution has fixed-rate liabilities. Other than selling the floating-rate security, what can this institutional investor do to assure that the interest rate earned on the floating-rate security will not fall below a predetermined level?
7. Interest rate swaps and interest rate agreements can be viewed as a package of other contracts. Discuss.

Index

About the Editors

Frank J. Fabozzi is visiting professor of finance at the Sloan School of Management at MIT. The editor of *The Journal of Portfolio Management,* Dr. Fabozzi has authored and edited over 25 books on investment management including *The Institutional Investor Focus on Investment Management* and *Managing Institutional Assets,* both from the Ballinger Division of Harper & Row, Publishers.

T. Dessa Fabozzi is vice president and manager of Client Analytics in the Financial Strategies Group of Merrill Lynch Capital Markets. Dr. Fabozzi is the co-author of *Bond Markets, Analysis, and Portfolio Strategies* and co-editor of *Advances in Bond Analysis and Portfolio Strategies.*

The Institutional Investor Series in Finance

The Institutional Investor Series in Finance has been developed specifically to bring you — the finance professional — the latest thinking and developments in investments and corporate finance. As new challenges arise in this fast-paced arena, you can count on this series to provide you with the information you need to gain the competitive edge.

Institutional Investor is the leading communications company serving the global financial community and publisher of the magazine of the same name. Institutional Investor has won 36 major awards for distinguished financial journalism — including the prestigious National Magazine Award for the best reporting of any magazine in the United States. More than 560,000 financial executives in 170 countries read Institutional Investor publications each month. Thousands more attend Institutional Investor's worldwide conferences and seminars each year.